Strand Book Store $20.00

D1768773

Inclusiveness in India

Other titles from IDE-JETRO:

Masahisa Fujita (*editor*)
ECONOMIC INTEGRATION IN ASIA AND INDIA

Masahisa Fujita (*editor*)
REGIONAL INTEGRATION IN EAST ASIA
From the Viewpoint of Spatial Economics

Daisuke Hiratsuka (*editor*)
EAST ASIA'S DE FACTO ECONOMIC INTEGRATION

Momoko Kawakami and Timothy J. Sturgeon (*editors*)
THE DYNAMICS OF LOCAL LEARNING IN GLOBAL VALUE CHAINS
Experiences from East Asia

Akifumi Kuchiki and Masatsugu Tsuji (*editors*)
FROM AGGLOMERATION TO INNOVATION
Upgrading Industrial Clusters in Emerging Economies

Akifumi Kuchiki and Masatsugu Tsuji (*editors*)
INDUSTRIAL CLUSTERS IN ASIA
Analyses of Their Competition and Cooperation

Akifumi Kuchiki and Masatsugu Tsuji (*editors*)
THE FLOWCHART APPROACH TO INDUSTRIAL CLUSTER POLICY

Hisayuki Mitsuo (*editor*)
NEW DEVELOPMENTS OF THE EXCHANGE RATE REGIMES IN DEVELOPING COUNTRIES

Mayumi Murayama (*editor*)
GENDER AND DEVELOPMENT
The Japanese Experience in Comparative Perspective

Nobuhiro Okamoto and Takeo Ihara (*editors*)
SPATIAL STRUCTURE AND REGIONAL DEVELOPMENT IN CHINA
An Interregional Input–Output Approach

Hiroshi Sato and Mayumi Murayama (*editors*)
GLOBALIZATION, EMPLOYMENT AND MOBILITY
The South Asian Experience

Takashi Shiraishi, Tatsufumi Yamagata and Shahid Yusuf (*editors*)
POVERTY REDUCTION AND BEYOND
Development Strategies for Low-Income Countries

Tadayoshi Terao and Kenji Otsuka (*editors*)
DEVELOPMENT OF ENVIRONMENTAL POLICY IN JAPAN AND ASIAN COUNTRIES

Hiroko Uchimura (*editor*)
MAKING HEALTH SERVICES MORE ACCESSIBLE IN DEVELOPING COUNTRIES

Koichi Usami (*Editor*)
NON-STANDARD EMPLOYMENT UNDER GLOBALIZATION
Flexible Work and Social Security in the Newly Industrializing Countries

Mariko Watanabe (*editor*)
RECOVERING FINANCIAL SYSTEMS
China and Asian Transition Economies

Inclusiveness in India
A Strategy for Growth and Equality

Edited by

Shigemochi Hirashima
Professor Emeritus, Meiji-Gakuin University, Japan

Hisaya Oda
Professor, Ritsumeikan University, Japan

and

Yuko Tsujita
Associate Senior Research Fellow, IDE-JETRO, Japan

Selection and editorial matter © Shigemochi Hirashima, Hisaya Oda and Yuko Tsujita 2011

Individual chapters © the contributors 2011

All rights reserved. No reproduction, copy or transmission of this publication may be made without written permission.

No portion of this publication may be reproduced, copied or transmitted save with written permission or in accordance with the provisions of the Copyright, Designs and Patents Act 1988, or under the terms of any licence permitting limited copying issued by the Copyright Licensing Agency, Saffron House, 6–10 Kirby Street, London EC1N 8TS.

Any person who does any unauthorized act in relation to this publication may be liable to criminal prosecution and civil claims for damages.

The authors have asserted their rights to be identified as the authors of this work in accordance with the Copyright, Designs and Patents Act 1988.

First published 2011 by
PALGRAVE MACMILLAN

Palgrave Macmillan in the UK is an imprint of Macmillan Publishers Limited, registered in England, company number 785998, of Houndmills, Basingstoke, Hampshire RG21 6XS.

Palgrave Macmillan in the US is a division of St Martin's Press LLC, 175 Fifth Avenue, New York, NY 10010.

Palgrave Macmillan is the global academic imprint of the above companies and has companies and representatives throughout the world.

Palgrave® and Macmillan® are registered trademarks in the United States, the United Kingdom, Europe and other countries.

ISBN 978–0–230–29023–5

This book is printed on paper suitable for recycling and made from fully managed and sustained forest sources. Logging, pulping and manufacturing processes are expected to conform to the environmental regulations of the country of origin.

A catalogue record for this book is available from the British Library.

A catalog record for this book is available from the Library of Congress.

10 9 8 7 6 5 4 3 2 1
20 19 18 17 16 15 14 13 12 11

Printed and bound in the United States of America

Contents

List of Tables	ix
List of Figures	xii
Notes on the Contributors	xv
Preface	xvi

Introduction: Inclusiveness in India – A Challenging Strategy for Growth and Equality   1
Shigemochi Hirashima, Hisaya Oda and Yuko Tsujita

Recent economic performance: background to the inclusive growth strategy	3
What does the government mean by 'inclusive growth'?	8
India's past development strategies	10
Challenges in current inclusive growth strategies	12
Structure of volume and major findings	15
Concluding remarks	27

PART I   GROWTH–POVERTY LINKAGE AND INCOME–ASSET RELATIONSHIP IN THE INCLUSIVE GROWTH STRATEGY

1   Infrastructure, Economic Growth and Interstate Disparity in India   35
Hisaya Oda

Introduction	35
Descriptive analysis of growing income disparities across Indian states	36
Infrastructure and economic growth	40
Empirical analysis	44
Constraints for the provision of infrastructure: the case of Bihar	50
Findings and conclusion	56

vi Contents

2 **Changes in Land Distribution and Non-agricultural Growth in India** 62
   Shigemochi Hirashima and Kensuke Kubo

   Introduction 62
   Changes in the distribution of land and assets in the 1980s and 1990s 65
   Methodology and data 73
   Results 76
   Interpretation of results 82
   Conclusion 84

3 **Financial Inclusion and Poverty Alleviation in India: An Empirical Analysis Using State-wise Data** 88
   Takeshi Inoue

   Introduction 88
   A history of financial inclusion in India 89
   Financial inclusion and poverty conditions 93
   Selected literature review 98
   Model and data 100
   Empirical results 101
   Some concluding remarks 104

PART II DISPARITY IN ACCESS TO SOCIAL SERVICES

4 **Health Inequality in India: Results from NSS data** 111
   Seiro Ito

   Introduction 111
   Data 112
   Estimates by expenditure quintiles 113
   Concluding remarks 126
   Appendix: NSS data 129

5 **The Implications of Migration and Schooling for Urban Educational Disparity: A Study of Delhi Slum Children** 136
   Yuko Tsujita

   Introduction 136
   Data collection and profile of children 139
   School attendance and type 142

Out-of-school children	147
School costs	152
Migration and school attendance	156
Results and discussion	160
Conclusions	164
Acknowledgements	165

PART III ISSUES OF WEAKER SECTIONS IN THE INCLUSIVE GROWTH STRATEGY

6 Electric Light and Minorities: The Provision of Semi-public Goods to Weaker Sections in India   175
Norio Kondo

Introduction	175
Muslims and social infrastructure	177
Theoretical background and data	184
Results and analysis	194
Concluding remarks	204

7 Challenges for Inclusive Sustained Employment: An Attempt to Organize Female Embroidery Homeworkers in Delhi   210
Mayumi Murayama

Introduction	210
Theorizing homeworkers	214
Overview of homeworkers in India	216
Interventions by SEWA Delhi in organizing embroidery homeworkers	221
Survey findings	226
Conclusion	235

PART IV PERSPECTIVES FOR OVERCOMING UNDERDEVELOPMENT: A CASE-STUDY OF BIHAR

8 Historical Origins of Underdevelopment and a Captured Democracy: An Analytical Narrative of Bihar   243
Kazuki Minato

Introduction	243
The political economy of underdevelopment in Bihar	246

	The burden of historical legacies	253
	Much ado about nothing: the protection of *bataidari* rights	259
	Divide et impera: welfare schemes for the underprivileged	261
	Conclusion	265
	Acknowledgements	266
9	**Interstate Disparity in India and Development Strategies for Backward States** *Prabhat P. Ghosh*	270
	Introduction	270
	Trends in regional disparity	271
	Development strategy, asymmetric federalism and regional disparities	274
	Growth of the Bihar economy	281
	Towards an alternative development strategy	290
	Conclusion	293
Index		297

List of Tables

I.1	Evaluation of change over time by *Mukhiya*, or village leaders, in Bihar	23
I.2	Chronology of physical and social infrastructure development in villages in Bihar	25
I.3	Ordered logit estimation of the implementation of five rural development programmes at the village level	26
1.1	Cross-state comparison of per capita electricity consumption	43
1.2	A summary of descriptive statistics of sample data	45
1.3	Regression results for growth of real per capita NSDP	47
1.4	Relative income gap between Bihar and other states	50
1.5	Comparison of state-wise per capita revenue capacity in 2006/7	53
2.1	Variable definitions	75
2.2	Comparison of variable means across sub-samples: buyers of land vs non-buyers	77
2.3	Comparison of variable means across sub-samples: sellers of land vs non-sellers	79
2.4	Probit results for land purchase	80
2.5	Probit results for land sales	81
3.1	Number of indebted households	92
3.2	Outstanding household debt	92
3.3	Definitions and sources of variables	102
3.4	Empirical results	103
A4.1	Expenditure quintile	135
A4.2	All-India sample size of each variables	135
5.1	Socio-economic background of children	141
5.2	School learning facilities and environment in 2006/7	144
5.3	The distribution of type of school attended by children who currently go to school	145

5.4	Completed years of education by students who dropped out	148
5.5	Reasons for dropping out (multiple answers)	148
5.6	Reasons for never-attended (multiple answers)	151
5.7	Average monthly expenditure per reporting student going to government school, by item of expenditure (Rs)	152
5.8	OLS estimates of government school children's monthly educational expenditure	155
5.9	Migration-related issues	158
5.10	Participation in pre-schooling programmes	159
5.11	Logistic regression of the effects of migration on school attendance	161
6.1	Percentage of urban population (%)	183
6.2	Average percentage of the population of Hindu and weaker sections in four states, 2001 (%)	189
6.3	Variables	191
6.4	Electric light – weaker sections and diversity: sub-district level analysis in Bihar, Gujarat, Uttar Pradesh and West Bengal	195
6.5	Electric light – weaker sections and diversity: town-level analysis in Bihar, Gujarat, Uttar Pradesh and West Bengal	196
6.6	Electric light – weaker sections and diversity: town-level analysis in Gujarat	198
6.7	Electric light – weaker sections and diversity: town-level analysis in Bihar	199
6.8	Electric light – weaker sections and diversity: town-level analysis in Uttar Pradesh	200
6.9	Electric light – weaker sections and diversity: town-level analysis in West Bengal	201
7.1	Extent of control of production for non-agricultural sector home-based workers (%)	218
7.2	Household characteristics	228
7.3	Social profile of embroidery workers	230
7.4	Earnings by embroidery workers	232

7.5	Differences in perception	235
8.1	Caste and political representation in Bihar	250
8.2	Voting patterns of upper castes, upper backward castes and Muslims	251
8.3	Voting patterns of lower backward castes and scheduled castes	252
8.4	Landownership by caste in Bihar	253
8.5	Important dates and events in Bihar politics, 2005–9	255
8.6	Caste composition of scheduled castes in Bihar	263
9.1	Per capita GSDP of major Indian states	282
9.2	Index of duality of economy of Bihar and India	284
9.3	Human Development Index of major Indian states, 1981, 1991 and 2001	285
9.4	Poverty ratios in Bihar and India	286
9.5	Literacy rates in Bihar and India	287
9.6	Infant mortality rate and expectation of life in Bihar and India	289

List of Figures

I.1	Per capita income and poverty ratio	4
I.2	Trend of Gini coefficients	5
I.3	Correlate of growth rate and initial income level	6
1.1	Ratio of the average income of the three richest states to that of the poorest states	37
1.2	Convergence or divergence of the state-wise growth rates	38
1.3	Cumulative income distribution and Lorenz curves of India	39
1.4	Coefficients of variation of per capita NSDP for 1960/1–2005/6	40
1.5	State-wise household electrification and income level	44
1.6	Relationship between per capita plan outlay and levels of income	55
2.1	Lorenz curves for consumption expenditure and asset holdings	66
2.2	Changes in asset distribution inequality, 1981/2 to 1991/2	68
2.3	Changes in asset distribution inequality, 1991/2 to 2002/3	69
2.4	Changes in land distribution inequality, 1983 to 1993/4	70
2.5	Changes in land distribution inequality, 1993/4 to 2004/5	70
2.6	Wealth levels and changes in land distribution inequality	71
2.7	Non-agricultural growth and changes in land distribution inequality	71
2.8	Composition of assets in rural India by class, 2002/3	72
3.1	Population group-wise distribution of branches	94
3.2	Population group-wise distribution of credit accounts (in thousands)	95

List of Figures xiii

3.3	Population group-wise distribution of deposit accounts (in thousands)	96
3.4	Population group-wise distribution of credit amount (in Rs crore)	96
3.5	Population group-wise distribution of deposit amount (in Rs crore)	97
3.6	Population group-wise distribution of percentage of population below the poverty line (% of persons)	98
4.1	Latrine type: none or pit = 1, other = 0	115
4.2	Water source: bottles, wells, tankers, tank, pond, river, others = 1, piped water = 0	116
4.3	Water treated: no = 1, yes = 0, conditional on not using piped water	117
4.4	Water treatment: filter, cloth screen, disinfectant, other = 1, uv, resin, reverse osmosis, boiling = 0, conditional on having water treated	118
4.5	Prenatal: government, private = 1, no = 0, conditional on being pregnant	119
4.6	Institutional births: government, private = 1, home, no birth = 0, conditional on being pregnant	120
4.7	Perinatal expenditure: Rs, conditional on being pregnant	121
4.8	Perinatal expenditure: Rs, conditional on utilization	122
4.9	Inpatient care: OOP expenditure, government and other reimbursement (Rs, conditional on being admitted to a hospital)	123
4.10	Outpatient care: OOP expenditure, government and other reimbursement (Rs)	124
4.11	Inpatient medicine expenditure: inside and outside hospitals (Rs)	125
4.12	Outpatient medicine expenditure: inside and outside hospitals (Rs)	126
A4.1	Sampling design of NSS	130
5.1	Attendance ratio (%)	143
5.2	Estimated minimum percentage of over-age children (%)	149

6.1	Houses with electric light *vis-à-vis* urban population/size of town, 2001	193
8.1	Sectoral composition of Bihar's economy	247
8.2	Rice yields in Bihar and West Bengal	248
8.3	Measures of electoral competition in the Bihar Assembly elections	254

Notes on the Contributors

Prabhat P. Ghosh is Professor at the Asian Development Research Institute, Patna, India.

Shigemochi Hirashima is Professor Emeritus, Meiji-Gakuin University, and Visiting Professor, Nihon Fukushi University, Japan.

Takeshi Inoue is Associate Senior Research Fellow of the Area Studies Centre, Institute of Developoing Economies, IDE-JETRO, Japan.

Seiro Ito is Director of the Development Strategies Studies Group, Development Studies Centre, Institute of Developing Economies, IDE-JETRO, Japan.

Norio Kondo is Director of the South Asian Studies Group, Institute of Developing Economies, IDE-JETRO, Japan.

Kensuke Kubo is Associate Senior Research Fellow at the Development Studies Centre, Institute of Developing Economies, IDE-JETRO, Japan.

Kazuki Minato is Research Fellow at the Area Studies Centre, Institute of Developing Economies, IDE-JETRO, Japan.

Mayumi Murayama is Deputy Director-General at the Interdisciplinary Centre, Institute of Developing Economies, IDE-JETRO, Japan.

Hisaya Oda is Professor at the Faculty of Policy Science, Ritsumeikan University, Japan.

Yuko Tsujita is Associate Senior Research Fellow at the Area Studies Centre, Institute of Developing Economies, IDE-JETRO, Japan.

Preface

India's development process started with the centrally planned economic framework placing development as a priority in the capital goods sector. This was a unique and challenging development strategy at that time compared with other developing countries. India has been unique also in placing equal weight on growth and equity in development process at the outset.

The assessment of the development performance during the centrally planned period prior to 1991 is mixed. Those who advocate the advantage of market economy have been critical of the persistent low growth rate of GDP. However, India should be recognized as a developing country that has been successful in maintaining democracy under civilian governments as a secular state. India is also exceptional among many developing countries in that she has been successful in diversifying her economy into a country with a full-fledged industrial structure. The skewed allocation of resources for higher education enabled India to establish a strong higher middle class in the field of science and technology for the development of the capital goods industry.

However, the cost of this strategy has been the slow development of the physical as well as social infrastructure and low efficiency under strong bureaucratic regulations. Although the balance of growth and equity has been the watchword of India as a 'socialistic state of society', India's performance in terms of overcoming social inequality has remained poor. In the face of this reality, India started introducing market principles towards the latter half of the 1980s and declared the final departure from the centrally planned economy in 1991.

The performance of the Indian economy after the reform of 1991 gives an impression that India was successful in getting out of the low-growth trap during the preceding period of planned economy. The higher growth rate has also resulted in the reduction of poverty in all states of India. However, in spite of the remarkable performance in terms of GDP growth rate and poverty reduction, regional disparity in terms of consumption, income and assets has been widening. The Inclusive Growth Strategy (IGS) set forth in 2006 appears to illustrate the strong determination of the Union Government in response to this situation.

The basic idea behind Inclusive Growth is not new. It had already been made explicit by Jawaharlal Nehru in 1947 and Manmohan Singh in 1991. Nor is it an Indian version of a PRSP (Poverty Reduction Strategy Paper). It is beyond the strategy for poverty reduction in economic terms. The real challenge of IGS is how to overcome the inherent social inequality in the process of growth. The study of IGS demands, therefore, a multidimensional, structural and long-term approach. In fact, the IGS covers a wide range of issues: stepping up the investment in infrastructure and agriculture; promoting employment, credit supply and urban renewal; and empowerment of socially discriminated segments of population, gender and minorities.

Although we could not cover all these issues in a comprehensive manner, we think we could shed some light on some of the crucial parts of the issues. We will leave the summary of our major findings to the Introduction, and the detailed analyses to the following chapters. However, it may be worthwhile to mention briefly the nature of this volume.

First, this is the outcome of a research project carried out by the Institute of Developing Economies, Japan, in the fiscal years 2008 and 2009. It should be added, however, that this volume could not have come about without joint field research with the Asian Development Research Institute, Patna, India.

Second, this is not a study of the Indian economy in general, but an IGS-specific study.

Third, this is a collection of chapters where every author shares an appreciation of the importance of the socio-political and structural dimensions of the issues the IGS set forth.

Fourth, in two chapters (Chapters 8 and 9) as well as a part of Chapter 1, Bihar, for a long time the least developed state in terms of per capita GDP, is specifically discussed.

Fifth, we have important chapters discussing the issues of employment and empowerment of women (Chapter 7), the state of the Muslim minority (Chapter 6), the relationship between poverty and health (Chapter 4) and financial inclusion (Chapter 3) and between migration and education (Chapter 5). Each chapter explores the new frontier of the issues that should be elaborated further in future study.

Sixth, the growing regional disparity has been the main issue discussed in two chapters. Chapter 1 examines the issue by focusing on the relationship between public investment and the level of infrastructure. Chapter 2 demonstrates, first, that the disparity of asset holding is more serious compared to that of consumption and income. Second, the growing disparity after the reform, despite higher GDP growth and poverty reduction, is observed in the period where agricultural growth was decelerated and non-agricultural growth was accelerated. The chapter finds also that the transaction of land through markets has not yet shown the direction to improve the social structure.

The objective that IGS has set forth, because of its challenging but novel nature in comparison with PRSP, for instance, would take time and patience. The inherent social inequality cannot be overcome in a short period of time. In this context, we would like to close this Preface by quoting the latter part of Para. 151 of the memorable Budget Speech delivered by Manmohan Singh on 24 July 1991:

> I shall be firm when it comes to defending the interests of this nation. But I promise that in dealing with the people of India I shall be soft hearted. I shall not in any way renege on our nation's firm and irrevocable commitment to the pursuit of equity and social justice. I shall never forget that ultimately all economic processes are meant to serve the interests of our people. It is only through a commitment to social justice and the pursuit of excellence that we can mobilise the collective will of our people for development, to give it a high moral purpose and to keep alive the spirit of national solidarity. The massive social and economic reforms needed to remove the scourge of poverty, ignorance and disease can succeed only if backed by a spirit of high idealism, self sacrifice and dedication.

This volume has greatly benefited from the Asian Development Research Institute (ADRI), Patna. We would like to express our sincere appreciation to Shaibal Gupta, Prabhat P. Ghosh, Sunita Lall and Sudip K. Pandey, to mention a few names at the ADRI, for their academic support and cooperation, which enriches our understanding of Bihar. Shivnath Prasad Yadav and Shashi Ranjan Kumar played leading roles in fieldwork in rural Bihar. We are indebted to Takeo Masuda for excellent administrative support, and Miyuki Kato and Ayumi Takahashi for data-entry and miscellaneous administrative support. Masahiro Okada at IDE-JETRO and Gemma Papageorgiou at Palgrave Macmillan provided timely arrangement for the publication of this volume. Last, but not least, we would like to thank Ritsuko Takakusagi, Noriko Wakabayashi, Lingua Guild Inc., Keith Povey and our English editors for their tremendous help with finalizing the editorial work, as well as anonymous referees for their helpful comments on an earlier draft.

Shigemochi Hirashima
Hisaya Oda
Yuko Tsujita

Introduction: Inclusiveness in India – A Challenging Strategy for Growth and Equality

Shigemochi Hirashima, Hisaya Oda and Yuko Tsujita

As the second largest consumer market in the world, the Indian economy has been enjoying high economic growth in recent years. Consequently, its role in the world, both economically and politically, has been expanding. It is, however, commonly pointed out that social and economic disparities across, for example, geographical, socio-economic, ethnic and gender lines have widened during this period. Inclusive growth, broadly defined as rapid growth benefiting every section of society, has been the main strategy pursued by the present Union Government of India. Unfortunately, the existing literature on inclusive growth is overwhelmingly concentrated on the trend and extent of inequality, particularly the economic aspects of regional inequality. This volume goes far beyond the conventional analysis of economic inequality and intends to critically examine inclusive growth in a wide range of social, economic and geographical areas.

The characteristics of our approach to inclusive growth are mainly threefold. First, multidimensional aspects of disparity are examined. This volume covers a wide range of social and economic development issues, vulnerable sections of the population and underdeveloped states, most of which have not been thoroughly analyzed in terms of disparity. Although this volume focuses on only one country, India, a close look at one particular developing country from multiple aspects provides a comprehensive picture of various forms of disparity and deepens our insight into understanding the processes of economic and social development in a particular context. Second, this volume explores the structural factors behind the increasing disparities. To do so, we have made extensive use of in-depth fieldwork and interviews, although each chapter has taken a different methodological approach, either qualitative, or quantitative, or a mix of both. The case studies include rural Bihar, one of India's most underdeveloped states (Introduction, Chapters 1, 8 and 9) and Delhi urban slums or resettlement colonies (Chapters 5 and 7). Some chapters have empirically examined secondary data, such as the census of India (Chapter 6) and the National Sample Survey (Chapters 2, 3 and 4). These chapters, although they demonstrate causal relations, have also benefited from the authors' own fieldwork or local interviews in Bihar and elsewhere by looking into the reasons for or causes of the growing disparities. It goes without saying that the primary and secondary data used in this volume are the most recent available. Third, policy implications are discussed. The existing literature on inclusive growth has paid insufficient attention to policy implications, mainly due to the difficulty of extracting implications from merely attending to the trend and degree of economic inequality. In this volume, structural dimensions in the growth process have been incorporated into an analysis of social and economic development, which enables us to suggest policy implications and argue for possible approaches to achieve inclusive growth.

So much academic work has been done under the heading of 'inclusive growth' in recent years, particularly since the term 'inclusive growth' appeared in a government document in 2006. Some recent reviews on inclusive growth tend to discuss the main challenges in a variety of sectors, including agriculture, social and physical infrastructure, employment and manufacturing (e.g., Dev, 2007; Dev and Rao, 2009; World Bank, 2006). A pioneering work on inclusive growth by K. N. Raj (Mody, 2006) paid close attention to the political processes involved in inclusive growth with a focus on the intermediate classes, including small businesses, the large and middle peasantry, and labour in the public sector. According to Raj, the intermediate classes are expected to play a spillover role in distributing the fruits of growth to the poor. However, the existing literature, in general, tends to be too comprehensive, so it does not deepen the analysis of the structural aspects of the disparities behind the birth of inclusive growth. Moreover, not all of the work is necessarily inclusive growth-specific; it sometimes overlaps with work under the Poverty Reduction Strategy Paper (PRSP) initiated by the IMF and World Bank. In this volume, we have tried to focus specifically on inclusive growth and on the issues detailed in the later sections of this chapter, so that our work can contribute to a better understanding of inclusive growth. The basic difference between PRSP and inclusive growth lies, in our understanding, in the way that the socio-political dimension is incorporated into the growth process.

This volume is not a comprehensive study on the subject. Instead, it is selective in nature so that we can understand the idea behind the birth of inclusive growth. We have tried to raise relevant questions for the successful implementation of this challenging strategy. An attempt has been made in each chapter to deepen our understanding of the nexus between sector/area issues and inclusive growth, provide a structural dimension to the analysis of disparities and suggest possible approaches and/or constraints to achieve inclusive growth. With this approach, many useful insights have been obtained with respect to the state of inequality that is deeply rooted in Indian society and sometimes, by implication, in the minds of the people. Consequently, we have raised more questions than answers. We also admit that our attempt is far from adequate, so many other important areas and issues have been left for future study. Nevertheless, this volume is written with the firm conviction, that the successful implementation of inclusive growth can lead India to achieve a sustainable society with pride and social dignity.

The remainder of this introductory chapter is organized as follows. First, the recent economic performance is examined. Second, the definition of the current government's inclusive growth is summarized. Third, India's past development strategies are argued, so as to highlight the difference between the inclusive growth of today and the development strategies of the past. Fourth, the challenges of inclusive growth in the post-reform period are discussed. Fifth, the structure of the volume and the major findings from each chapter are briefly summarized. Finally, concluding remarks are presented.

Recent economic performance: background to the inclusive growth strategy

The Indian economy has been enjoying high economic growth in recent years. India's economic performance since 2003/4 has been particularly impressive with an average of around 8 per cent economic growth in terms of net domestic product. This should be compared with the low growth rate of 3.0 to 3.5 per cent during the state planning period, which Raj Krishna labelled 'the Hindu rate of growth'. Then a series of deregulatory policies, starting in the mid-1980s and taking their final form in 1991, shifted the course of the Indian economy from a lower to a higher growth trajectory. Because of the higher and relatively stable economic growth and future prospects backed by the second largest consumer market in the world, India is regarded as an emerging economic power and is celebrated as a member of BRICs (Brazil, Russia, India and China). In fact, the size of the Indian economy in terms of purchasing power parity (PPP)-based national income is already the fourth largest in the world after the United States, China and Japan.

At the national level, higher economic growth has translated into higher per capita income growth. As indicated by Figure I.1, per capita income has steadily increased, as has the rate of growth. In turn, higher per capita income has had a positive impact on poverty reduction. The Planning Commission estimates the headcount poverty ratio declined from 54.9 per cent in 1973/4 to 27.5 per cent in 2004/5 at the national level.[1] Both urban and rural headcount poverty ratios improved over the same period. Although not shown here, other poverty indicators such as the poverty gap and the squared poverty gap indices also reveal similar trends. At the state level, both rural and urban areas in all states witnessed a reduction in the poverty ratio over the same period.

The Indian economy seems to be on the right track in terms of achieving higher economic growth and reducing poverty. However, a detailed analysis of state-wise income and poverty data reveals a different picture, namely that of increasing interstate disparity. Figure I.2 shows the Gini

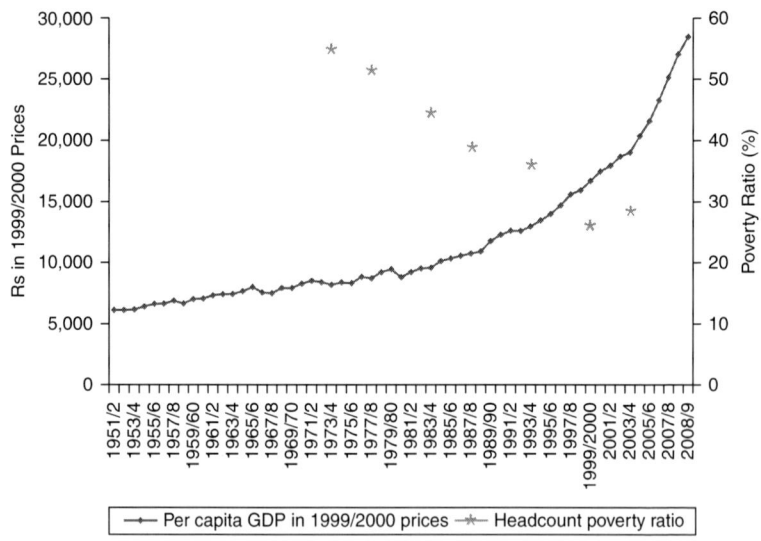

Figure I.1 Per capita income and poverty ratio

Note: The headcount poverty ratio for 1999/2000 is not directly compatible with earlier estimates due to a difference in the reference periods. Per capita GDP is used as a proxy for per capita income.
Sources: Indiastat database (www.indiastat.com) and Dev and Ravi (2007).

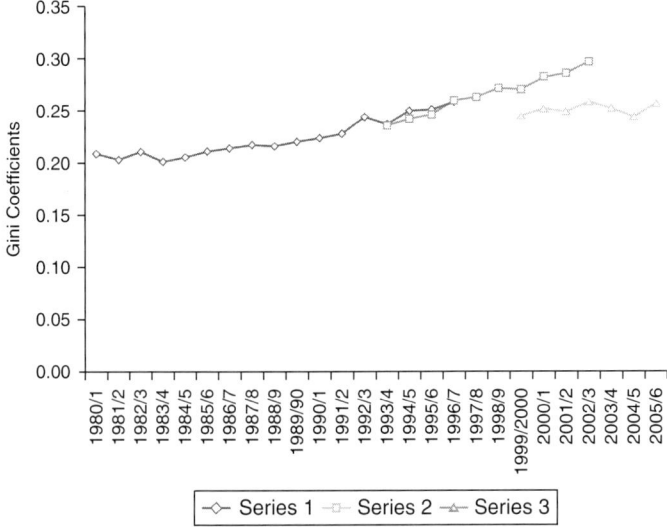

Figure I.2 Trend of Gini coefficients

Note: Gini coefficients are calculated using real per capita NSDP. Series 1 is based on 1980/1 constant prices, Series 2 on 1993/4 constant prices, Series 3 on 2000/1 prices.
Source: Indiastat database (www.indiastat.com).

coefficients for state-wise disparity measured in real per capita net state domestic product (NSDP) from 1980/1 to 2004/5. During this period, the Gini coefficient increased continually from 0.209 in 1980/1 to 0.257 in 2005/6 (the figure was 0.296 based on 1993 constant prices), indicating a widening income gap across Indian states. The coefficient of variation of real per capita NSDP shows a similar trend (see Chapter 1). Both of these results confirm the existence of rising income disparities across Indian states.

For the income disparity to decline, low-income states need to grow faster than high-income states. However, as evidenced in Figure I.3, which indicates the relationship between initial income levels and the average growth rates of states, there is no such trend. On the contrary, the figure shows that several low-income states record slow growth while some high-income states grow faster. Thus, the initial income gap not only persists but has also been widening due to differences in subsequent economic growth rates.

In terms of the growth–poverty nexus, a number of studies point to the fact that several of the low-growth states also show low poverty

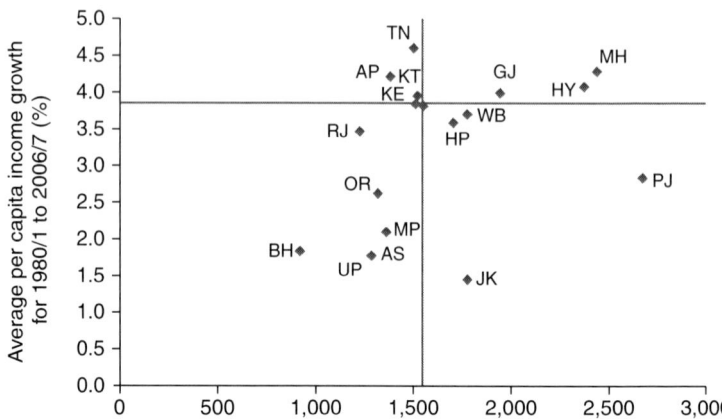

Figure I.3 Correlate of growth rate and initial income level

Note: Figures are based on real per capita NSDP in 17 major states, namely: Andhra Pradesh (AP), Assam (AS), Bihar (BH), Gujarat (GJ), Haryana (HY), Himachal Pradesh (HP), Jammu and Kashmir (JK), Karnataka (KT), Kerala (KE), Madhya Pradesh (MP), Maharashtra (MH), Orissa (OR), Punjab (PJ), Rajasthan (RJ), Tamil Nadu (TN), Uttar Pradesh (UP), and West Bengal (WB). The vertical and horizontal lines indicate all-India averages.
Source: Indiastat (www.indiastat).

elasticity (e.g., Purfield, 2006). As noted above, poverty ratios at both the national and state levels have been continually declining. However, low poverty elasticity implies that the rate at which poverty is being reduced in response to economic growth is low.

In investigating interstate income disparity, an emerging but not well documented fact is widening intrastate disparity. For example, the per capita income level in Patna, the most affluent district in Bihar, was, in 2006/7, 8.6 times that of Sheohar, an underdeveloped district in the same state (Government of Bihar, 2010), while the difference was only 3.3 times in 1998/9 (Government of Bihar, 2007). What is worse is that the deprivation in Bihar, not just in monetary terms but in other respects, relative to other states, is striking. For example, the census of India 2001 shows that the literacy rate for males, females and scheduled caste (SC) females are 94.2 per cent, 87.9 per cent and 82.7 per cent, respectively, in Kerala, where social indicators are high, while the corresponding figures in Bihar are 59.7 per cent, 33.6 per cent and 15.6 per cent, respectively. The female literacy rate of Musahar, one of the most deprived SCs in Bihar is only 3.9 per cent. This clearly demonstrates that the difference across gender and castes is much larger in

Bihar than Kerala. The state of inequality in Bihar, which is even greater and worse than in some better-off states over time, is concealed by the general tendency to neglect growing intrastate disparities. On the whole, and even with the recent high economic growth in India as a whole, inter- and intrastate disparities and socio-economic deprivation persist in many forms.

Furthermore, disparity is manifested not only spatially but also, for instance, in terms of caste, religion and gender. (See Chapter 6 for religious minorities and Chapter 7 for gender.) For example, even after the long-term implementation of affirmative action programmes that provide a quota system whereby a certain proportion of posts or seats are reserved in public sector employment and higher educational institutions, the socio-economic deprivation of scheduled castes and scheduled tribes (SC/STs) has been clearly apparent (e.g., Borooah and Iyer, 2005; Kijima, 2006). Overcoming the inherent social inequality that is deeply rooted in rural India, where two-thirds of the total population live, is another genuine objective of inclusive growth. In fact, Indian village communities do not consist of farming households alone; they also contain as many as 40 per cent non-farming households, some of which have traditionally been distinguished from farm households on the basis of caste (the so-called *Jajimani* system). Economic disadvantage and social discrimination against lower castes in the caste hierarchy might not have diminished as fast as the social division of labour. Inclusive growth in our understanding is to question the nature of growth processes and their impact on the socio-political structure of society. It, therefore, has to be a broad-based approach, with a focus on the social dimension of these processes and their distributional consequences. In rural India, one more dimension of disparity has to be looked into, namely the disparity in terms of asset holding position. In fact, we found out that the disparity in asset holding, in particular land, measured in terms of Gini coefficient is much higher than that of consumption and income between cultivators and non-cultivators, and between higher castes and SC/ST/OBC (Hirashima, 2009; Chapter 2).

A growth process which reduces inequality is important in many ways. Empirical evidence suggests that inequality in income and assets has an adverse effect on a wide range of different kinds of socio-economic deprivation (Wilkinson and Pickett, 2007). Inequality is also associated with unequal opportunities, further leading to wasted productive potential and the inefficient allocation of resources, while also inhibiting sound institutional development (World Bank, 2005). Moreover, the importance of politics and its consequences cannot be ignored in a democratic country. Inequality in India has been an issue ever since before Independence. As courting the rural votebank has been important politically, a wide range of rural poverty alleviation programmes have been carried out, mainly since the 1970s. Furthermore, the current Union Government, led by the Indian National Congress, is perceived as having been swept into power by voters from the lower socio-economic strata of society who had not adequately benefited from the economic growth touted by the previous ruling party who campaigned under the slogan 'Shining India'. In fact, the slow growth and persistent socio-economic inequality in less-developed states and regions have already led to an escalation in terrorism by some ultra-left-wing groups, such as the Naxalites. If current inequalities continue, their political costs will become higher. As widely argued in the literature, instability is detrimental to economic growth. It also poses a more serious threat to a heterogeneous country, like India, that is composed of many religious, ethnic and linguistic groups. Given this fear, it is easy to understand why the current Union Government has employed the concept of 'inclusive growth' to focus in its policy on economic growth and equity.

Higher economic growth in the post-reform period has translated into per capita income growth. However, trickle-down theory has not worked for the poor. The extent of poverty reduction in the 1990s and afterwards slowed down in comparison with that of the 1980s (Dev and Ravi, 2007; Himanshu, 2007). Many proponents of the belief that a higher GDP growth rate would trickle down and alleviate social inequality expected this to occur in the post-reform period. The condition of inherent social inequality has shown slow improvement during the pre-reform period as well as the post-reform period. The tension between growth and inclusion is further intensified by the recent trend that *haves* can access better-quality private infrastructure and services while *have-nots* have no access or only access to an inferior quality of public or even informal infrastructure and services. Inclusive growth strategies face both persistent age-old problems and emerging challenges. The realization of these challenges posed by inclusive growth is, in fact, reflected in the development priorities manifested in the current Five-Year Plan (2007/8–2011/12).

What does the government mean by 'inclusive growth'?

To our knowledge, the term 'inclusive growth' first appeared explicitly in the Union Government's Approach Paper to the 11th Five-Year

Plan (2007/8–2011/12). Under the specific chapter on inclusive growth, the document states:

> The strategy of inclusive growth proposed in this paper can command broad-based support only if growth is seen to demonstrably bridge divides and avoid exclusion or marginalization of large segments of our population. These divides manifest themselves in various forms: between the haves and the have-nots; between rural and urban areas; between the employed and the under/unemployed; between different states, districts and communities; and finally between genders. (Government of India, 2006a: 71)

This concept has been more clearly articulated in the Prime Minister's statement given in his foreword to the document 'Report to the People' prepared by the United Progressive Alliance, the ruling coalition of the Union Government. It states,

> The key components of our strategy of 'inclusive growth' have been to:
>
> (a) Step up investment in rural areas, in rural infrastructure and agriculture;
> (b) Increase credit availability to farmers and offer them remunerative prices for their crops;
> (c) Increase rural employment, providing a unique social safety net in the shape of the National Rural Employment Guarantee Programme;
> (d) Increase public spending on education and health care, including strengthening the mid-day meal programme and offering scholarships to the needy;
> (e) Invest in urban renewal, improving the quality of life for the urban poor;
> (f) Socially, economically and educationally empower scheduled castes, scheduled tribes, other backward classes, minorities, women and children; and
> (g) Ensure that, through public investment, the growth process spreads to backward regions and districts.

This strategy of 'inclusive growth' combines empowerment with entitlement and investment. Education empowers, improved health care empowers, employment guarantees entitle, fulfilling quota obligations entitles. Through a combination of offering entitlement, ensuring empowerment and stepping up public investment, our Government has sought to make the growth process more inclusive. (UPA, 2007: 5–8)

Although the concept of inclusive growth does not seem to be limited only to reducing inequality with respect to income/expenditure, inclusive growth as presented by the government offers only broad definitions and focuses more on listing the areas and sectors concerned. The World Bank (2006) has emphasized the speed and pattern of growth, having defined inclusive growth as sustainable, long-term, broad-based high growth benefiting the poor in absolute terms. The government of India has elsewhere further made it clear that the strategy of inclusive growth involves achieving a particular growth process with objectives of inclusiveness and sustainability rather than the employment of conventional strategies which only address some aspects of inclusion (Government of India, 2008: 5). This implies that the goal of the growth process is to distribute the benefits of growth to the weaker sections of society and to increase their overall wellbeing. Accordingly, the government, as in past planning and government documents, established specific short-run targets in a large number of areas of social and economic development. This seems, however, to be oriented towards development rather than inclusiveness. More fundamentally, it is not clearly stated what factors could have contributed to the growing disparities and for how long these disparities might have been increasing. It is, therefore, not sufficiently clear how inclusive growth can be achieved, particularly at and for the bottom social and economic milieux.

India has a long history of redressing unequal opportunity for the weaker sectors of society. For instance, affirmative action programmes to mitigate the disadvantages of SCs and STs have been carried out since Independence and even during the British colonial period in some presidency areas or princely states. Now the question arises as to whether there is any distinctive difference between 'inclusive growth' in the pre-reform and post-reform periods. Let us briefly review India's development strategies in the pre-reform period so as to demonstrate the contention that inclusive growth has existed since Independence.

India's past development strategies

India's development policy was unique in two respects in comparison to other developing countries. First, from the very beginning under the first Prime Minister Pandit Nehru's socialist vision and as a principle of nation building, India assigned equal weight to both growth and equity in its development planning process. Second, India opted to develop its economy by giving preference to the development of the capital goods sector over the consumer goods sector. As a result of this unique strategy, India was able to diversify its industrial structure much faster than other developing countries, many of which have still not succeeded in developing a fully fledged industrial structure. The development of heavy industry demanded the faster development of higher education, with particular emphasis on the natural sciences. Even though this skewed allocation of resources to higher education supported the growth of heavy industry and, later, the information technology industry, the trade-off in this unique development strategy was a delay in the provision of basic education. Also, it has to be pointed out that the development of heavy industry in India was achieved without much direct support from the agricultural sector. This is evidenced by the extremely low correlation coefficient between the growth rate of the industrial sector and that of the agricultural sector, although the overall GDP growth rate was significantly influenced by the performance of the agricultural sector (Hirashima, 2008) until recently when the economy started to shift rapidly towards services and industries in terms of value added.

The equal weight policy to growth and equity was not rigorously implemented, even under the state-led planning process. Growth in the first place remained low. Unlike East Asian countries, the industrial sector in India could not play a leading role in economic growth and poverty alleviation. The adaptation of capital-intensive technology led to a residual absorption of labour in the industrial sector, particularly the labour-intensive manufacturing sector. Some measures that were adopted with the aim of promoting equity in the industrial sector were introduced during the planning period. The regional dispersal of industrialization, following policies of protection for small-scale industry, freight equalization of inputs such as coal, iron and cement, industrial licensing in favour of the private sector to help them set up in less developed areas, the location of public enterprises in underdeveloped areas and so on, seem, though, to have achieved little. In the short run, the agricultural sector also failed to play a vital role in development. The effect of the 'green revolution' was confined to the irrigated north-east regions in the initial phase, although it did the spread to some other regions, particularly in the 1980s. The higher growth in outputs, crop diversification, and the growth of agricultural productivity resulted in higher wage levels and triggered rapid growth in the non-agricultural sector through input, output and consumption linkages (Fujita, 2002). A serious concern, however, is that agricultural development has been accompanied by inter-regional and inter-household disparity (Bhalla and Singh, 2001). The recent low growth in the output of major cereals is partly attributable to the low growth in output in 'left out' regions, such as Bihar, where the irrigation ratio, the precondition for the adaptation of new seed and fertilizer technology, is still low. The regions where agricultural investments are urgently required in order to maintain the self-sufficiency of major food grains for all, which is getting difficult even amid a decline in per capita consumptions of cereals in the country, often overlap with places where the public distribution system, including the distribution of subsidized food to the poor, is relatively dysfunctional, and nutrition-related indicators are low. Underdeveloped regions are burdened with multiple-faceted problems of development.

Drèze and Sen (2002) assessed the three most important tasks facing India, which were identified by the first Prime Minister Pandit Nehru in his well-known speech 'Tryst with Destiny' on the eve of Independence. The following were primarily chosen on the basis of their impact on the conditions of the poor in India: (1) a focus on the practice of democracy and the guarantee of various freedoms to the citizens of India, (2) the removal of the social inequality and backwardness that characterized British India and (3) the achievement of economic progress. From this perspective, independent India's worst marks are in the area of removing social inequality. This is evident from such factors as the slow spread of basic education, health, drinking water, sanitation and pervasive disparities between different socio-economic classes, genders, and regional and geographical areas. It is noteworthy that these deficiencies occurred during the pre-reform period when the state was expected to play a more active role in economic and social development.

On the whole, the main thrust of inclusive growth remains more or less the same in both the pre- and post-reform periods. Hanumantha Rao points out that it is neither a new nor a novel idea, and stands for 'equitable development' or for 'growth with social justice', which have always been the watchwords of development planning in India (Rao, 2009). The basic principles behind inclusive growth have been explicit for a long time.

Challenges in current inclusive growth strategies

Although the principal ideas of inclusive growth have remained much the same since the pre-reform period, there seem to be a few distinct differences in the circumstances surrounding the pursuit of inclusive growth in the post-reform period. On the one hand, the economic and political climate in the post-reform period seems to have been endowed with the potential to reduce disparities. Recent higher economic growth enables the government to raise revenue so that it can finance the bigger budgets which the inclusive growth strategy requires, mainly through higher tax revenues and a larger borrowing capacity, both of which, in fact, as a share of GDP have, on aggregate, risen for state governments in the 2000s. Politically, quite a few caste/religion-based or -supported parties have increasingly voiced their own demands, interests and rights, and even come into power, especially at the state level. In the villages, economic, social and political mobility has undergone changes in the local power structure over the years, particularly through the emergence of some intermediate and backward castes, even in underdeveloped states (e.g., Lieten and Srivastava, 1999, for Uttar Pradesh; and Gupta, 2001, for Bihar), although the extent to which this has happened varies from village to village.

On the other hand, overall economic policy in the post-reform period is for market forces to drive economic growth. Inclusive growth in the post-reform period has been tenaciously adopted with this form of growth strategy in mind. In the 11th Five-Year Plan document, it is clear that the provision of economic and social infrastructure and services tends to be reliant on the private sector or on public–private partnerships (PPP). The rational of public sector participation, or PPP, is mainly the public sector's inefficiency and the lack of resources. Critics argue that the current model of PPP is inclined to privatization (Datta, 2009) or that it contains a built-in mechanism to move towards privatization (CBGA *et al.*, 2009) even in essential service delivery to the poor at the grassroots level. In fact, despite the government's emphasis on care for the vulnerable and the poor who are more likely to depend on public services and infrastructure, development expenditure on aggregate by state governments, both as a share of GDP and of total expenditure, has not significantly increased, and social expenditure at the aggregated states level, both as a share of GDP and total expenditure, has declined since the late 1990s and risen since 2005/6 only to the level of the late 1990s. Worse still, underdeveloped states tend to be in a weaker fiscal position. This contradictory trend of stagnating expenditure at the level of the state while revenues have increased can be attributed not only to the Fiscal Responsibility and Budget Management Act, 2003, under which the government sought to take measures to reduce both the revenue and the fiscal deficits, but also, implicitly, to the recognition that the role of the government had changed from that of a major player to that of being just one player or facilitator among many in social and economic development through the PPP.

The inclusive growth strategy is predicated on market-led growth. Nevertheless, the government has emphasized the political consideration that the interplay of market forces alone is unlikely to remedy disparities stemming from social and economic divisions. Quality infrastructure and services affordable to anyone and maximizing everyone's quality of life with limited public finances remain major challenges.

It is well known that the higher attainment of social welfare in the state of Kerala is the result of active public intervention. It is, however, argued that the active role of the private sector is not negligible in the development of various basic services and welfare schemes, and the stereotypical dichotomy of the market versus the government misses complementary relationships between the two (Drèze and Sen, 2002; Sato, 2004). It is implied that decentralization could be a policy that would help to enhance these complementary relationships. A series of legal provisions to promote decentralization and empower democratic representation in local bodies have been amended since the 1990s. The involvement of the community at the grassroots level is expected to play an important role in improving the delivery system of essential services and poverty alleviation. At the same time, the central government has increasingly controlled state governments by increasing the amount it allocates to the Central Plan and Centrally Sponsored Scheme, in which each state government shares a certain proportion of the budget and carries out the same programmes all over the country. The shift in decision-making and in the allocation of funds to local communities often translates into different democratic participatory processes and differences in the degree to which programmes formulated by the central government are implemented (see the case of rural Bihar in the latter section of this chapter). Unfortunately, as we have argued, the inclusive growth strategy does not sufficiently address how development and poverty alleviation programmes can be implemented adequately, efficiently, accountably and transparently at the grassroots level. The government, with some degree of decentralization, has tried to improve programme implementation for the poor, such as by creating new institutions for new programmes, introducing bank transfers for a variety of beneficiaries, and other innovations, but they cannot necessarily provide a panacea for a wide range of problems facing people at the grassroots level. There might be growing momentum to reframe how inclusiveness can be achieved in a participatory fashion through mutually compatible and complementary relationships between the government, local institutions, the private sector, NGOs and so on.

Structure of volume and major findings

The present government's strategy of inclusive growth, as a broad-based strategy, pays attention to the following diverse areas: rural areas and farmers, employment and the safety net, education and health, the urban deprived, scheduled castes and scheduled tribes (SC/STs), other backward classes (OBCs) and minorities, women and children, and backward regions and districts. Although this volume is not comprehensive in nature, it has tried to touch upon as many of the above areas as possible.

This volume contains nine chapters in four parts. The three chapters in Part I and the two chapters in Part II deal with selected issues concerning key elements in inclusive growth. The two chapters in Part III take up the issue of the weaker sections of the population. The last two chapters in Part IV try to understand the historical and structural constraints on inclusive growth by examining possible explanations for the situation in the lowest income state in India, namely Bihar.

Growth poverty linkages and income–asset disparity in the inclusive growth strategies

Part I discusses growth, poverty and disparity across states in terms of their physical infrastructure (Chapter 1), assets, particularly land holdings, non-agricultural growth (Chapter 2) and institutional finance (Chapter 3).

Despite the importance of physical infrastructure development in economic growth (e.g., Straub, 2008), India's infrastructure development has lagged far behind economic growth. Public–private partnerships have been promoted, particularly in the transportation and power sectors. This is mainly due to financial constraints in the public sector and the leading role expected of the private sector in infrastructure development. Financing patterns, however, are still dominated by the public sector. In 2006/7, public investments were 4.23 per cent of GDP, while the private sector accounted for only 1.20 per cent of GDP (Government of India, 2006a: 11).

In this context, Chapter 1 examines the relationship between inter-state income disparity and infrastructure provision. The chapter first analyzes the growing income gap between richer and poorer states and presents several forms of evidence. Then, using a panel data for 17 states, econometric analysis demonstrates that the disparity across states can be explained by differences in the level of infrastructure provision.

In addition, the chapter discusses why the infrastructure is inadequate in some states. The case of Bihar, an underdeveloped state, is considered. It argues that deficiencies in infrastructure result from a weak fiscal position, the state's poor management of public expenditure and the low level of fiscal assistance from the central government. The chapter concludes that, despite efforts by the central government under the slogan of 'inclusive growth', current policies towards backward states are not only ineffective at redressing the gap between richer and poorer states, but may even increase this gap.

Common observable features among high poverty states such as Bihar, Madhya Pradesh (MP), Orissa, Rajasthan and Uttar Pradesh (UP) are a higher share of agriculture in the NSDP and in the total labour force, and a lower agricultural growth rate. The majority of the population, nearly 60 per cent of the country's workforce, is still principally engaged in agriculture, even though agriculture's contribution to GDP has declined to around 20 per cent. It is pointed out that agricultural growth is more effective than non-agricultural growth for reducing the poverty of the poor (World Bank, 2007). However, the recent economic growth in India is led by the non-agricultural sector, and there is no doubt that non-agricultural sector growth will play an important role in both accelerating economic growth and the alleviation of poverty.

Chapter 2 argues for the importance, when discussing poverty, vulnerability and disparity in rural India, of including the situation with regard to a household's assets. The chapter starts by demonstrating, first, that the disparity in assets, particularly in land, is far greater than the disparity in consumption and income. This finding raises a basic question regarding the methodology of poverty analysis, since the conventional approach has been confined only to levels of consumption and income. Second, the disparity, as measured in terms of the Gini coefficient in consumption, income and assets, declined in the 1980s, while it increased in the 1990s and early 2000s. The hypothesis was that the increase in disparity after the reform occurred when agricultural growth decelerated and non-agricultural growth accelerated (Hirashima, 2009). Chapter 2 tested this by using a more rigorous statistical analysis and confirmed the validity of this causal relationship. The policy implications of this finding are, therefore, that we recognize the significant role of agricultural growth in the context of disparity and try to enhance it. Simultaneously, we should accelerate non-agricultural growth while at the same time mitigating any factors that increase disparity. Third, it is documented that almost 90 per cent of rural assets are held in the form of land, buildings and livestock. It has also been found that the assets situation is the most important issue with regard to disparity in rural India. In fact, the average value of assets of a non-cultivator household was only 27 per cent that of a cultivator household at the all-India level. Also, the average value of assets of the scheduled castes was 27 per cent that of the higher castes in 2002 (*ibid.*). This difference is mainly attributable to how the ownership of land, which has been the symbol of prestige, power and wealth in rural India, is distributed. It was thought, therefore, that the direction of change in a social structure could be examined by analyzing trends in market transactions in land. It is presumed that social inequality in rural India might be changed if the buyer of land is a smaller peasant or a landless non-farmer and the seller is a wealthy farmer or a landlord. This chapter's findings show that most of India has taken the opposite path, the exceptions being those states where land reform was enforced in the past, notably West Bengal. The chapter also confirms that, due to the fact that land values are growing faster than is the case with rental income from the land, it has become more difficult for landless and smaller peasants to acquire land within the economic and institutional framework that presently determines behaviour in India's land market.

Financial inclusion is broadly defined as the process of ensuring access to and the use of basic formal financial services to all people at an affordable cost. In India, there have been various measures to encourage financial inclusion since the late 1960s. These have evolved from such schemes as the nationalization of commercial banks; the policy of credit lending to priority sectors such as agriculture, small-scale industries, the self-employed and weaker sections in the pre-reform periods; measures in the post-reform period such as the promotion of microfinance in collaboration with self-help groups (SHGs), largely formed by poor women, and the linking of SHGs with banks; and, finally, the issuing of Kisan credit cards, which help farmers buy inputs and meet their other production needs. This has contributed to some extent in that institutional finance has gradually increased and is estimated to have outweighed non-institutional finance over this period.[2] Meanwhile, indebtedness in terms of the number of households and the total amount of debt has increased over these years. It is estimated that nearly half the farm households were in debt (Government of India, 2007: 58). It is increasingly being reported that indebtedness has triggered a spate of farmer suicides, particularly in drought-prone areas. The government has taken initiatives such as debt waivers and debt-relief schemes for farmers.

Against this background, Chapter 3 analyzes, through the use of panel data regression models, whether financial inclusion measures have a statistically significant relationship to poverty conditions. For empirical analysis, the chapter used unbalanced panel data for 25 states and union territories covering seven time periods between 1973–4 and 2004–5. The model was specified to examine the impact of financial inclusion on poverty reduction. Following the relevant literature, the number of bank branches is regarded as the measure of physical access to financial services, while the number of bank accounts, the size of the deposits and the amount of credit are used to measure people's use of financial services. The econometric analysis in this chapter shows that these variables, except for the number of credit accounts, have a statistically significant negative relationship with the poverty ratio in rural and urban areas, even when controlling for outputs, government expenditure and the inflation rate. Accordingly, although some policy-makers have concerns about the progress of financial inclusion, the results in this chapter suggest that both access to and the use of financial services have actually contributed to the alleviation of poverty in rural and urban India.

Disparity in access to social services

In Part II, the disparity in access to social services, namely health and education, is investigated. Drèze and Sen (1995) argued that the government pursued an over-regulated economic policy and took no major initiative towards radical change in social policy in the pre-reform period. The basic provision of primary health care and basic education is therefore still incomplete. For example, in the census of India 2001 health and education indicators, such as life expectancy at birth (64.1 years) and adult literacy (65.2 per cent), remain low due to depressed figures in less developed states and in lower socio-economic strata. These low figures can be partly attributable to low public expenditure. Although the government has acknowledged that the majority of the poor depend upon public systems, and national policies regarding both health and education set a target for public expenditure equalling 6 per cent of GDP, this level has never been achieved. It was the private sector that eventually met this target (Tilak, 1995; World Bank, 1995). In fact, the 11th Five-Year Plan stated that private sector participation, or the PPP, is frequently mentioned, even in some areas of basic health and education provision (Government of India, 2008). Moreover, even if public expenditure is distributed in these sectors, the distribution of facilities, qualified human resources (i.e., medical professionals and teachers) and the quality of training or treatment seem to be inadequate and insufficient. The mismatch between resources and achievement due to the system of health and education provision among others is also serious. As the quality of basic health and education services in the public sector has fallen over the years, the affluent have increasingly tended to turn to the private sector. In contrast, the less privileged still depend on public services. As the supply side of health and education shifts towards a dichotomy of service providers based on one's economic status, the demand side is analyzed in Chapters 4 and 5. Both chapters have identified to what extent the quantity of basic provision has progressed and the household expenditure for such provision, and have discussed the challenges this situation poses for policy.

Using NSS household-level data, Chapter 4 examines the public's use of the health service. Health is considered paramount to wellbeing, but the disparities among the population with regard to health have been a lingering issue in the socio-economic development of India. As it is difficult to assess disparity by looking at state averages, the chapter summarizes health information by income quintile on a state-by-state basis. This chapter follows the central government's priorities and focuses on the sanitation infrastructure, pre-natal health, and medical expenditure and finance in rural India. It finds that: (1) water connections have improved while appropriate water treatment is mostly lacking, (2) the lack of toilets on household premises remains a challenge, (3) mean expenditure for births is high across income levels, (4) pre-natal checks are associated with lower mean expenditure for births and after birth, (5) mean in-patient expenditure plus expenditure on medicines outside the hospital, both conditional on admission, are high and pose serious risks for rural households, (6) government reimbursement for medical services is concentrated on low-income groups but is still not enough to cover costs, (7) the use of private insurance remains negligible and (8) there is substantial variation within states and union territories, which cannot be assessed using state averages. The author argues for more focused campaigns on preventive medicine, the establishment of a finance mechanism for the poor, and the need for decentralization within states.

The importance of education lies in the fact that disparities in the quality and quantity of education a child can receive are likely to affect a wide range of opportunities in the course of that person's life and for future generations. Recent and wide-ranging efforts to achieve the universalization of elementary education have been made with increasing urgency in the legal, financial and political areas. While these efforts have proved somewhat effective in rural areas with a rapid increase in enrolment in elementary schools, the situation has stagnated or even deteriorated in the urban areas of a large number of states. India is still a less urbanized country, in which only around 30 per cent of the population live in urban areas. However, with an increase in the growth of the urban population and in the volume of rural-to-urban migration, urban poverty has become worse in recent years.

Chapter 5 examines whether and how migration has an effect on the school attendance of urban slum children at their destination. It is argued that migration tends to affect school attendance adversely, particularly for children in migrant households who are disadvantaged by reason of their caste, religion, or gender. The chapter shows that, among the slum children, the problem of children never attending school is more critical than students dropping out. Apart from questions of caste or gender, school admission barriers for migrants who want to enter school become more difficult to overcome because of a lack of preparation for formal schooling at the pre-school age, such as the obtaining of a birth certificate, the completion of health-related programmes and attendance at pre-primary classes. The chapter, therefore, emphasizes the importance of parental awareness on pre-school programmes in the preparation for formal schooling and highlights the need to improve government schools, since the overwhelming majority of children can neither meet the admission criteria of private schools nor afford to attend them.

Issues of the weaker sections of the population in the inclusive growth strategies

Part III focuses specifically on weaker and more vulnerable populations in the context of inclusive growth. Chapter 6 discusses a religious minority (Muslims) in terms of the provision of a semi-public good (electricity), while Chapter 7 analyzes female homeworkers in terms of gender and employment.

The need for equity across caste, religion, gender, etc. has been recognized from early on. As discussed earlier, the system of quotas for public sector jobs and for higher education for SC/STs has evolved to expand education and employment quotas for OBCs. These quotas have been further extended to SC/STs in the Indian parliament, and to SCs, STs, OBCs and women in *panchayat* (local democratic institutions) to ensure that deprived groups are represented in government. In general, however, these underprivileged groups have continued to be relatively deprived even long after the implementation of the reservation policy (Deshpande, 2001; Kijima, 2006). At the same time, it is pointed out that the benefits of reservation policies has been disproportionally distributed and the disparity among underprivileged groups has also widened over the years (Mendelsohn and Vicziany, 1998). It finds that some SC/STs, even if few in number, experienced upward mobility. Underprivileged groups of Muslims, while generally categorized as OBCs, do not seem to benefit from the reservation system when compared to Hindu OBCs, who far outnumber Muslims. Muslims, comprising about 13 per cent of the population, are subject to occasional violence along religious lines, which has been instigated by the rise of Hindu nationalism in response to changing secular values. The Sachar Committee, established in 2005 and tasked with reporting on the socio-economic state-of-affairs of Muslims, provides the most comprehensive picture to date of Muslims in India (see Government of India, 2006b).

The analysis in Chapter 6, which is based on a theoretical analysis, confirms the relatively deprived living conditions faced by the Muslim population. The study utilized two theories, 'weak voice theory' and 'heterogeneity theory', to examine the relation between the provision of semi-public goods, namely, electric light, and the status of religious minorities, with a particular focus on Muslims. The former theory posits that the social weakness of a community explains the lower provision of public goods, while the latter theory locates the reason in lower levels of demand articulation and a lack of collective action by a certain group in a mixed community. Statistical analysis of the census of India 2001 data for four individual states – Gujarat, Bihar, Uttar Pradesh and West Bengal – as well as a pooled analysis of the four states supported the 'weak voice theory' interpretation for Muslims, with some limitations which depended on the socio-political structure of each state. On the other hand, the 'heterogeneity theory' was not confirmed by the analysis.

The recent high economic growth has not generated adequate employment opportunities in the formal sector, a situation often referred to as 'jobless' growth. Much empirical analysis has proved that the high economic growth of recent years is associated with a decline in the growth of employment opportunities and a fall in average earnings (see NCEUS, 2009, for reviews). The incidence of poverty among casual labourers and the self-employed is estimated to be higher than for regular workers in urban areas, while the incidence of poverty for agricultural labourers is higher than that for the self-employed in agriculture and the self-employed in the non-agricultural sector in rural areas (Sundram and Tendulkar, 2003). More than 90 per cent of the workforce is in the unorganized sector, even though this sector is estimated to contribute to half India's GDP (NCEUS, 2009).[3] The creation of adequate employment opportunities and the provision of better economic and social security for economically and socially disadvantaged populations in the society is a prerequisite for making growth 'inclusive'. Although some legal provision has been made in recent years to promote social security and safety nets for those who work in the unorganized sector, there is no doubt that it is difficult to assimilate informal sector workers in growth processes. Homeworkers represent a particular sub-section of the informal workforce. These workers carry out paid work for firms/ businesses or their intermediaries, typically on a piece-rate basis, generally provide the means of production and their workplace by themselves, and are overwhelmingly female (ILO, 2002).

Chapter 7 provides an analysis of a case study describing an attempt by embroidery homeworkers to organize to eliminate middlemen and to ensure better piece-rates, and explores the outstanding challenges that homeworkers face in order to achieve empowerment. The analysis suggests that although the negotiated piece-rates were relatively better than the rates workers could get from middlemen, the economic benefits were limited due to an irregular supply of work in the face of stiff competition from the middlemen. The programme, nevertheless, did begin to change the perceptions and attitudes of members towards women's empowerment. The chapter argues that the next challenge is to make the programme economically sustainable without sacrificing its social objectives.

Perspectives for overcoming underdevelopment: the case of Bihar

Finally, Part IV focuses on the state of Bihar, one of the least developed states in India. Bihar used to be endowed with natural resources.[4] However, colonial legacies (Frankel, 1989), the central government's agricultural and industrial policies (Ghosh, in this volume) and the negative interaction between the state's politics and its economy (Minato, in this volume), among other reasons, are often listed as the main causes of Bihar's social and economic underdevelopment. Bihar, as was pointed out earlier, continues to lag further and further behind other states in terms of economic and social indicators (see Chapter 9).

However, it is clear that poverty in Bihar *has* declined, albeit at a slower rate than in other states, and the state has experienced positive economic growth, although at a slower pace than elsewhere. In a survey conducted in 80 villages in five districts in Bihar, in which *Mukhiyas*, the heads of *Gram Panchayat* (the lowest tier of the rural self-government system) and village leaders assessed changes in their villages in the last decade, 77 out of 80 of the respondents concluded that their villages were relatively better off than ten years ago.[5] The main reasons given for this assessment were increased employment opportunities outside the village, followed by access to education (Table I.1). It is reported

Table 1.1 Evaluation of change over time by *Mukhiya*, or village leaders, in Bihar

Name of district	Per capita GDDP (Rs)	Ranking in the livelihood potential index (out of 38 districts)	No. of surveyed villages	No. of better-off villages	Most important reasons (up to three) for being better-off in the last ten years					
					Outside jobs	Access to education	Access to roads	Agricultural productivity	Wage rates	Social conditions
Bhagalpur	8,059	21	16	16	7	12	9	2	4	6
Rohtas	7,056	2	16	15	5	11	8	6	3	2
East Champaran	6,784	34	16	14	9	4	6	7	8	3
Madhubani	5,639	31	16	16	11	8	9	7	3	4
Kishanganj	5,355	10	16	16	14	8	2	11	3	2
Total	7,168	–	80	77	46	43	34	33	21	17

Note: The per capita gross district domestic product (GDDP) is an average of 2003–4 and 2004–5 at 1999/2000 prices. The GDDP total is the state average. Other reasons receiving few responses, such as access to electricity (7), private irrigation (7), political conditions (6), public irrigation (5), access to health (5) and so on were excluded from the table.

Sources: IDE-ADRI Survey (2008–9) and Government of Bihar (2009).

that all villages supplied seasonal labour to prosperous urban and rural areas outside the state, and that two-thirds of the villages served as a source of domestic and international long-term labour migration. As out-migration is not a recent phenomenon in Bihar (de Haan, 2002), it is presumed that those who traditionally did not leave the villages, particularly those in relatively underdeveloped areas, might have gained access to the labour market outside the state where there are more employment opportunities.

Access to education has been improved with the establishment of new schools and the appointment of new teachers by *panchayats*. In a survey of 80 government primary and upper primary schools in the same villages mentioned above, the provision of cooked mid-day meals in government schools, which began in Bihar in 2005, much later than in the majority of other states, has been implemented in 82.8 per cent of the surveyed schools, even though they are not regularly served in many schools. It is reported that school attendance, particularly of the lower castes, has tended to increase in these mid-day meal-implementing schools. Since the current state government, giving high priority to 'development', was sworn in during 2006, infrastructure development has progressed rapidly with new investments being made in electricity, schools and, to some extent, access to roads (Table I.2). Economic growth in Bihar has improved in very recent years, and the situation is better, particularly in sectors such as construction, hotels, restaurants, communication and trade.

Although public investment has increased and assisted in the development of the rural physical and social infrastructure, disparities across districts, blocks, *Gram Panchayats* and revenue villages within the state still remain. For example, all 80 surveyed villages are accessible to the main hamlet of the village by road. However, only 32.5 per cent (26 villages) are connected by *pukka* (paved or non-pitched) road, and accessibility to the main hamlet does not mean accessibility to the periphery of the villages, where the hamlets of lower caste groups tend to be located.[6] Table I.3 shows what factors determine the implementation of the five main rural development programmes in the surveyed villages, namely the National Rural Employment Guarantee Scheme (public works), the Backward Regions Grant Fund (the provision of financial resources for supplementing and covering existing development programmes to redress regional imbalances), the Twelfth Finance Commission Grant (mainly the installation of solar lights), Indira Awas Yojana (housing) and the Total Sanitation Campaign (toilet construction).[7] The dependent variable has a value from zero to five, depending

Table I.2 Chronology of physical and social infrastructure development in villages in Bihar (N = 80)

Year	Public primary/ upper primary schools (% in parentheses)	Electrified villages (% in parentheses)[1]	Accessibility to the main hamlet by road (% in parentheses)	
	Year established	Year electrified	Length of accessible years	
Before 1947	9 (11.3)	0 (0.0)		
1948–59	24 (30.0)	2 (4.2)		
1960–9	19 (23.8)	4 (8.3)		
1970–9	9 (11.3)	7 (14.6)		
1980–9	3 (3.8)	5 (10.4)	More than 5 years	56 (70.9)
1990–2005	3 (3.8)	11 (22.9)	1 to 5 years	19 (24.1)
2006–	13 (16.3)	19 (39.6)	Less than 1 year	4 (5.1)
Total	80	48[2]	Total	80[3]

Notes: [1] If any household is electrified, as per the government's old definition, the village is defined as an electrified village.
[2] If one of the government's new definitions of an electrified village 'more than 10% of households are electrified' is adopted, the number of electrified villages falls to 44.
[3] The year of accessibility for one village is missing.
Source: IDE-ADRI Survey (2008–9).

upon how many rural development programmes have been carried out in 2008/9 by scoring one for each programme. The difference at district and village levels is clear. Among the five surveyed districts, Bhagalpur and Madhubani districts are significantly less likely to have implemented the programmes. At the village level, villages with a hospital nearby or electrified villages tend to carry out rural development programmes. This implies that rural development programmes are run in places that are more easily accessible by road or are closer to a town (see Oda and Tsujita, 2011, for details). The overall relative wealth of villagers, represented by the ratio of households with tractors, also plays a significant role in programme implementation. On the whole, it is clear that relatively more developed villages tend to carry out rural development programmes.

At the same time, it is intriguing that the role of the *mukhiya* is not negligible when it comes to programme implementation. The programmes tend to have been executed in villages where the *mukhiya* himself/herself is a resident of the village and is from a scheduled caste. The development programmes often intend to target the poor, who are generally from the SCs. The SC *mukhiya*'s own initiatives seem to be more important than the proportion of SC beneficiaries in the villages.

Table I.3 Ordered logit estimation of the implementation of five rural development programmes at the village level

Variables	Dependent variable Value: minimum 0 to maximum 5 (score 1 if each programme has been implemented in the fiscal year 2008/9)	
	Coefficient	Robust standard errors
Bhagalpur district dummy	−2.167***	0.593
Madhubani district dummy	−2.734***	0.640
Hospital dummy	4.103***	1.555
Electrified village dummy	0.873*	0.464
Ratio of household with holding tractors	22.134**	9.720
Mukhiya SC dummy	2.211**	0.821
Mukhiya village resident dummy	1.028*	0.512
cut 1	−4.832	1.113
cut 2	−3.639	0.906
cut 3	−1.430	0.681
cut 4	1.118	0.621
cut 5	4.549	0.862
No. of observations	80	
Log likelihood	−84.49	
LR Chi-square	60.61	
Pseudo R^2	0.21	

Notes: ***, ** and * indicate significance at 1%, 5% and 10%, respectively. The explanatory variables are selected using the forward stepwise method. See note 7 for the examined variables. The dependent variable's mean is 3.29 (std dev. is 0.97).

At the household level, there is inequality in that only 23.4 per cent of households are estimated to have electricity even within our survey definition of electrified villages, which regards a village as electrified if there is any household that has electricity (48 villages, see Table I.2). The uneven distribution of benefits from public investment and development initiatives at the village level seems generally to reflect the existing socio-economic structure at the grassroots level. This implies that public investment, paradoxically, reinforces the existing rural socio-economic structure if growth cannot adequately address inequality. In fact, deep-rooted fundamental problems of inequality, such as the distribution of landholdings and the empowerment of lower castes, are not dealt with in the state's policies.

Chapter 8 deals with the political economy of underdevelopment in the state of Bihar. It attempts to document and explain the mechanism behind the seemingly inconsistent and contradictory coexistence over the past decades of low growth performance, a high incidence of poverty and substantial socio-economic inequality, on the one hand, and persistent inertia in a competitive democracy, on the other. Although many people have had high hopes for the future of Bihar after the demise of the Lalu Prasad Yadav-Rabri Devi duo's 'jungle *raj*', this chapter argues that it will be a formidable task to get rid of the deep-rooted causes of persistent poverty and inequality. Based on two accounts of the fierce controversy over the Nitish Kumar government's initiatives, the chapter suggests that, even if Bihar succeeds in escaping from its prolonged economic stagnation at the macro level, the great majority of landless and marginal peasants in the rural areas, who are of a low caste or scheduled caste background, will be left further behind.

In Chapter 9, Bihar's backwardness is elaborated from a long-term perspective. In addition to India's colonial legacy, which affected the pattern of regional development in India, the central government's development policies, such as freight equalization, and its agricultural and food policy have adversely affected Bihar's economy. Having an agrarian-based economy, Bihar was further disadvantaged during the post-reform period, when the state was replaced by the market as the main driver of economic growth. The chapter emphasizes the need for active state involvement and investment in high priority development areas, including agriculture, human resource development, infrastructure to help integrate markets and more efficient poverty alleviation programmes.

Concluding remarks

The goal of overall economic performance in the post-reform period has ostensibly been successful in achieving higher economic growth and in reducing poverty in general, but at the same time it has increased disparities in many socio-economic respects. The idea of inclusive growth is not new in independent India which has always tried to balance growth and equity. The change that is most characteristic of inclusive growth in the post-reform period is the pursuit of the principle of market-oriented growth with the financial constraints that this places on any chance of improving the lives of the vulnerable or weaker members of society. As economic reforms have been progressing slowly due to social, political and economic conflicts, the empowering of weaker sections, the removal of inequality and the solution to deep-rooted structural problems are time-absorbing and painstaking tasks by the same token. Hence, inclusive growth requires a very long-term political and financial commitment, which can be shared by central and state governments, local institutions, the private sector, NGOs, etc. at various levels from the centre to the grassroots.

A common observation has emerged from the chapters that there still exist many challenges if we are to reduce disparities in the process of social and economic development. A closer look at particular states, communities, wealth-groups, land buyers/sellers, women's associations, slum dwellers, etc. in this volume has revealed that various forms of disparity are commonly derived from interrelated disadvantages, for instance, in the economic, social, cultural, geographic and political arenas and so forth. The structural bottleneck to overcome inequality is also embedded in policy intervention, the delivery institutions of development programmes, rampant corruption and/or a combination of these three. Inclusive growth strategies cannot avoid tackling these interrelated structural problems.

The challenges the country faces are far more complex now than during the pre-reform period. Poor or vulnerable populations are more likely to suffer from changes brought about by global and internal economies, such as changes in the informalization of the labour market, increasing environmental degradation and the spread of HIV/AIDS or new communicable diseases. Since inclusive growth has to provide an answer not only to accumulated problems but also to new problems arising out of a rapidly changing global economy, it demands more time and patience. However, as long as the objective of inclusive growth is seriously and sincerely pursued by the government, people might be able to persevere and attain its goals.

Acknowledgements

We are grateful to anonymous referees for their helpful comments on an earlier draft. We are also deeply indebted to the Asian Development Research Institute, Patna, for their collaboration in a series of field surveys in rural Bihar. Needless to say, we are solely responsible for any errors.

Notes

1. Based on the Planning Commission's website (planningcommission.nic.in/data/datatable/Data0910/tab.%2019.pdf). The figure in 2004/05 is based on uniform recall period. It should be noted that the Government of India (2009) recommended a new method to measure poverty and re-estimated the headcount ratio as 41.8 per cent in rural areas and 25.7 per cent in urban areas

in 2004/5. Even though the new estimation turned out to be higher than conventional estimations, the extent of poverty reduction over the decade remains more or less the same.
2. It is noted that Informal finance in the rural areas is likely to be significantly underestimated (Jones, 2008).
3. The organized sector in India refers to the public sector, and non-agricultural enterprises or employees in the private sector in which more than ten employees work together. The remainder constitutes the unorganized sector.
4. Bihar was bifurcated in 2000 into Bihar and Jharkhand, and almost all the minerals and forests fell to the share of Jharkhand.
5. Eighty villages are selected as follows. First, five districts, one each from the five groups of districts with respect to rankings on the livelihood potential index, are selected. The livelihood potential index is composed on the basis of the availability of land per rural household, cropping intensity, agricultural productivity, the number of bovines per thousand capita and the percentage of the urban population (ADRI, undated.). Second, four blocks in each district are randomly selected. Third, four *Gram Panchayats* (GP) in each block are randomly selected. Finally, the selection of the revenue village is made during a field visit, after reaching the GP. One revenue village is selected in each GP based on two criteria: (1) caste composition and (2) the size of the population, which best represents that particular GP.
6. Of the 80 villages, 38 are inaccessible by vehicle during the monsoon months. The rest are connected by *kachcha* (unpaved or pitched) road (20 villages), *kharanja* (brick-paved) road (30 villages), *kharanja* and *pukka* road (3 villages) and *kachcha* and *kharanja* road (1 village), respectively.
7. In the ordered logit estimation, the explanatory variables are selected by forward stepwise methods. The considered variables are number of households, district dummies (Rohtas, Kishanganj, Bhagalpur, Madhubani and East Champaran), *mukhiya*'s caste/religion dummies (general caste, middle and upper caste (OBC and general castes), lower castes (extremely backward castes and SCs), SC, Muslim), the *mukhiya*'s level of education, the *mukhiya*'s age, a *mukhiya*'s sex dummy (one for male and zero otherwise), a *mukhiya*'s political affiliation dummy (one if the *mukhiya* is affiliated to any political party and zero otherwise), a *mukhiya*'s residential dummy (one if the *mukhiya* is a resident of the village and zero otherwise), the distance from the district headquarters, the distance from the block headquarters, the ratio of households that have a significant source of livelihood off the farm, an international migration dummy (one if any villager has gone abroad for work and zero otherwise), a long-term domestic migration dummy (one if any villager has gone outside the state for work for more than one year and zero otherwise), the ratio of electrified households within the village, a self-help group dummy (one if there is any functional self-help group in the village and zero otherwise), an agricultural cooperative dummy (one if there is any functional agricultural cooperative and zero otherwise), a road dummy (one if the main hamlet is accessible by *pukka* road and zero otherwise), the ratio of agricultural labourers' households, the ratio of landless households, the ratio of SC households, the ratio of households with a marketable surplus of their main crop, a flood dummy (one if more than half of the village's agricultural land suffers from floods or waterlogging and zero otherwise), an irrigation dummy (one if

more than half of the village's cultivable land is irrigated and zero otherwise), the ratio of households with fodder cutters, the ratio of households with a tractor, the ratio of households with a cultivator, a hospital dummy (one if there is a hospital in the village and zero otherwise) and an electrified village dummy (one if any household is electrified and zero otherwise).

References

Asian Development Research Institute (ADRI) (Undated) *Poverty and Social Assessment: A Districtwise Study of Bihar*, sponsored by the Bihar Rural Livelihood Promotion Society Patna, mimeo.
Bhalla, G. S. and Gurmail Singh (2001) *Indian Agriculture: Four Decades of Development*, New Delhi: Sage.
Borooah, Vani K. and Sriya Iyer (2005) 'Vidya, Veda and Barna: The Influence of Religion and Caste on Education in Rural India', *Journal of Development Studies*, 41 (8), pp. 1369–404.
Centre for Budget and Governance Accountability (CBGA), National Social Watch Coalition and Wada Na Todo Abhiyan (eds) (2009) *How Inclusive is the Eleventh Five Year Plan?: People's Mid-Term Appraisal. A Review of Selected Sectors*, mimeo.
Datta, Amrita (2009) 'Public–Private Partnerships in India: A Case for Reform?', *Economic and Political Weekly*, 45 (33), pp. 73–8.
de Haan, Arjan (2002) 'Migration and Livelihoods in Historical Perspective: A Case Study of Bihar, India', *Journal of Development Studies*, 38 (5), pp. 115–42.
Deshpande, Ashwini (2001) 'Caste at Birth? Redefining Disparity in India', *Review of Development Economics*, 5 (1), pp. 130–44.
Dev, Mahendra (2007) *Inclusive Growth in India: Agriculture, Poverty, and Human Development*, New Delhi: Oxford University Press.
_____ and N. Chandrasekhara Rao (eds) (2009) *India: Perspectives on Equitable Development*, New Delhi: Academic Foundation.
_____ and C. Ravi (2007) 'Poverty and Inequality: All India and States, 1983–2005', *Economic and Political Weekly*, 42 (6), pp. 509–21.
Drèze, Jean and Amartya Sen (1995) *India: Economic Development and Social Opportunity*, New Delhi: Oxford University Press.
_____ (2002) *India: Development and Participation*, 2nd edn, Oxford: Oxford University Press.
Frankel, Francine R. (1989) 'Caste, Land and Dominance in Bihar: Breakdown of the Brahmanical Social Order', in F. R. Frankel and M. S. A. Rao (eds), *Dominance and State Power in Modern India: Decline of a Social Order*, vol. 1, Delhi: Oxford University Press.
Fujita, Koichi (2002) 'Indian Agriculture: Technology, Policy and Structural Change', in H. Esho (ed.), *Contemporary South Asia 2: Future of Economic Liberalization*, Tokyo: University of Tokyo Press, pp. 97–119 (original in Japanese, 'Indo nogyoron: gijutsu, seisaku, kozohenka').
Government of Bihar (2007) *Economic Survey 2006–07*, March, Finance Department.
_____ (2009) *Economic Survey 2008–09*, February 2009, Finance Department.

_____ (2010) *Economic Survey 2009–10*, March 2010, Finance Department.
Government of India (2006a) *Towards Faster and More Inclusive Growth: An Approach to the 11th Five Year Plan (2007–2012)*, Planning Commission, New Delhi: Oxford University Press.
_____ (2006b) *Social, Economic and Educational Status of the Muslim Communities of India: A Report*, Prime Minister's High Level Committee Cabinet Secretariat, November.
_____ (2007) *Report of the Expert Group on Agriculture Indebtedness*, Banking Division, Department of Economic Affairs, Ministry of Finance, July.
_____ (2008) *Eleventh Five Year Plan 2007–12. Volume I. Inclusive Growth,* Planning Commission, New Delhi: Oxford University Press.
_____ (2009) *Report of the Expert Group to Review the Methodology for the Estimation of Poverty*, Planning Commission, New Delhi: Oxford University Press.
Gupta, Shaibal (2001) 'New Panchayats and Subaltern Resurgence', *Economic and Political Weekly*, 36 (29), pp. 2742–4.
Himanshu (2007) 'Recent Trends in Poverty and Inequality: Some Preliminary Results', *Economic and Political Weekly*, 42 (6), pp. 497–508.
Hirashima, S. (2008) 'Crucial Role of Indian Agriculture in Development: A Japanese Perspective', in S. K. Bhaumik (ed.), *Reforming Indian Agriculture: Towards Employment Generation and Poverty Reduction: Essays in Honour of G. K. Chadha*, New Delhi: Sage, pp. 315–41.
_____ (2009) 'Growth–Poverty Linkage, Income–Asset Relation in Regional Disparity: Evidence from Pakistan and India', *Pakistan Development Review*, Papers and Proceedings, 48 (4), pp.357–378.
International Labour Office (ILO) (2002) *Women and Men in the Informal Economy: A Statistical Picture*, Geneva: ILO.
Jones, J. Howard M. (2008) 'Informal Finance and Rural Finance Policy in India: Historical and Contemporary Perspectives', *Contemporary South Asia*, 16 (3), pp. 269–85.
Kijima, Yoko (2006) 'Caste and Tribe Inequality: Evidence from India, 1983–1999', *Economic Development and Cultural Change*, 54 (2), pp. 369–404.
Lieten, G. K. and Ravi Srivastava (1999) *Unequal Partners: Power Relations, Devolution and Development in Uttar Pradesh*, Indo-Dutch Studies on Development Alternatives 23, New Delhi: Sage.
Mendelsohn, Oliver and Marika Vicziany (1998) *The Untouchables: Subordination, Poverty and the State in Modern India*, Contemporary South Asia 4, Cambridge: Cambridge University Press.
Mody, Ashoka (ed.) (2006) *Inclusive Growth: K. N. Raj's Essays on Economic Development in the Economic Weekly and Economic Political Weekly*, Hyderabad: Orient Longman.
National Commission for Enterprises in the Unorganized Sector (NCEUS) (2009) *The Challenge of Employment in India: An Informal Economy Perspective. Volume I - Main Report*, New Delhi: NCEUS.
Oda, Hisaya and Yuko Tsujita (2011) 'The Determinants of Rural Electrification: The Case of Bihar, India', *Energy Policy*, 39 (6), pp. 3086–95.
Purfield, C. 2006. 'Mind the Gap: Is Economic Growth in India Leaving Some States Behind?', IMF Working Paper WP/06/103.
Rao, Hanumantha C. H. (2009) 'Inclusive Growth: Recent Experience and Challenges Ahead', *Economic and Political Weekly*, 44 (13), pp. 16–21.

Sato, Hiroshi (2004) 'Social Security and Well-Being in a Low-income Economy: An Appraisal of the Kerala Experience', *Developing Economies*, XLII-2, pp. 288–304.

Sundram, K. and Suresh Tendulkar (2003) 'Poverty among Social and Economic Groups in India in the 1990s', *Economic and Political Weekly*, 38 (59), pp. 5250–63.

Straub, Stephane (2008) 'Infrastructure and Growth in Developing Countries: Recent Advances and Research Challenges', Policy Research Working Paper No. 4460, Washington, DC: World Bank.

Tilak, J. B. G. (1995) *Costs and Financing of Education in India: A Review of Issues, Problems and Prospects*, Thiruvananthapuram: Centre for Development Studies.

United Progressive Alliance (UPA) (2007) *Report to the People UPA Government 2004–07*, (pmindia.nic.in/).

Wilkinson, Richard G. and Kate E. Pickett (2007) 'The Problems of Relative Deprivation: Why some Societies do Better than Others', *Social Science and Medicine*, 65, pp. 1965–78.

World Bank (1995) *India: Policy and Finance Strategies for Strengthening Primary Health Care Services*, Population and Human Resource Division, South Asia Country Department II (Bhutan, India, Nepal), Washington, DC: World Bank.

—— (2005) *World Development Report 2006: Equity and Development*, Washington, DC: World Bank.

—— (2006) *India: Inclusive Growth and Service Delivery: Building on India's Success*. Development Policy Review, Report No. 34580-IN, Washington, DC: World Bank.

—— (2007) *World Development Report 2008: Agriculture for Development*, Washington, DC: World Bank.

PART I

Growth–Poverty Linkage and Income–Asset Relationship in the Inclusive Growth Strategy

1
Infrastructure, Economic Growth and Interstate Disparity in India

Hisaya Oda

Introduction

The Indian economy has been growing in recent years. Though slow growth was once referred to as the 'Hindu rate of growth', now India has been moving forward at faster speeds. For the five years from 2002/3 to 2007/8, the real per capita net national product grew annually at around 7 per cent on average. Although growth slowed in 2008/9 due to the global financial crisis triggered by the crash of subprime loans, the economy showed a steady increase and demonstrated its robustness. India's economic growth rate may not be comparable to China's, but the 'big sleeping elephant' finally awoke and has started trotting. Because of its rapid and relatively stable economic expansion and its population exceeding 1 billion, India has been regarded as one of the promising emerging countries in the global era. Against the background of such high economic growth, however, lies a growing concern over deteriorating income inequality in various spheres: regional disparity – that is, interstate disparity, rural-urban disparity, social class disparity (inequality between Hindu caste and outcaste) and so on. While many studies highlight the widening disparity in India and its negative implication in recent years,[1] inequality issues, in fact, are not new to India. Since her independence or even in the pre-Independence era, inequality has topped the agendas of India's policy-makers. The dilemma facing India now is an old and traditional one, the dilemma between growth and distribution. India's economic policy has vacillated in the balance between them. Now, in the present context, a further problem is that inequality has been rising despite several attempts to redress it.

There are ample reasons for India to take inequality issues seriously. To a country with numerous ethnicities, languages, religions and social classes, growing imbalances among the different groups accentuate discontent, leading to political and economic turmoil and posing serious threats to the stability and sustainability of society. Aware of negative stimuli arising from worsening income disparities, the 11th Five-Year Plan under the leadership of Manmohan Singh of United Progressive Alliance (UPA) government reiterates the importance of social equality and regional balance while achieving higher economic growth. The idea of such balanced growth is introduced as 'inclusive growth', which has become the main slogan of the 11th Plan.

Differences in growth between rich and poor states contribute to growing income inequality. An important question becomes how to explain those differences in growth? Several studies argue that one of the factors influencing economic growth is the availability of state infrastructure (Nagaraj *et al.*, 1998; Mitra *et al.*, 2002; Ghosh and De, 2005). We are of the same view that infrastructure does matter, and the inequality of infrastructure provision is a source of income disparity. In order to supplement the existing arguments and highlight the important role of infrastructure in this regard, this chapter examines the widening income gap between rich and poor states, and explains it through differences in the availability of infrastructure. The provision of infrastructure is then analyzed with regard to fiscal viewpoints.

The chapter is organized as follows: the second section presents evidence of growing interstate income disparities in India. The third section discusses the source of economic growth of Indian states. It examines income inequality by highlighting the role of infrastructure in growth. In the fourth section, the evidence from econometric studies is presented. The fifth section analyzes factors limiting the supply of infrastructure. In particular a case of Bihar, the least developed state in India, is considered. The sixth section presents concluding remarks.

Descriptive analysis of growing income disparities across Indian states

This section provides evidence of growing income disparities across Indian states. First, we examine the trend of net state domestic product (NSDP) per capita, which is used as a proxy for income per capita in this chapter, to illustrate the growing gaps between rich states and poor states. Figure 1.1 indicates the ratio of the average income per capita of the three richest states to that of the three poorest states. The ratio was around 2 until the mid-1970s. Then it started increasing gradually. The graph shows no tendency for the ratio to decline. A couple of studies

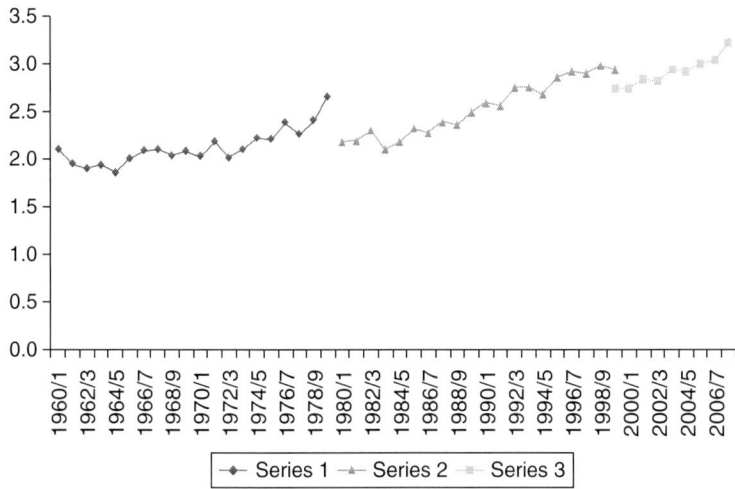

Figure 1.1 Ratio of the average income of the three richest states to that of the poorest states

Note: Figures are calculated using real per capita NSDP. Series 1 is based on 1970/1 constant prices, Series 2 is on 1980/1 constant prices and Series 3 is on 1999/2000 constant prices.
Source: Calculation by the author based on the data from Indiastat (www.indiastat.com).

comment on this by referring to the economic liberalization and reform initiated since the mid-1980s. Their usual explanation for the widening gaps between rich and poor states is that the reform has brought economic benefits to the former while the latter are being left behind (Bhattacharya and Sakthivel, 2004; Kumar, 2004).

Next, let us examine interstate income disparity by examining the relationship between the initial level of income of each state and the growth rate of real per capita NSDP of the corresponding state. According to the economic theory of convergence, poor states tend to grow faster than rich ones, narrowing the initial income gap between the former and the latter. This type of convergence is known as β-convergence (Barro and Sala-i-Martin, 1992). When β-convergence exists, the initial level of income and the growth rate of subsequent years should be negatively correlated. More strictly, this is the concept of unconditional (absolute) convergence.[2] This means that all the states will eventually reach the same steady state income level. Figure 1.2, which is the same graph as appears in the Introduction of this book (see Figure I.3), shows the relationship between the initial income levels and growth rates of selected Indian states. A casual observation of Figure 1.2 indicates a non-negative

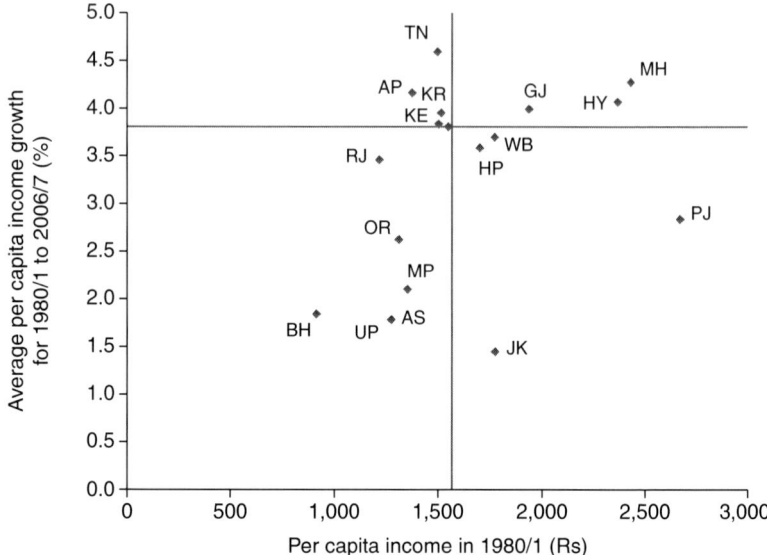

Figure 1.2 Convergence or divergence of the state-wise growth rates

Note: Figures are based on real per capita NSDP of 17 major states, namely Andhra Pradesh (AP), Assam (AS), Bihar (BH), Gujarat (GJ), Haryana (HY), Himachal Pradesh (HP), Jammu and Kashmir (JK), Karnataka (KT), Kerala (KE), Madhya Pradesh (MP), Maharashtra (MH), Orissa (OR), Punjab (PJ), Rajasthan (RJ), Tamil Nadu (TN), Uttar Pradesh (UP) and West Bengal (WB). The vertical and horizontal lines indicate all-India average.
Source: Calculation by the author based on the data from Indiastat (www.indiastat).

association between them, rejecting the existence of β-convergence (unconditional). This means that the initial income gap between rich states and poor states tends to remain. There is even a possibility that the gap will increase further. The analysis of β-convergence across the states of India has been a popular topic. Many analyses confirm absolute divergence of income. See Singh *et al.* (2003) for a brief summary of these studies.

One widely used measure for inequality is the Gini coefficient. It is calculated by the difference between the Lorenz curve and the 45 degree line, which indicates the case of perfect equality. Figure 1.3 shows income distributions by Lorenz curves for 1960/1, 1990/1 and 2005/6, based on the state-wise real per capita NSDP for the respective years.[3] As can be observed, the Lorenz curve diverges from the 45 degree line, and the deflection of the Lorenz curve becomes larger with the passage of time, indicating growing income inequality. The resulting Gini coefficients of

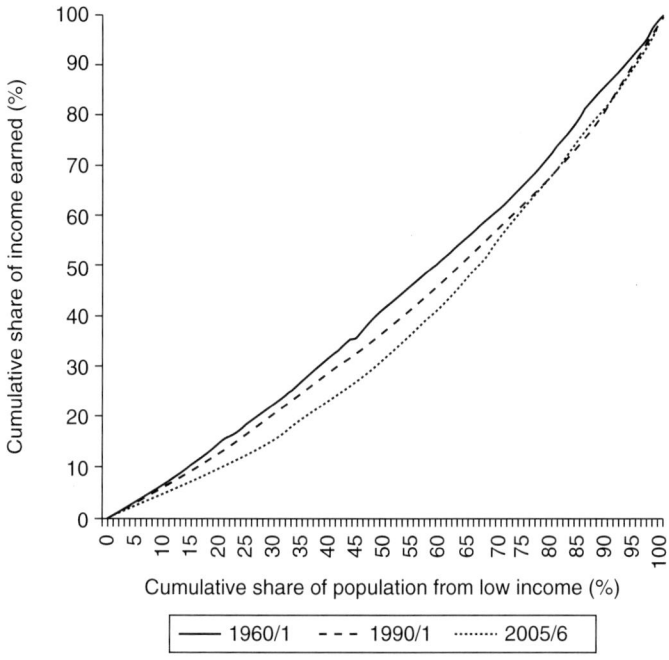

Figure 1.3 Cumulative income distribution and Lorenz curves of India

Note: Figures are based on real per capita NSDP.
Source: Calculation by the author based on the data from Indiastat (www.indiastat.com).

interstate inequality are 0.122 in 1960/1, 0.161 in 1980/1, 0.183 in 1990/1, 0.212 in 2000/1 and 0.241 in 2005/6 (the Lorenz curves of 1980/1 and 2000/1 are not shown in Figure 1.3).[4] A very rough examination of these figures might reveal that income inequality across the Indian states is not only increasing but also the speed of increment is accelerating. Our Gini figures are consistent with those noted by Ahluwalia (2002), which also show increasing regional disparities with accelerated speeds. As for consumption inequality, Deaton and Drèze (2002) and Singh *et al.* (2003) also find increasing interstate inequality.

The coefficients of variation (CV) of state-wise income per capita also show the same tendency of worsening disparities in Figure 1.4. The CV measures the dispersion from the national average per capita income and can serve as another indicator of interstate inequality. The CV here is population weighted, and calculated by using real per capita NSDP.[5] If it declines over time, it suggests the existence of σ-convergence among

40 *Infrastructure, Growth and Interstate Disparity*

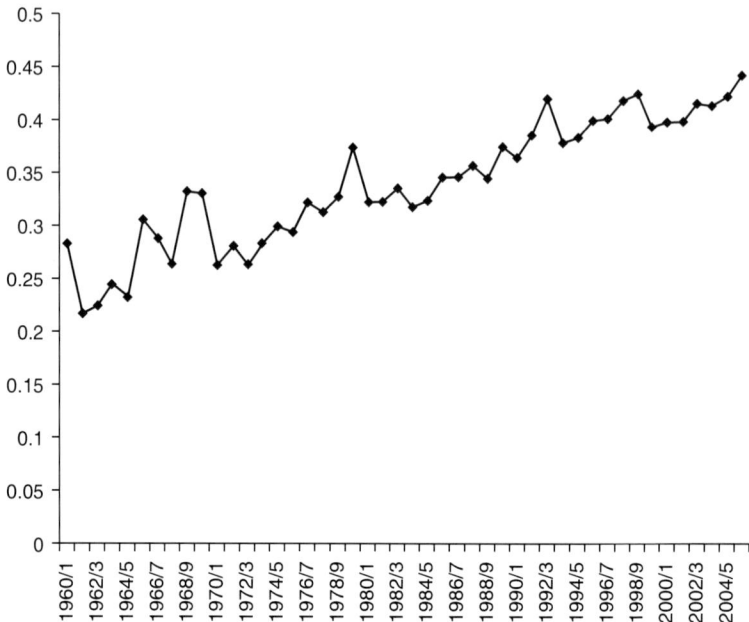

Figure 1.4 Coefficients of variation of per capita NSDP for 1960/1–2005/6

Note: Figures are based on real per capita NSDP
Source: Calculation by the author based on the data from Indiastat (www.indiastat.com).

states, meaning narrowing disparities across states (Barro and Sala-i-Martin, 1992).[6] Figure 1.4 is not indicative of the existence of σ-convergence, but rather shows a diverging trend since the early 1970s. This supports the findings of Cashin and Sahay (1996) and Ghosh and De (2004). Ghosh and De (2004) claim that, in addition to the increasing trend, the CVs have recorded a significant upward shift after 1991/2 – that is, post-reform decades – but our data do not show such a tendency.

The descriptive analyses and evidence presented in this section reveal that interstate income inequality has been increasing. This is a very alarming sign for the Indian authorities, whose prime objective is growth with equal distribution. In the following section, we now turn to identify the source of income inequality.

Infrastructure and economic growth

Infrastructure is critically important in the early stage of economic development, and its roles are manifold. Infrastructure is not only a productive input to production, but it also creates an environment that contributes to higher productivity. Without proper infrastructure, it is not possible for the country or the region to enjoy sustainable economic growth. In this chapter, we hypothesize that infrastructure inserts positive impacts on growth, and different levels of infrastructure provision lead to different growth patterns, causing income inequalities across the states of India.

Brief review of literature

Existing literature has emphasized the role of infrastructure in economic development.[7] Infrastructure directly and indirectly affects economic activities through various channels. Classical theory stresses that infrastructure as a form of public capital is an important factor of input (Rosenstein-Rodan, 1943; Murphy *et al.*, 1989). It increases the productivities of labour and private investment, thereby enhancing production capacity (Aschauer, 1989).[8] In particular, given the limited accumulation of infrastructure in developing countries, its marginal products are higher. This constitutes a basic rationale for promoting infrastructure projects in developing countries. The higher accumulation of infrastructure also 'crowds in' private investment (Agenor, 2004). When a private business makes a decision on where to invest, the condition of infrastructure in potential sites influences its decision to a great extent. In the era of globalization, infrastructure endowments are increasingly becoming important for all countries, including developing ones, to attract foreign direct investment.

In order to illustrate indirect impacts arising from infrastructure provision, let us consider the case of electricity supply to rural areas first. Electricity makes it possible for farmers to use irrigation pumps and other agricultural equipment, thereby increasing the productivity in the rural sector. This is a sort of direct effect of infrastructure. However, infrastructure can provide more to the rural sector. For example, electric lights enable children in villages to study at night, contributing to the accumulation of human capital (Barnes, 1988). Another case is the building of road networks. Roads link villages with cities, making the movement of agricultural products easier and the cost of transportation less (Binswagner *et al.*, 1989; Zhang and Fan, 2004).[9] They also contribute to the expansion of the market, as products can be transported to remote places which would not have been accessible without a road network. Furthermore, along with the improvement of public transportation, roads allow children to go to school more easily in rural areas where schools are sometimes not conveniently located and children must walk for hours to reach them.

In the Indian context, studies generally find a positive relationship between infrastructure and economic activities. Using the national data and constructing an infrastructure index, Sahoo and Dash (2009) find a positive influence of infrastructure stocks on economic growth in India. At the state level, Ghosh and De (2004, 2005) provide empirical evidence that initial differences in infrastructure endowments determine the levels of state output in subsequent years. A similar implication was also presented by Nagaraj *et al.* (2000). Mitra *et al.* (2002) analyze a relationship between the level of infrastructure provision and total factor productivities in the Indian manufacturing sector, and find a positive correlation between them. As for the impact of infrastructure on poverty reduction, Datt and Ravallion (2002) show that the speed of poverty reduction tends to be faster in the states with better infrastructure. The review of existing literature confirms that infrastructure provision is critically important as a condition for economic development, and that the level of infrastructure endowments affects economic performance and poverty reduction.

State-wise provision of infrastructure: the case of electricity

In this sub-section, we provide an overview of the state-wise provision of infrastructure in India through the electricity supply. No one questions the importance of electricity supply in economic development. For the private sector, a stable and reliable electricity supply is vital to their economic activities. Likewise, it is almost impossible to live without electricity in the modern era. Lack of electricity definitely lowers the quality of our lives. Cross-country comparison reveals a low level of electric supply in India in terms of both quantity and quality. India's per capita electricity consumption was 543kWh in 2007,[10] which was lower than the Asian average of 705kWh, and even lower than the African average of 578kWh in the same year (IEA, 2009). India's transmission and distribution loss (T&D loss) of electricity is around 27 per cent, which is higher than the average of low-income countries (24 per cent). It is the highest among BRICs countries (China 6 per cent, Russia 12 per cent and Brazil 17 per cent).[11] This high T&D loss indicates a low quality of electricity infrastructure. Obviously, the low level and quality of electricity supply has negative implications on the nation's economic development by setting a ceiling on economic activities.

While the average level of electricity supply in India is low at the international standard, interstate inequality in electricity supply has been observed. Among the 17 major states,[12] per capita electricity consumption of states such as Punjab (1,506kWh) and Gujarat (1,331kWh) was more than 1,000kWh in 2006/7 (Table 1.1). On the other hand, it was less than 100kWh in Bihar, the lowest of all. Bihar's consumption was 147kWh in 1999/2000, but it declined to 91kWh in 2006/7. This might be due to the bifurcation of the state in 2000 into Bihar and Jharkhand.[13] Since the division, now that Jharkhand is considered relatively more developed, the separation has had a negative implication on Bihar's development process. Clearly high-income states with developed industrial sectors (Gujarat) and/or with intensive irrigation networks (Punjab, Haryana) tend to consume more.

Per capita electricity consumption is directly related to the coverage of household electrification. While recent data are not available, according to the 2001 census, the rate of household electrification is higher among high-income states in the western region (Punjab, Haryana and Gujarat; see Figure 1.5), and lower among low-income states in the eastern region (Bihar, Jharkhand and Orissa). Punjab attains the highest coverage (91.9 per cent), followed by Haryana (82.9 per cent), while Bihar's coverage is lowest (10.3 per cent), Jharkhand being the second lowest (24.9 per cent).

Table 1.1 Cross-state comparison of per capita electricity consumption

States	(kWh)		
	1994/5	1999/2000	2006/7
Andhra Pradesh	371.0	434.0	802.4
Assam	104.0	101.2	175.1
Bihar	130.0	146.7	91.0
Gujarat	599.0	840.9	1330.8
Haryana	478.0	530.2	1208.2
Himachal Pradesh	251.0	340.0	872.0
Jammu and Kashmir	211.0	269.3	758.6
Jharkhand	n.a.	n.a.	659.2
Karnataka	363.0	367.0	805.5
Kerala	236.0	315.0	440.8
Madhya Pradesh	334.0	353.1	581.7
Maharashtra	499.0	571.6	975.4
Orissa	321.0	334.3	664.7
Punjab	785.0	924.1	1506.3
Rajasthan	266.0	339.5	590.7
Tamil Nadu	431.0	548.0	1079.9
Uttar Pradesh	197.0	179.1	340.5
West Bengal	176.0	206.9	396.8
India	319.0	364.5	671.9

Source: Indiastat (www.indiastat.com).

44 Infrastructure, Growth and Interstate Disparity

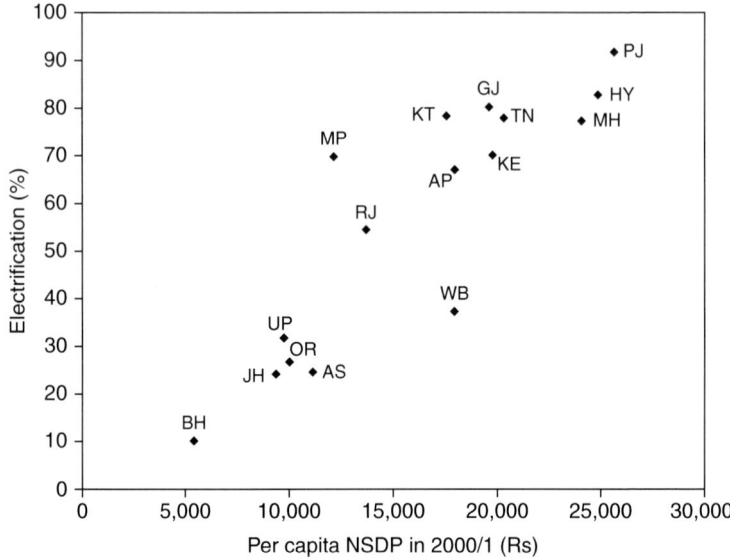

Figure 1.5 State-wise household electrification and income level

Note: AP: Andra Pradesh, AS: Assam, BH: Bihar, GJ: Gujarat, HY: Haryana, JH: Jharkhand, KT: Karnataka, KE: Kerala, MP: Madhya Pradesh, MH: Maharashtra, OR: Orissa, PJ: Punjab, RJ: Rajasthan, TN: Tamil Nadu, UP: Uttar Pradesh, WB: West Bengal.
Sources: Census of India (2001) and Indiastat (www.indiastat.com).

Empirical analysis

Data and methodology

Our empirical analysis focuses on the relationship between the availability of infrastructure and economic growth of the states of India, and aims to deduce explanations for income disparity. The study uses data on the 17 major states of India[14] from 1970/1 to 2006/7. These states account for around 85 per cent of the nation's GDP and 90 per cent of its total population.

The dependent variable is the ten-year average of real per capita NSDP growth, except for the period from 2000/1 to 2006/7 for which the six-year average growth is used instead. We use a ten-year average to avoid short-term fluctuations of growth, which easily influence regression outcomes. For each state, four average growth rates are obtained. Our estimated equation takes the following form:

$$GRPC_{it,it+10} = \alpha + \beta \ln y_{it} + \gamma X_{it} + \mu D + u_{it}$$

where $GRPC_{it,it+10}$ represents the ten-year average annual growth rate of real per capita NSDP for state i, t is the initial year of each ten-year period (i.e. t = 1970, 1980, 1990 and 2000), y_{it} is the initial level of real per capita NSDP for state i and X_{it} is a vector of explanatory variables. It includes the availability of infrastructure and the level of human capital for state i at the time of t. As for the variable representing infrastructure, we use per capita consumption of electricity. We also employ state-wise national highway density and road density for infrastructural variables as alternatives to electricity consumption. As a proxy for human capital, state-wise effective literacy rates are employed. X_{it} also includes inflation rates in order to account for the impact of macro instability on economic growth. State-level NSDP deflators are used as a proxy for these. D is a vector of dummy variables. The first dummy accounts for the impact of economic reforms and takes D = 1 for $t \geq 1990$ and 0 otherwise. The second is the bifurcation dummy. It assigns D = 1 for $t \geq 2000$ for three states that experienced bifurcation of the state and 0 otherwise. The three states are Bihar, Madhya Pradesh and Uttar Pradesh. The bifurcation dummy is included to consider possible impacts due to the separation of the state. α is the constant term and u_{it} is the error term. A summary of descriptive statistics of each variable is given in Table 1.2.

Data on net state domestic product (NSDP) are obtained from the CD-ROM version of *Domestic Products of States of India: 1960–61 to 2006–07* (2nd updated edition), published by EPW Research Foundation. Using these data, we construct an annual series of real per capita NSDP and

Table 1.2 A summary of descriptive statistics of sample data

Variable	Obs	Mean	Standard deviation	Min	Max
Growth rate of real per capita NSDP (%/100)	68	0.030	0.018	–0.005	0.077
Log of initial real per capita NSDP (constant at 1999/2000 prices)	68	9.252	0.426	8.132	10.165
Log of per capita electricity consumption (kWh)	68	5.062	0.868	2.964	6.750
Log of national highway density (km per 1,000 sq km of area)	51	3.489	0.791	1.131	4.682
Log of road density (km per 1,000 sq km of area)	68	6.278	0.869	3.689	8.229
Literacy rates (%/100)	68	0.499	0.166	0.217	0.909
Inflation rate (%/100)	68	0.073	0.022	0.033	0.118
Reform dummy	68	0.5	0.504	0	1
Bifurcation dummy	68	0.044	0.207	0	1

calculate ten-year average annual growth rates of each state. State-level deflators are derived on the basis of the gap between constant and current NSDPs, and are translated into state-level inflation rates. Data on per capita electricity consumption, literacy rates and road density are obtained from the Indiastat database (www.indiastat.com). Per capita electricity consumption data are also supplemented by various *Economic Surveys*, Government of India. Data on national highways by state are from Das (2005).

Since the data set has the form of a panel, we employ three different techniques for estimation: pooled OLS, fixed-effects models and random-effects models.

One might question the use of per capita consumption of electricity as the variable for infrastructure endowments. In response to this enquiry, we note the legitimacy of using electricity consumption as follows. First, electricity is considered the most important utility in economic activities from agriculture to manufacturing. A study by the World Bank stresses that among transportation, telecommunications and electricity, economic activities are most constrained by lack of electricity (World Bank, 2005). Second, electricity consumption measures the state and economic role of infrastructure better than other factors. For example, consider the case of road density, which is popularly used as an infrastructure variable. Unlike electricity consumption, road density is influenced by many factors, such as geographical condition, population and so on. There is also a quality issue. It is almost impossible to know the quality of roads just by looking at road density figures. Some roads are nicely paved and some are paved but full of holes. On the other hand, the use of electricity consumption is less susceptible to these problems. Third, a couple of studies indicate that there is a high correlation between electricity supply and the state of other types of infrastructure. For example, Calderon and Serven (2004) report that the correlation coefficient of power generating capacity and tele-density (telecommunication) is 0.94. Esfahani and Ramirez (2003) also present a similar finding.

Results

Table 1.3 displays the estimates of our regression analyses. The three different panel estimation techniques are applied. As a result, fixed-effects and random-effects estimations are rejected in favour of pooled OLS. Along with the estimates of pooled OLS, we report the results of fixed effects and random effects with relevant test statistics for reference purposes (Eq. (2) and Eq. (3) respectively).

Table 1.3 Regression results for growth of real per capita NSDP

	Dependent variable: growth rates of real per capita NSDP					
Variables	Eq(1)	Eq(2)	Eq(3)	Eq(4)	Eq(5)	Eq(6)
Log of initial real per capita NSDP	−0.0087* [0.0052]	−0.0235* [0.0143]	−0.0087** [0.0038]	−0.0157** [0.0067]	−0.0073 [0.0061]	−0.0014 [0.0061]
Log of per capita electricity consumption	0.0110*** [0.0024]	0.0098 [0.0076]	0.0110*** [0.0019]	0.0098** [0.0041]		
Log of highway density					0.0075*** [0.0023]	
Log of road density						0.0011 [0.0029]
Literacy rates	0.0217 [0.0162]	0.0480 [0.0587]	0.0217* [0.0128]	0.0419** [0.0174]	0.0150 [0.0208]	0.0278 [0.0224]
Inflation rate	−0.2215*** [0.0788]	−0.2405** [0.0867]	−0.2215*** [0.0748]	−0.2254*** [0.0700]	−0.2797*** [0.0845]	−0.2664*** [0.0797]
Bifurcation dummy	0.0073* [0.0040]	0.0095 [0.0058]	0.0073* [0.0041]	0.0045 [0.0044]	0.0121** [0.0048]	0.0149*** [0.0048]
Partition dummy	−0.0231*** [0.0061]	−0.0201** [0.0076]	−0.0231*** [0.0069]	−0.0258*** [0.0057]	−0.0268*** [0.0054]	−0.0253*** [0.0060]
Constant	0.0573 [0.0445]	0.1873* [0.1067]	0.0573* [0.0347]	0.1217** [0.0485]	0.0825 [0.0533]	0.0351 [0.0595]
No. of observations	68	68	68	51	51	68
Estimation method	Pooled OLS	Fixed effects	Random effects	2SLS	Pooled OLS	Pooled OLS
Fisher test		0.61 [F(16, 45)]				
Hausman test			2.97 [χ2 (5)]			
Breusch and Pagan LM test			1.60 [χ2 (1)]			
R-sqr	0.663	0.601	0.663	0.585	0.584	0.571

Notes: *** Significance at 1% level, ** significance at 5% level, * significance at 10% level. Figures in squared brackets are cluster-robust standard errors. For 2SLS, instruments are exogenous variables, one-time lagged per capita electricity consumption and literacy rate variables.

Estimates by pooled OLS are shown in Eq. (1). The result shows a positive and statistically significant impact of per capita electricity consumption, the level of infrastructure provision, on the ten-year averages of real per capita NSDP growth. This finding of the positive and significant relationship is consistent with those of existing studies such as Nagaraj *et al.* (1998) and Bandyopadhyay (2006).[15] In our case, a 1 per cent increase of electricity consumption increases the per capita real NSDP growth by 0.011 percentage points. Seemingly, this figure is small, but if we consider the significant gap in electricity consumption among Indian states, which is evident in Table 1.1, we may notice that the impact of infrastructure provision has a considerable effect on economic growth. For example, if electricity consumption doubled – that is, a 100 per cent increase – it would raise annual per capital real NSDP by 1.1 per cent.

In order to check the robustness of the result, we also run two-stage least squares regressions (2SLS). The instruments used are one-time lagged per capita electricity consumption and one-time lagged literacy rate. The result given in the column of Eq. (4) confirms a positive and statistically significant relationship between the ten-year averages of real per capita NSDP growth and per capita electricity consumption. A 1 per cent increase of electricity consumption increases the real per capita NSDP growth by 0.0098 percentage points.

In order to see the impact of other types of infrastructure on economic growth, national highway density and road density (both in kilometres length per 1,000 km^2 of area) are used as a proxy for the availability of infrastructure. The estimated results reported in Eq. (5) show that the impact of the availability of infrastructure by the density of national highways is positive and significant. This suggests the importance of transportation networks in economic development. However, when another type of transportation network is employed as an infrastructural variable, it reveals a different picture. In the column of Eq. (6), the estimate on road density indicates a positive but not statistically significant impact of infrastructure on economic growth. Purfield (2006) reports a similar result while Nagaraj *et al.* (1998) find otherwise. Probably this indeterminacy is a reflection of the fact that road density is influenced by such factors as geographical condition, population and so on, which are not necessarily linked with economic activities. In addition, as already touched upon, there is an issue of quality when using 'road density' as an infrastructure variable, as 'road' includes any kind of road in the state, and road density may not be a good indicator representing the level of infrastructure. These might result in a not statistically significant relationship between the availability of road network and economic growth.

Note that both highway density and road density are indicators to scale the level of transportation-related infrastructure. However, their impacts differ, as the former seems a more relevant measure that accounts for quantity and quality of infrastructure, while the latter may not do so.

The coefficient on the initial level of real per capita NSDP is negative and significant in Eq. (1) and Eq. (4) when electricity consumption is used as an infrastructural variable, but it becomes insignificant when other types of infrastructures are added. Though the result is not robust, it leaves a possibility that conditional β-convergence does exist, meaning that each state reaches its respective steady state income level. The influence of literacy rates on real per capita NSDP growth is positive but statistically insignificant in Eq. (1). However, using one-time lagged literacy rate as the instrument, the effect becomes positive and significant, shown in the column of Eq. (4). This finding is important, as the imbalance in human capital formation has been observed across the states. Both physical as well as social infrastructure can explain differences in economic growth at the state level. The provision of such infrastructure, therefore, affects interstate income inequality. The impact of inflation rates is always positive and significant. The result is robust. Since the state economy suffers from higher inflation, sound macroeconomic policies to check the price and prevent fluctuation are imperative.

The estimated coefficient of the reform dummy is positive and almost robust. The result implies that the overall impact of economic liberalization since the beginning of 1990s on the states' economy is positive. However, it should be remembered that the degree of the impact is not uniform. As the second section of this chapter describes, some states benefited from the economic reform while others have not been recipients of economic rewards, creating the gap between the former and the latter. The effect of bifurcation is always negative and statistically significant. This result may indicate that the economies of three states (Bihar, Madhya Pradesh and Uttar Pradesh) have been negatively affected by the separation of part of the state. For example, Bihar lost 54 per cent of its state territory but only 25 per cent of the state population due to the departure of Jharkhand (ADRI, 2008). As Table 1.4 in the next section shows, Jharkhand's per capita NDSP is more than twice Bihar's. Only simple mathematics are necessary to understand the negative implication of bifurcation, as the relatively developed region compared to the rest of Bihar became a new state, leaving the majority of population behind at the same time. However, there is a caveat in interpretation of the estimate on the bifurcation dummy, as the three states have been characterized by slow growth and low income levels.

50 Infrastructure, Growth and Interstate Disparity

Table 1.4 Relative income gap between Bihar and other states

	Per capita NSDP (current prices, Rs)		Income disparity in 1999/2000 (base: Bihar = 1)	Income disparity in 2005/6 (base: Bihar = 1)	Comparison of disparity up (+)/ down (−)
	1999/2000	2005/6			
Andra Pradesh	15,507	26,211	2.69	3.33	+
Assam	12,269	18,598	2.13	2.36	+
Jharkhand	12,747	19,066	2.21	2.42	+
Gujarat	18,864	34,157	3.27	4.34	+
Haryana	21,966	38,832	3.81	4.93	+
Karnataka	16,758	27,291	2.91	3.47	+
Kerala	19,294	30,668	3.35	3.89	+
Madhya Pradesh	12,384	15,647	2.15	1.99	−
Maharashtra	23,340	37,081	4.05	4.71	+
Orissa	10,567	17,299	1.83	2.20	+
Punjab	25,615	34,929	4.44	4.44	−
Rajasthan	13,477	17,863	2.34	2.27	−
Tamil Nadu	19,378	29,958	3.36	3.80	+
Uttar Pradesh	9,405	13,262	1.63	1.68	+
West Bengal	15,826	25,223	2.74	3.20	+
India Average	15,839	25,716	2.75	3.27	+
Bihar	5,766	7,875	1.00	1.00	n.a.

Source: Government of India, Ministry of Finance, *Economic Survey 2007/08*.

Therefore, the negative sign on the bifurcation dummy may simply reflect the negative impact of partition of the state, or it may be a sign that the three states are just behind others in the post-reform period. Probably the result reflects both effects.

The empirical results obtained here are suggestive of a positive impact of infrastructure on economic growth. Accordingly, differences in the infrastructure endowment across the states of India explain the divergence of growth rates of real per capita NSDP, and hence growing interstate income disparities.

Constraints for the provision of infrastructure: the case of Bihar

This section aims to outline factors that constrain infrastructure provision. The case of Bihar is considered here.

Bihar: the state left behind

Bihar is often portrayed as one of the BIMARU states. 'BIMARU' is a coined acronym consisting of the initial letters of Bihar, Madhya Pradesh, Rajasthan and Uttar Pradesh, the four low-income states. The sound of 'BIMARU' happens to resemble *'bimar'* in Hindi, which means *sick*. Though 'BIMARU' is a derogatory expression, it well describes the current situation of Bihar.

A cross-state comparison using data on per capita income in 2005/6 shows that Bihar's income is less than one-fifth of Haryana, the state with the highest per capita income. A striking fact is that the relative income gap between other states and Bihar tends to be widening. Among 16 states listed in Table 1.4, the relative income gap became larger in 12 states, while the gap was narrowed in only three states (Madhya Pradesh, Rajasthan and Punjab) between 1999/2000 and 2005/6. The income gap is just one indicator that demonstrates Bihar's backwardness. As for the poverty ratio, Bihar's headcount poverty ratio in 2003/4 was 41.5 per cent on average, with 43.1 per cent in rural and 31.7 per cent in urban areas (Dev and Ravi, 2007). These figures easily surpass the Indian averages of 28.3 per cent, 29.2 per cent and 26.0 per cent, respectively. Since Bihar is the third most populous state in India with 87.25 million people, the state accommodates 16.5 per cent of the total below the poverty line (BPL) population of India.[16] In addition, the social sector of Bihar is also undeveloped.[17] This is another factor that limits the economic growth of Bihar.

We have already examined the interstate disparity in electricity supply in the third section of this chapter. As Table 1.1 shows, there is a huge gap in per capita electricity consumption across the states, Bihar's consumption being the lowest. An alarming fact is that the gap of Bihar's electricity consumption vis-à-vis that of high-income states is way over the income gap. For example, Bihar's per capita income in 2005/6 was about one-fifth of Haryana's per capita income, but in terms of electricity consumption, Bihar's was less than one-13th of Haryana's and one-16th that of Punjab. This highlights Bihar's state of undeveloped infrastructure. Clearly, lack of infrastructure has constrained the state's economic performance. Another indicator that reveals the inadequacy of infrastructure in Bihar is the Relative Infrastructure Development Index, provided by the Centre for Monitoring Indian Economy (CMIE). The index is a weighted average of various infrastructure measures, including power generation, irrigation, transportation and telecommunication, education, health and banking facilities. Taking the Indian average as 100, Bihar's index was 61.0 in 2001. The figure is the second lowest after Jharkhand (52.3). The highest score was obtained by Punjab (212.3), followed by Kerala (195.4). An important question to be asked is: what causes the shortage of infrastructure in Bihar? We look into this question in the next sub-section.

The state of the state revenue

Inadequate stocks of infrastructure reflect the weak fiscal position of the Bihar government. Bihar has been suffering from persistent fiscal deficits. Other Indian states are also in the same situation, but the problem has been at a critical stage for a quite long period in Bihar, as a report by the World Bank points out (World Bank, 2007).

The fundamental problem of persistent fiscal deficits is due to the state's lack of its own revenue-generating capacity. In India, the state revenue consists of its own tax and non-tax revenue, plus fiscal supports from the central government. In the case of Bihar, the ratio of own revenue to total state revenue has been declining in recent years. The ratio was 27.8 per cent in 2002/3, but it reduced to 19.6 per cent in 2007/8 (Government of Bihar, 2008). The state finance of Bihar is becoming increasingly dependent on transfers and grants from the centre.

Since the rural sector is predominant in the Bihar economy and the urban sector is undeveloped, the taxation bases in Bihar are limited. As a result, per capita own revenue of the state finance remains at a low level. In 2006/7, per capita own revenue of the Bihar government was Rs 535.6 (see Table 1.5). This figure was the lowest among all states. It is even surprising to notice that per capita own revenue of low-income states like Uttar Pradesh and Orissa is far larger than that of Bihar. It should be noted that the gap between Uttar Pradesh and Bihar in this regard is more than that which the difference of per capita income level can explain. This might imply lack of revenue efforts by the government of Bihar.

The central fiscal transfers to the states mainly consist of the share of divisible central taxes, such as income taxes by the Finance Commission, fiscal assistance from the Planning Commission, and Central and Centrally Sponsored Plan Schemes by the central government ministries.[18] The transfer by the Finance Commission is designed, in principle, to adjust fiscal imbalances between the centre and the states (vertical distribution), and to reduce interstate fiscal disparities (horizontal distribution). It usually accounts for the largest portion in the state revenue. The amount of transfer is based on the formula recommended by the Finance Commission (FC) every five years, at the time

Table 1.5 Comparison of state-wise per capita revenue capacity in 2006/7

	Per capita own revenue (a) (tax + non-tax)		Per capita net transfers from centre (b)	Per capita revenue (a + b)	
	Rs (current prices)	Relative disparity		Rs (current prices)	Relative disparity
Andra Pradesh	3,825.2	7.1	1,625.0	5,450.2	2.3
Gujarat	4,107.0	7.7	1,321.6	5,428.6	2.3
Haryana	5,875.2	11.0	937.0	6,812.2	2.9
Jharkhand	1,563.7	2.9	1,756.7	3,320.4	1.4
Karnataka	5,020.8	9.4	1,749.8	6,770.6	2.9
Kerala	3,885.7	7.3	1,851.1	5,736.8	2.4
Madhya Pradesh	1,871.5	3.5	1,744.6	3,616.1	1.5
Maharashtra	4,384.7	8.2	1,380.7	5,765.4	2.4
Orissa	1,947.6	3.6	2,516.3	4,463.9	1.9
Punjab	6,019.4	11.2	1,540.3	7,559.7	3.2
Rajasthan	2,322.2	4.3	1,673.1	3,995.3	1.7
Tamil Nadu	4,742.0	8.9	1,421.2	6,163.2	2.6
Uttar Pradesh	1,620.3	3.0	1,506.9	3,127.2	1.3
West Bengal	1,602.0	3.0	1,328.3	2,930.3	1.2
Bihar	535.6	1.0	1,838.2	2,373.8	1.0

Source: ADRI (2008).

of writing, by the 12th Finance Commission (TFC). The sharing criteria under the recommendation of the TFC are the following: The share of the states to the central tax revenue is 30.5 per cent, 1 per cent up from the 11th Finance Commission (EFC); the share to the states is distributed according to the weights assigned by the TFC: income distance from the national average 50 per cent, population 25 per cent, area 10 per cent, tax effort 7.5 per cent, fiscal discipline 7.5 per cent. The weights assigned by the EFC were income distance 62.5 per cent, population 10 per cent, area 7.5 per cent, infrastructure index (infrastructure distance from the national average) 7.5 per cent, fiscal discipline 7.5 per cent, tax effort 5 per cent. Though the TFC did not assign any weight to infrastructure index, these changes are favourable to low-income and populous states like Bihar, as far as Table 1.5 indicates. Bihar is the third largest recipient of devolutions from the centre. The high level of Bihar's share confirms the commission's prioritized distribution of central taxes to low income states. The amount of central transfers to Bihar is comparable to those of richer states, or even surpasses them, but it is important to notice that per capita total revenue is still lowest among major states due to lack of the state's own revenue. Currently the transfer is based on the recommendation by the 13th Finance Commission. The tendency observed in the TFC still remains.

Plan expenditure and the provision of infrastructure

Equally as important as the Finance Commission transfers is the fiscal assistance from the Planning Commission, which is disbursed among the states either in the form of grants or lending in line with the five-year plan:[19] the central piece of India's development plan. The Planning Commission's fiscal assistance directly affects the state's public investments in physical and social infrastructure. While the central government recognizes the importance of the Planning Commission's transfers in the economic development of the states, the states' share in the total plan expenditure has been declining. The share was high at 94.5 per cent under the first Five-Year Plan (1951/2 to 1955/6), but it comes down to 40.8 per cent under the 11th Five-Year Plan (2007/8 to 2011/12) (ADRI, 2008). There is no question that the declining tendency in the total plan expenditure has a negative implication on low-income states, including Bihar.

In addition to the shrinking shareable pool of funds, another issue pertaining to Bihar is the inadequacy in the horizontal distribution of central assistance. The amount of per capita plan expenditure on Bihar is projected to be Rs 6,566 (based on 2006/7 prices) during the 11th Five-Year Plan, the lowest among the major states of India. It is reported that this tendency has continued since the fifth Five-Year Plan (1974/5 to 79/80) (ADRI, 2008). In general, the amount of per capita plan expenditure of less developed states is lower. When graphed with per capita income, this relation becomes apparent. Figure 1.6 shows the relationship between per capita income and per capita amount of plan expenditure under the 11th Five-Year Plan. The diagram indicates that low-income states tend to receive lower amounts of plan outlay, while high-income states receive more. Given this situation, low-income states face considerably difficulties in catching up with high-income states. Although the central transfers and assistance play an important role in the economic development of the states and reducing fiscal disparities across them, it is ironical that certainly the current policy has limitations and, in fact, tends to widen the income gap between rich and poor states rather than narrowing it.

Simply increasing the amount of plan expenditure or budget for development, however, does not necessarily increase the supply of infrastructure. The limited budget is certainly a constraint for low-income states, but there is an issue of the state government's capacity to execute

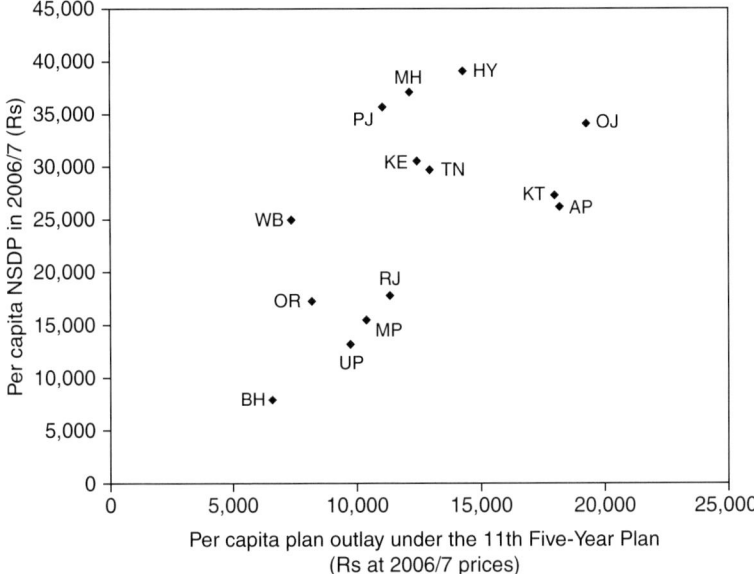

Figure 1.6 Relationship between per capita plan outlay and levels of income

Note: AP: Andra Pradesh, AS: Assam, BH: Bihar, GJ: Gujarat, HY: Haryana, JH: Jharkhand, KT: Karnataka, KE: Kerala, MP: Madhya Pradesh, MH: Maharashtra, OR: Orissa, PJ: Punjab, RJ: Rajasthan, TN: Tamil Nadu, UP: Uttar Pradesh, WB: West Bengal.
Sources: Government of India (2007) and Indiastat (www.indiastat.com).

development projects. The World Bank reports that Bihar's capacity for resources utilization for development purposes is the lowest in India (World Bank, 2007). It writes, 'Cross-state comparison shows Bihar and Uttar Pradesh ranked the lowest, spending approximately one-fourth the per capita level of the top states – Karnataka, Gujarat and Punjab.' This under-utilization and inefficiency pose a serious constraint to development. The low level of utilization of central funds is another factor to explain insufficient stocks of infrastructure. In sum, Bihar needs a fundamental reform not only to increase revenue capacities but also enhance the state capacity to utilize funds efficiently.

Lack of infrastructure is not attractive to private businesses at all. Given the current poor state of infrastructure,[20] Bihar cannot expect large-scale private investment.[21] In particular, it is extremely difficult to attract foreign direct investment to Bihar. This is evident if one examines figures of the approved FDI cases. The amount of FDI flowing into Bihar from August 1991 to December 2007 was just 0.25 per cent of the total FDI approved by the central government.[22] On the other hand, Maharashtra accounted for 19.3 per cent of the total. High-income states with high levels of infrastructure endowments are the favourite destinations for private businesses, including foreign ventures. Greater investment contributes to the state economy and to the state tax revenue as well. The state government in turn becomes encouraged, and uses their increased resources to create a more favourable investment climate. The private sector then responds to this by investing more in the state. This spiral process creates further disparities across the states.

Findings and conclusion

This chapter has analyzed a growing interstate income disparity by focusing on the relationship between infrastructure provision and economic growth. First, the chapter has confirmed that the income gap indeed has been widening. Several measures are used to verify this trend. Second, the chapter has investigated the relationship between infrastructure and economic growth. Our results show a positive impact of infrastructure on economic growth. This result confirms that imbalances in the provision of infrastructure can explain income inequality, and is consistent with findings in the existing literature. Third, taking up the case of Bihar, the least developed state, the chapter has identified factors that constrain the accumulation of infrastructure from fiscal viewpoints. The chapter has argued that, in the light of weak fiscal positions facing low-income states, the current policies, though they have been weighted towards low-income states, are not conducive to narrowing the existing gap but they might be rather in the direction of widening it unintentionally. The chapter has also pointed out that lack of the state government's management capacity constrains the accumulation of infrastructure.

India's economic liberalization policy in the era of globalization has brought economic prosperity to the country. However, the fruits from economic liberalization are not distributed equally among the states. Ironically, those benefits are not delivered to low-income states with limited stocks of infrastructure but to already high-income states with better infrastructure endowments, causing worsening income disparities. In the pre-liberalization period, domestic factors mainly explain interstate disparities. In the post-liberalization period, and also under the process of globalization, external factors such as FDI and international trade become increasingly important to the state economy, and they tend to widen the disparities across the states. Considering the power of these factors and the ongoing situation, the redressal of income disparities needs more active central government interventions to low-income states as what their governments can do is limited in the short-run. This is noted in the 11th Five-Year Plan as 'the role of centre in promoting equity among states, therefore, assumed added importance in the post-liberalization era' (Government of India, 2007). The central government alone cannot remedy the situation. At the same time, the state government efforts are required in many areas from achieving fiscal soundness by increasing own revenue to building public expenditure management capacity. There is no solution that works in the short run to achieve equity. The solution simply depends on the continued efforts by both the central and the state governments.

Not solely through our negligence but also because of limitation of space, a view from the political economy in infrastructure provision has been missed in our analysis. We are fully aware of its role in public provision as discussed by such as Persson and Tabellini (1999). In particular, the case of Bihar would provide a good subject for research in the future. We mainly focus on the interstate income disparity, which is just one aspect of inequalities that exist in India. In fact, inequality arises over many dimensions. Of course, inequalities between rural and urban, inequalities among social classes and intrastate disparities are also critical issues, demanding closer attention and investigation.

Notes

1. There are a number of studies focusing on inequality issues in India. Papers that examine interstate inequality include, for example, Das and Barua (1996), Singh *et al.* (2003), Bhattacharya and Sakhivel (2004) and Ghosh and Gupta (2009).
2. The other concept is conditional convergence. It is defined such that the income of each state converges to the 'respective' steady state income level. If a country's income position is away from its steady state, then the country grows faster. See Mankiw *et al.* (1992).
3. For deriving Lorenz curves and Gini coefficients, we did not consider the intrastate distribution of income; that is, we assumed that each individual's income in a state is equal to the average real per capita NSDP of the state. This assumption may not produce precise Gini coefficients, but it would be fine just to see the changing trend of income inequality across states.
4. These figures seem lower than one might expect. When Gini coefficients are calculated based on personal consumption data, they tend to be higher, as they account for intrastate variations. For example, Gini coefficients reported in Dev and Ravi (2007) are 0.263 for rural and 0.346 for urban in 1999/2000, and 0.269 for rural and 0.350 for urban in 2004/5. Figures reported by Gajwani *et al.* (2006), however, are even lower than ours. For example, the Gini coefficient in 2000, based on nominal consumption expenditure, is 0.168.

5. The CV is calculated as follows:

   $CV = \dfrac{\sqrt{\sum_{i=1} w_i(X_i - \bar{X})^2}}{\bar{X}}$ where X_i is the real per capita NSDP of state i, $\bar{X}$ the average real per capita NSDP and w is the population weight of state i.
6. One might be confused with the relationship between σ-convergence and β-convergence. Barro and Sala-i-Martin (1992) shows that β-convergence is a necessary condition for β-convergence, but not a sufficient condition. That initially poor states grow faster than rich ones does not guarantee the narrowing income gap between them.
7. A good review of literature on this topic is Gramlich (1994). See Straub (2008) for recent developments.
8. Aschauer (1989) examined the impact of infrastructure on the US productivity, and concluded that the US's productivity slowdown in the 1970s and 1980s resulted mainly from slower growth in infrastructure accumulation. The timing of his publication coincided with the advent of endogenous growth theory, with some papers emphasizing the role of public capital in growth process, such as Barro (1990).
9. Binswanger *et al.* (1989) find a positive impact of roads on the reduction of transportation cost and the productivity increase in the rural sector of India. Zhang and Fan (2004) also find a positive impact of road infrastructure on agriculture productivity in rural India.
10. There is a considerable gap between the consumption figure in IEA (2009) and that reported by the Indian government. According to the government data, the per capita electricity consumption in 2006/7 was 671.9kWh. Even with this figure, the level of consumption is still low.
11. T&D loss data are from the World Bank (2007).
12. The 17 states are Andhra Pradesh, Assam, Bihar, Gujarat, Haryana, Himachal Pradesh, Jammu and Kashmir, Karnataka, Kerala, Madhya Pradesh, Maharashtra, Orissa, Punjab, Rajasthan, Tamil Nadu, Uttar Pradesh and West Bengal.
13. At the same time, Madhya Pradesh was split into Madhya Pradesh and Chhattisgarh, and Uttar Pradesh was bifurcated into Uttar Pradesh and Uttarakhand.
14. The 17 states are the same ones noted in reference 12 above.
15. Both studies report a positive and statistically significant relationship between per capita economic growth and per capita electricity consumption. Bandyopadhyay (2006) uses per capita industrial electricity consumption. Utilizing per capita power generation, Lall (2007) also finds a similar result.
16. The author's calculation based on the poverty ratios and population data at the time of 2003/4.
17. It is reported that of the 100 most backward and poorest districts in the country, 38 districts are in Bihar (Government of India, 2003). Since there are 38 districts in Bihar, all districts in the state are listed.
18. See Vithal and Sastry (2001) and Krishna (2007) for details on the fiscal relationship between the central government and the states of India.
19. The distribution of normal central assistance through the Planning Commission is based on the *Gadgil* formula weighted towards poorer states. In addition to normal assistance, there are other forms of assistance by the Planning Commission. These are distributed mainly at the discretion of the

commission. Central and centrally sponsored schemes (CSS) operated by the central government ministries do not have a specific formula. Since the state government needs to contribute a 25 per cent share of total scheme costs, it is often criticized in that only high-income states can afford to receive the CSS (Vithal and Sastry, 2001).
20. In fact, there are other factors that discourage private investment in Bihar. Those include natural calamities such as heavy floods due to monsoon rain and unfavourable security situations in rural areas caused by Naxalites.
21. A World Bank study points to this fact (World Bank, 2008). It reports that Bihar accounted for only 0.4 per cent of the total private projects under implementation at the time of the survey.
22. Data from *Indiastat* database (www.indiastat.com). The original data come from the Ministry of Commerce and Industry, Government of India.

References

ADRI (2008) *Joint Memorandum of Political Parties & Academic/Professional Organizations of Bihar to 13th Finance Commission*, Asian Development Research Institute, Patna, Bihar.
Agenor, Pierre-Richard (2004) *The Economics of Adjustment and Growth*, Cambridge, MA: Harvard University Press.
Ahluwalia, M. (2002) 'State Level Performance Under Economic Reforms in India', in Anne Krueger (ed.), *Economic Policy Reforms and the Indian Economy*, Chicago, IL: University of Chicago Press.
Aschauer, D. A. (1989) 'Is Public Expenditure Productive?', *Journal of Monetary Economics*, 23 (2), pp. 177–200.
Bandyopadhyay, S. (2006) 'Rich States, Poor States: Convergence and Polarisation in India', Discussion Paper Series, Department of Economics, University of Oxford.
Barnes, D. F. (1988) *Electric Power for Rural Growth: How Electricity Affects Rural Life in Developing Countries*, Boulder, CO: Westview Press.
Barro, R. J. (1990) 'Government Spending in a Simple Model of Endogenous Growth', *Journal of Political Economy*, 98 (S5), pp. 103–25.
_____ and X. Sala-i-Martin (1992), 'Convergence', *Journal of Political Economy*, 100 (2), pp. 223–51.
Bhattacharya, B. B. and S. Sakthivel (2004) 'Regional Growth and Disparity in India: Comparison of Pre-and Post Reform Decades', *Economic and Political Weekly*, 6 March, pp. 1071–7.
Binswanger, H. P., S. R. Khandkur and M. R. Rosenzweig (1989) 'How Infrastructure and Financial Institutions affect Agriculture Output and Investment in India', Policy Research Working Paper Series 163, World Bank, Washington, DC.
Calderon, Cesar, and Luis Serven (2004) 'The Effects of Infrastructure Development on Growth and Income Distribution', Policy Research Working Paper No. 3400, World Bank, Washington, DC.
Cashin, P. and R. Sahay (1996) 'Internal Migration, Center-State Grants, and Economic Growth in the States of India', *IMF Staff Paper*, 43 (1), pp. 123–71.
Das, K. (2005) 'Infrastructure and Growth in a Regional Context: Indian States since the 1980s', Working Paper No. 165, Gujarat Institute of Development Research, Gota, Ahmedabad.

Das, S. K. and A. Barua (1996) 'Regional Inequalities, Economic Growth and Liberalisation: A Study of the Indian Economy', *Journal of Development Studies*, 32 (3), pp. 364–90.

Datt, Gaurav, and Martin Ravallion (2002) 'Is India's Economic Growth Leaving the Poor Behind?', *Journal of Economic Perspectives*, 16 (3), pp. 89–108.

Deaton, A. and J. Drèze (2002) 'Poverty and Inequality in India: A Re-Examination', *Economic and Political Weekly*, 7 September, pp. 3729–48.

Dev, M. S., and C. Ravi (2007) 'Poverty and Inequality: All India and States, 1983–2005', *Economic and Political Weekly*, 42 (6), pp. 509–21.

Esfahani, Hade Salehi, and Maria Teresa Ramirez (2003) 'Institutions, Infrastructure, and Economic Growth', *Journal of Monetary Economics*, 70, pp. 443–77.

Gajwani, K., R. Kanbur and X. Zhang (2006) 'Patterns of Spatial Convergence and Divergence in India and China', paper presented at the Annual Bank Conference on Development Economics (ABCDE), St Petersburg, 18–19 January.

Ghosh, B. and P. De (2004) 'How do Different Categories of Infrastructure Affect Development? Evidence from Indian States', *Economic and Political Weekly*, 16 October, pp. 4645–57.

_____ (2005) 'Investigating the Linkage between Infrastructure and Regional Development in India: Era of Planning to Globalization', *Journal of Asian Economics*, 15, pp. 1023–50.

Ghosh, P. P. and C. D. Gupta (2009) 'Political Implications of Inter-State Disparity', *Economic and Political Weekly*, 27 June, pp. 185–91.

Government of Bihar, Finance Department (2008) *Economic Survey 2007/08*, New Delhi.

Government of India, Planning Commission (2003) *Report of the Task: Identification of Districts for Wage and Self-Employment Programmes*, New Delhi.

_____, Planning Commission (2007) *Eleventh Five-Year Plan*, New Delhi.

_____, Ministry of Finance (2008) *Economic Survey 2007/08*, New Delhi.

Gramlich, Edwar M. (1994) 'Infrastructure Investment: A Review Essay', *Journal of Economic Literature*, 32 (3), pp. 1176–96.

International Energy Agency (IEA) (2009) *Key World Energy Statistics 2009*, Paris, France.

Krishna, S. (2007) *From Centre to State: Finance Commission Transfers in India*, Centre for Federal Studies, Hamdard University, New Delhi.

Kumar, Sanjay (2004) 'Impact of Economic Reforms on the Indian Electorate', *Economic and Political Weekly*, 17 April, pp. 1621–30.

Lall, S. V. (2007) 'Infrastructure and Regional Growth, Growth Dynamics and Policy Relevance for India', *The Annals of Regional Science*, 41 (3), pp. 581–99.

Mankiw, N. G., D. Romer and D. N. Weil (1992) 'A Contribution to the Empirics of Economic Growth', *Quarterly Journal of Economics*, 107 (2), pp. 407–37.

Mitra, Arup, Aristomene Varoudakis and Marie-Ange Veganzones-Varoudakis (2002) 'Productivity and Technical Efficiency in Indian States' Manufacturing: The Role of Infrastructure', *Economic Development and Cultural Change*, 50 (2), pp. 395–426.

Murphy, Kevin, Andrei Shleifer and R. Vishny (1989) 'Industrialization and the Big Push', *Journal of Political Economy*, 97, pp. 1003–26.

Nagaraj, R., A. Varoudakis and M. A. Veganzones (1998) 'Long Run Growth Trends and Convergence across Indian States', OECD, Technical Paper, No. 131.

_____ (2000) 'Long-Run Growth Trends and Convergence across Indian States', *Journal of International Development*, 12 (1), pp. 45–70.

Persson, Torsten, and Guido Tabellini (1999) 'The Size and Scope of Government: Comparative Politics with Rational Politicians', *European Economic Review*, 43, pp. 699–735.

Purfield, C. (2006) 'Mind the Gap – Is Economic Growth in India Leaving Some States Behind?', IMF Working Paper WP/06/103.

Rosenstein-Rodan, Paul (1943) 'Problems of Industrialization of Eastern and Southeastern Europe', *Economic Journal*, 53, pp. 202–11.

Sahoo, P. and R. K. Dash (2009) 'Infrastructure Development and Economic Growth in India', *Journal of the Asia Pacific Economy*, 14 (4), pp. 351–65.

Singh, N., L. Bhandari, A. Chen and A. Khare (2003) 'Regional Inequality in India: A Fresh Look', *Economic and Political Weekly*, 15 March, pp. 1069–73.

Straub, Stephane (2008) 'Infrastructure and Growth in Developing Countries: Recent Advances and Research Challenges', Policy Research Working paper No. 4460, World Bank, Washington, DC.

Vithal, B. P. R. and M. L. Sastry (2001) *Fiscal Federalism in India*, Delhi: Oxford University Press.

World Bank (2005) *Investment Climate Surveys*, ongoing project, World Bank, Washington, DC.

_____ (2007) *World Development Indicators 2007*, CD-ROM, World Bank, Washington, DC.

_____ (2008) *Bihar: Towards a Development Strategy*, a World Bank report, World Bank, Washington, DC.

Zhang, X. and S. Fan (2004) 'How Productive Is Infrastructure? A New Approach and Evidence from Rural India', *American Journal of Agricultural Economics*, 86 (2), pp. 492–501.

2
Changes in Land Distribution and Non-agricultural Growth in India

Shigemochi Hirashima and Kensuke Kubo

Introduction

It is well known that there is an overwhelming tendency for the rural poor in India to be landless (e.g., Walker and Ryan 1990). While landlessness is one outcome of poverty, it is also viewed as a reason for persistent poverty. Land ownership may present rural landless households with a way out of poverty, but the majority of families in need are not in a position to take such a route. This chapter sheds some light on whether or not this path out of poverty is still important, and to what extent it is an option for the rural poor in the context of India's recent economic growth.

The notion that land ownership can alleviate rural poverty is supported by evidence that land ownership is correlated with access to credit and investment in both physical and human capital. These investments open the way to new income opportunities, including self-employment or salaried employment in the non-agricultural sector (Lanjouw and Shariff, 2004). At the same time, land by itself is a productive asset that can increase the potential earning power of rural households. A skilled cultivator can generally attain a higher standard of living from operating his farm than from participating as a wage worker in the agricultural labour market.

The effect of land ownership on the alleviation of poverty is severely limited, however, if the markets for land and credit operate in such a way that a landless household cannot profitably purchase land with borrowed funds. This phenomenon has indeed been observed in the South Asian context (Hirashima, 1978, 2008). One factor is that the market price of land tends to be higher than the discounted future flow of farm returns, because of the power and prestige associated with land ownership (Basu, 1986; Hirashima, 2009). Farmland prices are also affected by expectations of growth in the non-agricultural sector. Landless households, because they lack assets that they can use as collateral, can seldom borrow funds at competitive interest rates from formal credit institutions.

Taken together, the imperfections and peculiarities of the land and credit markets imply the following. Landless villagers must borrow at a higher interest rate than existing landowners in order to purchase farmland whose price is inflated by its value from non-agricultural uses. The existence of such market imperfections has been one of the motives behind land reform legislation in post-Independence India. However, unlike successful land reforms elsewhere in Asia – particularly in Japan and Taiwan – the Indian land reform has been limited in its ability to redistribute land to the most disadvantaged rural residents. In Indian states where land distribution remains particularly skewed, such as Bihar, land reform remains on the policy agenda. However, the political establishment in these states has continued to prevent significant reforms from taking place (Bandhopadhyay, 2009).[1]

While the prospect for significant land redistribution fades, there is some evidence that the distribution of land in rural India is gradually deteriorating. As we discuss in the first section, survey data show a slight increase in inequalities in the ownership of land and assets during the 1990s and early 2000s. We find that this increasing inequality occurred across the board. States that are relatively wealthy (in terms of per capita output) were just as likely as poorer states to see increasing inequalities in the distribution of assets and land. At the same time, there is some indication that states with high rates of non-agricultural growth experienced larger increases in inequality. Thus, it is likely that the increasing inequality in the distribution of land during the 1990s was somehow associated with growth in the non-agricultural sector.

This raises the following question. What is the relationship between non-agricultural growth and changes in land distribution? There are two scenarios under which growth in the non-agricultural sector can coincide with a deterioration of the distribution of land, and these have different implications for the welfare of the landless and marginally landowning rural households. First, growth in the non-agricultural sector increases demand for land for industrial, commercial and residential use. This is especially true around cities and large towns. This increased demand tends to raise land prices and widen the gap that may already exist between the market price of land and its value as a productive asset for cultivators. Thus, landless households may be shut out of the market for buying farmland, and inequalities in land distribution may be exacerbated by non-agricultural growth.

On the other hand, non-agricultural development may make land ownership less important to rural residents if it involves increased employment in the manufacturing and service sectors. In particular, if members of the landless and marginally landowning households are able to access new employment opportunities, they may find it easier to escape poverty through regular employment than through owner-cultivation. Such individuals may be better off as a result of non-agricultural growth, even if there is no increase in the amount of land they own. In fact, when land ownership becomes less important for the landless and the marginal landowners, less land will move into their hands, and more land will be released by them. This may contribute to an increased inequality in land ownership.

In this chapter, we pursue the question of which of these two scenarios most accurately describes the changes in rural India during the 1990s and 2000s, which have been characterized by growth in the non-agricultural sector and a slight increase in inequality of land ownership. Clearly, the two explanations have different implications for the evaluation of India's recent experience of growth. If the first scenario holds, it is likely that a significant portion of the rural population has been deprived of access to land ownership, and this would raise concerns about the desirability of unregulated development in the Indian countryside. On the other hand, if the second scenario holds, it is likely that non-agricultural development, as well as overall economic growth, has made all sections of society generally better off.

In order to evaluate these competing scenarios, we examine data collected in 2003 by the National Sample Survey Organization as part of its 59th round survey. We make use of information from the *Situation Assessment Survey of Farmers*, a 'first of its kind' survey that collected information on various aspects of farming. The survey covered rural households that carried out any agricultural activity – no matter how small – on their own operational land holding. One part of the survey asked respondents about land transactions during the preceding agricultural year. By examining the characteristics of the households who purchased or sold land, it is possible to infer the state of the land market in the different parts of the country that have been experiencing varying degrees of non-agricultural economic growth. These inferences, in turn, allow us to draw conclusions about the impact of non-agricultural development on marginal and landless rural households.

To summarize briefly, we find that in states with high rates of non-agricultural growth, the market for land is characterized by a movement away from agricultural fundamentals, as reflected in the type of household that is more likely to buy land. Specifically, we find that households that are more enthusiastic about farming are less likely to be buyers in such states. Although our data do not contain information on the price of land, we can infer from this that non-agricultural demand has been raising the price beyond what is affordable for the landless and marginal households. This is corroborated by our finding that households engaged primarily in agricultural labour are less likely to buy land in states where there is high non-agricultural growth. We also find that in states with a history of strong land reform legislation, agricultural labour households have a better chance of acquiring land.

These findings support the view that non-agricultural growth has been accompanied by a tendency for the landless and marginally landholding households to be excluded from having the opportunity to buy land. On the other hand, they do not rule out the possibility that non-agricultural growth has provided sufficient employment opportunities to landless and marginal households and thus land ownership has become less important to them as a source of livelihood. Citing evidence from previous studies, we argue that landless and marginal households have not benefited greatly from the newly generated non-agricultural employment opportunities.

The remainder of the chapter is organized as follows. In the next section, we discuss the changes in land distribution at the state level during the 1980s and 1990s; the third section describes the data and methodology; in the fourth section, we present the main statistical results from the NSS data; the fifth section presents an interpretation of the results; and the final section concludes.

Changes in the distribution of land and assets in the 1980s and 1990s

Land is by far the most important asset in rural India. This section presents a snapshot of how the ownership of land is distributed, along with that of assets in general. Figure 2.1 compares the distribution of the stock of owned assets with that of the annual flow of consumption expenditure. The graphs were constructed from data collected by the National Sample Survey Organization (NSSO) in large-scale household surveys. From the respective Lorenz curves, it is obvious that the distribution of assets is considerably more unequal than that of consumption

66 Changes in Land Distribution

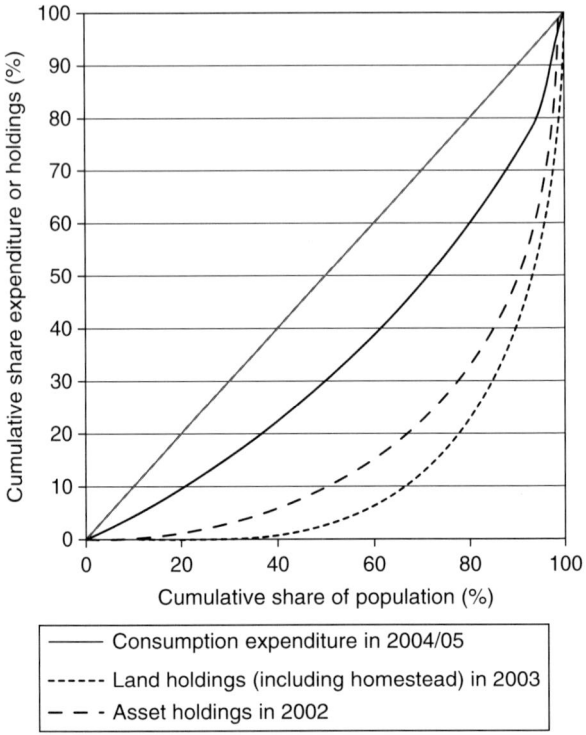

Figure 2.1 Lorenz curves for consumption expenditure and asset holdings
Source: Computations based on NSSO (2005; 2006a; 2006b).

spending. Moreover, land is more unequally distributed than is the case with assets as a whole. While the Gini coefficient for consumption expenditure in 2004/5 was 0.31, the corresponding values for total assets (in 2002) and land (in 2003) were 0.62 and 0.76, respectively (Subramanian and Jayaraj, 2006; Rawal, 2008).

In order to understand why assets are more unequally distributed than consumption expenditure, it is necessary to recognize that many poorer households totally depend on labour income to meet their consumption needs. Since human capital is not included in the NSSO's definition of household assets, the graph for total assets in Figure 2.1 may overstate the degree of inequality in earning potential among rural households. On the other hand, the Lorenz curve for consumption expenditure may fail to incorporate intertemporal aspects of poverty such as vulnerability. If poorer households are more vulnerable to income shocks, it is possible that the Lorenz curve built on the basis of consumption expenditure over a single period understates the true level of inequality. The amount of assets a household owns is closely related to how well it can cope with intertemporal aspects of poverty. Thus, the Lorenz curve for asset holdings may contain information on inequality that is missing from its consumption-based counterpart.

It is important to keep in mind that data on the distribution of land and assets suffer from two major problems. The first is the problem of possible under-reporting. As a result of land reform policies such as ceilings on land holdings, many large landowners are known to have superficially transferred some of their ownership through *benami* transactions, whereby holdings are re-registered under the names of non-existent individuals (Mearns, 1999). Since such schemes are used only by those with holdings above the specified ceiling, under-reporting is likely to exert a downward bias on indices of inequality. The second problem is that the assets are only measured in gross terms; liabilities are not netted out. This is because the liabilities reported by households for the NSSO's *All-India Debt and Investment Survey* (which is also the source for the data on the distribution of assets) appear to be grossly under-reported. Subramanian and Jayaraj (2006) compare the estimates for total household debt from the NSSO survey with estimates based on the amount of outstanding loans reported by financial institutions. It turns out that the former estimates are only around a quarter of the latter. Since the relationship between under-reporting and the amount of assets a household may own is unknown, it is not possible to know in which direction the estimates of net assets are biased. Thus, researchers such as Subramanian and Jayaraj work mostly with data on gross assets.

With these caveats in mind, and assuming that the under-reporting bias does not change significantly over time, we next examine how inequalities in asset and land distribution have changed over time. Figures 2.2 and 2.3 show how inequalities regarding assets changed during the 1980s and 1990s. Here, states are the unit of observation. Figure 2.2 maps the Gini coefficient for the distribution of assets for 1981/2 onto the corresponding figure for 1991/2. With the exception of Madhya Pradesh and Rajasthan, all states lie below the 45 degree line, implying that inequalities in asset distribution fell during the 1980s in most of India. It is interesting to note that the same pattern holds for both high-poverty and low-poverty states. Figure 2.3 presents a contrasting picture. In more than half the states, the degree of inequality increased between 1991/2 and 2002/3. While the states that experienced the largest

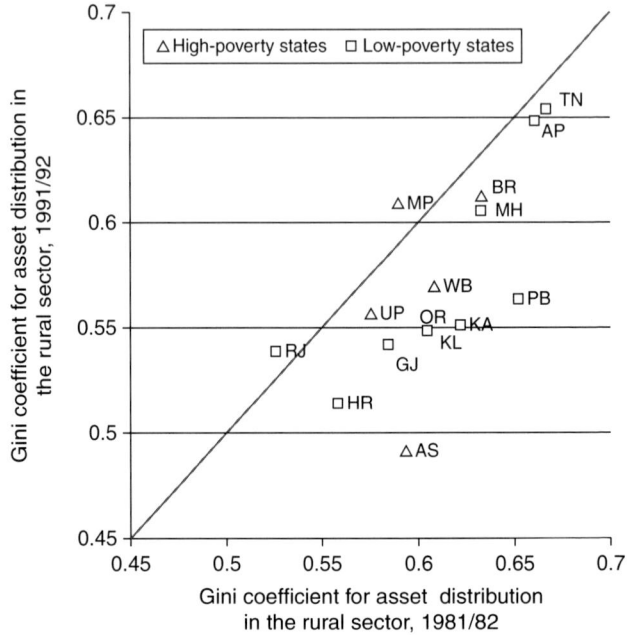

Figure 2.2 Changes in asset distribution inequality, 1981/2 to 1991/2

Notes: [1] 'High poverty states' are those with a poverty headcount ratio of 40% or higher in 1993/94. The remaining states are defined as 'low poverty states'.
[2] State acronyms: AP=Andhra Pradesh, AS=Assam, BR=Bihar (includes Jharkhand), GJ=Gujarat, HR=Haryana, KA=Karnataka, KL=Kerala, MP=Madhya Pradesh (includes Chhattisgarh), MH=Maharashtra, OR=Orissa, PB=Punjab, RJ=Rajasthan, TN=Tamil Nadu, UP=Uttar Pradesh (includes Uttarakhand), WB=West Bengal.
Sources: From data in Subramanian and Jayaraj (2006), Sen and Himanshu (2003), and Himanshu (2007).

increase in inequality (those furthest away from the 45 degree line) belong to the low-poverty category, there were only two high-poverty states (Bihar and Madhya Pradesh) where inequality decreased.

Figures 2.4 and 2.5 present analogous plots for the Gini coefficient for land distribution. In Figure 2.4, we find that land distribution tended to become more equal during the 1980s, especially in states with initially high inequality. As we turn to Figure 2.5, we see that the Gini coefficient increased slightly in many states during the 1990s and the first half of the 2000s.

In Figures 2.6 and 2.7, we plot the changes in the Gini coefficient between 1993/4 and 2004/5 against two variables representing economic conditions in each state: per capita net state domestic product (NSDP)

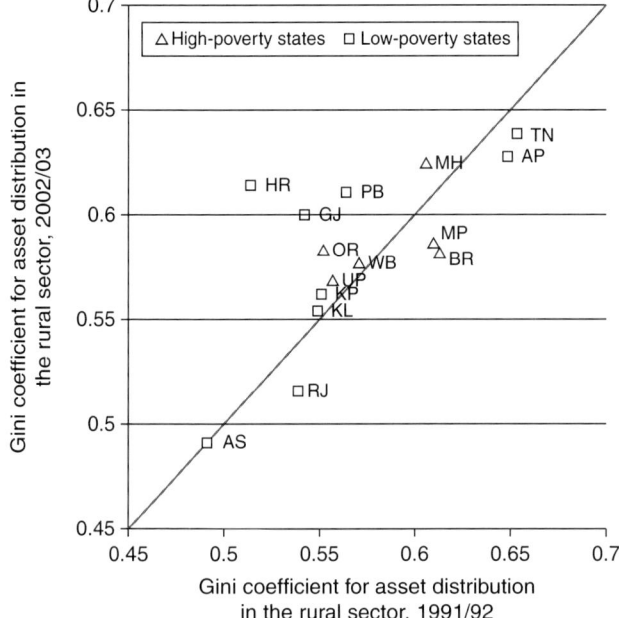

Figure 2.3 Changes in asset distribution inequality, 1991/2 to 2002/3

Notes: [1] 'High poverty states' are those with a poverty headcount ratio of 40% or higher in 1993/94. The remaining states are defined as 'low poverty states'.
[2] State acronyms: AP=Andhra Pradesh, AS=Assam, BR=Bihar (includes Jharkhand), GJ=Gujarat, HR=Haryana, KA=Karnataka, KL=Kerala, MP=Madhya Pradesh (includes Chhattisgarh), MH=Maharashtra, OR=Orissa, PB=Punjab, RJ=Rajasthan, TN=Tamil Nadu, UP=Uttar Pradesh (includes Uttarakhand), WB=West Bengal.
Sources: From data in Subramanian and Jayaraj (2006) and Himanshu (2007).

and the growth in non-agricultural NSDP.[2] From Figure 2.6, we see that inequalities in the distribution of land tended to increase, regardless of initial wealth levels. In Figure 2.7, with the exception of the north-eastern border state of Arunachal Pradesh, there appears to be a positive relationship between non-agricultural growth and changes in land distribution inequality. Thus, it is likely that this increase was somehow associated with growth in the non-agricultural economy.

In Figure 2.8, we graph the composition of assets in rural India, based on the NSSO *Debt and Investment Survey* for 2002/3, presented by Subramanian and Jayaraj (2006). The share of each type of asset in the total is presented separately for different asset-holding classes. The most striking aspect is that the share of land is quite high, particularly for the

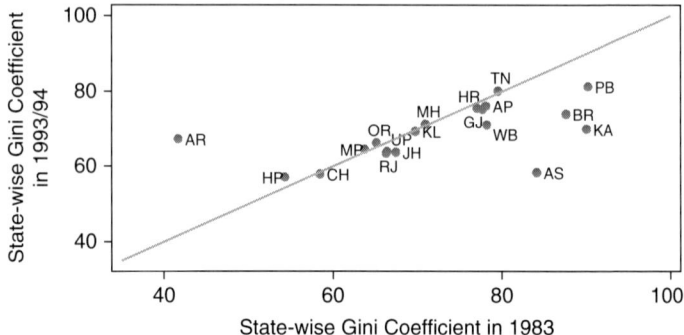

Figure 2.4 Changes in land distribution inequality, 1983 to 1993/4

Notes: [1] The Gini coefficients were calculated from the unit-level data of the Employment and Unemployment Survey, Rounds 38 and 50, National Sample Survey Organization.
[2] State acronyms: AP=Andhra Pradesh, AR=Arunachal Pradesh, AS=Assam, BR=Bihar, CH=Chhattisgarh, GJ=Gujarat, HR=Haryana, HP=Himachal Pradesh, JH=Jharkhand, KA=Karnataka, KL=Kerala, MP=Madhya Pradesh, MH=Maharashtra, OR=Orissa, PB=Punjab, RJ=Rajasthan, TN=Tamil Nadu, UP=Uttar Pradesh (includes Uttarakhand), WB=West Bengal.

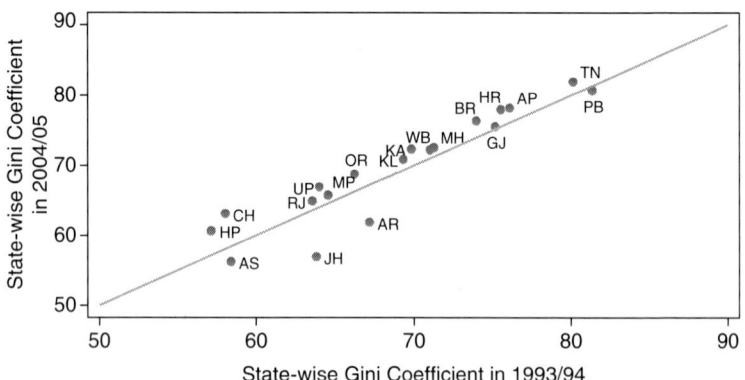

Figure 2.5 Changes in land distribution inequality, 1993/4 to 2004/5

Notes: [1] The Gini coefficients were calculated from the unit-level data of the Employment and Unemployment Survey, Rounds 50 and 61, National Sample Survey Organization.
[2] State acronyms: AP=Andhra Pradesh, AR=Arunachal Pradesh, AS=Assam, BR=Bihar, CH=Chhattisgarh, GJ=Gujarat, HR=Haryana, HP=Himachal Pradesh, JH=Jharkhand, KA=Karnataka, KL=Kerala, MP=Madhya Pradesh, MH=Maharashtra, OR=Orissa, PB=Punjab, RJ=Rajasthan, TN=Tamil Nadu, UP=Uttar Pradesh (includes Uttarakhand), WB=West Bengal.

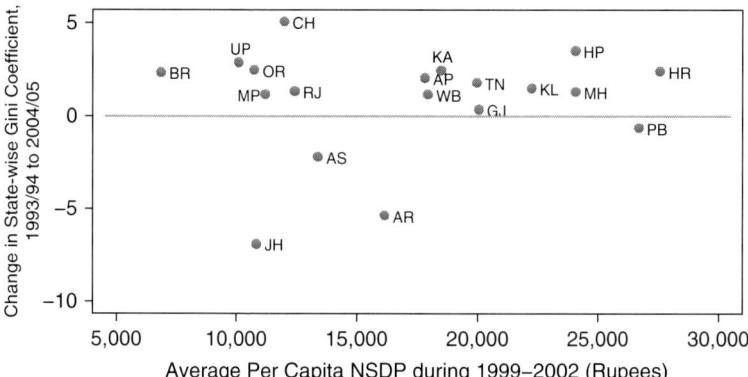

Figure 2.6 Wealth levels and changes in land distribution inequality

Notes: [1] Changes in Gini coefficients were calculated from the unit-level data of the Employment and Unemployment Survey, Rounds 50 and 61, National Sample Survey Organization.
[2] Net State domestic product (NSDP) data are from the National Statistics Office.
[3] State acronyms: AP=Andhra Pradesh, AR=Arunachal Pradesh, AS=Assam, BR=Bihar, CH=Chhattisgarh, GJ=Gujarat, HR=Haryana, HP=Himachal Pradesh, JH=Jharkhand, KA=Karnataka, KL=Kerala, MP=Madhya Pradesh, MH=Maharashtra, OR=Orissa, PB=Punjab, RJ=Rajasthan, TN=Tamil Nadu, UP=Uttar Pradesh (includes Uttarakhand), WB=West Bengal.

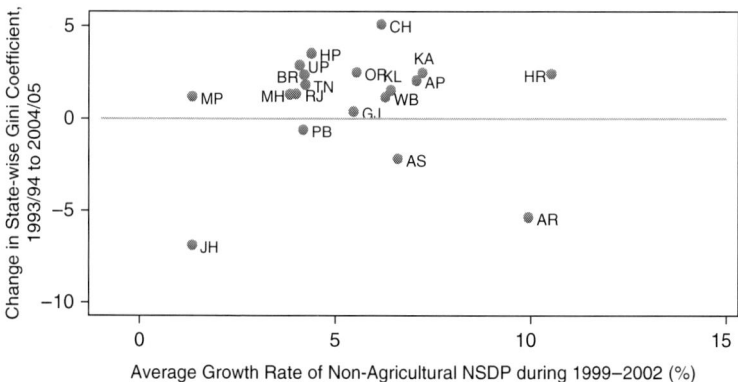

Figure 2.7 Non-agricultural growth and changes in land distribution inequality

Notes: [1] Changes in Gini coefficients were calculated from the unit-level data of the Employment and Unemployment Survey, Rounds 50 and 61, National Sample Survey Organization.
[2] Net State domestic product (NSDP) data are from the National Statistics Office.
[3] State acronyms: AP=Andhra Pradesh, AR=Arunachal Pradesh, AS=Assam, BR=Bihar, CH=Chhattisgarh, GJ=Gujarat, HR=Haryana, HP=Himachal Pradesh, JH=Jharkhand, KA=Karnataka, KL=Kerala, MP=Madhya Pradesh, MH=Maharashtra, OR=Orissa, PB=Punjab, RJ=Rajasthan, TN=Tamil Nadu, UP=Uttar Pradesh (includes Uttarakhand), WB=West Bengal.

72 Changes in Land Distribution

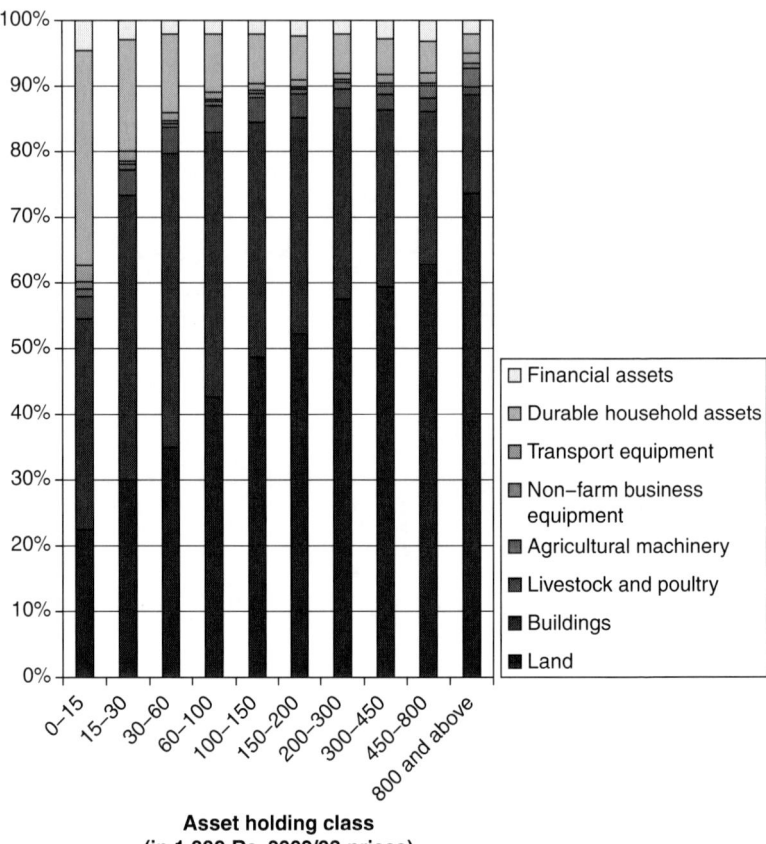

Figure 2.8 Composition of assets in rural India by class, 2002/3

Notes: Figures in the bar graphs are percentage shares.
Source: From data in Table 5a of Subramanian and Jayaraj (2006).

larger asset holders. In the upper-most grouping (assets of 250,000 Rs and higher), land makes up roughly 73 per cent of total assets in value terms. By contrast, the smallest asset holders keep only around 18 per cent of their assets in land, the majority being held in the form of buildings (most often homes) and other durable household assets. This is the reason why, in Figure 2.1, the Lorenz curve for land lies far below that for total assets.

The changes in the Gini coefficient reveal that the distribution of the ownership of assets and land became more unequal during the 1990s and early 2000s. We also find that the increase in inequality in terms of the ownership of land tended to be high in states that experienced high growth in the non-agricultural sector. In order to examine the relationship between non-agricultural growth and land distribution in greater depth, we now examine household-level data from the National Sample Survey.

Methodology and data

The state-level evidence reviewed in the previous section suggests that the increase in inequalities in the ownership of land in rural India during the 1990s and early 2000s can partly be attributed to growth in the non-agricultural sector over the same period. As mentioned in the introduction, there are two possible scenarios that can give rise to this relationship: (1) increased non-agricultural (industrial, commercial and residential) demand for land may raise land prices, especially around cities and large towns, to such an extent that landless and marginally owning households lacking self-financing capabilities and access to cheap capital are denied the opportunity to buy land; and (2) employment generation in the non-agricultural sector may make land ownership less attractive to landless and marginally owning rural households as a source of livelihood, so that land ownership becomes more concentrated in the hands of existing landowners.

The statistical analysis introduced in this section investigates whether or not the first of these scenarios is supported by the data. We use household-level data from a nationally representative sample survey of farm households to address this question. In the data, called the Situation Survey of Farmers ('Schedule 33') in the NSS 59th round, a farm household is broadly defined as including a rural household that carries out some form of agricultural activity on land that it operates.

The survey covers the following topics: (1) the characteristics of the household and its members; (2) knowledge of farming practices and institutions; (3) details regarding possessed land and irrigation; (4) access to and use of farm inputs and new technologies; (5) the use of loans; (6) the purchase and sale of assets, including agricultural land; (7) farm and non-farm income, excluding labour income; and (8) consumption expenditure. For each household in the survey, we are able to observe whether or not it sold or purchased any land and relate that action to other variables. Also, we are able to merge the household-level data with various state- and region-level variables of interest.

Our basic strategy is to identify the kind of household that is likely to participate in land transactions. The methodology is closest to that of Deininger *et al.* (2009) who examined the causes and consequences of land sales transactions in India. Unlike Deininger *et al.* (*ibid.*) who observed all transactions that occurred during a period of almost 20 years, we only observe transactions that occurred during the one-year reference period for the survey. Thus, land transactions are recorded with lower frequency in our data. However, we utilize a much larger and more comprehensive sample, due to the wide coverage of the NSS survey. As a result, we are able to incorporate various regional variables of interest and to interact them with other variables at the household level.

The state and regional variables that we employ are the following: (1) the growth rate of non-agricultural net state domestic product (NSDP) during the three-year period prior to the survey; (2) a land reform variable constructed by adding up the number of land-related laws passed since independence, using data from Besley and Burgess (2001); and (3) a variable representing a regional climate shock, measured as the occurrence of a rainfall deficiency of greater than 10 per cent on average during the three years prior to the survey for each sub-division as defined by the Indian Meteorological Department (IMD).[3]

The aim is to see if the average characteristics of land buyers and sellers exhibit any peculiarities that are distinct from those of non-traders, and to see if these peculiarities vary between 'high non-agricultural growth states', 'strong land reform legislation states', 'rainfall-deficient regions' and the all-India average. By observing the peculiarities of land-trading households, it is possible to make inferences about the functioning of regional land markets. The data is further subjected to analysis by probit regression.

The definitions of the variables are given in Table 2.1. The household-level variables can be classified as follows: (1) characteristics of the household head (age, primary education completion (*Age, PrimEdu*); (2) the broad caste community of the household (one of the following: scheduled tribes, scheduled castes, other backward classes, or other communities (*ST, SC, OBC, OthComm*); (3) whether or not the household is classified as a household engaged primarily in agricultural labour (*AgLabour*); (4) variables concerning the agricultural knowledge/curiosity/progressiveness of the farmer (whether the farmer answered in the affirmative when asked if he/she 'likes farming as a profession'; the number of sources of information on agriculture accessed by the farmer as a ratio to the mean value within the same NSS stratum[4] (*LikeFarm, AgInfo*); (5) the area of land owned by the household

Table 2.1 Variable definitions

Variable name	Definition
Household-level	
Age	Age of head of household
PrimEdu	Equals one if head of household completed primary education
ST	Equals one if household belongs to a scheduled tribe
SC	Equals one if household belongs to a scheduled caste
OBC	Equals one if household belongs to the 'other backward caste' category
OthComm	Equals one if household belongs to a community other than the ones mentioned above
AgLabour	Equals one if the primary source of household income is agricultural labour
LikeFarm	Equals one if the respondent (usually the head of the household) likes farming as a profession
AgInfo	Number of sources of information on agriculture accessed by the household, as a proportion of the average within the NSS stratum
LandOwned	Area of land owned in hectares
MedShare	Annual medical expenditure as a proportion of annual consumption expenditure
LoanShare	Loans outstanding as a proportion of annual consumption expenditure
CultInc	Annual net income from cultivation in Rs
LiveInc	Annual net income from livestock in Rs
BusInc	Annual net income from non-farm business in Rs
State/region-level	
LandRef	Cumulative number of land reform laws passed between 1948 and 1992
NonAgGro	Equals one if the average growth rate of the state's net domestic product in the non-agricultural sector during 1999–2002 was greater than 5%
RainDef	Equals one if the annual rainfall during 2000–2 was less than 90% of the average during 1970–2002

(*LandOwned*); (6) annual medical expenditure as a proportion of total consumption expenditure,[5] as a measure of health shocks (*MedShare*); (7) the outstanding loan balance as a ratio to annual consumption expenditure (*LoanShare*); (8) income from self-employment[6] (cultivation, animal husbandry and non-farm business (*CultInc*, *LiveInc*, *BusInc*). These household-level variables are combined with the three state- and region-level variables described earlier. *LandRef* counts the cumulative number of land reform laws in each state,[7] *NonAgGro* is an indicator for an annual non-agricultural NSDP growth rate of 5 per cent or higher during 1999–2002, and *RainDef* is an indicator for a rainfall deficiency of greater than 10 per cent during 2000–2.

Results

Mean comparisons

Table 2.2 presents sample means and sub-sample means for variables at the level of the household. This is done separately for buyers and non-buyers of land. From the full sample averages, we find that buyers are slightly older and less likely to belong to a scheduled caste. Scheduled castes are socially disadvantaged classes; they have been given explicit recognition by the Indian government. Purchasers of land are less likely to be agricultural labourers, tend to 'like farming' and access more sources of information on agriculture. They also tend to own more land. The high value of loans observed for these buyers is probably attributable to loans obtained for the purpose of acquiring land.

Turning to the sub-sample for strong land reform states (hereafter, 'land reform states'), we find that the scheduled caste and agricultural labourer variables are no longer significantly different when we compare buyers of land with non-buyers. In fact, the point estimate for the means suggests a higher occurrence of *SC* and *AgLabour* households as buyers. This may be due to the success of land reform legislation in promoting opportunities for members of disadvantaged groups to purchase land. On the other hand, the *LikeFarm* and *AgInfo* variables are not significantly different when we compare buyers and non-buyers, which may be due to rigidities in the land market caused by land reform. The areas of land owned by buyers and non-buyers in land reform states are roughly the same, which suggests that land reform weakens the tendency of ownership to become concentrated.

The salient results for the high non-agricultural growth states (hereafter, 'non-agricultural growth states') are that buyers are less likely to be *AgLabour* households, and that the *LikeFarm* variable is no longer significantly different when we compare buyers and non-buyers. Although the difference is not statistically significant, the point estimate for mean non-farm business income (*BusInc*) is higher for buyers, unlike in the full sample. This suggests that in non-agricultural growth states, enthusiasm for farming (as proxied by *LikeFarm*) is less relevant, and non-farm income is more relevant when it comes to the purchase of land. This

Table 2.2 Comparison of variable means across sub-samples: buyers of land vs non-buyers

Variable	Full sample		Sub-samples					
			Strong land reform states		High non-agricultural growth states		Rainfall-deficient regions	
	non-buyer (n = 44,175)	buyer (n = 147)	non-buyer (n = 4,863)	buyer (n = 26)	non-buyer (n = 19,804)	buyer (n = 73)	non-buyer (n = 15,116)	buyer (n = 60)
Age	46.52	49.12*	46.25	53.31**	46.65	51.09**	47.06	47.22
PrimEdu	0.40	0.45	0.48	0.58	0.41	0.47	0.38	0.52
ST	0.13	0.14	0.09	0.03**	0.17	0.09	0.16	0.25
SC	0.17	0.11*	0.29	0.41	0.16	0.18	0.13	0.02***
OBC	0.43	0.46	0.07	0.00***	0.32	0.31	0.40	0.38
OthComm	0.27	0.29	0.55	0.56	0.34	0.42	0.31	0.35
AgLabour	0.20	0.11***	0.20	0.23	0.23	0.11**	0.21	0.16
LikeFarm	0.18	0.32***	0.22	0.40	0.19	0.23	0.17	0.45***
AgInfo	0.32	0.54***	0.41	0.47	0.37	0.53*	0.32	0.62***
LandOwned	1.16	1.92***	0.49	0.50	1.01	1.86**	1.58	2.75**
MedShare	0.06	0.07	0.05	0.12*	0.05	0.09*	0.06	0.07
LoanShare	0.33	0.81***	0.14	0.20	0.36	0.93*	0.50	1.06
CultInc	2342	3732**	1786	2135	2293	3212	2816	3592
LiveInc	235	−159	195	25*	289	566	295	−1195
BusInc	485	423	993	420**	598	939	475	968

Notes: [1] 'Strong land reform states' are those where the number of land reform laws passed during 1948–92 is greater than nine. 'High non-agricultural growth states' are those where the growth rate of the net state domestic product in the non-agricultural sector during 1999–2002 was 5% or higher. 'Rainfall-deficient regions' are Indian Meteorological Department sub-divisions (roughly similar to states in size), where the average annual rainfall during 2000–2 was less than 90% of the average during 1970–2002.
[2] ***, ** and * indicate that the difference between the means is greater than zero at a significance level of 1%, 5% and 10%, respectively.

is consistent with the possibility that land prices in non-agricultural growth states have been driven up by industrial, commercial and/or residential demand.

In Table 2.3, we look at differences between the sellers of land and non-sellers. First of all, sellers are more likely than non-sellers to have completed primary education. This may reflect a tendency among more educated households to move out of agriculture. We also find that sellers are significantly less likely to be scheduled tribe households. This partly reflects the legal restrictions placed on transactions in tribal land. Sellers are also less likely to be households engaged in agricultural labour, even after controlling for the size of the holdings. Sellers are likely to be larger land-holders, especially in the land reform states. This is an indication of the equalizing effect of land reform.

The variable *MedShare* has a higher value for sellers than for non-sellers, which suggests that some sales were made in response to negative health shocks. In high non-agricultural growth states and rainfall-deficient states, the *LoanShare* variable is significantly higher for sellers in comparison to non-sellers. In the case of rainfall-deficient states, this may indicate the existence of distress sales by indebted households in response to climate shocks.

Probit regression

Tables 2.4 and 2.5 present the results of the probit regressions. In Table 2.4, the dependent variable is an indicator for the household's participation in the market as a buyer of land. First, we find that households in non-agricultural growth states are significantly more likely to purchase land, all else being equal. On the other hand, households in rainfall-deficient states are less likely to buy land. This may be because land transactions are more common in states with non-agricultural growth, while they are less common in rainfall deficient states.

Turning to the characteristics of the household, scheduled caste households and households engaged primarily in agricultural labour are both less likely to buy land. Agricultural labour households are even less likely to buy land in high agricultural growth states, as can be seen from the significantly negative coefficient on the interaction term *AgLabour*NonAgGro*. This suggests that agricultural labourers are crowded out of the land market in such states. On the other hand, the negative impact of belonging to an agricultural labour household is weakened in land reform states and rainfall-deficient states. This may be because in those states larger landowners find land ownership less attractive as a target for investment.

Table 2.3 Comparison of variable means across sub-samples: sellers of land vs non-sellers

	Full sample		Strong land reform states		Sub-samples			
					High non-agricultural growth states		Rainfall-deficient regions	
Variable	non-seller (n = 44.216)	seller (n = 106)	non-seller (n = 4.864)	seller (n = 25)	non-seller (n = 19.817)	seller (n = 60)	non-seller (n = 15.136)	seller (n = 40)
Age	46.52	48.97	46.27	51.74	46.66	48.17	47.07	45.00
PrimEdu	0.40	0.65***	0.48	0.92***	0.41	0.72***	0.38	0.65**
ST	0.13	0.02	0.09	0.02***	0.17	0.01***	0.16	0.00***
SC	0.17	0.12	0.29	0.07***	0.16	0.11	0.13	0.16
OBC	0.43	0.44	0.07	0.10	0.32	0.33	0.40	0.45
OthComm	0.27	0.42***	0.55	0.81***	0.34	0.55**	0.31	0.38
AgLabour	0.20	0.02***	0.20	0.03***	0.23	0.03***	0.21	0.02***
LikeFarm	0.18	0.32**	0.22	0.23	0.19	0.34*	0.17	0.38*
AgInfo	0.32	0.54***	0.41	0.43	0.37	0.54*	0.32	0.61***
LandOwned	1.16	1.84***	0.49	0.83***	1.01	1.41	1.58	1.74
MedShare	0.06	0.10***	0.05	0.11***	0.05	0.09***	0.06	0.09
LoanShare	0.33	0.69***	0.14	0.51	0.36	0.66**	0.51	0.96***
CultInc	2344	3493	1780	3554**	2294	3369	2816	4138
LiveInc	234	491	195	31***	289	758	290	408
BusInc	484	1290	991	696	596	1916	475	1354

Notes: [1] 'Strong land reform states' are those where the number of land reform laws passed during 1948–92 is greater than nine. 'High non-agricultural growth states' are those where the growth rate of the net state domestic product in the non-agricultural sector during 1999–2002 was 5% or higher. 'Rainfall-deficient regions' are Indian Meteorological Department sub-divisions where the average annual rainfall during 2000–2 was less than 90% of the average during 1970–2002.
[2] ***, ** and * indicate that the difference between the means is greater than zero at a significance level of 1%, 5% and 10%, respectively.

Table 2.4 Probit results for land purchase

	Coefficient	Standard error	Marginal effect	Standard error
LandRef	−0.0060	0.0161	0.0000	0.0001
NonAgGro	0.2760**	0.1271	0.0017**	0.0008
RainDef	−0.3279**	0.1618	−0.0016**	0.0007
Age	0.0038	0.0029	0.0000	0.0000
PrimEdu	−0.0122	0.0778	−0.0001	0.0004
ST	0.0952	0.1854	0.0006	0.0012
ST * LandRef	0.0023	0.0394	0.0000	0.0002
ST * NonAgGro	−0.3598	0.2639	−0.0013**	0.0006
ST * RainDef	0.2839	0.3167	0.0023	0.0035
SC	−0.4830**	0.2364	−0.0018***	0.0007
SC * LandRef	0.0141	0.0290	0.0001	0.0002
SC * NonAgGro	0.4960*	0.2542	0.0053	0.0046
SC * RainDef	−0.3240	0.3420	−0.0012	0.0008
AgLabour	−0.6548*	0.3838	−0.0023***	0.0008
AgLabour * LandRef	0.1010**	0.0488	0.0005**	0.0002
AgLabour * NonAgGro	−0.4290**	0.2140	−0.0015***	0.0004
AgLabour * RainDef	0.9855**	0.4879	0.0206	0.0225
LikeFarm	−0.1809	0.2064	−0.0008	0.0008
LikeFarm * LandRef	0.0778**	0.0344	0.0004**	0.0002
LikeFarm * NonAgGro	−0.5937***	0.2084	−0.0017***	0.0004
LikeFarm * RainDef	0.9151***	0.3208	0.0179	0.0142
AgInfo	0.0709	0.1390	0.0004	0.0008
AgInfo * LandRef	0.0389*	0.0207	0.0002*	0.0001
AgInfo * NonAgGro	−0.2174	0.1552	−0.0010*	0.0006
AgInfo * RainDef	0.4237**	0.2070	0.0039	0.0030
LandOwned	0.0212***	0.0055	0.0001***	0.0000
LoanShare	0.0628***	0.0184	0.0003***	0.0001
MedShare	0.1322	0.1666	0.0007	0.0009
LargeBusInc	0.0196	0.1131	0.0001	0.0006
Constant	−2.9022	0.1288		

Notes: [1] The dependent variable equals one if the household reported purchasing land during 2002/3, and zero otherwise. The number of households in the sample is 43,334 and the number of households reporting a land purchase is 147 (0.34%).
[2] To calculate the marginal effects, the mean value was used for the continuous variables and a value of zero was used for the dichotomous variables.
[3] ***, ** and * represent statistical significance at the 1%, 5% and 10% levels, respectively.

Households where the head of household likes farming as an occupation (those with *LikeFarm* equal to one) are less likely to buy land in non-agricultural growth states. However, this significantly negative effect is weakened or reversed in land reform states and rainfall-deficient states. This finding suggests that in high non-agricultural growth states, there

Table 2.5 Probit results for land sales

	Coefficient	Standard error	Marginal effect	Standard error
LandRef	0.0317	0.0195	0.0001	0.0001
NonAgGro	0.3014*	0.1800	0.0008	0.0006
RainDef	0.0737	0.2299	0.0002	0.0006
Age	0.0022	0.0037	0.0000	0.0000
PrimEdu	0.1964**	0.0937	0.0005**	0.0003
ST	0.1413	0.2492	0.0004	0.0008
ST * LandRef	−0.0902	0.0964	−0.0002	0.0002
ST * NonAgGro	−0.6138**	0.2547	−0.0007***	0.0002
ST * RainDef	−0.9365**	0.4619	−0.0008***	0.0002
SC	−0.4828	0.3796	−0.0008	0.0004
SC * LandRef	0.0423	0.0370	0.0001	0.0001
SC * NonAgGro	−0.2664	0.3158	−0.0005	0.0004
SC * RainDef	0.9260*	0.4838	0.0098	0.0124
AgLabour	−0.6532***	0.2434	−0.0010***	0.0003
AgLabour * LandRef	−0.0215	0.0393	−0.0001	0.0001
AgLabour * NonAgGro	0.2956	0.2708	0.0011	0.0014
AgLabour * RainDef	−0.2501	0.3718	−0.0004	0.0005
LikeFarm	0.0818	0.1807	0.0002	0.0005
LikeFarm * LandRef	−0.0041	0.0281	0.0000	0.0001
LikeFarm * NonAgGro	0.0111	0.2211	0.0000	0.0006
LikeFarm * RainDef	0.0867	0.2859	0.0002	0.0009
AgInfo	0.1731	0.1621	0.0005	0.0005
AgInfo * LandRef	0.0126	0.0217	0.0000	0.0001
AgInfo * NonAgGro	−0.2379	0.1722	−0.0004*	0.0003
AgInfo * RainDef	0.2346	0.2476	0.0008	0.0010
LandOwned	0.0161**	0.0071	0.0000**	0.0000
LoanShare	0.0397***	0.0135	0.0001**	0.0000
MedShare	0.3683***	0.1153	0.0009***	0.0003
LargeBusInc	0.1120	0.1169	0.0003	0.0004
Constant	−3.3779***	0.1524		

Notes: [1] The dependent variable equals one if the household reported selling land during 2002/3, and zero otherwise. The number of households in the sample is 43,334 and the number of households reporting a land sale is 106 (0.24%).
[2] To calculate the marginal effects, the mean value was used for the continuous variables and a value of zero was used for the dichotomous variables.
[3] ***, ** and * represent statistical significance at the 1%, 5% and 10% levels, respectively.

is a tendency for land not to be allocated to the most enthusiastic agriculturalists. On the other hand, in land reform states and rainfall-deficient states, where the ownership of a large area of land is a less attractive investment, the allocation of land to enthusiastic farmers is more likely. Similarly, farmers with better access to agricultural information (i.e., those with a higher value for *AgInfo*) are more likely to buy land only in land reform states and rainfall-deficient states. *LandOwned* has a significantly positive coefficient, suggesting that, on average, larger owners are more likely to purchase land.

In Table 2.5, the dependent variable indicates that the household sold land during the one-year reference period. First, we can see that households in non-agricultural growth states are more likely to sell land. This reflects the higher activity in the market for land in those states.

Turning to the characteristics of the household, we find that households with higher education levels (*PrimEdu* equal to one) are more likely to sell land. This is consistent with our earlier finding from mean comparisons; there may be a tendency for higher-educated households to move out of agriculture. Another prominent pattern is that scheduled tribe households are less likely to sell land. As mentioned in the mean comparisons section, this reflects the government's regulation of transactions in tribal land. Scheduled caste households are likely to sell land only in rainfall-deficient states. On the other hand, households engaged in agricultural labour seem less likely to sell land. This may be due to the fact that their initial holdings are relatively small.

As in the case of land purchases, households with larger land holdings and higher loan-to-consumption ratios are more likely to sell land. Some land sales are thought to be the result of indebtedness. Finally, households with higher medical bills (*MedShare*) are more likely to sell land. This may reflect the need to sell land in response to a negative health shock.

Interpretation of results

The mean comparisons and probit regressions yield some insight into the nature of land transactions in rural India. From the perspective of our research topic, it is interesting to see that non-agricultural growth has a significant impact on who it is who buys land. Specifically, we found that both agricultural labourers and enthusiastic agriculturalists are less likely to buy land in states with high non-agricultural growth. This implies that the effect of non-agricultural growth on land distribution is not only inequitable, it may also be inefficient, as land tends to be kept out of the hands of the most enthusiastic farmers.

Non-agricultural growth is expected to have an impact on the land market through its effect on the price of land. Non-agricultural growth states are likely to experience a larger increase in the land price, as industrial, commercial and residential demand competes against agricultural demand for the use of land. The increase in the price of land may be so high that farmers do not find it profitable to acquire new plots of land for purely agricultural purposes. There is some supporting evidence that points in this direction. Studies by Hirashima (1978, 1996, 2000) describe how the rent-to-price ratio for farmland in India and Pakistan has been decreasing over time, partly due to the growing importance of non-agricultural uses. More recently, the study of farmland prices by Kumar *et al.* (2005) finds that the distance to a town, as well as the share of non-agricultural value-added in the local economy, has a large positive effect on land prices.

There is also some indication that land prices have increased more rapidly in areas affected by non-agricultural growth. According to a survey co-sponsored by the Institute of Developing Economies and the Asian Development Research Institute, there was a roughly twofold increase in the nominal price of agricultural land between 1998 and 2008 in the largely agricultural state of Bihar. Meanwhile, in some rural areas near the city of Bangalore in the southern state of Karnataka, where information technology and other industries have been booming in recent years, the state government's valuation of land (called the 'guidance value') increased more than twofold in a single annual revision (*The Hindu*, 2007). Such anecdotal evidence suggests that the increase in the price of land has been greater in areas of high non-agricultural growth.

Given that growth in the non-agricultural sector may tend to prevent landless and marginally owning households (many of whom engage in agricultural labour) from having the opportunity to buy land, a natural question is whether or not the same households have been able to take advantage of the increased employment opportunities created by non-agricultural growth. While our data do not contain information on non-agricultural employment, some evidence pertaining to this question can be found in the existing literature. Kijima and Lanjouw's (2005) study, which uses data from a different NSSO survey, finds that the power of non-agricultural growth to reduce poverty has been limited, at least during the 1990s. The beneficiaries of non-agricultural employment growth tended to be those with relatively high levels of education and social status. Kijima and Lanjouw (*ibid.*) also find that the rise in agricultural wage rates has been more effective in reducing poverty than non-agricultural growth *per se*.

Of course, non-agricultural growth may contribute to poverty reduction among landless and marginal households by raising demand for manual labour (such as at construction sites), therefore also putting upward pressure on the agricultural wage. The point we wish to emphasize is that the positive effect of the generation of employment opportunities as a result of non-agricultural growth and any resulting wage increases must be weighed against the negative effect of reduced accessibility to agricultural land.

What, then, are the policies that can be used to ensure that landless and marginally landowning households are not made worse off by growth in the non-agricultural sector? An obvious option is to improve the basic education system so that members of landless and marginal households have greater access to higher-paying non-agricultural jobs.

Another policy recommendation is implied by our statistical results. We found that in states with more enactment and greater enforcement of land reform legislation, there is less of a tendency for land transactions to lead to an unequal distribution of land ownership. Moreover, households engaged in agricultural labour and enthusiastic farmer households are more likely to buy land in such states than in the other states. Thus, land reform legislation, even if it was enacted decades earlier, appears to be effective in controlling the negative effects of non-agricultural growth on the distribution of land. While the strengthening of land reform continues to be difficult in those states where it has remained weak, our results provide additional evidence on why it may be a good idea to pursue it with increased urgency.

Conclusion

Following a period of equalization in the 1980s, inequalities in the distribution of land increased during the 1990s. This chapter has explored the implications of this change on landless and marginally landowning households by analyzing nationally representative data from the National Sample Survey, which contains information on land transactions. Employing mean comparisons and probit regressions, we have found that in states of high non-agricultural growth there tend to be fewer agricultural labourers or enthusiastic farmers buying land. This can be interpreted in the following way. In the non-agricultural growth states, the demand for commercial, industrial, or residential land is of such a magnitude that the price of agricultural land tends to rise above what a skilled and enthusiastic farmer is willing to pay. This is reflected in their low level of participation as buyers. This, in turn, provides an answer for why relatively fewer households that are engaged in agricultural labour buy land in non-agricultural growth states. They are effectively denied the opportunity to buy land.

There is no doubt that the development of the non-agricultural sector plays an important role in income growth and poverty eradication in India because it increases employment and self-owned business opportunities and raises wages for agricultural labourers. However, there may be some scope for policy intervention. In particular, land reform and land-use legislation, including regulations that govern the conversion of agricultural land, if properly and strictly enforced, may insulate the agricultural land market to some extent from developments in the non-agricultural sector. This would lower land prices for landless and marginal landowning households and give them more opportunities to cultivate their own land. With the right policy tools, balanced growth between agriculture and industry can be achieved in conjunction with a reduction in poverty.

Notes

1. The success of agricultural land reform in Japan is attributable to a combination of factors, apart from the fact that it was imposed on the country by a post-war occupying force. Hirashima (1982) points out how, prior to land reform, productivity levels were equalized across regions and across individual farms so that significant disruptions in production were avoided during the reform process. In addition, widespread tenancy disputes and tight government control over production and distribution during the pre-war and wartime years weakened the incentive of landowners to cling to their titles (see also Dore, 1959). These observations may provide some hints as to why land reforms in some Indian states, including West Bengal and Kerala, have met with some success while in others they have failed.
2. Data on net state domestic product were obtained from the Central Statistics Office via the Reserve Bank of India's *Handbook of Statistics on the Indian Economy*.
3. IMD subdivisions are roughly similar in size to states. The rainfall data used for variable construction were obtained from the Indian Meteorological Department via the Indian Institute of Tropical Meteorology.
4. An NSS stratum is an artificial regional partition employed by the NSS for sampling purposes. It is roughly equivalent in size and population to a district.
5. Data on consumption are collected using two reference periods: a 30-day period for food and other high-frequency items and a 365-day period for low-frequency items, including medical goods and services. Total consumption expenditure was estimated as an annual figure.
6. Unfortunately, Schedule 33 of the 59th round does not contain a module for wage income.
7. Land legislation is mainly a state matter in India.

References

Bandhopadhyay, D. (2009) 'Lost Opportunity in Bihar', *Economic and Political Weekly*, 44 (47), pp. 12–14.

Basu, Kaushik (1986) 'The Market for Land', *Journal of Development Economics*, 20, pp. 163–77.

Besley, Timothy and Robin Burgess (2000) 'Land Reform, Poverty Reduction, and Growth: Evidence from India', *Quarterly Journal of Economics*, 115 (2), pp. 389–430.

Deininger, Klaus, Songqing Jin and Hari K. Nagarajan (2009) 'Determinants and Consequences of Land Sales Market Participation: Panel Evidence from India', *World Development*, 37 (2), pp. 410–21.

Dore, R. P. (1959) *Land Reform in Japan*, London: Oxford University Press.

Himanshu (2007) 'Recent Trends in Poverty and Inequality: Some Preliminary Results', *Economic and Political Weekly*, 42 (6), pp. 497–508.

The Hindu (2007) 'Sharp Revision in Guidance Value in Bangalore Rural', 23 November.

Hirashima, Shigemochi (1978) *The Structure of Disparity in Developing Agriculture: A Case Study of the Pakistan Punjab*, Tokyo: Institute of Developing Economies.

Hirashima, Shigemochi (1982) 'Growth, Equity and Labor Absorption in Japanese Agriculture', in Shigeru Ishikawa, Saburo Yamada and Shigemochi Hirashima (eds), *Labour Absorption and Growth in Agriculture: China and Japan*, Bangkok: ILO/ARTEP.

Hirashima, Shigemochi (1996) 'Asset Effects in Land Price Formation in Agriculture: The Experience from South Asia', *Pakistan Development Review*, 35 (4), pp. 963–76.

Hirashima, Shigemochi (2000) 'Issues in Agricultural Reforms: Public Investment and Land Market Development', *Economic and Political Weekly*, 35 (43/4), pp. 3879–84.

Hirashima, Shigemochi (2008) 'The Land Market in Development: A Case Study of Punjab in Pakistan and India', *Economic and Political Weekly*, 43 (42), pp. 41–7.

Hirashima, Shigemochi (2009) 'Growth–Poverty Linkage, Income–Asset Relation in Regional Disparity: Evidence from Pakistan and India', *Pakistan Development Review*, 48 (4), pp. 357–78.

Kijima, Yoko and Peter Lanjouw (2005) 'Economic Diversification and Poverty in Rural India', *Indian Journal of Labour Economics*, 48 (2), pp. 349–74.

Kumar, Parmod, Basanta K. Pradhan and A. Subramanian (2005) 'Farmland Prices in a Developing Economy: Some Stylized Facts and Determinants', *Journal of International and Area Studies*, 12 (2), pp. 93–113.

Lanjouw, Peter and Abusaleh Shariff (2004) 'Rural Non-Farm Employment in India: Access, Incomes and Poverty Impact', *Economic and Political Weekly*, 39 (40), pp. 4429–46.

Mearns, Robin (1999) 'Access to Land in Rural India: Policy Issues and Options', World Bank Policy Research Working Paper No. 2123.

NSSO (National Sample Survey Organization) (2005) *Household Assets and Liabilities in India (as on 30.06.2002)*, Report No. 500 (based on data of the 59th Round *All-India Debt and Investment Survey*). Ministry of Statistics and Programme Implementation, New Delhi: Government of India.

NSSO (2006a) *Household Ownership Holdings in India, 2003*, Report No. 491 (based on data of the 59th Round *Land and Livestock Holdings Survey*). Ministry of Statistics and Programme Implementation, New Delhi: Government of India.

NSSO (2006b) *Level and Pattern of Consumer Expenditure, 2004–05*, Report No. 508 (based on data of the 61st Round *Consumer Expenditure Survey*). Ministry of Statistics and Programme Implementation, New Delhi: Government of India.

Rawal, Vikas (2008) 'Ownership Holdings of Land in Rural India: Putting the Record Straight', *Economic and Political Weekly*, 43 (10), pp. 43–7.

Sen, Abhijit and Himanshu (2003) 'Poverty and Inequality in India: Getting Closer to the Truth', Centre for Economic Studies and Planning, Jawaharlal Nehru University.

Subramanian, S. and D. Jayaraj (2006) 'The Distribution of Household Wealth in India', UNU-WIDER Research Paper No.2006/116.

Walker, Thomas S. and James G. Ryan (1990) *Village and Household Economies in India's Semi-arid Tropics*, Baltimore, MD: Johns Hopkins University Press.

3
Financial Inclusion and Poverty Alleviation in India: An Empirical Analysis Using State-wise Data

Takeshi Inoue

Introduction

Financial development is considered to be an integral factor in a country's economic growth. Indeed, cross-country studies such as King and Levine (1993), Demirgüç-Kunt and Maksimovic (1996) and Levine and Zervos (1998), among others, find that higher levels of financial development are significantly and robustly associated with faster rates of economic growth (Bhattacharya and Sivasubramanian, 2003: 905). Moreover, there is much evidence for a strong and causal relationship between the depth of the financial system on the one hand and the investment, growth and total factor productivity on the other hand (Claessens, 2005: 2). Much of this evidence has focused on the importance of overall financial development. In many developing countries, however, the financial system at large does not cater to the needs of all customers, which tends to be skewed towards those already better off (*ibid.*: 2). Accordingly, in addition to financial development, 'financial inclusion' has received a great deal of attention as of late.

Generally speaking, financial inclusion can be defined as the process of ensuring access to and usage of basic formal financial services for all people at an affordable cost. Basic formal financial services include credit, savings, insurance, payments and remittance facilities. Without access to these services, people often resort to using high-cost informal financial sources, and a lack of financial inclusion likely exerts a disproportionally negative impact on low-income groups. Therefore, the promotion of financial inclusion is considered to play an important role in alleviating poverty and reducing income inequalities within a country.

In India, the concept of financial inclusion can be traced back to the social control of the banking sector that started in the 1960s. Since then, various measures have been undertaken to promote financial inclusion. Of late, in April 2005, the Reserve Bank of India (RBI), India's central bank, formally announced that financial inclusion would be one of their primary policy objectives. This announcement has brought more attention to the issue and has sparked a growth in literature on financial inclusion in India. Several empirical studies have focused on the degree of progress in financial inclusion and have examined its relation to relevant variables such as economic growth and infrastructure development. Based on these previous studies, this chapter aims to analyze empirically the link between financial inclusion and poverty reduction by using panel data for 25 Indian states and union territories from 1973–4 to 2004–5.

The chapter is organized as follows: the following section summarizes the history of financial inclusion measures in India; the third section examines developments in financial inclusion and the poverty ratio; and the fourth section reviews relevant prior research. We then present an empirical analysis of the possible relationship between financial inclusion and poverty reduction. The fifth section provides a brief explanation of the model and the definitions and sources of the data; and the sixth section shows the empirical results. Lastly, the concluding remarks summarize the main findings of the study.

A history of financial inclusion in India

In India, since the late 1960s, there have been various initiatives undertaken to expand formal financial services to rural areas (RBI, 2008: 303). These could be categorized broadly into the following three time phases by their characteristics: the first phase running throughout the 1980s, the second phase spanning the early 1990s through March 2005 and the third phase beginning in April 2005 (*ibid*.: 304).

During the first phase of financial inclusion initiated by bank nationalization in 1969, some measures were taken at different points in time to expand the outreach of banking facilities and to increase the flow of credit to rural areas (*ibid*.: 303). The measures were mainly composed of a branch licensing policy, the establishment of Regional Rural Banks (RRBs) and the introduction of priority sector lending. For example, the branch licensing policy put emphasis on the expansion of banking facilities in rural and unbanked areas, and in fact contributed in promoting branch openings in rural and semi-urban areas, which increased the share of total branches from 62.6 per cent in 1969 to 77.3 per cent in 1991 (Rao, 2007: 355–6). Also, the RRBs, the commercial banks set up in 1975 to cater to the credit needs of the rural poor, successfully expanded their branch network in rural areas comprising more than 40.0 per cent of the total number of rural branches of commercial banks, although this advance was limited in that it only constituted around 2.0 per cent of banking sector credits (Joshi, 2006: 85, 92). Moreover, under priority sector lending, bank credit extended to priority sectors such as agriculture, small-scale industries, industrial estates, road and water operators, retail traders, small businesses, professionals, self-employed persons and education, and weaker sections increased from Rs 659 crore (18.2 per cent of a total net bank credit) in 1969 to Rs 40,475 crore (42.4 per cent) in 1989 (Shajahan, 1998: 2750–1).[1] The number of priority sector accounts also increased from 7.8 lakhs to 331 lakhs during the same period (*ibid*.: 2751).[2]

With the onset of the economic reforms of the early 1990s, however, systematic financial sector reforms were implemented which placed more emphasis on the efficiency and profitability of the banking system that had allegedly been neglected in earlier decades (Chavan, 2007: 3219). As a result, attempts towards financial inclusion also underwent significant modification in the 1990s. Specifically, in 1991, the branch licensing policy was relaxed and the banks were allowed to close down loss-making branches in urban, metropolitan and rural centres in the case that these centres were being served by two other commercial banks except the RRBs (Sen and Vaidya, 1997: 43).[3] Also, in 1992, the RRBs were permitted to lend 40.0 per cent of fresh advances to their clients outside the target groups such as small and marginal farmers, agricultural labourers and artisans, and this proportion was increased to 60.0 per cent of fresh lending from 1994 (Joshi, 2006: 88). Moreover, coverage of priority sectors was increased by adding many new sectors and segments, which would indirectly affect the share of credit to areas traditionally deemed priority sectors when the concept was first introduced (Rao, 2007: 356).

While these state control initiatives were de-emphasized, financial inclusion in its second phase was encouraged mainly by the promotion of microfinance called the SHG-Bank linkage programme (RBI, 2008: 304). This programme was launched by the National Bank for Agriculture and Rural Development in 1992 to facilitate collective decision-making by the poor and to provide 'door step' banking (*ibid*.: 305). Under the programme, financially excluded people, especially the poor women, establish self-help groups, engage in promoting their banking habits and conduct transactions with the banks (i.e., credit and deposit facilities). Since its inception, the SHG-Bank linkage programme has seen rapid expansion. As of March 2007, 50 commercial banks, 96 RRBs and 352 cooperative banks participated in this programme, and the number of bank-linked self-help groups increased from 255 in 1992–3 to 29 lakhs in 2006–7, while the cumulative bank loan increased from Rs 0.3 crore to Rs 18,047 crore during the same period (*ibid.*: 330). During the second phase, the Kisan Credit Cards (KCCs) were also introduced to provide adequate and timely credit from the banking sector to the farmers, who would then be able to purchase agricultural inputs and draw cash for their production needs (RBI, 1999: 1.25). In every year since, 80 to 90 lakhs of KCCs have been issued and in 2007–8 the cumulative number of total KCCs amounted to 761 lakhs.

The third phase of financial inclusion began in April 2005, when the RBI explicitly used the term 'financial inclusion' as a major policy objective in their Annual Policy Statement for the year 2005–6 (RBI, 2008: 304). In this statement, while recognizing concerns about the banking practices that tend to exclude vast sections of the population in particular pensioners, the self-employed and those employed in the unorganized sector, the RBI urged the banks to review their existing practices and provide banking services to all segments of the population on an equitable basis (RBI, 2005b: 39; Leeladhar, 2006: 76).

For example, the RBI advised the banks to make available a basic 'no-frills' banking account with low or nil minimum balance as well as charges to expand the outreach of such accounts to vast sections of the population. The RBI also asked the banks to consider the introduction of a General Credit Card facility in rural and semi-urban areas. With a view to providing hassle-free credit, this facility entitles the holder to withdraw up to the credit limit of Rs 25,000 without insistence on security or purpose (Leeladhar, 2008: 1509). Moreover, in order to ensure that persons belonging to low-income groups do not encounter difficulties in opening bank accounts, the know-your-customer procedure for opening accounts has been simplified for those accounts with balances not exceeding Rs 50,000 and credit limits not exceeding Rs 100,000 annually (RBI, 2008: 306).

Have these initiatives actually encouraged access to and/or usage of formal financial services in India? The All-India Debt and Investment Survey (AIDIS) by the National Sample Survey Organization (NSSO) indicates some interesting features on the progress of financial inclusion by looking at patterns of household debt (see Tables 3.1 and 3.2). Table 3.1 shows the number of households indebted to different credit agencies. This table shows that the number of households indebted to institutional sources increased sharply between 1961 and 1991 in rural areas and

Table 3.1 Number of indebted households (in lakh)

	Rural			Urban		
	Institutional agencies	Non-institutional agencies	Total	Institutional agencies	Non-institutional agencies	Total
1961	75 (17.4)	356 (82.6)	431	NA	NA	NA
1971	76 (23.9)	242 (76.0)	318	NA	NA	NA
1981	89 (49.0)	93 (51.2)	182	23 (45.6)	27 (53.5)	50
1991	181 (66.7)	114 (41.9)	271	50 (61.1)	39 (48.7)	81
2002	198 (50.6)	229 (58.5)	392	52 (52.2)	52 (52.8)	99

Notes: [1] Institutional agencies are composed of the government, cooperative societies and commercial banks, whereas non-institutional agencies are composed of landlords, agricultural moneylenders and professional moneylenders.
[2] Figures in parentheses show the percentage for total number of indebted households.
[3] 'NA' in the table indicates that there is no relevant data.
Sources: NSSO (1998a, 1998b, 2005) and RBI (1965, 1977, 1987, 2008).

Table 3.2 Outstanding household debt (in Rs crore)

	Rural			Urban		
	Institutional agencies	Non-institutional agencies	Total	Institutional agencies	Non-institutional agencies	Total
1961	413 (14.8)	2376 (85.2)	2789	NA	NA	NA
1971	1094 (29.2)	2658 (70.8)	3752	NA	NA	NA
1981	3794 (61.3)	2399 (38.7)	6193	1813 (60.0)	1210 (40.0)	3023
1991	14215 (64.0)	7996 (36.0)	22211	10662 (70.0)	4570 (30.0)	15232
2002	63648 (57.1)	47820 (42.9)	111468	49060 (75.1)	16266 (24.9)	65327

Notes: [1] Institutional agencies are composed of the government, cooperative societies and commercial banks, whereas non-institutional agencies are composed of landlords, agricultural moneylenders and professional moneylenders.
[2] Figures in parentheses show the percentage for total number of indebted households.
[3] 'NA' in the table indicates that there is no relevant data.
Source: RBI (2008).

between 1981 and 1991 in urban areas in absolute terms, as well as the share of total indebted households. A detailed analysis suggests that this can be explained mainly by the high growth of households indebted to commercial banks. Thereafter, the number of households indebted to institutional agencies continued to increase, although the share of institutional sources declined between 1991 and 2002 in both rural and urban areas with a concurrent increase in the share of non-institutional sources.

We can also find similar trends in the pattern of households' outstanding debts in Table 3.2. Specifically, the proportion of household debt owed to institutional sources has increased in both rural and urban areas in absolute terms. This was mainly due to the high growth in households' debts to commercial banks. In relative terms, however, the share of institutional sources-owed debt by rural households declined between 1991 and 2002, while the share of non-institutional sources increased correspondingly. These trends in institutional and non-institutional credit sources can be taken to imply that financial inclusion in India has been successfully promoted to a certain extent, although results are still far from satisfactory.

Financial inclusion and poverty conditions

In the previous section, we showed that there have been a variety of initiatives taken in the expansion of financial services to rural India, mainly through commercial banks. In addition, according to data from the AIDIS, we found that institutional sources increased with regard to household debt, among which commercial banks played a leading role. Hence, this section first examines the movements for financial inclusion in India from the early 1980s by using relevant data on commercial banks. This section also reviews how poverty conditions have changed during the surveyed period because poverty reduction is one of the major goals of financial inclusion.

Since access to financial services is not synonymous with the use of financial services, it is necessary to distinguish between these two different concepts, namely access, or the possibility of using financial services, and the actual use of financial services (Beck, Demirgüç-Kunt and Martinez Peria, 2007: 236). Following Beck, Demirgüç-Kunt and Martinez Peria (2007), we regard the number of bank branches as the indicator with which to measure physical access to formal financial services, while the number of bank accounts and the amount of credit and deposit are utilized to measure the actual use of formal financial services.

In India, the scheduled commercial banks have steadily increased their branches from 8,262 in 1969 to 77,699 in 2008. Figure 3.1 illustrates the population group-wise distribution of commercial bank branches during the period from 1969 to 2008.[4] In all areas, rural branches showed the most growth and reached their peak of 35,389 (57.9 per cent of total branches) in 1993. Subsequently, however, they have started to decrease, and so has the share of total branches, which is considered to reflect changes in the branch licensing policy since the early 1990s

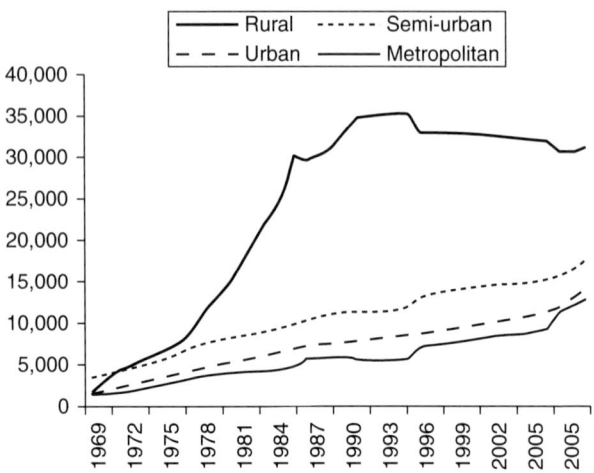

Figure 3.1 Population group-wise distribution of branches
Source: RBI (2009).

as discussed earlier. In contrast, bank branches in other areas such as semi-urban, urban and metropolitan increased even after the 1990s, and have steadily expanded their shares in total. As of March 2008, the number of bank branches in metropolitan areas is the smallest among all areas, but the average growth rate in these areas from 1990 to 2008 is the highest.

Next, we move on to examine another measure of financial inclusion, the actual use of financial services. The total number of credit accounts has increased from 43 lakhs in 1972 to 11 crore in 2008, whereas the total number of deposit accounts has increased from 3.5 crore to 58 crore during the same period. Figures 3.2 and 3.3 illustrate the population group-wise distribution of credit and deposit accounts during the period from 1980 to 2008, respectively. In the last three decades, the number of credit accounts has been volatile in all places, especially in rural and metropolitan areas (see Figure 3.2). That is, during the 1980s, credit accounts increased in all areas, especially in rural areas. Entering the 1990s, however, they showed decreased or stagnant trends across all areas and recorded the highest rates of reduction in rural areas. Since 2000, credit accounts have again begun to increase in all areas and have registered the highest rates of growth in metropolitan areas. In March 2008, the number of credit accounts in metropolitan areas exceeds that of rural areas for the first time. Compared to credit accounts, deposit accounts

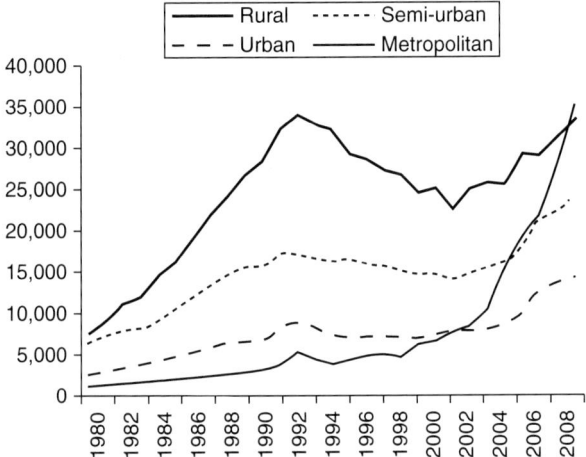

Figure 3.2 Population group-wise distribution of credit accounts (in thousands)
Source: RBI (2009).

have shown relatively steady growth trends (see Figure 3.3). Even in the 1990s, the growth rates remained positive in all areas though they were lower relative to those in the 1980s. Of all areas, the metropolitan areas showed the highest growth rates in the 1990s and this trend has continued since 2000.

Credit and deposit amounts are also a measurement device to determine the extent of financial services usage. The total credit amount has increased from Rs 56 billion in 1972 to Rs 24,170 billion in 2008, whereas the total deposit amount has increased from Rs 83 billion to Rs 32,499 billion during the same period. Figures 3.4 and 3.5 depict the population group-wise distribution of credit and deposit amounts during the period from 1980 to 2008, respectively. The credit amount has consistently increased in all areas since 1980 (see Figure 3.4). In particular, metropolitan areas comprise a 50.0 per cent share of the total amount on average, followed by urban, semi-urban and rural areas. Similarly, the deposit amount has continuously increased in all areas, among which metropolitan areas have the highest proportion, followed by urban, semi-urban and rural areas (see Figure 3.5). These figures commonly show that there are growing regional differences in terms of credit and deposit, and the difference between metropolitan areas and the other areas has expanded over time.

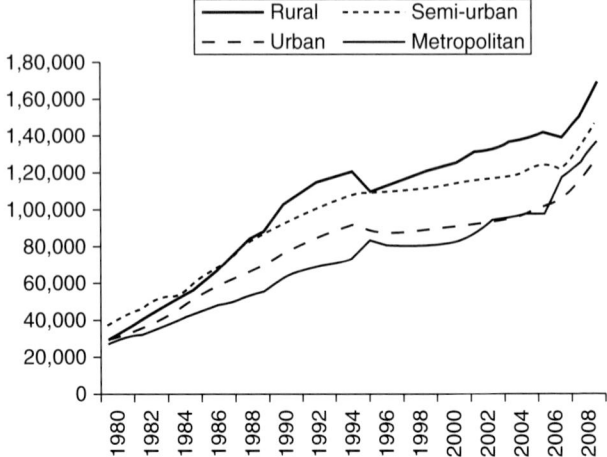

Figure 3.3 Population group-wise distribution of deposit accounts (in thousands)
Source: RBI (2009).

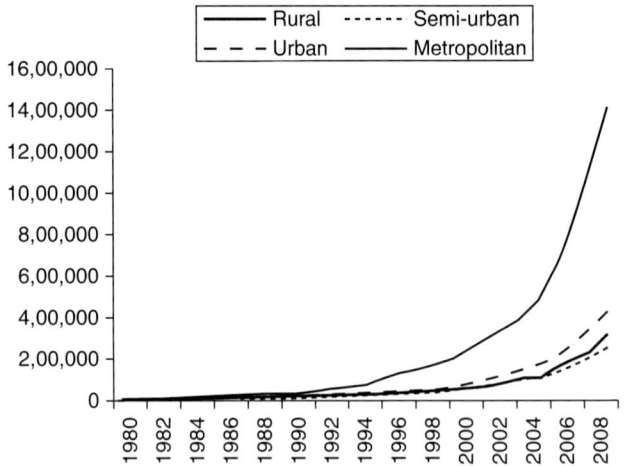

Figure 3.4 Population group-wise distribution of credit amount (in Rs crore)
Source: RBI (2009).

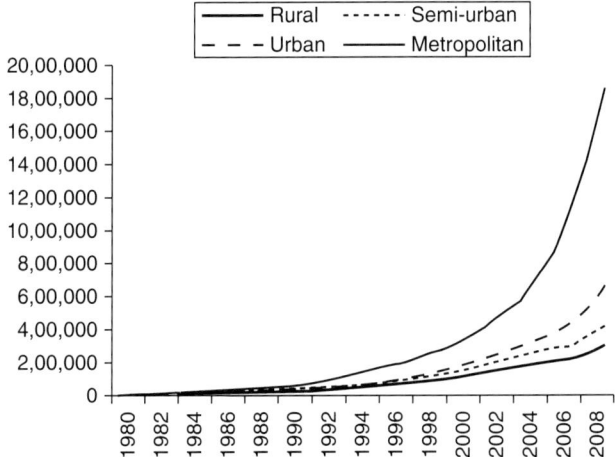

Figure 3.5 Population group-wise distribution of deposit amount (in Rs crore)
Source: RBI (2009).

Lastly, we review the trend of poverty conditions in India. Figure 3.6 illustrates the population group-wise distribution of poor people, measured by the percentage of the population below the poverty line.[5] This figure shows that the poverty ratio unanimously declined between 1973–4 and 1999–2000, but began to increase between 1999–2000 and 2004–5 in both rural and urban areas. Throughout the entire period, the poverty ratio in rural areas has been consistently higher than that in urban areas except in 1993–4, whereas in terms of the change rate, rural areas show a larger reduction in the poverty ratio than urban areas on average.

To sum up, financial inclusion in India was encouraged mainly in rural areas until the late 1980s. As the figures show, however, metropolitan areas have since experienced a significant bump in financial inclusion in terms of both access to and usage of financial services. These structural changes are considered to reflect the government's policy changes towards the banking sector as well as the environment surrounding commercial banks. On the other hand, with regard to poverty conditions, it is found that the poverty headcount ratio, having been in decline since 1973–4, began to increase between 1999–2000 and 2004–5 in both rural and urban areas. According to data from the AIDIS, the share of non-institutional sources-owed household debt increased between 1991 and 2002, especially in rural areas. Therefore, the trend of the poverty ratio is generally in line with that of household debt.

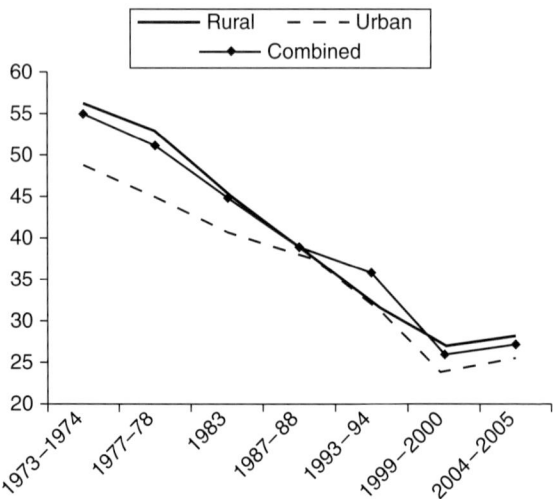

Figure 3.6 Population group-wise distribution of percentage of population below the poverty line (% of persons)
Sources: RBI (2009) and Indiastat.com (www.indiastat.com/).

Selected literature review

The relationship between financial development and economic growth has received much attention in a large amount of the literature. From a theoretical viewpoint, some economists argue that more developed financial systems assist in mobilizing savings, facilitating investment and promoting growth, whereas others propose that economic growth creates additional demands on financial services, which in turn may bring about more developed financial systems (Shan and Morris, 2002: 154). Besides, of late there has been a rise in the amount of literature on the relationship between financial development, poverty reduction and income inequality, such as Jalilian and Kirkpatrick (2002), Beck, Demirgüç-Kunt and Levine (2007), Clarke et al. (2006) and so on. As this chapter pays special attention to financial inclusion, in this section we survey the relevant prior studies on the link between financial inclusion and either economic growth or poverty reduction.

To begin with, Beck, Demirgüç-Kunt and Martinez Peria (2007) provide a set of banking sector outreach indicators and then analyze the determinants of the proposed indicators. To indicate access to financial services, they present data on the number of branches and ATMs per capita and per square kilometre. They also present data on the number of loan and deposit accounts per capita and the average loan and deposit size relative to GDP per capita to measure the actual use of credit and deposit services. After verifying the validity of the outreach indicators, they explore the empirical association between these indicators and an array of variables previously found to affect financial sector depth. Using a broad cross section including India, they find that the outreach indicators are significantly determined by per capita GDP, the quality of governance, the credit information environment and the communications infrastructure.

Next, the RBI (2008) empirically examines the relationship between financial inclusion and economic growth in general and infrastructure development in particular. This is based on state-wise data for nine Indian states for the period 2001 to 2006. Here, the savings and credit accounts per 100 persons are used as proxy indicators of financial inclusion, while per capita income is taken as an indicator of economic growth; electricity consumption, in milliwatts per 100,000 persons, and road lengths, in kilometres, are also used to measure infrastructure development. Empirical results indicate that there is a two-way relationship between financial inclusion and economic and infrastructure developments. That is, financial inclusion has a positive effect on economic growth, while economic growth and infrastructure development seem to promote financial inclusion.

Burgess and Pande (2005) evaluate the importance of the state-led branch expansion programme in India by examining its impact on the poverty ratio in rural and urban areas. They state that, due to the introduction of the new branch licensing policy in 1977, rural branch expansion was relatively higher in financially less developed states between 1977 and 1990, and that the reverse was true both before 1977 and after 1990. Based on these observations, by using panel data for 16 states for the period from 1961 to 2000, they empirically analyze how the increase in the number of branches in rural unbanked locations affects the poverty headcount ratio and report that, when evaluated at the sample mean, rural branch expansion can explain a 14.0 to 17.0 percentage point decline in the rural headcount ratio, but it does not affect urban poverty.

Finally, Bhandari (2009) measures progress towards financial inclusion in India in the form of the growth of deposit bank accounts and calculates Spearman's rank correlation between the state-wise growth in bank accounts and the percentage changes in below-poverty-line population. Using the data from 1999–2000 and 2004–5 for Indian states and union territories, Bhandari finds that changes in the poverty ratio and the growth of bank accounts are negatively correlated in both rural and urban areas, but that the coefficients are statistically insignificant. Therefore, he concludes that the provision of banking services to the maximum number of people is unsuccessful as a poverty reduction strategy.

As mentioned above, the prior literature surveyed measures the extent of financial inclusion from data relating to the banking sector, such as the number of branches, the number of credit and deposit accounts and/or the amount of credit and deposit. We utilize all of these variables to assess both the amount of access to and usage of formal financial services. This differs from the reviewed literature such as Burgess and Pande (2005), Bhandari (2009) and RBI (2008), which use either the bank branch or the bank account as the measure of financial inclusion. Among the literature, Beck, Demirgüç-Kunt and Martinez Peria (2007) use all of the relevant variables to measure the degree of financial inclusion and explores its relation to per capita GDP, institutional quality, the credit information environment and so on. Unlike Beck, Demirgüç-Kunt and Martinez Peria (2007), we apply each of the financial inclusion measures to find their impact on poverty reduction in India.

Model and data

This section provides a brief explanation of the empirical model as well as the definitions and sources of the variables. To assess the relationship between financial inclusion and poverty conditions in India, we employ panel data regression methodology using unbalanced panel data for 25 states and union territories covering seven time periods between 1973–4 and 2004–5.[6,7] Our model specification is as follows:

$$y_{it+1} = \alpha + \beta_i x_{it} + \gamma_i z_{it} + \mu_i + e_{it} \tag{1}$$

where y_{it+1} is the poverty condition; x_{it} is a proxy for financial inclusion; z_{it} is a vector of control variables; μ_i is the state fixed effect; e_{it} is random disturbance; and i and t stand for the region and time period, respectively. In order to mitigate the potential problem of reverse causality, the dependent variable is set in period $t + 1$, while the other variables are set in period t. Logarithmic values are used for each explanatory variable but not for poverty conditions, so parameter estimates give the magnitude of semi-elasticity of poverty reduction with respect to the explanatory variables.

Poverty conditions are measured using the percentage of the population below the poverty line. We use this ratio in rural and urban areas separately. The data is obtained from RBI (2009) and the websites of the Planning Commission and Indiastat.com.

Financial inclusion is measured by the number of bank branches, the number of credit and deposit accounts and the amount of credit and deposit, respectively. The number of bank branches is a proxy for physical access to financial services, and the other criteria are indicative of actual usage of financial services. The data are obtained from various issues of *Banking Statistics* and *Basic Statistical Returns of Scheduled Commercial Banks in India* published by the RBI. Since the primary objective of financial inclusion is to alleviate poverty conditions by promoting the provision of financial services, we expect financial inclusion to be associated with a lower poverty ratio.

Equation (1) also includes control variables to avoid any possible omitted variables. Here, we consider the net state domestic product (NSDP), state government expenditure and inflation rate at all-India levels as the control variable. The NSDP and inflation rate are taken from RBI (2009), while state expenditure is taken out of various issues of the *RBI Bulletin*, RBI (2004) and RBI (2006). We assume that both higher income levels and larger government expenditures have a positive impact on poverty reduction, whereas higher inflation has an adverse impact on the poor.

Each variable is expressed as follows: POVUR and POVRU represent the poverty ratio in urban and rural areas, respectively; OFF is the logarithm for the number of bank branches per 100,000 persons; DEAC and CRAC are the logarithms for the number of deposit and credit accounts per 100,000 persons, respectively; DEAM and CRAM are the logarithms for the ratio of the deposit and credit amounts in per cent of NSDP, respectively; Y is the logarithm for NSDP per 100,000 persons; EXP is the logarithm for state government expenditure per 100,000 persons; and INF is the growth rate of the Wholesale Price Index (WPI). The abbreviations, definitions and sources of each variable are listed in Table 3.3.

Empirical results

Table 3.4 shows the results of panel data estimation. The Hausman test results indicate that the random-effect model is preferable to the fixed-effect model in all cases except for Column 7. The first two columns report the regression results of Equation (1) using OFF as the measure of financial inclusion. Here, we examine the effect of physical access to financial services on rural poverty in Column 1 and urban poverty in Column 2. In both regressions, the coefficients of OFF are significantly estimated to be at a negative value; it suggests that easier access to

Table 3.3 Definitions and sources of variables

Variables	Definition	Sources
POVRU	The percentage of the population below the poverty line in rural areas	RBI (2009) and the websites of the Planning Commission (www.planningcommission.gov.in/) and Indiastat.com (www.indiastat.com/)
POVUR	The percentage of the population below the poverty line in urban areas	
OFF	The log of the state-wise number of scheduled commercial bank branches per 100,000 persons	Various issues of *Banking Statistics* and *Basic Statistical Returns of Scheduled Commercial Banks in India* published by the RBI (state-wise population and NSDP from RBI (2009))
DEAC	The log of the state-wise number of deposit accounts per 100,000 persons	
CRAC	The log of the state-wise number of credit accounts per 100,000 persons	
DEAM	The log of the ratio of the state-wise deposit amount in per cent of NSDP	
CRAM	The log of the ratio of the state-wise credit amount in per cent of NSDP	
Y	The log of net state domestic product (NSDP) at constant prices (base:1999–2000) per 100,000 persons	RBI (2009) (state-wise population from RBI (2009))
INF	Inflation rate throughout all of India calculated from WPI (%)	
EXP	The log of the state government total expenditure per 100,000 persons	RBI (2004, 2006) and various issues of the *RBI Bulletin* (state-wise population from RBI (2009))

formal financial services has a positive impact on poverty alleviation in both rural and urban areas. This is partly consistent with Burgess and Pande (2005), which states that branch expansion can explain the decline in the rural poverty ratio, but does not affect urban poverty. Furthermore, with regard to the control variables, the results show that the coefficients on Y, EXP and INF in rural areas as well as EXP in urban areas are statistically significant with expected sign, although output and inflation rates are not significant in urban areas.

Table 3.4 Empirical results

	POVRU	POVRU	POVRU	POVRU	POVRU	POVRU	POVRU	POVRU	POVRU	POVRU
OFF	-5.738 (0.011)									
DEAC		-3.808 (0.054)	-5.877 (0.000)	-3.669 (0.010)						
CRAC					-1.381 (0.207)	-0.635 (0.483)				
DEAM							-10.943 (0.001)	-3.691 (0.013)		
CRAM									-4.137 (0.001)	-1.927 (0.048)
Y	-13.591 (0.001)	-2.460 (0.529)	-12.694 (0.003)	-3.320 (0.377)	-10.878 (0.012)	-1.380 (0.707)	-9.348 (0.112)	-1.482 (0.680)	-10.972 (0.008)	-2.296 (0.490)
EXP	-2.961 (0.010)	-5.142 (0.000)	-1.576 (0.244)	-3.858 (0.003)	-4.042 (0.002)	-5.625 (0.000)	5.360 (0.194)	-2.428 (0.173)	-1.291 (0.371)	-4.051 (0.001)
INF	1.006 (0.013)	0.063 (0.846)	0.864 (0.003)	0.047 (0.879)	1.236 (0.002)	0.327 (0.289)	0.658 (0.083)	0.139 (0.643)	1.000 (0.009)	0.258 (0.385)
Constant	113.190 (0.000)	57.471 (0.002)	154.682 (0.000)	88.365 (0.000)	103.278 (0.000)	51.055 (0.009)	87.471 (0.001)	47.270 (0.003)	92.731 (0.000)	49.467 (0.001)
Observations	127	127	127	127	127	127	127	127	127	127
R-squared	0.661	0.667	0.689	0.670	0.663	0.633	0.886	0.669	0.688	0.622
F ratio	0.000	0.000	0.000	0.000	0.000	0.000	0.000	0.000	0.000	0.000
Hausman	0.000	0.019	0.005	0.002	0.000	0.000	0.133	0.008	0.004	0.000
Model	Random	Random	Random	Random	Random	Random	Fixed	Random	Random	Random

Note: Numbers in parentheses show p-values.

Next, Columns 3 to 6 display the results of regression using either DEAC or CRAC as the measures of financial inclusion. These variables are indicative of the actual use of formal financial services. The empirical results show that the coefficients of deposit accounts are significantly estimated to be of negative value, while the coefficients of credit accounts are negative as expected, but become insignificant. These results suggest that the improved usage of financial services only in the form of deposit accounts reduces the poverty ratio in both rural and urban India. This is in contrast to the results of Bhandari (2009) in which changes in the poverty ratio and the growth of deposit accounts are insignificantly correlated, although the methodologies employed are different. Concerning the control variables, the results are the same as those in the first two columns except for EXP in Column 3, which is now statistically insignificant.

Lastly, Columns 7 to 10 report the results of regression using either DEAM or CRAM as the measure of financial inclusion. Like the cases of DEAC and CRAC, financial inclusion is expressed in the form of actual use of formal financial services. The empirical results show that the coefficients of deposit and credit are significantly estimated to be at a negative value, suggesting that greater use of financial services in the form of deposit and credit also alleviate the poverty condition in both areas. Regarding the control variables, as shown in Columns 7 and 8, the coefficients become insignificant in all variables except for INF in Column 7. In Columns 9 and 10, however, the results are the same as those of Columns 3 and 4; that is, Y and INF in rural areas as well as EXP in urban areas are statistically significant with expected sign, with the others also showing the expected sign but becoming insignificant.

In summation, Table 3.4 indicates that in general financial inclusion variables, excluding the variable for the number of credit accounts, have a significant negative association with the poverty ratio in both rural and urban areas. Considering the results of each component of financial inclusion variables, it is suggested that easier access to and greater use of formal financial services have a positive impact on poverty alleviation throughout India.

Some concluding remarks

Financial inclusion is generally defined as the process of ensuring access to and usage of basic formal financial services to all people at an affordable cost. In India, there have been various measures taken to encourage financial inclusion since the late 1960s. Although new measures in the form of microfinance, such as the SHG-Bank linkage programme, have been implemented as a result of economic liberalization since the early 1990s, commercial banks still play a pivotal role in the promotion of financial inclusion in India. Accordingly, in this chapter, after reviewing the relevant data, we analyzed whether financial inclusion measures have a statistically significant relationship with poverty conditions by estimating panel data regression models.

According to relevant data on commercial banks, it was found that financial inclusion in India was encouraged mainly in rural areas until the late 1980s, but subsequently metropolitan areas have experienced a significant bump in financial inclusion. On the other hand, with regard to poverty conditions, it was also found that the poverty headcount ratio, having been in decline since 1973–4, began to increase between 1999–2000 and 2004–5 in both rural and urban areas.

For empirical analysis, we use unbalanced panel data for 25 states and union territories covering seven time periods between 1973–4 and 2004–5. The model was specified to examine the impact of financial inclusion on poverty reduction. Following the relevant literature, the number of bank branches is regarded as the measure of physical access to financial services, while the number of bank accounts and the amount of deposit and credit are used as the measure of usage of financial services. The econometric results show that these variables, excluding the variable for the number of credit accounts, have a statistically significant negative relationship with the poverty ratio in rural and urban areas even when controlling for output, government expenditure and inflation rate. Accordingly, although some policy-makers have concerns about the progress of financial inclusion, the results in this chapter suggests that both access to and usage of financial services have actually contributed in alleviating poverty conditions in both rural and urban India.

In this study, we attempted to focus on the relationship between financial inclusion measures on the one hand, and the poverty ratio on the other. However, these measures make up only one part of basic financial services, and thus may only partially reflect the degree of financial inclusion in a country. It is necessary to develop new indicators to measure financial inclusion from different viewpoints. In addition, although we have examined the direct link between financial inclusion and the poverty ratio, the relevant literature points out that finance could serve to relieve poverty through a variety of routes. Therefore, more work will be needed to re-examine the link between financial inclusion and the poverty ratio considering relevant variables.

Notes

1. A crore is equal to 10 million (10,000,000).
2. A lakh is equal to one hundred thousand (100,000).
3. In October 2009, the RBI took a big step by freeing bank branch openings in towns and villages with populations of up to 50,000, while the scheduled commercial banks (other than the RRBs) were enjoined to ensure that at least one third of such branch expansions happen in underbanked districts of underbanked states (Subbarao, 2010: 5).
4. Population groups such as, rural, semi-urban, urban and metropolitan are defined as places having populations of: under 9,999; 10,000 to 99,999; 100,000 to 999,999; and over 1,000,000, respectively (RBI, 2009: 483).
5. In 2004–5, there were two types of measurement for population below the poverty line: the Uniform Reference Period (URP) and the Mixed Reference Period (MRP). In this chapter, we use a poverty ratio based on URP.
6. The 25 states and union territories covered in this study are as follows: Andhra Pradesh, Arunachal Pradesh, Assam, Bihar, Gujarat, Haryana, Himachal Pradesh, Jammu & Kashmir, Karnataka, Kerala, Madhya Pradesh, Maharashtra, Manipur, Meghalaya, Nagaland, Orissa, Punjab, Rajasthan, Tamil Nadu, Tripura, West Bengal, Andaman & Nicobar Islands, Chandigarh, Delhi and Pondicherry.
7. The time periods are 1973–4, 1977–8, 1983, 1987–8, 1993–4, 1999–2000 and 2004–5.

References

Beck, T., A. Demirgüç-Kunt and R. Levine (2007) 'Finance, Inequality and the Poor', *Journal of Economic Growth*, 12 (1), pp. 27–49.

Beck, T., A. Demirgüç-Kunt and M. S. Martinez Peria (2007) 'Reaching Out: Access to and Use of Banking Services across Countries', *Journal of Financial Economics*, 85 (1), pp. 234–66.

Bhandari, A. K. (2009) 'Access to Banking Services and Poverty Reduction: A State-wise Assessment in India', *IZA Discussion Paper* 4132.

Bhattacharya, P. C. and M. N. Sivasubramanian (2003) 'Financial Development and Economic Growth in India', *Applied Financial Economics*, 13 (12), pp. 905–9.

Burgess, R. and R. Pande (2005) 'Do Rural Banks Matter? Evidence from the Indian Social Banking Experiment', *American Economic Review*, 95 (3), pp. 780–95.

Chavan, P. (2007) 'Access to Bank Credit: Implications for Dalit Rural Households', *Economic and Political Weekly*, 42 (31), pp. 3219–24.

Claessens, S. (2005) 'Access to Financial Services: A Review of the Issues and Public Policy Objectives', *Policy Research Working Series* 3589, Washington, DC: World Bank.

Clarke, G. R. G., L. C. Xu and H.-F. Zou (2006) 'Finance and Income Inequality: What Do the Data Tell Us?', *Southern Economic Journal*, 72 (3), pp. 578–96.

Demirgüç-Kunt, A. and V. Maksimovic (1996) 'Financial Constraints, Uses of Funds, and Firm Growth: An International Comparison', *Policy Research Working Paper Series* 1671, Washington, DC: World Bank.

Jalilian, H. and C. Kirkpatrick (2002) 'Financial Development and Poverty Reduction in Developing Countries', *International Journal of Finance and Economics*, 7 (2), pp. 97–108.

Joshi, D. P. (2006) *Social Banking: Promise, Performance and Potential*, New Delhi: Foundation.

King, R. and R. Levine (1993) 'Finance and Growth: Schumpeter might be Right', *The Quarterly Journal of Economics*, 108 (3), pp. 717–37.

Leeladhar, V. (2006) 'Taking Banking Services to the Common Man: Financial Inclusion', *RBI Bulletin*, January, pp. 73–7.

Leeladhar, V. (2008) 'The Indian Banking Industry: A Retrospect of Select Aspects', *RBI Bulletin*, September, pp. 1501–10.

Levine, R. and S. Zervos (1998) 'Stock Markets, Banks and Economic Growth', *American Economic Review*, 88 (3), pp. 537–58.

National Sample Survey Organization (NSSO) (1998a) *Indebtedness of Rural Households as on 30.6.1991: Debt and Investment Survey*, no. 420, New Delhi: NSSO, July.

National Sample Survey Organization (1998b) *Indebtedness of Urban Households as on 30.6.1991: Debt and Investment Survey*, no. 421, New Delhi: NSSO, July.

National Sample Survey Organization (2005) *Household Indebtedness in India as on 30.06.2002; All India Debt and Investment Survey*, no. 501, New Delhi: NSSO, December.

Rao, K. G. K. S. (2007) 'Financial Inclusion: An Introspection', *Economic and Political Weekly*, 42 (5), pp. 355–60.

Reserve Bank of India (RBI) (1965) 'All India Rural Debt and Investment Survey, 1961–62', *RBI Bulletin*, September, pp. 1296–393.

Reserve Bank of India (1977) *Indebtedness of Rural Households and Availability of Institutional Finance: All India Debt and Investment Survey 1971–72*, Mumbai: RBI, April.

Reserve Bank of India (1987) *All India Debt and Investment Survey, 1981–82: Assets and Liabilities of Households as on 30th June 1981*, Mumbai: RBI, September.

Reserve Bank of India (1999) *Annual Report 1998–1999*, Mumbai: RBI, August.

Reserve Bank of India (2004) *Handbook of Statistics on State Government Finances*, Mumbai: RBI, July.

Reserve Bank of India (2005a) *Annual Policy Statement for the year 2005–06*, Mumbai: RBI, April.

Reserve Bank of India (2005b) *Mid-Term Review of Annual Policy Statement for the year 2005–06*, Mumbai: RBI, October.

Reserve Bank of India (2006) *State Finances: A Study of Budgets 2006–07*, Mumbai: RBI, December.

Reserve Bank of India (2008) 'Financial Inclusion', *Report on Currency and Finance 2007–08*, September, pp. 294–348.

Reserve Bank of India (2009) *Handbook on Statistics of Indian Economy 2008–09*, Mumbai: RBI.

Reserve Bank of India (various issues) *Banking Statistics: Basic Statistical Returns*, Mumbai: RBI.

Reserve Bank of India (various issues) *Basic Statistical Returns of Scheduled Commercial Banks in India*, Mumbai: RBI.

Sen, K. and R. R. Vaidya (1997) *The Process of Financial Liberalization*, Delhi: Oxford University Press.

Shan, J. and A. Morris (2002) 'Does Financial Development "Lead" Economic Growth', *International Review of Applied Economics*, 16 (2), pp. 153–68.

Shajahan, K. M. (1998) 'Priority Sector Bank Lending: Some Important Issues', *Economic and Political Weekly*, 33 (42–3), pp. 2749–56.

Subbarao, D. (2010) 'Financial Inclusion: Challenges and Opportunities', *RBI Bulletin*, January, pp. 1–10.

Thorat, U. (2007) 'Financial Inclusion: The Indian Experience', *RBI Bulletin*, July, pp. 1165–72.

World Bank (2008) *Finance for All? Policies and Pitfalls in Expanding Access*, Washington, DC: World Bank.

PART II
Disparity in Access to Social Services

4
Health Inequality in India: Results from NSS Data

Seiro Ito

Introduction

Health is considered to be paramount to wellbeing. Good health directly enhances welfare, but also increases the chance of being wealthy by raising people's innate productivity. With a booming economy, people in good health should benefit from increased opportunities. It is therefore essential in reducing socio-economic inequality to provide quality health care to the underprivileged population.

Disparity in health care utilization has been a lingering issue in socio-economic development of India. Starting with National Health Policy set in 1985, Government of India (GOI) expanded the network of government hospitals throughout the nation. The public health care system comprised of a three-tier structure, with the primary health care provided by Primary Health Centres (PHCs), each intended to serve 30,000 residents. Secondary and tertiary functions are placed in larger hospitals in towns and cities.

The results, however, were far below those envisaged in 'Health for All' (MHFW, 2002). It is well documented that government hospitals, especially remotely placed PHCs and Subcentres, are understaffed and plagued with absenteeism due to misplaced incentive schemes and strong labour unions. Rural residents show their preference for untrained yet friendly local quacks over medical professionals at PHCs in large villages, who may be rude and often out of the office. This has led the GOI to admit 'gross underutilization of the existing health infrastructure at the primary level' (MHFW, 2005: 4). The MHFW (2005) attributes the failure to poor governance, the dysfunctional role of the state, lack of a strategic vision and weak management. The National Rural Health Mission (NRHM), started in 2005, seeks to provide universal access to equitable, affordable and quality health care, which is accountable and responsive to the needs of the people. One of its special focuses is on child and maternal health and population stabilization.

Despite being the top priority in national policies and widely shared deep concerns over their disparity, health statistics are seldom shown below the state level. Almost all publications give results with national or state averages (see, for example, Radwan, 2005; World Bank, 2005; IIPS, 2006; Ito, 2009). There do exist studies based on micro-level data, but these are local studies that do not represent the nation as a whole. When we are considering the disparity, discussions based on highly aggregated levels defeat their purpose and can mask important variability within each state. Given the size of states, it is prudent to confirm what we can learn at the below-state level.

Using NSS household-level data, this chapter examines the health service utilization. We follow central government's priority and focus our attention on sanitary infrastructure, perinatal health, medical expenditure and finance in rural India. We break down households into five expenditure classes to understand the variability masked in the state averages. Given that health shocks are endogenous to expenditure levels through unobservable ability, we do not examine the number of incidences or prevalence of certain diseases. Instead, we condition on the health shocks and focus on the aftermath of health shocks. Health shocks we consider are pregnancy, serious symptoms that may lead to hospitalization and less serious ailments that may result in outpatient visits.

It is found that, for rural households, (1) water connection requires improvement and appropriate water treatment is almost lacking, (2) lack of a toilet on household premises remains a challenge, (3) mean birth expenditure is large across the income levels, (4) a prenatal check is associated with lower mean birth and postnatal expenditure, (5) mean inpatient expenditure plus medicine expenditure outside the hospital, both conditional on admission, is large, (6) government reimbursement for inpatient medical services of the poor is negligible and (7) use of private insurance remains negligible. We argue for more focused campaigns on preventive medicine and establishment of finance mechanisms for the poor.

Data

We use household-level data from the National Sample Survey (NSS), 60th Round, Schedule 25.0 (NSS 60-25.0), which was collected in 2004.

This dataset focuses primarily on health care services utilization. While it comprises of rural and urban sectors, we will use only the rural sector where the health problem is more pronounced.

The NSS 60–25.0 sample is based on 73,868 households from 35 states. The rural sample consists of 47,302 from 4,755 villages/blocks. Some states and Union Territories (UTs) (namely, Delhi, Goa, Chandigarh, Dadra and Nagar Haveli, Daman and Diu, Lakshadweep and Pondicherry) draw small sample that is less than 100 households. We will not take these states and UTs into our consideration in the analysis, yet we will produce graphs for them.

Sample collection is designed to be representative of the society in each state, while at the same time trying to make sure that households with higher health care needs (households that experienced hospitalization in the last year, households with a child less than five years old, households with elderly more than 60 years old) are included.

We defer discussions on technical issues related to the dataset to the appendix. We note here that, while NSS 60–25.0 did not collect detailed income data, it asked simplified monthly expenditure questions to get a rough estimate of household expenditure level. We will rely on this information to get the per capita expenditure, national-level expenditure quintiles and classify households into each wealth class. This allows us to relate the accessibility, expenditure and utilization of health care services to some measure of wealth when we consider the health inequality. All the data we used are adjusted for respective sampling probabilities, so we can interpret the data as the representative sample.

Estimates by expenditure quintiles

In browsing through the trends at below state level, we use expenditure quintiles to group the households. In NSS 60–25, a set of simplified questions on monthly expenditure is attached. Each household answers to these questions, and we use them as a proxy of household incomes. The precision of such proxy remains to be seen, but measurement errors in monthly expenditure may not be seriously damaging, if the errors are randomly distributed for each wealth level with mean zero, which we assume to be so. This follows since we use them to classify households into wealth classes, and we average within classes, hence errors also get rounded. As the data collection is design-based, we will use appropriate weights to estimate quintile averages.[1]

Infrastructure

We begin the browsing tour with socio-economic statistics. In the first panel of the graphs, we depicted in the vertical axis the proportion of households which has no latrine or has a pit latrine. All other types of modern toilet facilities are coded as 0, so we are looking at the proportion of households with pre-modern toilet facilities.

In each graph, information of each state is shown. We take the wealth (expenditure) classes defined by per capita expenditure quintiles in the horizontal axis. As we move from left to right, the wealth level of each class becomes larger. We use the common wealth class classification among the states and, by normalizing the population size, the width of each wealth class shows the proportions of respective wealth classes in each state. Given that we are going to summarize the information by wealth classes, we interchangeably use the terms 'wealth classes' and 'wealth levels'.

We have arranged the drawing order of states by the proportion of the two bottom wealth classes: graphs are drawn for states with the largest proportion of two bottom classes to smallest. In Punjab, for example, almost a half of sample is in the class V. We have set the background colours such that lower the expenditure levels, darker the background colour becomes. This allows one to browse the figures and get an idea of wealth levels and distribution by the darkness of background. Chhattisgarh, another example, the poorest state defined by our drawing order, along with Orissa, indicates that the share of lowest income quintile is almost 50 per cent. In some figures, some graphs are superimposed with a cross sign. These are states with small sample, defined by 75 or less. These are marked due to a concern over sampling errors.

Hygiene-related variables show a well-established pattern in Figure 4.1. In most of the states, even at the high-income level, latrines are either pits or nonexistent. The level of lack of modern toilet facilities is strikingly high. In the first row of graphs, which show the six poorest states, the proportions of pre-modern toilets for two poorest wealth classes are almost one. Most states show the negative correlations with the wealth levels, but the pattern seems to indicate a discrete drop between the top wealth class and the second to the top, implying that use of modern toilets becomes suddenly widespread after passing a certain wealth threshold.

When we look at the water sources in Figure 4.2, pre-modern water facilities (defined here as anything other than piped water) are pervasive in dark coloured states. Again, most of within-state correlation is negative with wealth levels. Some southern states (Andhra Pradesh, Karnataka and Tamil Nadu) are overachieving, given their graphs are darker than

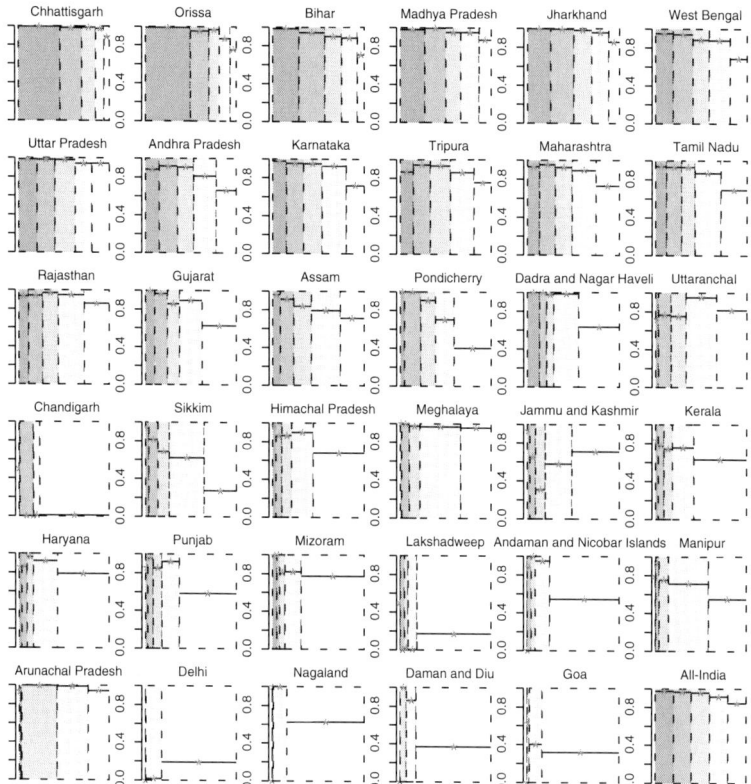

Figure 4.1 Latrine type: none or pit = 1, other = 0

Notes: [1] The lowest quintile is shaded with the darkest grey. The highest quintile is shaded with the lightest grey.
[2] Width of quintiles indicates the proportion of each quintiles in each state.
[3] States are ordered by the relative size of two lowest quintiles in each state.

other states. We also note that within-state variation is not large relative to between-state variation.

Lack of an hygienic water source translates into unsafe and unclean water at the household level. When we look at the practice of water treatment in Figure 4.3, a high percentage of households across the wealth classes do not treat water. Even with the few who treat the water, methods of treatment show that majority uses the non-chemical process such as cloth screens and other filtering (Figure 4.4). In Figure 4.4, the proportion includes, among the households who claim to treat water, households not using UV, resin, reverse osmosis, boiling, or disinfectants.[2]

116 *Health Inequality in India*

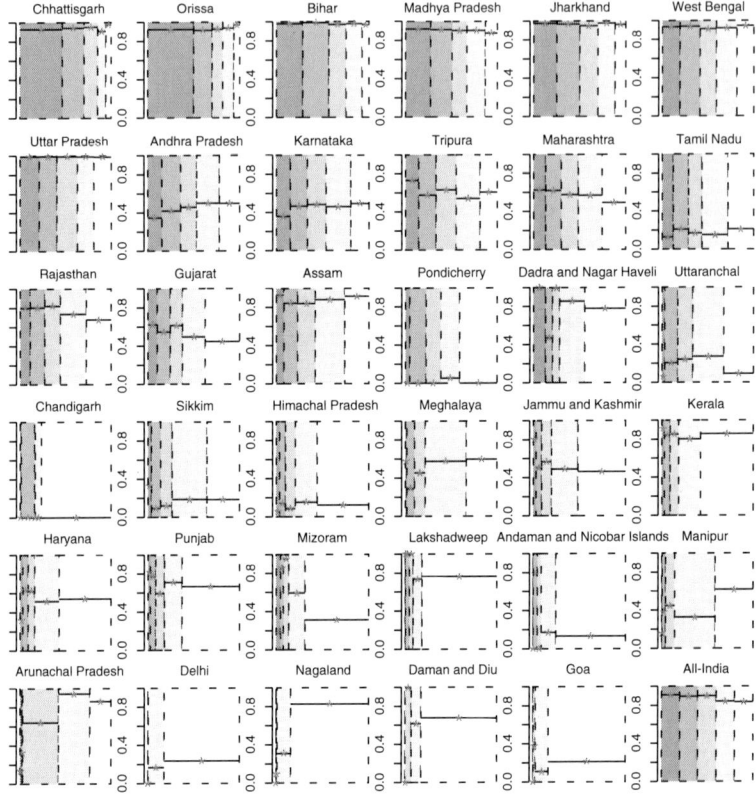

Figure 4.2 Water source: bottles, wells, tankers, tank, pond, river, others = 1, piped water = 0

These factors combine together to indicate that a lack of toilets may threaten the unprotected water source that the majority of the poorer population uses.

Perinatal health

Perinatal health is a top priority in NRHM. Although not shown here to save space, pregnancy is not correlated with wealth levels, suggesting that perinatal health is an across-the-board issue for Indians. In Figure 4.5, prenatal health care, defined as at least one visit to a clinic prior to giving a birth, is utilized by the majority of the population. This is especially so in the southern states of Andhra Pradesh, Karnataka, Kerala and Tamil Nadu, and in West Bengal, where the communist government reigns.

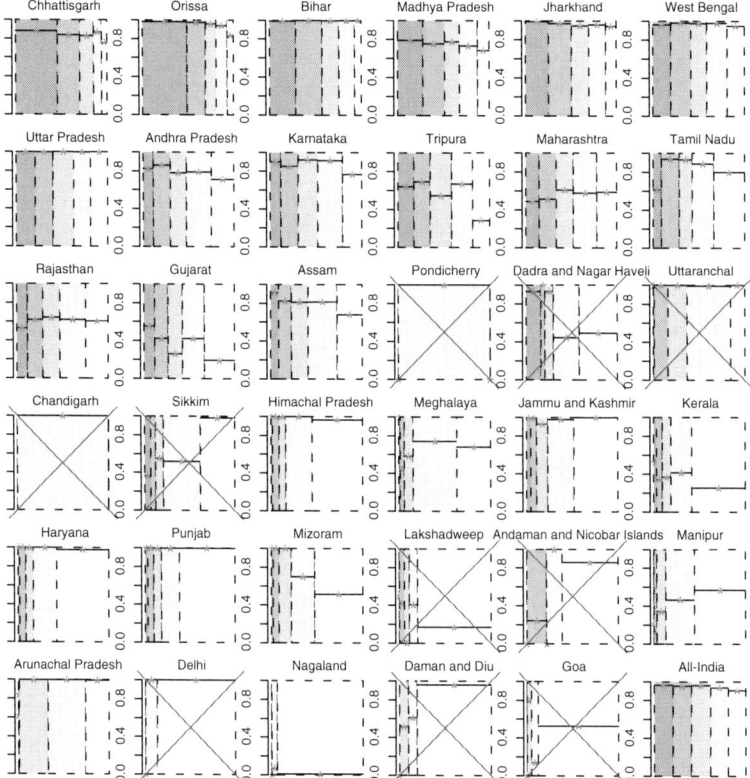

Figure 4.3 Water treated: no = 1, yes = 0, conditional on not using piped water

Notes: [1] Sample is selected conditional on having water treated.
[2] Samples with no sample matching the category is either left as blank.
[3] Samples with size less than 75 are superimposed with across.

Other states show either a weak positive correlation with wealth levels or relatively low level of utilization.

Institutional births (Figure 4.6) remain an issue; as shown, a general positive correlation exists with wealth levels in most of the states. Aforementioned states Andhra Pradesh, Karnataka, Kerala, Tamil Nadu and West Bengal fare well in institutional births, with Kerala outperforming superbly.

When we look at the mean perinatal expenditures in Figure 4.7, where we select the sample conditional on being pregnant, it is generally above Rs 1,000 even with the lowest wealth quintile. If we condition

118 *Health Inequality in India*

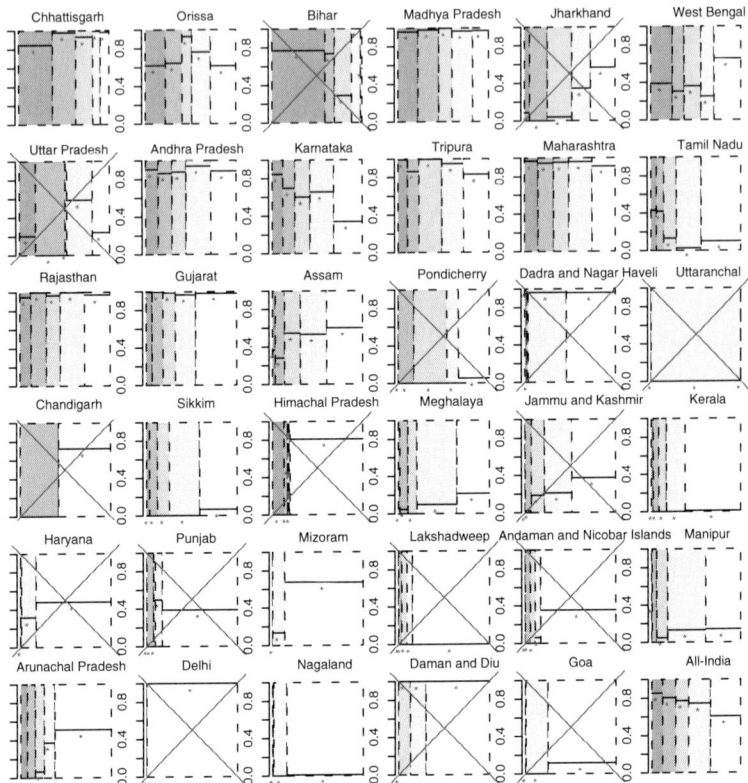

Figure 4.4 Water treatment: filter, cloth screen, disinfectant, other = 1, uv, resin, reverse osmosis, boiling = 0, conditional on having water treated

Notes: [1] Sample is selected conditional on having water treated.
[2] See the note of Figure 4.3

the sample on utilization of respective services, Figure 4.8 shows that mean expenditure increases. This increase is most pronounced in poorer states. This suggests that there are more mothers in poorer states that do not utilize the perinatal health care services. Among prenatal, birth and postnatal health care, the most significant expenditure increase between Figure 4.7 and Figure 4.8 comes from birth-related expenditure. When mothers in poorer states give birth in hospital, births generally come expensive, suggesting an adverse event.

It would be interesting to see if having prenatal health care is associated with lower birth and postnatal expenditure. To do so, one can plot

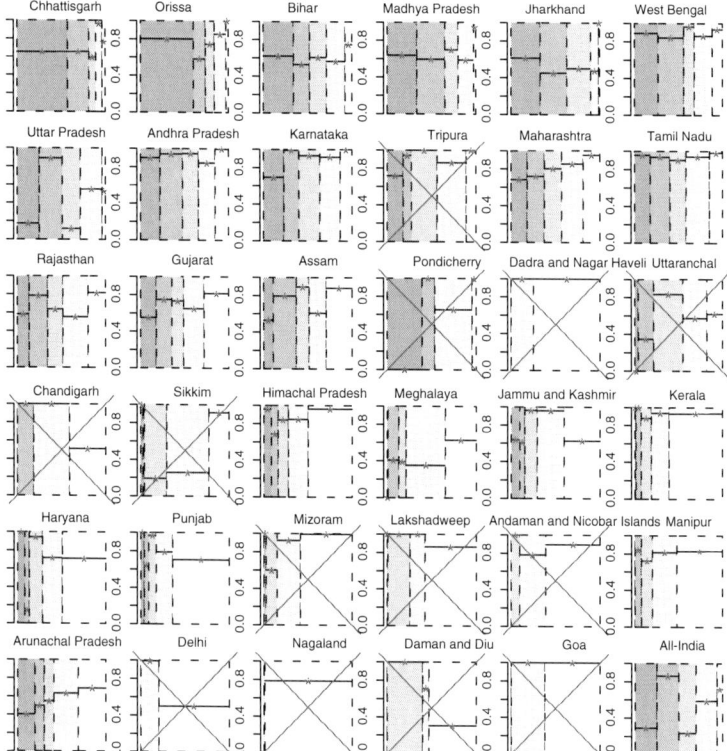

Figure 4.5 Prenatal: government, private = 1, no = 0, conditional on being pregnant

Notes: [1] Sample is selected conditional on being pregnant.
[2] See the note of Figure 4.3

utilization of prenatal health care against birth and postnatal expenditure. However, to save space, we simply compare the median expenditure among prenatal care takers and non-takers. In birth expenditures, median takers pay less than the median non-takers. Median birth expenditure is greater (by Rs 59) for prenatal non-takers. This gives a good ground for focusing more on preventive care in prenatal health.[3]

Household health expenses and finance in inpatient care

Hospitalization poses a major financial burden on households. Conditional on being admitted to a hospital, Figure 4.9 shows the extent of burden. Each graph shows the layers of out-of-pocket (OOP),

120 *Health Inequality in India*

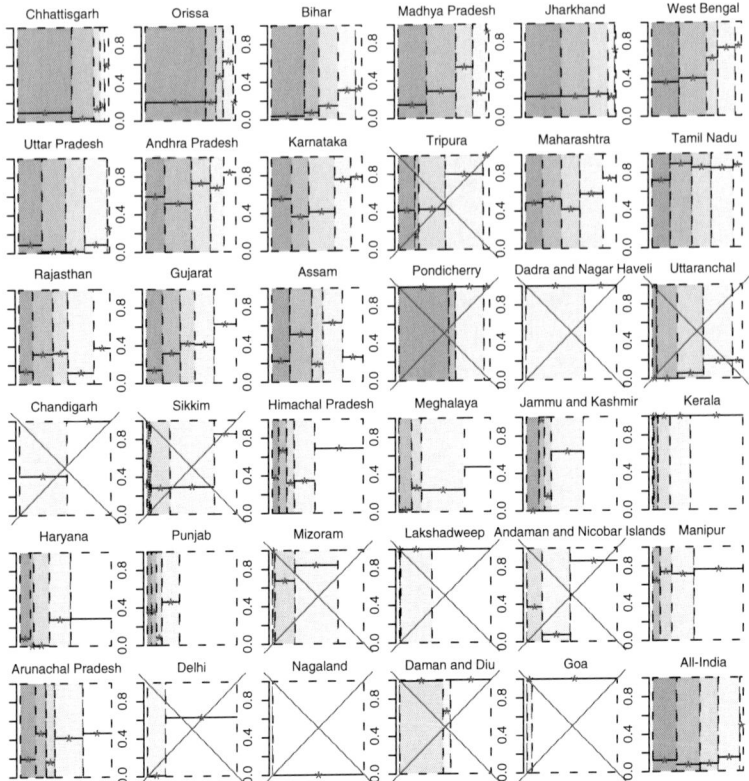

Figure 4.6 Institutional births: government, private = 1, home, no birth = 0, conditional on being pregnant

Notes: [1] Sample is selected conditional on being pregnant.
[2] Institutional births are births at health facilities. If the birth is institutional, it is coded as 1, otherwise 0. So the graphs show the proportions of institutional births.
[3] See the notes to Figure 4.3.

government reimbursement and other private reimbursement. In most of the states, the mean total payment for the lowest income quintile is in a 2,000 Rs band about Rs 4,000, which is about 10–20 months' worth of their per capita expenditure.

It is notable that mean total inpatient expenditure increases with wealth class, implying that poorer households receive the private secondary or tertiary care less than wealthier households. Take Punjab, for example: the mean total payments in the three lowest wealth classes are about Rs 5,000, while the top wealth class exceeds Rs 15,000, which is

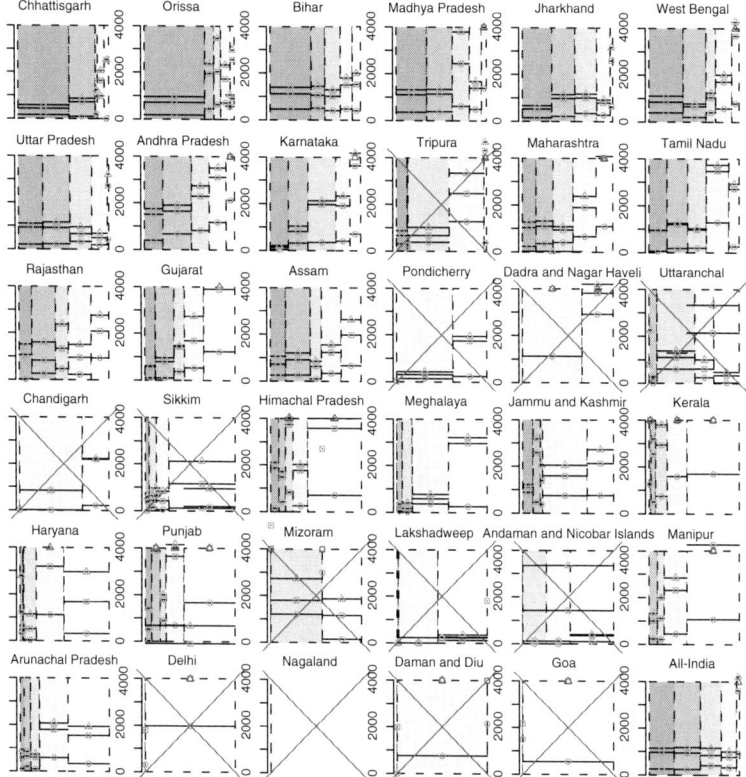

Figure 4.7 Perinatal expenditure: Rs, conditional on being pregnant

Notes: [1] In each quintile, expenditure is depicted as a cumulative sum of prenatal (□), birth (○) and postnatal (△) expenditure.
[2] Sample is selected conditional on being pregnant.

marked with △. Thus, the wealthiest spends on average three times more than the poorest three wealth classes. Except in Chhattisgarh, Sikkim, Manipur and Arunachal Pradesh, the lower wealth classes pay less in hospitalization. One may consider that this not as a problem if the differences originate due to the lower wealth classes choosing government hospitals that charge less than the private hospitals. Even so, as the quality of medical services is considered to be inferior in the government hospitals, this indicates that the poor are receiving lower-quality care. It is also natural to suspect that the poor, who are less educated and short on cash, may not understand the symptoms well or choose not to be admitted, both of which result in lower mean inpatient expenditure.

122 Health Inequality in India

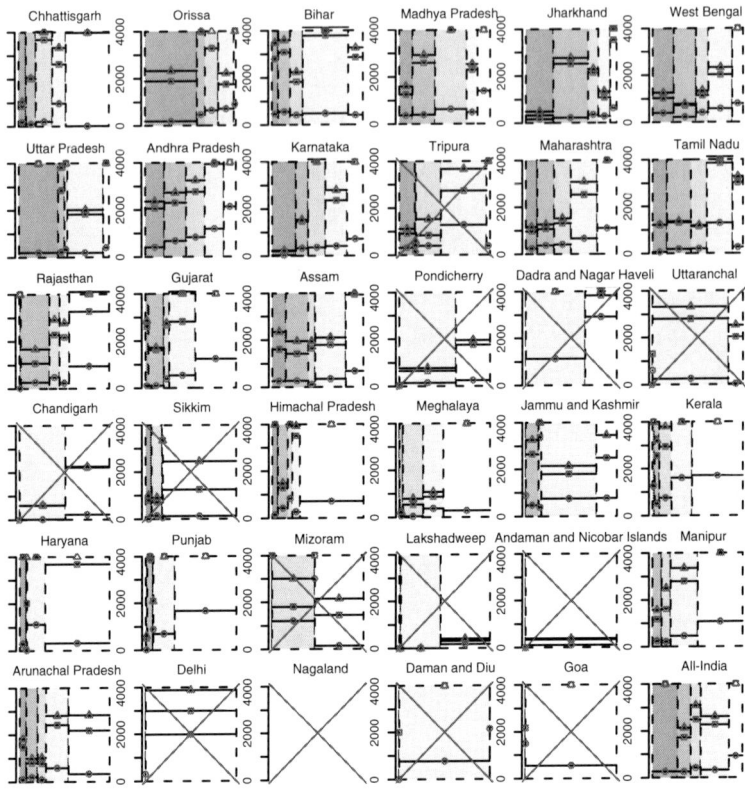

Figure 4.8 Perinatal expenditure: Rs, conditional on utilization

Notes: [1] In each quintile, expenditure is depicted as a cumulative sum of prenatal (o), birth (□), and postnatal (Δ) expenditure.
[2] Sample is selected conditional on using the respective health care services.

As one can see, almost all the expenditure comes from OOP. Formal third-party finances for hospitalization costs are almost nonexistent in Figure 4.10. The government reimbursement beneficiaries are concentrated at the second highest and top wealth classes. It is important to note that medical insurance plays almost no role in financing hospitalization, leaving a major health risk unattended.

Household health expenses and finance in outpatient care

Outpatient care for less severe ailments is more frequent and less costly than inpatient care. The general pattern in Figure 4.10 is that it is about Rs 200–400 across the wealth classes. The increasing pattern

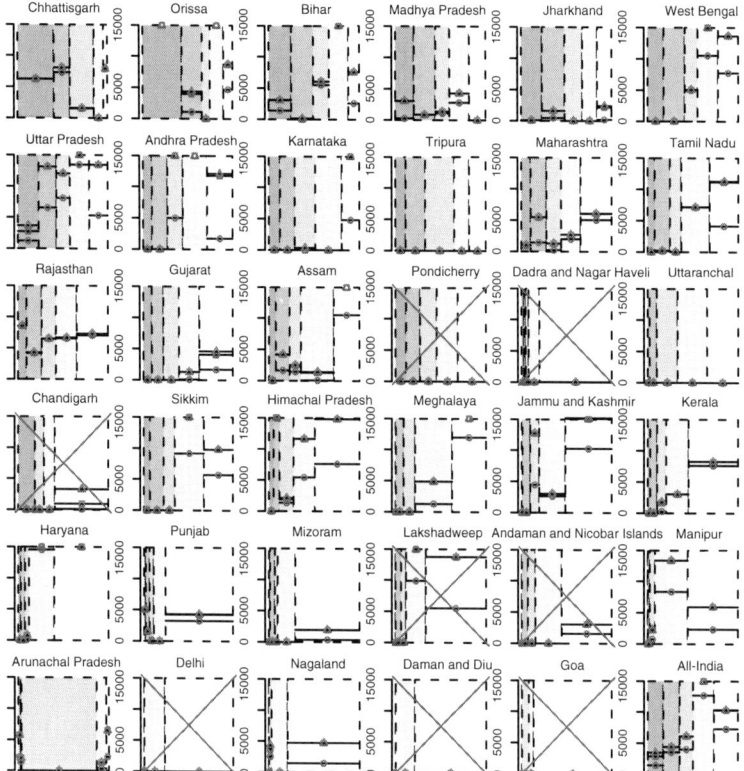

Figure 4.9 Inpatient care: OOP expenditure, government and other reimbursement (Rs, conditional on being admitted to a hospital)

Note:[1] In each quintile, expenditure is depicted as a cumulative sum of OOP expenditure (O), government reimbursement (□), and private and other reimbursement (Δ).
[2] Sample is selected conditional on being admitted to a hospital.

that we found in inpatient care costs is less pronounced with outpatient care. The majority of the Indian population has a good access to primary health care providers. One needs to exercise caution, however, as the NSS questionnaire does not ask about the qualification of the service providers. It is well known that untrained quacks play a major role in servicing primary health care in rural areas. As in inpatient care, there is little reimbursement from insurers.

An oft-heard complaint in government hospitals is that they are out of stock of free medicine. The patients are forced to buy the medicines

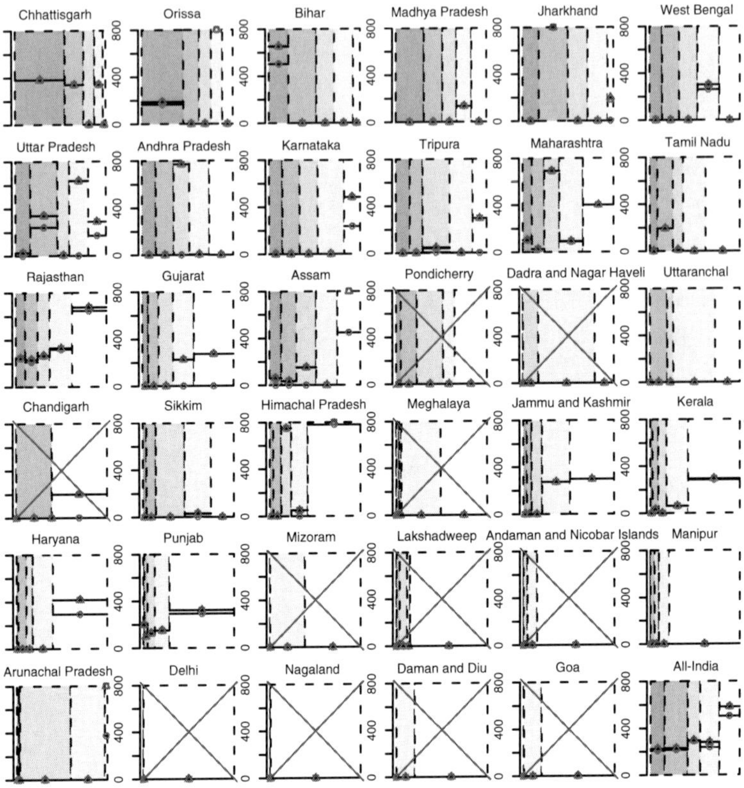

124　*Health Inequality in India*

Figure 4.10 Outpatient care: OOP expenditure, government and other reimbursement (Rs)

Notes: [1] In each quintile, expenditure is depicted as a cumulative sum of OOP expenditure (O), government reimbursement (□), and private and other reimbursement (Δ).
[2] Sample is selected conditional on using an outpatient department.

outside the hospitals. The markets for such over-the-counter (OTC) medicines are prevalent and are directly affecting the household health expenditure. In Figures 4.11 and 4.12, we layer the prescribed payments and OTC payments for inpatient and outpatient care, respectively. For outpatient care, the level of spending does not vary with wealth class, as minor ailments that are usually dealt with in primary health care do not require costly medicines. In Figure 4.11, we see that, except for Bihar, Chhattisgarh and Uttar Pradesh, OTC payments are smaller for lower quintiles, and the total inpatient medicine payments are smaller than in higher quintiles. This suggests that the poor have only prescribed

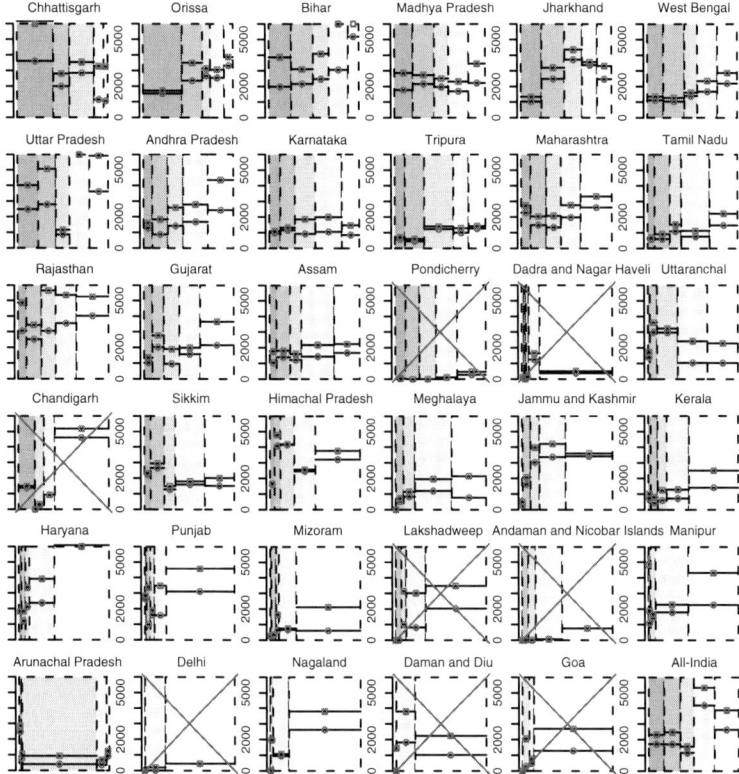

Figure 4.11 Inpatient medicine expenditure: inside and outside hospitals (Rs)

Notes: [1] In each quintile, expenditure is depicted as a cumulative sum of prescribed medicines (○) and OTC medicines (□).
[2] Sample is selected conditional on being admitted to a hospital.

medicines to rely on, while the wealthy choose to spend a significant amount on OTC medicines.

We see that the lowest quintile in most states spends around Rs 200 during the period of 15 days prior to the survey, due to health shocks that led them to seek outpatient medical care. OTC payments are not large relative to prescribed payments, except in Chhattisgarh, Bihar, Madhya Pradesh and West Bengal, which are medically backward states. This is another significant burden on poor households, as they face the risk of costs amounting to two to three days' worth of per capita expenditure within a 15-day window.

126 *Health Inequality in India*

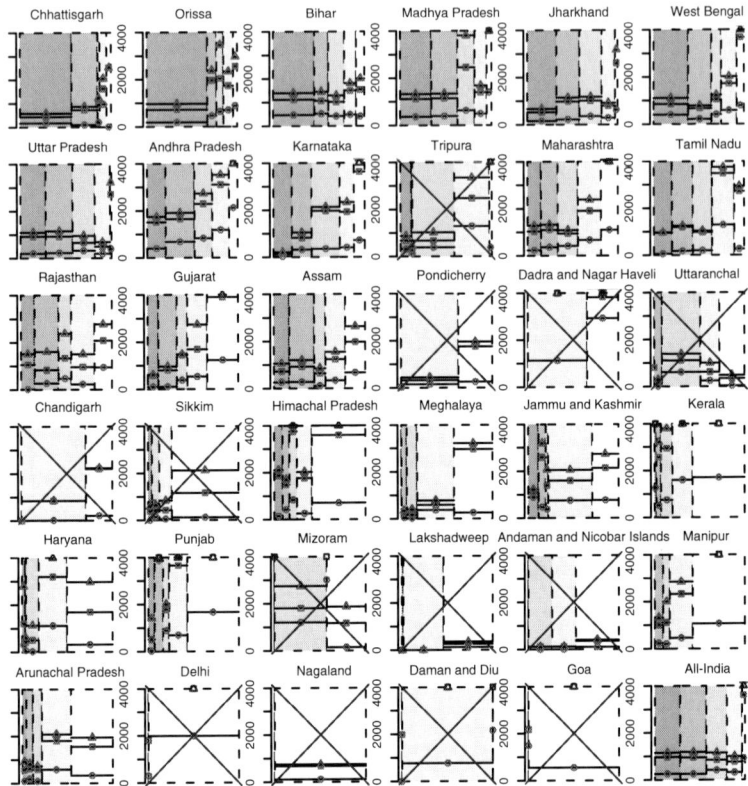

Figure 4.12 Outpatient medicine expenditure: inside and outside hospitals (Rs)

Notes:[1] In each quintile, expenditure is depicted as a cumulative sum of prenatal (○), birth (□), and postnatal (△) expenditure.
[2] Sample is selected conditional on being pregnant.

Concluding remarks

Using NSS data, this chapter has shown the extent of variability below state averages. It is seen that (1) water connection requires improvement and appropriate water treatment is almost lacking, (2) lack of toilets on household premises remains a challenge, (3) mean birth expenditure is large across the income levels, (4) a prenatal check is associated with lower mean birth and postnatal expenditure, (5) mean inpatient expenditure plus medicine expenditure outside the hospital, both conditional on admission, is large, (6) government reimbursement for inpatient medical services of the poor is negligible and (7) use of private insurance remains negligible.

By breaking down the state-level averages, we have seen that variability in medical expenditure is found across wealth classes. While the access to hygiene infrastructure shows relatively small variability across wealth classes, expenditure on perinatal care and inpatient care shows positive correlations with wealth levels. These are masked under the state averages that most researchers use. Expenditure on outpatient care and outpatient care medicines showed no correlation with wealth levels. We have evidenced that within state, in addition to between state, variation remains an important source of health inequality.

Within-state disparity poses a new agenda for welfare of the poor. It has been well noted that between-state disparity is an issue, and the central government has been spending more of its budget on backward states and UTs. The results of this chapter show that such an effort is not sufficient to reduce the disparity. Even in the rich states, such as Punjab or Haryana, state governments fail to ensure health care service utilization for the poorer segment of population. This may be deeply rooted in the Indian legislative system, where the state government does not easily give up the authority and budget to lower-level, local governments. As Ito (2009) stressed, the centralized governance system survives even after federalism slashed the power of central government; it survives within the state. The challenge remains big, as mere decentralization to much lower levels may end up in confusion if the adequate capacity and accountability have not been built up.

Within-state disparity of inpatient care expenditure is interpreted as due to difference in purchasing power. Clearly, there exists a need for a formal insurance scheme that provides nationwide services. As for publicly funded schemes, there are only two: Central Government Health Schemes (CGHS), provided mainly to central government employees, and Employee State Insurance Scheme (ESIS), provided to formal sector employees. In 2007, the policy-holders of CGHS accounted for 0.4 per cent of the entire population, while those of ESIS accounted for about 4 per cent. Public information on both schemes is very limited, and readers are referred to Rao (2005) for more details of CGHS and ESIS.

The vast majority of the rural population is outside these two schemes. The challenges in establishing health insurance in rural India are big: it needs to be affordable, well understood by rural residents, provides a reasonable cover for major diseases and injuries, accepted in major hospitals, to list a few. In addition, one needs to avert incentive problems for the insurance to be financially sustainable, such as adverse selection and moral hazard both by hospitals and patients. Micro-insurance, defined as small-scale insurance for the poor, provides some leading examples. However, there has not been a micro-insurance scheme which successfully scaled up beyond pilot levels, most probably due to incentive problems and the complexity of logistical operations. Health financing remains an important area for future policy research.

Notes

1. We used weighted quintile function in Hmisc package of R.
2. In Figure 4.4, proportions of each wealth class are different from previous figures. This is due to Figure 4.4 is based on selected samples which are conditioned on households which treat water.
3. Note the possible endogeneity of the estimates that more conscious pregnant women may opt for prenatal checks, resulting in lower birth expenditure even in the absence of prenatal checks, hence underestimating the impacts. As the health and non-health benefits of birth are not confined to birth-related expenditure, we can consider these numbers as the lower bound of estimated returns to prenatal checks.

References

Das, Jishnu and Jeffrey Hammer (2005) 'Which Doctor? Combining Vignettes and Item Response to Measure Clinical Competence', *Journal of Development Economics*, 78, pp. 348–83.

Gelman, Andrew and Hao Lu (2003) 'Sampling Variance for Surveys with Weighting, Poststratification and Raking', *Journal of Official Statistics*, 19 (2), pp. 133–51.

International Institute of Population Studies (IIPS) (2006) *The World Health Survey: India, 2003*, Mumbai.

Ito, Seiro (2009) 'Public Health Care System in India', in Masako Ii (ed.), *Health Care Systems in Asia*, Tokyo: Tokyo University Press (in Japanese).

Ministry of Health and Family Welfare (MHFW) (2002) *National Health Policy: 2002*, http://mohfw.nic.in/np2002

_____ (2005) *National Rural Health Mission: Meeting People's Health Needs in Rural Areas*,www.mohfw.nic.in/NRHM/Documents/Mission_Document.pdf

Radwan, Ismail (2005) 'India: Private Health Services for the Poor', Health, Nutrition and Population (HNP), Discussion Paper, World Bank, Washington, DC.

Rao, K. S. (2005) 'Health Insurance in India', in Ministry of Health and Family Welfare, *Financing and Delivery of Health Care Services in India*, National Commission on Macroeconomics and Health.

World Bank (2005) *Implementation Completion Report for Reproductive and Child Health Project*, World Bank, Washington, DC.

Appendix: NSS Data

Sampling design

NSS is a multi-stage stratified sample survey. Putting it rigorously, it is a quadruply stratified, cluster sampling survey (see Figure A4.1). First-stage units (FSUs) are villages listed in 1991 census. Villages and communities are initially stratified by states, which can be considered as the first stage stratification. In each state, in the second-stage stratification, FSUs are classified into rural and urban strata. As we focus on rural health, we discard all the urban strata. In a rural stratum, three classes of third stage strata are created according to population size to oversample small and large villages.

Within each third-stage strata, villages are sampled with a probability proportional to population size. This is the first cluster sampling phase. When a large community is chosen, a hamlet group is created and two hamlets are sampled. This is the second cluster sampling phase. Within each hamlet/village, four fourth-stage strata are created to capture the several aspects of health efficiently: households with hospitalization experience, households with infants, households with elderly and all other households. Within each fourth-stages strata, households are chosen. This constitutes the third cluster sampling phase, as a household is considered to be a cluster of individuals.

NSS is designed to cover the entire population of India, except for conflict-prone areas. This makes NSS an ideal resource in understanding socio-economic issues at the various aggregation levels. Due to confidentiality and privacy considerations, the raw data do not specify village names nor tehsil names. The lowest level one can identify is districts. However, as the design specifies, one can learn about the variability within districts. We can also study village-level variations if we

First stage units (FSUs): villages and urban clusters from 1991 census.

I. first stage stratification (**state**): states

II. second stage stratification (**sector**): geographical location
   1. rural
   2. urban

III. third stage stratification (**stratum**): population size of FSUs
   1. size 0 - 50 if there are more than 50 of them
   2. size more than 15000 if there are more than 4 of them
   3. other (general strata), starting as 3, 4, ...

IV. sampling of villages
   1. first cluster sampling phase: within each strata, FSUs are chosen by random sampling with probability proportional to size with replacement (PPSWR).
   2. second cluster sampling phase (optional, **segment**, **subblock**): hamlet group
      i. FSUs are divided into a hamlet group if estimated present population (**prspop**) is more than 1200.
      ii. 2 hamlet groups are chosen with simple random sampling without replacement (SRSWOR).

V. fourth stage stratification (second stage strata, SSS, **stratum2**): for each hamlet group households are randomly chosen according to (double the number if there is only 1 hamlet):
   1. at least one member hospitalized
   2. at least one child below 5 years old
   3. at least one member above 60 years and older
   4. other

VI. third cluster sampling phase
   1. at least one member hospitalized: 2 HHs
   2. at least one child below 5 years old: 1 HHs
   3. at least one member above 60 years and older: 1 HH
   4. other: 1 HH

Figure A4.1 Sampling design of NSS

Note: Words in a different type font (e.g. **state**) are variable names used in data set.

are not interested in identity of the village below district level. As stated in the first section, one rarely sees an analysis at the village level, let alone at the district level. Therefore, the extent of the lower level variability is relatively unknown, as it is generally averaged out at the higher aggregation level.

NSS explicitly specifies two stratification stages, at FSU or our third stage, and at household groups or our fourth stage. NSS documents refer to them as first-stage strata (FSS) and second-stage strata (SSS), respectively. From hereon, we will follow their terminology.

Means

In computing the statistics at the various aggregation level, NSS gives the complex formulae with many subscripts. One can, however, compute the means in a simpler and more interpretable manner if we build the concept from ground up.

- Hamlet means: in a hamlet h, households are selected form four second-stage strata (SSS), $s = 1,2,3,4$ each with $n_{h,s}$ observations. We denote each SSS have population of $N_{h,s}$.

$$\mu_h = \sum_{s=1}^{4} w_{h,s} \mu_{h,s}$$

$$= \sum_{s=1}^{4} \frac{w_{h,s}}{n_{h,s}} \sum_{i=1}^{n_s} x_{h,s,i}$$

$$= \sum_{s=1}^{4} \frac{N_{h,s}}{N_h} \frac{1}{n_{h,s}} \sum_{i=1}^{n_s} x_{h,s,i} \qquad (1)$$

$$= \frac{1}{N_h} \sum_{s=1}^{4} \frac{1}{P_{h,s}} \sum_{i=1}^{n_s} x_{h,s,i}$$

The weights are given as:

$$w_{h,s} = \frac{N_{h,s}}{N_h}, \quad N_h = \sum_{s=1}^{4} N_{h,s}, \quad p_{h,s} = \frac{n_{h,s}}{N_{h,s}}$$

- FSU means: In case of there being two hamlet groups (hgs) being sampled, as they are selected with simple random sampling without replacement (SRSWOR), we just take a simple mean of the two hamlet means. Rewriting N_h in (1) explicitly as $N_{j,h}$, an FSU mean is:

$$\mu_j = \sum_{h=1}^{2} w_{j,h} \mu_{j,h}$$

$$= \sum_{h=1}^{2} \frac{N_{j,h}}{\tilde{N}_j} \left(\frac{1}{N_{j,h}} \sum_{s=1}^{4} \frac{1}{P_{j,h,s}} \sum_{i=1}^{n_s} x_{h,s,i} \right) \qquad (2)$$

$$= \frac{1}{\tilde{N}_j} \sum_{h=1}^{2} \sum_{s=1}^{4} \frac{1}{P_{j,h,s}} \sum_{i=1}^{n_s} x_{j,h,s,i}$$

The weights are given as:

$$w_{j,h} = \frac{N_{j,h}}{\tilde{N}_j}, \quad \tilde{N}_j = \sum_{h=1}^{2} N_{j,h}, \quad p_{j,h,s} = \frac{n_{j,h,s}}{N_{j,h,s}}$$

To avoid cluttering notation, we assume that there is only one hamlet in a village, so FSU means are equal to hamlet means. We will therefore substitute h subscripts with j subscripts in (1) and ignore FSU mean formula (2).

- Stratum means: all sampled FSUs in first-stage stratum f is sampled with a probability proportional to size with replacement (PPSWR). If there are J FSUs selected, then:

$$\mu_f = \sum_{j=1}^{J_f} w_{f,j} \mu_{f,j}$$

For stratum f whose population (stratumsize) is N_f, the weights are given as:

$$w_{f,j} = \frac{\tilde{w}_{f,j}}{w_f}, \quad w_f = \sum_{j=1}^{J_f} \tilde{w}_{f,j}, \quad \tilde{w}_{f,j} = \frac{N_{f,j}}{N_j}$$

where we denote each FSU j's population size as $N_{f,j}$. The raw weight $\tilde{w}_{f,j}$ is divided with its sum, as its sum may fall short of adding up to one, which is typical in cluster sampling.

$$\mu_f = \sum_{j=1}^{J_f} \frac{N_{f,j}}{N_f} \frac{1}{w_f} \left(\frac{1}{N_{f,j}} \sum_{s=1}^{4} \frac{1}{p_{j,s}} \sum_{i=1}^{n_s} x_{j,s,i} \right)$$

$$= \frac{1}{N_f w_f} \sum_{j=1}^{J_f} \sum_{s=1}^{4} \frac{1}{p_{j,s}} \sum_{i=1}^{n_s} x_{j,s,i} \quad (3)$$

$$= \frac{1}{\tilde{N}_f} \sum_{j=1}^{J_f} \sum_{s=1}^{4} \frac{1}{p_{j,s}} \sum_{i=1}^{n_s} x_{j,s,i}$$

where

$$\tilde{N}_f = \sum_{j=1}^{J_f} N_{f,j}$$

(3) amounts to sums of each second-stage strata s in an FSU j is expanded with its sampling probability $p_{j,s}$, and total sum at the stratum level f is divided with the size of FSUs being sampled.

- District means: each state d is divided into one or more strata depending on the size.

$$\mu_d = \sum_{f=1}^{F_d} w_{d,f} \mu_{d,f}$$

The weights are given as:

$$w_{d,f} = \frac{N_{d,f}}{N_d}, \quad N_d = \sum_{f=1}^{F_d} N_{d,f}$$

So

$$\mu_d = \sum_{f=1}^{F_d} \frac{N_{d,f}}{N_d} \left(\frac{1}{\tilde{N}_{d,f}} \sum_{j=1}^{J_{d,f}} \sum_{s=1}^{4} \frac{1}{p_{j,s}} \sum_{i=1}^{n_s} x_{j,s,i} \right)$$

$$= \frac{1}{N_d} \sum_{f=1}^{F_d} \frac{1}{p_{d,f}} \sum_{j=1}^{J_{d,f_s}} \sum_{s=1}^{4} \frac{1}{p_{j,s}} \sum_{j=1}^{n_s} x_{j,s,i}$$

Where $p_{d,f}$ is sampling probability in stratum f:

$$p_{d,f} = \frac{\tilde{N}_{d,f}}{N_{d,f}}$$

- State means: each state t is divided into districts.

$$\mu_t = \sum_{d=1}^{D_t} w_{t,d} \mu_{t,d}$$

The weights are given as:

$$w_{t,d} = \frac{N_{t,d}}{N_t}, \quad N_t = \sum_{d=1}^{D_t} N_{t,d}$$

So

$$\mu_t = \sum_{d=1}^{D_t} \frac{N_{t,d}}{N_t} \left(\frac{1}{N_{t,d}} \sum_{f=1}^{F_d} \frac{1}{p_{t,d,f}} \sum_{j=1}^{J_{d,f}} \sum_{s=1}^{4} \frac{1}{p_{j,s}} \sum_{i=1}^{n_s} x_{j,s,i} \right)$$

$$= \frac{1}{N_t} \sum_{d=1}^{D_t} \sum_{f=1}^{F_d} \frac{1}{p_{t,d,f}} \sum_{j=1}^{J_{d,f}} \sum_{s=1}^{4} \frac{1}{p_{j,s}} \sum_{i=1}^{n_{ps}} x_{j,s,i}$$

The expansion factors $p_{j,s}$ and $p_{t,d,f}$ reflect that there was sampling at these stages, households and FSUs. All the other stage – that is, SSS, districts, states – are complete census in each of these levels, except for hamlet groups/sub-block stage where we have opted for simple averages as we are not provided with population size of each group.

Nonresponse

Nonresponse in the survey is treated as the following. Nonresponse occurs at the household level, hence, when there are $r_{j,s}$ nonresponses for SSS s, we have effective observations of size $\tilde{n}_{j,s} = n_{j,s} - r_{j,s}$. So the hamlet/village mean formula (1) becomes:

$$\mu_j = \sum_{s=1}^{4} w_{j,s} \tilde{\mu}_{j,s}$$

$$= \sum_{s=1}^{4} \frac{w_{j,s}}{\tilde{n}_{j,s}} \sum_{i=1}^{\tilde{n}_s} x_{j,s,i}$$

$$= \sum_{s=1}^{4} \frac{N_{j,s}}{N_j} \frac{1}{\tilde{n}_{j,s}} \sum_{i=1}^{\tilde{n}_s} x_{j,s,i} \qquad (1)$$

$$= \frac{1}{N_j} \sum_{s=1}^{4} \frac{1}{\tilde{p}_{j,s}} \sum_{i=1}^{n_s} x_{j,s,i}$$

We defined effective sampling probability $p_{j,s}$ as

$$\tilde{p}_{j,s} = \frac{\tilde{n}_{j,s}}{N_{j,s}}$$

This is justified if the nonresponse happens at random, or data is missing at random (MAR), because each statistic $\tilde{\mu}_{j,s}$ is consistent so long as deletion of observations is not correlated with its values $x_{j,s,i}$. This assumption may be too strong when the variable is related to health. For example, an ill individual may wish to withhold answers to the NSS interviewers. However, we have no other means to deal with this problem, and we consider it to be worthwhile to conduct investigation, rather than discarding the data altogether. Note also that all the state-level analysis also assumes MAR.

Table A4.1 Expenditure quintile

Class	Expenditure (Rs)
I	0–311
II	311–400
III	400–462
IV	462–610
V	610–

Table A4.2 All-India sample size of each variables

Variable	Number of observations
Latrine type	47,301
Water treated	47,301
Water source	47,296
Water treatment	10,078
Inpatient expenditure	20,534
Outpatient expenditure	19,149
Inpatient medicine expenditure	10,534
Outpatient medicine expenditure	47,301
Pregnant	6,578
Prenatal check	6,567
Birth	4,649
Postnatal check	4,615

5
The Implications of Migration and Schooling for Urban Educational Disparity: A Study of Delhi Slum Children

Yuko Tsujita

Introduction

It is widely acknowledged that there are disparities in education in India in terms of access to schools, the quality of schooling, and educational attainment, across spatial, social, economic, gender and ethnic lines, as well as in other respects. The lack or inadequacy of education is a serious issue, not only because education, particularly elementary education, is constitutionally and legally guaranteed as a fundamental right of children, but also because it is perceived to have a pivotal role in poverty alleviation. Much of the literature suggests that education has not only intrinsic value but also instrumental value in that it enhances the quality of life, helps people to earn more, improves their health and raises a person's awareness of their rights, etc. for themselves and the next generations. Disparities in the quality and quantity of education a child can receive, therefore, are likely to affect a wide range of opportunities in the course of one's life and, worse still, such disparities reinforce the socio-economic status quo for future generations.

A review of the literature in India, mainly dominated by analyses of rural children, suggests that poverty, or low incomes, adversely affects the quality and quantity of education one can receive (e.g., Drèze and Kingdon, 2001; Govinda, 2002). The direct and opportunity costs of education disproportionately burden children in lower-income households (Tilak, 2009). Much education research shows that school enrolment in India is closely associated with gender, caste and religion (e.g., Bhalotra and Zamora, 2010; Borooah and Iyer, 2005). Recent government education programmes have targeted girls, scheduled castes (SCs) and scheduled tribes (STs), in particular.

A recent and broad range of accelerated effort, including constitutional, legal, financial and political commitments, to achieve the universalization of elementary education show that attendance ratios for children aged six to 14 have significantly improved in rural areas (62.6 per cent in 1992/3 to 77.5 per cent in 2005/6), particularly for girls (52.2 per cent in 1992/3 to 73.4 per cent in 2005/6) (IIPS, 1998, 2007). Rural–urban disparity in school attendance has increasingly shrunk. However, this masks the fact that attendance rates in urban areas have stagnated, particularly among boys – that is, 85.3 per cent in 1992/3 to 85.4 per cent per cent in 2005/6 (*ibid.*), and they have even deteriorated in a large number of states. At the same time, it has become increasingly clear that there has been a *de facto* privatization of education. With the falling quality of education at government schools, many of those who can afford it turn to private schools. The emerging picture of elementary education in urban India implies that the opportunities and quality of education provided for disadvantaged people in urban areas seem to be much lower than for the affluent, and that such a disparity might have widened in recent years.

The total number of poor and undernourished individuals living in urban areas in developing countries has recently increased (Haddad *et al.*, 1999). Recent rapid urban population growth and a relative lack of attention to urban poverty have possibly exacerbated multidimensional deprivation, including deprivation regarding education. Likewise in Delhi, the capital city of India, with a large proportion of migrants from less developed regions of India, the headcount ratio of poverty marginally increased from 14.69 per cent in 1993/4 to 14.70 per cent in 2004/5. What is worse, the number of people living below the poverty line significantly increased from 1.6 to 2.3 million over the same period.[1] Urban poverty and slums often overlap and are mutually reinforcing (Mitra, 2003; Gupta *et al.*, 2009).[2] Although the population of the slums accounts for nearly a quarter of the total population in the metropolitan cities, the limited number of previous *ad hoc* attempts at slum studies in India has rarely been able to examine children's education.[3] Some limited research on slum children is basically confined to a school-based analysis (e.g., Tooley and Dixon, 2007) and to slum children in a few selected slums, as case studies (e.g., Aggarwal and Chugh, 2003; Banerji, 2000; Chugh, 2004; Husain, 2005; Jha and Jingram, 2005). As a result, the disparity within urban areas in terms of education is under-researched (Govinda, 2002).

There is often reluctance to regularize slums or informal settlements and provide basic infrastructure and services to such areas because slum dwellers are often regarded as temporary migrants (UN Millennium Project, 2005). Wratten (1995) has argued that the urban poor might be denied access to basic services because they lack political clout even if there has been some expansion in basic services and their quality has improved. The recent trend to outsource the provision of basic services to the private sector, under the name of private and public partnership, might prevent equitable accessibility and quality in services because certain groups lack economic clout, too. Slum dwellers might have no alternative but to share a limited and often degraded infrastructure or even to depend upon informal channels as a substitute for government services, including education.

Urban bias in infrastructure and service delivery is often emphasized in the existing literature. The argument about migration and education at a person's destination, therefore, indicates that migrants can enhance educational opportunities for children at their destination (e.g., UNDP, 2009). However, in India, the implication is that migrant children suffer when it comes to access to education at both ends, leaving rural schools and being unable to join or complete school at their urban destination (Chakrabarty, 2002; Smita, 2007). Nevertheless, studies on the impact of migration on children's education at their urban destination in India are limited to small-scale case studies (Govinda and Bandyopadhyay, 2008), despite the sizeable increase in migration, particularly rural-to-urban migration, in recent years (see Bhagat, 2009; Singh, 2009). The incidence of poverty among migrants tends to be lower than of that among non-migrants in the 1980s and 1990s (De Haan, 1997; Singh, 2009). Do these previous findings in urban areas in general still hold true for slum dwellers in recent years? With the recent worsening of urban poverty, and the stagnation or decline in schooling in urban areas, it is presumed that the large increase in rural-to-urban migration might have adversely affected school attendance among the lower echelons of the urban economy.

The purpose of this chapter, based on household surveys in Delhi, is to discuss the schooling of children aged five to 14 in slums, with a focus on whether, and if so how, migration affects slum children's school attendance. In this regard, the question of how migration has had an impact on the education of disadvantaged children in terms of caste, religion and gender is investigated. The analysis of this chapter contributes to filling a gap in the literature both on schooling in slum areas and on the impact of migration on children's education at destinations in urban India. This also enables me to extract policy implications that might improve school attendance in slum areas, viz. reduce disparities in school attendance in the light of stagnation or declining trends in school attendance in urban areas. The structure of the chapter is as follows. The second section will provide a brief context, describe the collection of data and detail certain characteristics among the slum children. The third section will present an overview of the attendance situation and types of school. The fourth section will analyze currently out-of-school children. The fifth section will argue that the costs of schooling act as constraints on school attendance. The sixth section will investigate the effects of migration on school attendance. A summary of the major findings is presented in the seventh section. The analytical methodology employed in this chapter is both qualitative, when describing schooling processes, and quantitative, in terms of generalizations about the findings.

Data collection and profile of children

Context and data collection

This study is based on data collected from a slum survey in Delhi, which was carried out by the author and two investigators from November 2007 to March 2008. The 2001 census showed that the slum population in Delhi was approximately 1.9 million, which is estimated to be 22.0 per cent of the total population (Government of Delhi, 2006). The total slum population Delhi is second only to those of Greater Mumbai slums. The literacy rate in Delhi slum areas (67.4 per cent), however, was far less than that in Greater Mumbai slum areas (83.0 per cent), and the proportion of the scheduled caste population in Delhi slums (26.1 per cent) was much larger than that of the Greater Mumbai slums (6.0 per cent) (Government of India, 2005a). There has been a sharp increase in the number of in-migrants to Delhi since the 1990s, in which nearly 70 per cent were from Uttar Pradesh and Bihar (Government of Delhi, 2006, 2009), two of the least developed and educationally backward states of India. Delhi slum dwellers, in sum, can be characterized by a concentration of the population among the lower socio-economic strata of society.

Three-stage stratified random sampling techniques were used. In the first stage, using the *Jhuggi-jhompadi* (notified slums) list prepared by the Municipal Corporation of Delhi, slum clusters with 200 or more households in all the nine revenue districts were considered. Since the sample was confined to a total of 50 clusters, due to time and financial constraints, the proportion of the number of clusters in each district to the total number was used as a weight in deciding the number of clusters to be selected from each district. Once the number of clusters to be selected from a particular district was estimated, specific clusters were randomly selected. In the second stage, the proportion of the number of households in each of the sample clusters to the total number of households in the 50 clusters was used as a weight in the distribution of 417 sample households across the city. In the final stage, after interviews with the *pradhan* (slum chief) or informal leaders in the selected clusters on the various socio-economic aspects of the slum and its dwellers, households were randomly selected for interviews. Of the 417 households, the number of children aged five to 14, which basically covers the age group covered by Delhi's compulsory education years, turned out to be 718 in 311 households: 417 boys and 301 girls.[4]

It should be noted that the slums surveyed are limited to notified slums. Because of this, the sample is unlikely to include the poorest of the poor, such as the homeless, the destitute and short-term, seasonal or new migrants.[5] It is also worth mentioning that only those who remain in the slums are covered in the survey, while some households might have moved out of the slums to better residential areas or returned to their place of origin. This is particularly relevant for non-migrants and long-term migrants.

Profile of slum children

The census of India indicated that a migration of more than five years constitutes a long-duration migration. Long-term migrants are perceived to have better access to information on job availability, government services and other matters concerning their livelihoods. Decisions on whether and to what extent a child is educated at elementary level are primarily taken by the household. By taking the duration of migration and the educational decision-making process into account, the total sample of children is divided into two groups on the basis that the highest age for the children in the sample is 14 years old. One group (153 children) consists of children in migrant households whose head of household migrated to Delhi within the last 14 years. The other group (557 children) consists of children in other households whose head of household migrated to Delhi more than 14 years ago or whose head of household is a non-migrant.

It is found that only 15.2 per cent of the total sample of children are second-generation Delhites whose head of household was born in Delhi, while most heads of household had migrated from less developed regions of India, such as Uttar Pradesh and Uttarakhand (47.9 per cent) and Bihar and Jharkhand (15.9 per cent).[6] The heads of households for children in migrant households tend to arrive in Delhi from a more limited number of regions of India, particularly from the above two states (41.8 per cent from Uttar Pradesh and Uttarakhand and 33.3 per cent from Bihar and Jharkhand) than the children in other households who have come from all over India and neighbouring countries. The overwhelming majority of the children's heads of households, regardless of their migration status and state of origin, have come from rural areas (87.2 per cent).[7] The reasons for migrating, according to the heads of household in the total sample, were mainly to look for work (57.7 per cent), followed by their being called by their family or to join their family (22.1 per cent). The head of a migrant household with children migrated more for economic reasons (75.2 per cent) than did their counterparts in other households (56.3 per cent). It is found that children in migrant households are more likely to possess a house and land at their parents' place of origin than children in other households (migrants only).[8] It seems that ties with their native place become increasingly weaker as migrants spend a longer time in Delhi.[9]

Table 5.1 shows the socio-economic characteristics of children in both categories. It shows that the composition of children in both migrant

Table 5.1 Socio-economic background of children

	Children in migrant HH	Children in other HH	Difference (other HH- migrant HH)
No. of children	153	557	
Mean household monthly income (Rs)	3,307.3	4,012.8	705.5***
	(1,402.1)	(2,071.6)	(177.7)
Mean household size (persons)	5.8	6.2	0.4***
	(1.3)	(1.5)	(0.1)
Children below the poverty line – households (%)	90.2	85.3	−4.9
Percentage of first-generation learners	43.1	41.3	−1.8
Percentage of females	42.5	40.8	−1.7
Percentage of Muslims	20.3	26.0	5.7
Percentage of scheduled castes/tribes	36.0	38.5	2.5
Percentage of other backward classes	36.6	33.2	−3.4

Notes: [1] The migration status of eight children is unknown.
[2] Standard deviations for the means are in parentheses.
[3] *** shows the difference to be significant at 1%, using a t test for mean household monthly income and mean household size, and a chi-squared test for the other variables.

and other households is similar in terms of gender, caste and religion. Moreover, the proportion of first-generation learners, which is defined as those for whom neither parent ever attended school, shows a similar ratio. It is, however, clear that the economic conditions of children in migrant households, such as their income levels and the incidence of poverty, defined as a percentage of the population below the poverty line in terms of monthly per capita expenditure, tend to be worse than those for children in other households.[10] The incidence of poverty among migrants in the lower echelons of the economy in this study contradicts previous findings on such incidence among migrants in general, the latter being less likely to be living below the poverty line (see, for example, De Haan, 1997; Singh, 2009).

School attendance and type

School attendance

The current attendance ratios at school, which refers to whether a child was attending any educational institution, including a pre-school or a non-formal school in the academic year 2007/8, is 72.0 per cent in the total sample.[11] This is much lower than the 90.3 per cent attendance ratio in Delhi in the National Sample Survey (NSS) in 2004/5 (Government of India, 2006: 84). It is often indicated in the education literature on India that girls and scheduled castes/tribes (SCs/STs) are less likely to attend schools. However, the attendance ratio for girls (74.6 per cent) is higher than that for boys (70.1 per cent). This follows a similar pattern to the attendance ratios across gender lines in the NSS Delhi as a whole – that is, 91.3 per cent for girls and 89.5 per cent for boys (ibid.: 82–3). Similarly, the attendance ratio for SC/STs, 73.1 per cent in the sample, is slightly higher than that for non-SC/STs, 70.6 per cent, though the attendance ratio for general castes (78.4 per cent) is significantly higher than that for other backward classes (OBCs) (64.5 per cent). The attendance ratio for Muslims, often regarded as an educationally backward community, is 64.7 per cent, which is significantly lower than that for non-Muslims – that is, mostly Hindu (74.4 per cent).[12] The gender, caste and religion patterns of attendance depict a different picture when migration status is taken into consideration.

The attendance ratio for children in migrant households is much lower (64.1 per cent) than that for children in other households (74.1 per cent). The difference is particularly sharp at the age of five: 15.0 per cent for children in migrant households and 50.0 per cent for

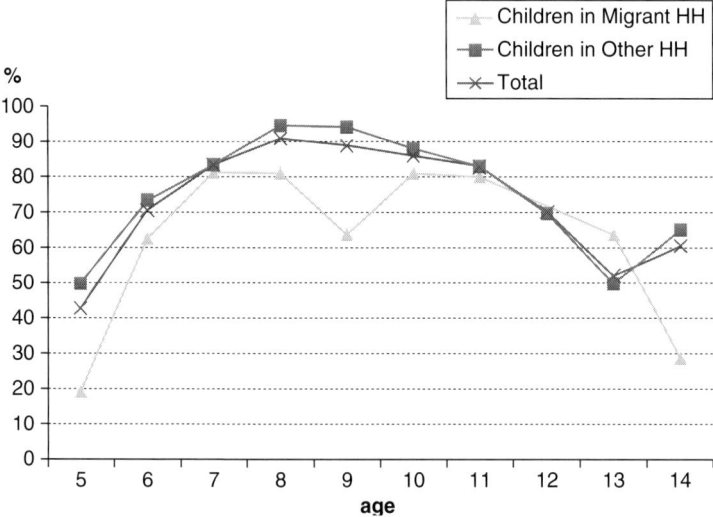

Figure 5.1 Attendance ratio (%)

children in other households (Figure 5.1). The issue of late admission will be discussed below.

Migration seems to have had a disproportionately negative impact on the schooling of girls and lower castes. The attendance ratios for girls, across migration status, are significantly different at 77.5 per cent for girls in other households when compared to 64.6 per cent for girls in migrant households, while the difference with respect to boys' attendance, across their migration status, is not significant. Similarly, the attendance ratio for SC/ST children in other households (78.0 per cent) is far higher than their counterparts in migrant households (52.7 per cent), while the attendance ratio for other caste groups is not significantly different, no matter what their migration status is. The relatively higher attendance for SCs/STs in other households affects the disadvantages Muslims suffer when it comes to school attendance for their children in the total sample and in the other households' sample, since SC/ST children are overwhelmingly non-Muslims; in other words, the attendance ratio for non-Muslims is different at 77.4 per cent for children in other households and 63.9 per cent for children in migrant households, while the attendance ratio for Muslims remains more or less the same, regardless of their migration status (64.5 per cent and 64.8 per cent for Muslims in migrant and other households, respectively).

Private schooling

It has become increasingly clear that the *de facto* privatization of education, reflected in the growing number of private schools and the increasing number of students enrolling there, has become prominent in a large number of states, particularly in urban areas. The NSS 2004/5 shows that 53.7 per cent of primary school and 50.1 per cent of upper primary school children attend private school in urban areas (Government of India, 2006: A49). As the quality of government school education has

Table 5.2 School learning facilities and environment in 2006/7

	Total	Delhi Government schools	Private aided schools	Private unaided schools
Total no. of schools[1]	4,742	2,923	310	1,450
Percentage of schools which have:				
A common toilet (%)	90.5	89.1	97.7***	91.5**
A girls' toilet (%)[2]	87.2	84.3	88.7	90.9***
A playground (%)	79.0	74.2	78.7	90.0***
No. of classrooms in good condition/ total no. of classrooms	0.853 (0.317)	0.786 (0.367)	0.917*** (0.254)	0.976*** (0.116)
No. of graduate teachers/total no. of teachers	0.831 (0.184)	0.797 (0.179)	0.868*** (0.131)	0.890*** (0.186)
Schools which have primary and/or upper primary classes only	3,093	2,061	120	912
Pupil–classroom ratio[3]	34.4 (31.9)	37.5 (36.2)	28.9** (23.3)	28.1*** (19.0)
Pupil–teacher ratio[3]	33.9 (19.9)	36.2 (21.5)	27.3*** (19.2)	29.5*** (14.5)

Notes: [1] Other types of school management (N = 59) are included in the total no. of schools.
[2] Girls' toilets are analyzed only for girls and co-educational schools.
[3] Since the number of students is available only from 1st to 8th class in the dataset, these two analyses are made for schools which have only primary and/or upper primary classes.
[4] The ***, ** and * mean differences from government schools are significant at 1%, 5% and 10%, respectively. Standard deviations appear in parentheses.
[5] For definitions of private aided and unaided schools, see note 13.
Source: District Information System for Education Delhi unit-level data.

deteriorated over the years, middle- and upper-class households tend to turn to private schooling for their children's education. Table 5.2 shows that school facilities and the learning environment in Delhi are generally more favourable in private schools than in government schools.[13] It has recently also been pointed out that the growth in private schools in slum areas is catering to the needs of low-income families, based on school surveys (Tooley and Dixon, 2007), though 'low income' is not defined. Based on their few slum surveys, Aggarwal and Chugh (2003), however, argue that enrolment in private schools is low, since very few families in slums could meet the expenses required. Table 5.3 shows that only 37 children (7.2 per cent of children currently going to school) attend private schools, including schools run by NGOs and religious charitable trusts. The children going to private school are concentrated in the lower classes and none of them studies beyond class six. Some parents in the household survey said that they used educational loans to finance private schooling and expressed uncertainty about until when they could afford to send their children to private school. The long-term

Table 5.3 The distribution of type of school attended by children who currently go to school

		Government school		Private school		Total	
		No.	Share (%)	No.	Share (%)	No.	Share (%)
Migration Status 1	Children in migrant households	91	92.9	7	7.1	98	100
	Children in other households	383	92.7	30	7.3	413	100
Migration Status 2	Household head – non-migrant children	68	85.0	12	15.0	80	100
	Household head – migrant children	412	94.3	25	5.7	437	100
Total		480	92.8	37	7.2	517	100

Notes: [1] Private school includes schools run by a religious-charity organizations or NGOs.
[2] The migration status 1 defined children in migrant households as those whose head of household migrated to Delhi within the last 14 years, while children in other households are those whose head of household migrated to Delhi more than 14 years ago or whose head of household is a non-migrant. The migration status 2 distinguishes between children on the basis of whether or not their head of household is a migrant.
[3] Chi-squared statistics for the independence of the distribution from migration status are 0.00 (n.s.) for migration status 1 and 8.76 (prob = 0.003) for migration status 2.

inability to pay prevents slum households from having continued access to private schools up to the higher classes.

The growing number of private schools around the slum areas pointed out by the school-based study does not mean that slum children can afford to attend these schools. Since the number of schools within the slums is limited due to constraints of space for schools, and slum areas in Delhi are often adjacent to other clusters of settlement, an explanation can be found in the fact that government housing and approved colonies for the middle class, in which children are more likely to attend private schools, exist near slums.[14] The association between the rise of private schools near slum areas and the absorption of slum children into such schools does not seem to be straightforward.

UNICEF's multiple state survey highlighted the bias against girls and lower castes in private schooling (Mehrotra, 2006). No such bias against gender is seen in the slum children sample, although there is a tendency towards caste bias.[15] Table 5.3 further suggests that a difference in terms of private schooling seems to be related to whether or not the head of household is a migrant rather than to a student's migration status as defined in this chapter. A similar pattern is found in which girls, general castes, SC/STs and non-Muslims in non-migrant households tend to attend private schools more than their counterparts in migrant households.[16] Although private schooling generally costs far more than government schooling, even some relatively lower-income households are not completely excluded from private schooling.[17] This implies that people on a very long-term stay in Delhi have more extensive information about schools and acquire the means to overcome admission criteria for their children. The exceptions are Muslims. It seems that Muslims are less likely to be in private school, no matter how many years they have lived in Delhi's slums.

On the whole, most children, regardless of their migration status, attend government school, even though some parents in slums have the notion that private schooling is somehow better than government schooling.[18] A hierarchical division of schools reflecting the socioeconomic status of the family has intensified over the years, therefore the kind of private school that even slum children can afford to study in is presumably unrecognized by the government since it charges lower fees but does not meet quality standards in terms of facilities and teachers. The survey found that only 54.2 per cent of class one to five children going to private school can write their own name accurately in any language, while 78.9 per cent of their counterparts in government school can do so. In fact, slum parents are not always happy with the quality of education in the private schools in that they had expected higher standards.[19] The analysis of the types of school attended also shows that government schools suffer from neglect because their students come from lower socio-economic strata and the schools themselves are provided with fewer resources. Although disparities in terms of the quality of the school are beyond the scope of this chapter, it is worthwhile emphasizing the importance of improvements in government education, since a large majority of children do not overcome barriers to admission criteria or parents cannot afford to send their children to private schools.[20]

Out-of-school children

The survey asked children currently out of school if they had ever attended an educational institution. If they had, they are regarded as 'drop-out' children. If not, they are regarded as 'never-attended' children.

Drop-out children

The proportion of children who have dropped out in the total is 6.5 per cent for children in migrant households and 8.6 per cent for children in other households. It might be worth noting that the drop-out rate from the gender-, caste- and religions-wise analysis shows no significant difference in the total sample. However, when the sample is confined to children in migrant households, the drop-out rate for SC/ST children (16.3 per cent) is much higher than that for general castes (2.9 per cent) and OBCs (0.0 per cent).

Age-wise, no student up to the age of eight has dropped out, regardless of their migration status, but after nine years old, the number of students dropping out gradually increases by age. This peaks at 14 years old, with as many as 57.1 per cent of children in migrant households and 26.1 per cent of children in other households of that age having withdrawn from school. Class-wise, among the children in other households who have dropped out of school, the number of children in terms of having completed class is largest in class five, followed by class four (Table 5.4). This implies that the transfer from primary to upper primary classes is not smooth. Drop-out children in migrant households have completed slightly lower classes, such as classes two, three and four, than children in other households. This can be related to the reasons for dropping out that are mentioned below.

The NSS 2004/5 for children aged five to 14 in urban areas indicated that children's income-generating activities are the most cited reason

Table 5.4 Completed years of education by students who dropped out

Class	No. of children in migrant HH		No. of children in other HH		Total	
	No.	%	No.	%	No.	%
1	0	0.0	2	4.3	2	3.4
2	3	30.0	3	6.4	7	12.1
3	3	30.0	7	14.9	10	17.2
4	2	20.0	10	21.3	12	20.7
5	1	10.0	17	36.2	18	31.0
6	1	10.0	4	8.5	5	8.6
7	0	0.0	2	4.3	2	3.4
8	0	0.0	1	2.1	1	1.7
9	0	0.0	1	2.1	1	1.7
Total	10	100.0	47	100.0	58	100.0

Note: The number of children in migrant and other HHs who dropped out is 10 and 48, respectively. The migration status of one class-2-completed-child is missing.

Table 5.5 Reasons for dropping out (multiple answers)

		All	Children in migrant HH	Children in other HH
1	Financial constraints	18	5	13
2	Own unwillingness	16	1	15
3	Own poor performance	9	1	8
4	Migration	4	2	2
5	Domestic chores	4	0	4
6	Household economic activities	3	0	3
7	Parents' negative perception	3	1	2
8	Lack of good company	3	0	3
9	Language problems	2	0	2
10	Family illness	2	0	2
11	Distance from school	1	0	1
12	Own bad behaviour	1	0	1
13	Disappeared and later found	1	0	1
14	NGO school was closed	1	0	1
15	No response	3	2	1

Notes: [1] The number of children in migrant and other HHs who dropped out is 10 and 48, respectively.
[2] 2 children in other households dropped out due to migration. They joined the household much later than the head of household, who migrated more than 14 years ago.

for a child dropping out, followed by parents' negative perceptions about education, and domestic chores (Government of India, 2006: A42). The reasons for slum children's drop-out rate, given in Table 5.5, seem to be slightly different. For children in migrant households, financial constraints are the dominant reason, while for children in other households, the child's own unwillingness is the reason most often given, closely followed by financial constraints, and the child's own poor performance. The issue of financial constraints is scattered across the classes, while a child's own unwillingness is concentrated among children moving from primary to upper primary classes (classes four, five and six), regardless of their migration status. Since the economic conditions of children in migrant households tend to be worse than those of children in other households, children in migrant households tend to have withdrawn from school a little earlier than children in other households.

One underlying reason for dropping out seems to be over-age. The ratio of over-age pupils is estimated to be 9.0 per cent and 14.3 per cent in 2007/8, at the primary and upper primary school levels respectively, in Delhi (Mehta, 2010: 97). Due to difficulties in obtaining the exact date of birth in the household survey,[21] Figure 5.2 estimated the minimum

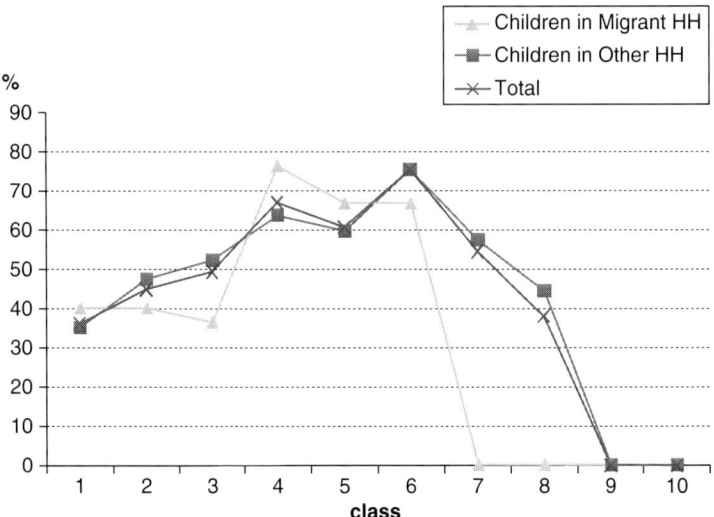

Figure 5.2 Estimated minimum percentage of over-age children (%)

Note: A pupil is regarded as overage if they have late being admitted and/or ever repeated the same class(es). For details, see note 22.

percentage of over-age children by class and migration status based on the parents' declaration of their children's age.[22] The estimated over-age rates for slum children are far higher (55.3 per cent for children in other households and 52.2 per cent for children in migrant households) than the average over-age rates in Delhi. With the admission to school being later than the official age of five and/or the repetition of the same class(es), the over-age problem is common, particularly in the earlier classes.[23] The rate goes up till class six and down towards the highest class, regardless of migration status. Estimated over-age rates after class seven are zero for children in migrant households, probably due to the fact that very few children survive till the higher classes. Even among children in other households, those surviving as higher-class students tend to be the standard age. This seems to be implicitly related to the prioritization of a student's academic performance as the underlying principle of schooling. The decision to drop out is sometimes taken *ex facto* by schools in a subtle way. Till recently academic performance has been one of the criteria for going up a class. What is more, all students in Delhi take the Central Board of Secondary Education exams at the end of classes ten and 12. Anecdotal evidence suggests that those who are less likely to pass are discouraged from turning up for the exam or from continuing school for some classes/grades before taking the exam, so that schools can raise their pass rate at the exams.[24] Academic performance appears to be a very important issue, even after the recent government 'no repetition up to class eight' policy was adopted.[25]

Never-attended children

The percentage of those who have never attended school is significantly different, at 29.4 per cent for children in migrant households and 17.2 per cent for children in other households. This is probably attributable to higher rates of 'never-attended' children among SC/STs (30.9 per cent) and OBCs (42.9 per cent) children in migrant households in comparison to general caste children in migrant households (11.4 per cent). The ratio of 'never-attended' children generally declines by age. Table 5.6 shows the reasons for never having attended school. While the NSS 2004/5 data for children aged five to 14 in urban areas shows that parents' negative perceptions about education are the most cited reason for 'never attended' (Government of India, 2006: A42), the main reason for slum children never attending school is financial constraints, regardless of a person's migration status. This is followed by parental misunderstandings about the admission age (under-age).

Table 5.6 Reasons for never-attended (multiple answers)

		All	Children in migrant HH	Children in other HH
1	Financial constraints	54	24	30
2	Under-age	30	9	21
3	Parental negative perception	17	1	16
4	Own unwillingness	7	4	3
5	Household economic activities	5	0	5
6	Domestic chores	3	1	2
7	Priority of boys' education	3	0	3
8	Distance from school	3	0	3
9	Disability	3	0	3
10	Death of a family member	1	1	0
11	No response	16	6	10

Note: The number of 'never-attended' children in migrant and other households is 45 and 96, respectively.

The second reason is particularly high (25 children) among five-year-olds, regardless of their parents' place of birth and migration status. This implies that not only migrant parents but also even some long-term migrants and non-migrants do not seem to understand the school age system properly.

Only 5.7 per cent of 'never-attended' children are engaged in paid work, while 10.3 per cent of children who have dropped out do paid work. In particular, 20.0 per cent of the children in migrant households who have dropped out are engaged in paid work. Moreover, no child below 11 years old works. It seems these findings support the argument that children who drop out then work (PROBE, 1999), rather than the conventional argument that children cannot go to school because of their work. This is also consistent with a previous study in slums (Banerji, 2000), which established that it is common for 'never-attended' children to be neither in school nor at work. The phenomenon of 'nowhere children' is particularly prevalent among children in migrant households.

It is observed that the ratio for 'never-attended' is much higher than that for those who have dropped out, regardless of a child's migration status. Although the existing literature tends to point out that dropping out is the main challenge to overcome in order to achieve universalization in elementary education, the magnitude of the 'never-attended' problem seems to be larger than the issue of drop-outs, particularly for children in migrant households in the lower echelons of urban society.

School costs

One of the main reasons for being out of school among slum children turns out to be financial constraints. School costs are often categorized into direct and indirect costs, such as foregoing earnings while attending school. This section, however, will restrict its focus to direct costs, particularly the costs for children going to a government school, since the overwhelming majority of children attend government schools.

It is widely acknowledged that government education is not free, even at elementary level. Children in migrant households are less likely to attend and, furthermore, the average monthly expenditure on education for children in migrant households going to government school (Rs 29.1) is much less than it is for children in other households (Rs 63.6). Table 5.7 shows the item-wise average monthly expenditure on education per child going to government school by migration status.

As a child is promoted to the upper classes, costs generally increase for three items: (1) uniforms and other clothing, (2) stationery, textbooks and books and (3) coaching/private tuition fees. First, uniforms are to be provided free for all students in government schools. However, not all children in government schools benefit from this scheme: 84.6 per cent

Table 5.7 Average monthly expenditure per reporting student going to government school, by item of expenditure (Rs)

Item of expenditure	Children in migrant HH			Children in other HH		
	Class I–V	Class VI–VIII	Class IX–X	Class I–V	Class VI–VIII	Class IX–X
Tuition fees and other required fees	5.0	10.3	10.0	7.0	14.5	21.7
Uniforms and other clothing	2.0	17.7	41.7	5.6	21.7	23.3
Stationery, textbooks and books	11.9	31.0	83.3	19.8	58.4	80.0
Meals, transportation and lodging	0.9	0.0	0.0	1.2	5.2	26.7
Coaching, private tuition fees	0.5	0.8	50.0	1.9	25.1	67.8
Parents' association fees	2.9	3.8	0.0	1.5	1.7	9.4
Others (e.g., school excursions)	0.0	0.0	0.0	0.1	0.1	0.8
Total	23.2	63.5	185.0	36.9	127.5	229.8
No. of observations	81	10	1	264	84	15

and 73.8 per cent of children going to government school in migrant and other households, respectively, were awarded uniforms for the last year either in kind or in cash. Children in migrant households are more likely to have benefited at primary school. However, they do not receive such benefits as often as children in other households above the upper primary school class (class six up). Second, textbooks are, as a matter of policy, to be provided free of charge to all students in government schools. It is again found, however, that 84.6 per cent and 73.8 per cent of government school children in migrant and other households are provided textbooks free. The pattern of benefits for textbooks, in relation to migration status and the benefiting classes, is also found with uniforms. Other than textbooks, the relatively high cost of stationery, particularly notebooks, pens, etc., when compared to other items is related to the local practice of rote memorization of what students learn at school, homework and/or tuition. Subsidies for stationery are only available for some students after sixth class. Parents' incomes must meet certain conditions, and last year's school attendance record, caste, religion and so on are also taken into consideration. Lastly, coaching and private tuition costs are high, particularly for children in other households. Only 5.5 per cent of children in migrant households who are going to government schools take coaching/private tuition, while 15.4 per cent of their counterparts in other migrant households do so. Class-wise, higher-class students tend to take private tuition, regardless of their migration status (66.7 per cent for the eighth class, 70.0 per cent for the ninth class and 50.0 per cent for the tenth class), and tuition costs increase as the class gets higher. Private tuition seems to be essential for achieving a better academic performance and probably those who take private tuition are likely to survive till the upper class. This may be viewed as a necessary cost to complete compulsory education in government schools.

So far, the emerging picture on education expenditure is that children in migrant households going to government schools are slightly more likely to benefit from incentive programmes, such as free uniforms and textbooks, and at the same time they are less likely to take private tuition, this being particularly so for the lower classes. It was also found in an analysis of income percentile-wise education costs, though not shown, that higher-income households tend to spend more on education. Therefore, children in migrant households seem to be at a disadvantage that is derived from their poorer economic condition than children in other households (Table 5.1).[26]

As Table 5.7 suggests, the difference in monthly education expenditure, across a student's migration status, is clear. What is also striking is the comparison between the same disadvantaged groups across migration status. For example, regardless of a student's migration status, the average monthly expenditure of Rs 58.1 for girls is slightly higher than Rs 55.6 for boys. However, the average expenditure for girls in migrant households is only Rs 27.4, which is significantly lower than the Rs 65.2 for girls in other households. Similarly, the average monthly expenditure of SC/STs of Rs 63.0 is slightly higher than that of the general castes (Rs 58.5) in the total sample, which masks the difference within SC/STs across a student's migration status: Rs 70.7 for children in other households and Rs 23.7 for children in migrant households.

An attempt has been made to explain the monthly education expenditure for a child going to a government school (the logarithm of each child's monthly educational expenditure) formally through the use of an OLS technique. The explanatory variables included continuous variables, such as the class/grade of the child and the monthly per capita household income. Household wealth is assumed to be an important determinant of household expenditure on education in India (e.g., Panchamukhi, 2005; Tilak, 2002). The other variables are dummy variables, including a tuition dummy (one for those who have taken tuition in the last year and zero otherwise), an incentive dummy (one for those who have benefited from any incentive programme in the last year and zero otherwise), an SC/ST dummy (one for SC/ST and zero otherwise) and an OBC dummy (one for OBC and zero otherwise) with 'general caste' as the comparison group, a girls dummy (one for female and zero for male) and a Muslim dummy (one for 'Muslim' and zero for other religions). A parental motivation dummy is also included: one for a university education or above as the parents' desired level of education for their child and zero otherwise – that is, the desired level of education is less than university level. The class/grade, income, tuition and motivation variables are expected to increase expenditure on education, whereas the other dummy variables are expected to reduce it. A regression analysis was carried out in the pooled sample and in two sub-samples: children in migrant households and children in other households, separately.

The results are given in Table 5.8. In all the regressions, class and tuition dummies are statistically significant with a positive coefficient. In the pooled sample, incentives tend to reduce education expenditure and household monthly per capita income tends to increase education expenditure. It is intriguing, when it comes to sub-samples, that the incentive dummy is statistically significant with a negative coefficient only for children in the migrant household, while monthly per capita household income is statistically significant with a positive coefficient

Table 5.8 OLS estimates of government school children's monthly educational expenditure

Dependent variable = monthly expenditure on education per child in logarithm	All	Children in migrant HH	Children in other HH
Constant	2.736***	3.186***	2.674***
	(0.153)	(0.210)	(0.185)
Monthly per capita HH income	0.000***	0.000	0.000***
	(0.000)	(0.024)	(0.000)
Tuition	0.756***	0.647***	0.704***
	(0.105)	(0.218)	(0.117)
Incentive	−0.220**	−0.556***	−0.158
	(0.096)	(0.137)	(0.111)
Class/grade	0.180***	0.100***	0.193***
	(0.017)	(0.028)	(0.193)
Motivation	0.050	0.143	0.011
	(0.067)	(0.096)	(0.011)
SC/ST	−0.020	−0.010	−0.066
	(0.080)	(0.124)	(0.066)
OBC	−0.008	−0.307***	0.051
	(0.081)	(0.113)	(0.096)
Muslim	0.053	0.051	0.001
	(0.080)	(0.117)	(0.093)
Girls	0.007	−0.025	−0.006
	(0.063)	(0.089)	(0.074)
No. of observations	476	91	379
Adjusted R^2	0.473	0.555	0.473

Note: Standard errors are in parentheses.***,** and * indicate significance at 1%, 5% and 10%.

only for the children in the other households. Parental motivation concerning their children's education has a positive effect on expenditure, though it is not statistically significant in any regression. Being a member of the lower castes (i.e., belonging to SC/STs and OBCs) has a generally negative effect on expenditure on education, except for OBC children in other households. Muslims tend to spend more than non-Muslims, even though the proportion of incentive beneficiaries in both categories is not significantly different. It is interesting that the coefficients and t-ratios of the Muslim dummy in any regression become much smaller, unlike SC/ST and OBC dummies, when the motivation dummy is excluded. This shows Muslims' willingness to pay is relatively easily mediated by parental motivation. The gender dummy in the pooled sample is positive, but it turns out to be negative in both sub-samples. When regressions were carried out separately for boys and girls in the migrant household sub-samples, incentives in the girls sub-sample tended to reduce expenditure to a larger extent than that for boys, while tuition in the boys' sub-sample tended to increase expenditure more than that for girls. It appears that in migrant households incentive programmes mitigate gender bias when it comes to expenditure on children. At the same time, tuition renders such a bias valid. Similar regressions have been carried out for both gender sub-samples in other households, separately. The percentage of girls in other households who benefited from an incentive is 85.4 per cent, which is higher than that for boys in other households (79.9 per cent). However, the girls' sub-sample shows that the incentive dummy still remains statistically not significant, though with a negative coefficient. It is noteworthy that the positive coefficient of monthly per capita household income is statistically significant and larger in the girls' sub-sample than that in the boys' sub-sample. This implies that expenditure borne by school-going girls in other households tends to be affected by a household's economic wealth, and, in fact, they are from slightly wealthier households than the boys in other households.

This section examined out-of-pocket expenditure for children going to government schools. Children in other households tend to spend more on education-related items than children in migrant households. Household economic wealth and tuition tend to increase education expenditure, particularly in children in other households, while incentives significantly reduce expenditure on education particularly for children in migrant households. It seems that caste and gender bias are expressed through expenditure on education, irrespective of migration status.

This analysis of expenditure covers only those who attend schools. The next section will find out what factors determine attendance, with a focus on migration.

Migration and school attendance

Framework of analysis
Review of literature
A large amount of the literature has investigated different aspects of school enrolment in rural India. The theory predicts that school enrolment increases when the net benefits of education outweigh its costs. School enrolment generally increases with parents' economic wealth and education level, particularly the mother's education level (Behrman

et al., 1999; Drèze and Kingdon, 2001; Duraisamy, 2002, to mention a few). Social inequalities stemming from caste, religion and gender tend to be reflected in lower schooling among the lower castes, Muslims and girls. The determinants for school enrolment studies evolved from paying attention to individual and household characteristics to a focus on the qualities of the schools involved (Drèze and Kingdon, 2001) and the broader effect of context in specific villages, such as land distribution and caste composition (Dostie and Jayaraman, 2006). Under favourable circumstances, the effects of disadvantage in terms of caste, religion, etc. are negligible (Borooah and Iyer, 2005; Husain, 2005). These excellent studies focus extensively on rural areas and enrolment, whereas the school attendance of children in urban slums is rarely examined. The neighbourhood school system is far more complex in urban areas and there are at least a few government schools that the same slum's children attend.[27] It is difficult to match a slum and attendance at any particular school, and the existing literature suggests that individual and household characteristics are better-performing variables than characteristics concerning a school or the area where people live, this section, therefore, will focus on individual and household characteristics to investigate the effect of migration on school attendance.

It is pointed out in the existing literature in India that there are two main obstacles to attending schools, particularly in relation to migrant children in slums. First, migrants tend occasionally to make long visits to their place of origin. These affect school attendance negatively (Jha and Jingram, 2005; Aggarwal and Chugh, 2003; Chugh, 2004). Table 5.9 shows that 30.7 per cent of children in migrant households have visited their parental place of origin in the last year, while this is so for only 14.9 per cent of children in other households. The average number of visit days is 27.2 days among children in migrant households who have visited their parents' place of origin in the last one year, with the longest duration being a sojourn of 27.3 days on average by children in migrant households who are currently attending school. It seems from the household survey that quite a few households tried to avoid visiting their place of origin for a long time as much as possible during school terms. A visit to one's place of origin would not be a major obstacle in elementary schooling.

Second, it is indicated that migrant children also face difficulties in understanding the language used at school, since it tends to be different from their mother tongue (Jha and Jingram, 2005). Hindi is the medium of instruction at school for all school-going children in the sample, regardless of school type and class. More than 90 per cent of children,

Table 5.9 Migration-related issues

	Total no. of children	No. of those who have visited their parental place of origin in the last one year	Average no. of visit days among children who have visited their parental place of origin in the last one year	Using Hindi at home	No of children who have a birth certificate
Children in migrant HH	153	47 (30.7)	27.2	138 (90.2)	25 (16.3)
Children in other HH	557	83 (14.9)	21.0	510 (91.9)	217 (39.0)
Total	710	130 (22.4)	23.3	648 (91.5)	242 (34.1)

Note: The total number of children in other HH who answered the question of language at home is 555. Figures in parentheses show the percentage of children in each category.

regardless of migration status, use Hindi at home (Table 5.9). This is attributable to the fact that the migrants are mainly from Uttar Pradesh/ Uttarakhand, Bihar/Jharkhand or other northern states, where Hindi is largely used at home or is an understandable language.

As indicated in the section on school attendance above, the attendance ratio at the age of five among children in migrant households is much lower than that for children in other households. One possible and critical reason for late admission is that parents face delays in obtaining a birth certificate or an alternative proof of identification (i.e., an affidavit), which was mandatory at the time of the survey for admission to any government school in Delhi,[28] although this sounds a flimsy reason for turning down an application.[29] In fact, only 16.3 per cent of children in migrant households have a birth certificate (Table 5.9), which is particularly low at 2.2 per cent for 'never-attended' children in migrant households. Children who were born in Uttar Pradesh/Uttarakhand and Bihar/Jharkhand are less likely to have a birth certificate than children born in Delhi.[30] This reflects the fact that migrant children were born largely in their parents' village where there was weak enforcement of the rule to register a birth with the civil authorities.[31]

It has been shown in this chapter that the out-of-school problem is closely linked to 'never-attended' children rather than to children who drop out. Recent education research in India implies that pre-school intervention, such as nutrition, health and basic learning, plays an important role in the life-cycle of children (Ramachandran *et al.*, 2009). Pre-school programmes would raise parents' awareness about children's formal schooling at the standard age and prepare children for formal schooling. Table 5.10 shows to what extent slum children have been involved in three pre-schooling health and educational intervention programmes. Compared to health services, including a course of polio drops and a whole set of immunization shots, attendance at nursery classes or *Anganwadi* (pre-primary school) under the Government of India's Integrated Child Development Services is much lower, although 60.9 per cent of children live in slums where at least one *Anganwadi* exists. In any cases, children in migrant households have less access to any pre-school programme than children in other households.

Estimation

To investigate the effects of migration and other related issues on school attendance, a logit analysis has been carried out. The following two dependent variables have been examined. One is the initial attendance of children, given value one if a child has ever attended school (i.e., 'drop-out' and 'currently attending') and zero otherwise ('never-attended'). The other is current attendance, given value one if a child is 'currently attending' and zero otherwise ('drop-out' and 'never-attended'). The unit of observation is the individual child. The effects of migration have been

Table 5.10 Participation in pre-schooling programmes

	Children in migrant HH		Children in other HH	
	Total no. of children who answered	Total no. of children who have completed the programme	Total no. of children who answered	Total no. of children who have completed the programme
Whole set of immunization shots	143	64 (44.8)	551	294 (53.4)
Course of polio drops	143	115 (80.4)	553	493 (89.2)
Attendance at *Anganwadi* or nursery classes	143	17 (11.9)	535	116 (21.7)

Note: Parentheses show the proportion of children to the total in each migrant status.

examined in four ways: (1) duration of migration – a migration dummy (one if the head of household migrated to Delhi within the last 14 years and zero otherwise); (2) the nexus of migration and disadvantaged groups – a migrant girls dummy (one for girls in migrant households and zero otherwise), a migrant lower castes dummy (one for SCs, STs or OBCs in migrant households and zero otherwise) and a migrant Muslim dummy (one for Muslims in migrant households and zero otherwise); (3) the head of household's place of origin with the head of household born in Delhi as the comparison group, regardless of the year of migration – (a) a less developed state dummy (one if the head of household is from a less developed state (so-called BIMARU states), including Uttar Pradesh/Uttarakhand, Bihar/Jharkhand, Madhya Pradesh/Chhattisgarh and Rajasthan, and zero otherwise), and (b) an 'other states' dummy (one if the head of household is from the rest of India and neighbouring countries and zero otherwise). This simultaneously enables me to compare the head of household's migration status – that is, migrants and non-migrants. Finally, I have looked at (4) a child's place of birth – a 'born in Delhi' dummy (one if a child was born in Delhi, irrespective of the head of household's migration status and zero otherwise). Also, all the available explanatory variables, including individual and household characteristics, and the migration-related issues based on the literature review in the previous section, have been considered so as to avoid bias from omitted variables, since the main purpose is to exam whether, and how, migration has affected children's schooling.

Results and discussion

The results are given in Table 5.11. As expected, household wealth has a significant positive effect on attendance, though the marginal effects are very small. Father's educational level also has a significant positive effect on attendance. A slightly surprising result is that the mother's education, in contrast to evidence from the existing literature suggesting that the mother's education plays a significant role in children's education, has no significant positive effect. At the same time, it appears that parents' higher motivation concerning their children's education plays a significant role in children's schooling. The coefficients of age turn out to be statistically significant with a positive sign in initial attendance. In other words, the probability of 'never-attended' decreases by age. It might be worth mentioning that access to schools might be affected by the slum's overall standard of living. However, none of the district and area (trans-Yamna area) dummies, although

Table 5.11 Logistic regression of the effects of migration on school attendance

Variables	Initial attendance		Current attendance	
	Dependent variable (1 for currently attending and dropping out and 0 for never-attended)		Dependent variable (1 for currently attending and 0 for dropping out and never-attended)	
	Coefficients	Marginal effect	Coefficients	Marginal effect
Age	0.357***	0.034***	0.044	0.007
	(0.051)	(0.005)	(0.039)	(0.006)
Monthly per capita	0.001***	0.000***	0.001***	0.000***
household income	(0.001)	(0.000)	(0.000)	(0.000)
Migration-related issues:				
Birth certificate	0.035	0.003	–0.154	–0.026
(having a birth certificate = 1)	(0.333)	(0.031)	(0.275)	(0.046)
No. of visit days to	–0.001	–0.000	0.008	0.001
place of origin	(0.013)	(0.001)	(0.012)	(0.002)
Hindi (using Hindi at	0.700*	0.084	0.535	0.099
home = 1)	(0.421)	(0.061)	(0.370)	(0.076)
Immunization	1.303***	0.130***	1.331***	0.220***
(completed the set of immunization shots and polio drops = 1)	(0.288)	(0.031)	(0.238)	(0.039)
Pre-schooling	0.295	0.026	0.477*	0.072*
(if ever attended pre-school = 1)	(0.323)	(0.027)	(0.285)	(0.039)
Parental education and motivation:				
Father's completed	0.136***	0.013***	0.123***	0.020***
years of schooling	(0.044)	(0.004)	(0.037)	(0.006)
Mother's education	0.139	0.014	0.074	0.012
dummy (illiterate = 1)	(0.382)	(0.039)	(0.333)	(0.056)
Motivation (university	0.937***	0.078***	1.318***	0.184***
and above as parents' desired level of education for a child = 1)	(0.336)	(0.025)	(0.293)	(0.033)
Underprivileged dummies:				
Girls	0.628**	0.058**	0.441*	0.071*
	(0.292)	(0.026)	(0.244)	(0.038)

(*continued*)

Table 5.11 Continued

Variables	Initial attendance		Current attendance	
	Dependent variable (1 for currently attending and dropping out and 0 for never-attended)		Dependent variable (1 for currently attending and 0 for dropping out and never-attended)	
	Coefficients	Marginal effect	Coefficients	Marginal effect
Low caste	0.166	0.016	−0.015	−0.002
	(0.329)	(0.033)	(0.278)	(0.045)
Muslim	−0.087	−0.008	−0.055	−0.009
	(0.340)	(0.034)	(0.287)	(0.048)
Migration dummies:				
Children in migrant HH	0.663	0.055	0.511	0.076
	(0.792)	(0.056)	(0.703)	(0.095)
Low caste in migrant HH	−0.667	−0.076	−0.866	−0.165
	(0.762)	(0.103)	(0.682)	(0.147)
Girls in migrant HH	−0.033	−0.003	−0.164	−0.028
	(0.555)	(0.054)	(0.497)	(0.088)
Muslim in migrant HH	−0.442	−0.049	0.350	0.052
	(0.665)	(0.086)	(0.610)	(0.081)
HH head migrated from BIMARU	−0.586	−0.051	−0.053	−0.009
	(0.425)	(0.033)	(0.338)	(0.054)
HH head migrated from other states	−0.773	−0.092	0.099	0.016
	(0.507)	(0.073)	(0.425)	(0.066)
Child born in Delhi	0.746**	0.087*	0.479	0.086
	(0.348)	(0.049)	(0.304)	(0.060)
Constant	−4.925***		−2.555	
	(1.024)		(0.847)	
No. of observations	633		633	
LR Chi-square	165.11		161.26	
Pseudo R^2	0.266		0.216	

Note: Standard errors are in parentheses. ***, ** and * indicate significance at 1%, 5% and 10%, respectively. 'Marginal effects were calculated using the mean values for the continuous explanatory variables, while the binary variables were set to zero.

not shown due to space constraints, has a statistically significant effect on attendance.

A longer visit to the parents' place of origin has a negative effect on initial attendance, though it is not statistically significant. Speaking Hindi at home has a significant positive effect on initial attendance, while immunization has a significant positive effect both on initial and current attendance. Most likely, this reflects the fact that parents who complete their children's immunization programme prior to formal schooling tend to be aware of the importance of education, and possibly children are less likely to suffer from communicable diseases and to be absent from school on health grounds. It is intriguing that obtaining a birth certificate has a positive impact on initial attendance, though it is not statistically significant. It seems to be important to possess it at the time of admission. Pre-school education also has a positive coefficient on attendance, and it is statistically significant on current attendance in particular. This can be interpreted as meaning that pre-school education plays an important role in formal schooling and at the same time it does not currently promote a smooth transition to formal schooling.

Bias against girls is not expressed in school attendance. In fact, girls are more likely to attend schools than boys. As incentive programmes tend to reduce education expenditure, incentives might be the reason why girls in general are more likely to attend schools. A lower-caste affiliation has a negative effect on current attendance, and religion (i.e. being a Muslim) has a negative effect on both initial and current attendance, though it is not statistically significant. On the one hand, it seems that lower-caste children are not so disadvantaged with regard to being admitted to school; however, they are less likely to remain in school than the general castes. On the other hand, Muslims are less likely to start and continue formal schooling. It has recently become widely acknowledged that the socio-economic conditions of Muslims have deteriorated over the years. As was found elsewhere in this chapter, non-migrant households, with the exception of Muslims, have advantages regarding attendance in private schools. Disadvantages in terms of attendance remain even after controlling for parents' motivation and there seem to be structural obstacles for Muslims when it comes to educating their children.

The migration dummy has a positive coefficient, though not significant, on attendance; however, the coefficients for all socially underprivileged migrant dummies turn out to be negative except for Muslim children in migrant households in terms of current attendance. Girls, lower castes and Muslims in migrant households are disadvantaged when it comes to initial attendance. Since the coefficients for migrant girls are negative in terms of current attendance, though not statistically significant, it seems that they, in comparison to boys in migrant households, face not only barriers regarding entry but also obstacles regarding their continuing in school. This also implies that gender bias seems to lie in whether or not they are migrants. As for children in households whose head is from a less developed region, the coefficients for such dummies are negative in both initial and current attendance. This result also indicates that children in non-migrant households are more likely to attend schools than children in households whose head is from a less developed region. However, children in non-migrant households are more likely to drop out than children in households whose head is from a non-less developed region. This might reflect the fact that Muslims account for a relatively higher proportion of non-migrant households (38.0 per cent) than that of the total sample (24.8 per cent). At the same time, it is clear that children who were born in Delhi, regardless of the head of household's migration status, are more likely to attend school, particularly initially, which is consistent with the fact that they are more likely to have a birth certificate and have completed the immunization programmes.

Conclusions

This chapter shows how migration affects school attendance and how migration and social disadvantage in terms of schooling are interrelated. Overall attendance in slums is much lower than that of Delhi as a whole. The attendance ratio is lower for children in migrant households than for children in other households. This mainly reflects a low attendance ratio for lower castes and females. In spite of the remarkable growth in private schools in urban areas, slum children largely depend upon government schools, though the proportion of these children in non-migrant households is slightly higher than that of children in migrant households. The importance of improving government schools for slum dwellers or disadvantaged people in the cities is not diminishing, since most slum dwellers do not overcome barriers to admission or cannot afford to send their children to private schools.

Among the out-of-school children, those who have never attended school by far outnumber those who drop out. There are quite a few children who are neither at school nor at work. This is especially the case for children in migrant households.

One of the major 'out-of-school' reasons is a lack of finance. Children in other households tend to spend more on education than children in migrant households. It has been pointed out that a household's economic wealth and private tuition fees tend to increase expenditure on education in children in other households, while incentives significantly reduce expenditure on education for children in migrant households. It seems that caste and gender bias are clearly expressed through expenditure on education, regardless of migration status. The implication is that the delivery of free uniforms and textbooks needs to be improved, since incentives play a significant role in lowering expenditure on education. It seems that private tuition is essential for children if they are to achieve a better academic performance and therefore continue their schooling but at the same time private tuition costs tend to increase expenditure on education significantly. Remedial classes in or outside school might be considered.

On the whole, migration tends adversely to affect school attendance. In particular, underprivileged children, in terms of gender, caste and religion, in migrant households are disadvantaged, especially regarding initial attendance. Apart from caste or gender attributes, migrant children in disadvantaged categories face further and greater hurdles when it comes to admission to school because of a lack of pre-school preparation, such as the obtaining of a birth certificate, the completion of an immunization shot, a polio drop course and pre-primary school. Universal elementary education or the reduction of disparities in school attendance in urban areas in a situation where urban poverty has recently been getting worse and there has been a sizeable increase in rural-to-urban migration can be achieved by taking urban-specific problems into account and by tackling education alongside other sectors such as health. The most important underlying implication seems to be raising awareness for parents with regard to schooling.

Acknowledgements

I would like to thank Rajan and Purushottam, who carried out the household survey. Shreekant Jha and Rajnish Kumar assisted me with data entry, processing and cleaning. I am also grateful to Kuldeep Singh, Satendra Kumar, Manoj Kumar and N. S. Kumar, who helped me in various stages of the fieldwork. Thanks also go to Arup Mitra for fruitful discussions. Last, but not least, I am deeply indebted to the slum dwellers who cooperated. Any errors are, however, my sole responsibility.

Notes

1. The Planning Commission (Government of India, 2009) assessed the methodology for an estimation of the degree of poverty in India, which turns out to be a 13.1 per cent headcount poverty ratio with 2.0 million people living below the poverty line in Delhi in 2004/5.

2. The Slum Areas (Improvement and Clearance) Act, 1956, defined slum areas on the basis of their being unfit for human habitation, cramped conditions, the faulty arrangement of streets, a lack of ventilation, light or sanitation facilities, or any combination of these factors, which are detrimental to safety, health or morals.
3. The NSS 58th round investigated the conditions of urban slums as a whole and the same round separately conducted a small sample survey round, with 217 households in slums and squats in Delhi, which is much smaller than my household survey. No question is asked about education (see Government of India, 2003, 2005b).
4. The structure of school education in Delhi is five-year primary, three-year upper primary, two-year secondary and two-year higher secondary within a national framework of a ten-year education. The age of admission is officially five years old, which means children should be five years old at the middle of the school year (at the end of September). According to the Constitution of India, and the Right of Children to Free and Compulsory Education Act, 2009, education is guaranteed up to 14 years old; this study, therefore, includes those who are 14 years old.
5. It is reported that the notified slums have better access to a wide range of basic facilities, including drinking water, electricity, roads (within the slums and in the approach to slums), latrines, drainage, underground sewage, garbage collection and so on than the non-notified slums, which have more than 20 households (Government of India, 2003).
6. In 2000, Uttar Pradesh and Bihar were each bifurcated into two states.
7. The proportions of heads of households who migrated from rural areas for children in migrant and other households (excluding non-migrants) are 84.3 per cent and 88.2 per cent, respectively. The incidence of poverty is more or less the same regarding the place of origin of migrant household heads, irrespective of their migration status: 84.8 per cent for urban-to-Delhi migrants and 86.3 per cent for rural-to-Delhi migrants.
8. The proportion of children in migrant households who have a house at their parent's place of origin is 69 per cent, which is significantly higher than that for children in other households, excluding non-migrants (47.1 per cent). Similarly, the proportion of children who have land at their parent's place of origin for children in migrant and other households, excluding non-migrants, is 26.8 per cent and 23.4 per cent, respectively.
9. The average number of years the head of household has spent in Delhi is 9.6 years for children in the migrant household group, which is naturally shorter than the 24.3 years for children in other households, excluding non-migrants.
10. The poverty line of Rs 56.64 per capita per month, on 1973/4 prices, has been adjusted to take account of price changes using the consumer price index for Delhi to update it for the year 2007/8, as per Planning Commission (Government of India, 1993). See also note 1.
11. It is noted that attendance is different from enrolment. The attendance status of children is cross-checked with the number of days a student was absent from school in the last term.
12. Out of a total of 540 non-Muslim children, 528 children (97.8 per cent) are Hindu.

13. Private schools in India are disaggregated into aided and unaided schools. The former are privately managed but a regular maintenance grant, mainly for teachers' salaries, is granted by the government, while the latter are managed and financed completely by private parties. Unaided schools are further classified into recognized and unrecognized schools, although all private schools are expected to be under the recognition, instruction and inspection of the state government.
14. The *Pradhans* said that there are only 12 government schools, one religious charity-based school and four NGO schools within the 50 surveyed slum areas, while there are 259 government schools and 29 private schools outside the slum areas but which slum children attend.
15. The percentage of private school attendance to total attendance, across gender lines, is 7.7 per cent for boys and 6.3 per cent for girls. Caste-wise, the percentages are 13.1 per cent for the general castes, 5.0 per cent for SC/STs and 4.5 per cent for OBCs.
16. The attendance ratios for private schools are, for example, 4.8 per cent for girls whose head of household is a migrant and 15.6 per cent for girls whose head of household is a non-migrant.
17. Except for the lowest income percentile group, almost every group has a child going to a private primary school. The average monthly education expenditure per child at the primary level (classes one to five) is Rs 33.6 for government schools, which is significantly lower than the Rs. 96.1 for private schools.
18. For example, 'Delhi's government schools are not good and the situation is getting worse. That is why I send my son to private school' (Kishan (alias), father of a 13-year-old) and 'It matters whether a child attends a government or private school' (Mohammad Iqbal (alias), father of one private- and one government-school-going child).
19. For example, Rajiv Kumar (alias), father of three children going to private school, revealed, 'Children have been admitted to a private school, but that school is not good for study. We are now planning to send them to another religious charity school.'
20. The Supreme Court ordered the Delhi government in 2004 to investigate whether private schools had complied with contracts to provide free education for the poor as a condition of their being allotted school land at a concessionary rate (Juneja, 2005), and it seems the private schools are slow to comply with their original contracts (Mallica, 2005). This seems to be a symptom of the Herculean task involved in meeting the mandatory provision of a 25 per cent reservation for disadvantaged children in private schools as stipulated in the Right of Children to Free and Compulsory Education Act, 2009.
21. The exact date of birth was not asked in the survey, since it took a long time or was usually impossible to find in the pre-test rounds of the survey. Moreover, it is not possible to cross-check the date of birth, due to the unavailability of an original birth certificate in most households.
22. Overage is estimated as follows. If a pupil has been late being admitted to school at class one and/or ever repeated the same classes, they are regarded as an overage child. Since the calculation is not based on the exact date of birth (see note 21), these figures can be regarded as an estimated minimum percentage of overage children.

23. 7.9 per cent of currently attending children have 'repeated', while 25.4 per cent of drop-out children have 'repeated' the same grade.
24. This point was made by the focus group discussion in a non-surveyed slum in November 2008.
25. The survey was carried out before the introduction of this policy in 2008/9. In this policy, any student who attends more than 75 per cent of school days and takes the final exam is entitled to go to the next higher class.
26. Education accounted for 8.0 per cent of monthly household expenditure in urban Delhi in 2006/7 (Government of India, 2008), while the proportion of education expenditure to total expenditure per month in this sample turned out to be 2.5 per cent for children in migrant households and 5.0 per cent for children in other households.
27. There are 2.8 primary and 2.6 upper primary schools on average, which children attend from the same slum, based on the interviews with the *Pradhans*.
28. Apart from fundamental reasons such as financial constraints, other possible administrative reasons for late admission can be related to the short window of time in which one can apply for admission. If parents are unaware, unavailable or unable to apply to schools during a specific and very short period of time, children in slum areas are less likely to be admitted later. This point was made by some households.
29. For example, Sunita (alias), mother of three school-age children in the household survey, said, 'My children are not in school because we cannot prove their date of birth. My brother, after gruelling months, succeeded in getting a signature from a Member of the Legislative Assembly in our constituency so as to admit the children to school, which later turned out to be invalid for school admission.'
30. The ratio of those who have a birth certificate is 57.6 per cent for children born in Delhi, 20.8 per cent for children born in Uttar Pradesh/Uttarkhand and 12.0 per cent for children born in Bihar/Jharkhand.
31. The NFHS in 2005–6 (IIPS, 2008a, 2008b, 2009) reported the proportions of under-five-year-old children who had a birth certificate as 55.1 per cent in Delhi, 5.0 per cent in Uttar Pradesh and 2.8 per cent in Bihar.

References

Aggarwal, Y. P. and Sunita Chugh (2003) *Learning Achievement of Slum Children in Delhi*, Occasional Paper 34, New Delhi: National Institute of Educational Planning and Administration.

Banerji, Rukmini (2000) 'Poverty and Primary Schooling: Filed Studies from Mumbai and Delhi', *Economic and Political Weekly*, 35 (10), pp. 795–802.

Behrman, Jere R., Andrew D. Foster, Mark R. Rsenzweig and Prem Vashishtha (1999) 'Women's Schooling, Home Teaching, and Economic Growth', *Journal of Political Economy*, 107 (4), pp. 682–714.

Bhagat, Ram B. (2009) 'Internal Migration in India: Are the Underclass More Mobile?', paper presented at the 26th IUSSP General Population Conference in Marrakech.

Bhalotra, Sonia and Bernarda Zamora (2010) 'Social Divisions in Education in India', in Rakesh Basant and Abusaleh Shariff (eds), *Oxford Handbook of Muslims: Empirical and Policy Perspectives*, New Delhi: Oxford University Press.

Borooah, Vani K. and Sriya Iyer (2005) 'Vidya, Veda and Barna: The Influence of Religion and Caste on Education in Rural India', *Journal of Development Studies*, 41 (8), pp. 1369–404.

"Chakrabarty, V. (2002) 'Education of Urban Disadvantaged Children', in R. Govinda (ed.), *India Education Report*, New Delhi: Oxford University Press.

Chugh, Sunita (2004) *Why Children Dropout? A Case Study of a Metropolitan Slum*, New Delhi: Bookwell.

De Haan, Arjan (1997) 'Rural-Urban Migration and Poverty: The Case of India', *IDS Bulletin*, 28 (2), pp. 35–47.

Dostie, Benoit and Rajshri Jayaraman (2006) 'Determinants of School Enrollment in Indian Villages', *Economic Development and Cultural Change*, 2 (January), pp. 405–21.

Drèze, Jean and Geeta Gandhi Kingdon (2001) 'School Participation in Rural India', *Review of Development Economics*, 5 (1), pp. 1–24.

Duraisamy, Malathy (2002) *Child Schooling and Child Work in Rural India*, Working Paper series No. 84, New Delhi: National Council of Applied Economic Research.

Government of Delhi (2006) *Human Development Report: Partnership for Progress*, New Delhi: Oxford University Press.

_____ (2009) *Economic Survey of Delhi 2008/09*, New Delhi: Government of NCT Delhi.

Government of India (1993) *Report of the Expert Group on Estimation of Proportion and Number of Poor*, New Delhi: Planning Commission.

_____ (2003) *Condition of Urban Slums 2002: Salient Features*, NSS 58th Round (July 2002–December 2002), New Delhi: National Sample Survey Organization.

_____ (2005a) Slum Population (640 cities and towns Reporting Slums) Vol. I, Census of India 2001, Series 1. Office of Registrar General and Census Commissioner, India, Department of Publication.

_____ (2005b) *Housing Condition in India: Household Amenities and Other Characteristic*, NSS 58th Round 8 (July 2002–December 2002), New Delhi: National Sample Survey Organization.

_____ (2006) *Status of Education and Vocational Training in India, NSS 61st Round (July 2004–2005)*, New Delhi National Sample Survey Organization.

_____ (2008) *Household Consumer Expenditure in India, 2006–07*, NSS 63rd Round (July 2006–June 2007), New Delhi: National Sample Survey Organization.

_____ (2009) *Report of the Expert Group to Review the Methodology for Estimation of Poverty*, November, Planning Commission.

Govinda, R. (ed.) (2002) *India Education Report*, New Delhi: Oxford University Press.

_____ and Madhumita Bandyopadhyay (2008) *Access to Elementary Education in India Country Analytical Review*, Consortium for Research on Educational Access, Transitions and Equity.

Gupta, Kamla, Fred Arnold and H. Lhungdim (2009) *National Family Health Survey (NFHS-3) 2005/06 Health and Living Conditions in Eight Indian Cities*, Mumbai: IIPS.

Haddad, L., M. T. Ruel and J. L. Barrett (1999) 'Are Urban Poverty and Undernutrition Growing? Some Newly Assembled Evidence', *World Development*, 27 (11), pp. 1891–904.

Husain, Zakir (2005) 'Analysing Demand for Primary Education: Muslim Slum Dwellers of Kolkata', *Economic and Political Weekly*, 40 (2), pp. 137–47.

International Institute for Population Sciences (IIPS) (1998) *National Family Health Survey (NFHS-2) 1998/99 volume I*, Mumbai: IIPS.

_____ (2007) *National Family Health Survey (NFHS-3) 2005/06 volume I*, Mumbai: IIPS.

_____ (2008a) *National Family Health Survey (NFHS-3) INDIA 2005/06 Uttar Pradesh. March 2008*, Mumbai: IIPS.

_____ (2008b) *National Family Health Survey (NFHS-3) INDIA 2005/06 Bihar. May 2008*, Mumbai: IIPS.

_____ (2009) *National Family Health Survey (NFHS-3) INDIA 2005/06 Delhi. February 2009*, Mumbai: IIPS.

Jha, Jyotsna and Dhir Jhingram (2005) *Elementary Education for the Poorest and Other Deprived Groups: The Real Challenge of Universalization*, New Delhi: Manohar.

Juneja, Nalini (2005) 'Exclusive Schools in Delhi: Their Land and the Law', *Economic and Political Weekly*, 40 (33), pp. 3685–90.

Mallica (2005) *'Poor' Children in 'Rich' Schools*, WP 2005/1, New Delhi: Institute of Social Studies Trust.

Mehta, Arun C. (2010) *Elementary Education in India Progress towards UEE: Analytical Tables 2007–08*, New Delhi: National University of Educational Planning and Administration.

Mehrotra, Santosh (2006) *The Economics of Education in India: The Challenge of Public Finance, Private Provision and Household Costs*, New Delhi: Sage.

Mitra, Arup (2003) *Occupational Choices, Networks, and Transfers: An Exegesis Based on Micro Data from Delhi Slums*, New Delhi: Manohar.

Panchamukhi, P. R. (2005) 'Household Expenditure on Elementary Education', in Santosh Mehrotra, P. R. Panchamukhi, R. Srivastava and R. Srivastava (eds), *Universalizing Elementary Education in India: Encaging the 'Tiger' Economy*, New Delhi: Oxford University Press.

PROBE (1999) *Public Report on Education in India*, New Delhi: Oxford University Press.

Ramachandran, Vimala, Kameshwari Jandhyala and Aarti Saihjee (2009) 'Through the Life Cycle of Children: Factors that Facilitate/Impede Successful Primary School Competition', in Rama V. Baru (ed.), *School Health Services in India: The Social and Economic Contexts*, New Delhi: Sage.

Singh, D. P. (2009) 'Poverty and Migration: Does Move Help?', in Ministry of Housing and Urban Poverty Alleviation (ed.), *India Urban Poverty Report 2009*, New Delhi: Oxford University Press.

Smita (2007) *Locked Homes Empty Schools: the Impact of Distress Seasonal Migration on the Rural Poor*, New Delhi: Zubaan.

Tilak, Jandhyala B. G. (2002) *Determinants of Household Expenditure on Education in Rural India*, Working Paper series No. 88, New Delhi: National Council of Applied Economic Research.

_____. (2009) 'Universalizing Elementary Education: A Review of Progress, Policies and Problems', Preet Rustagi (ed.), *Concerns, Conflicts, and Cohesions: Universalization of Elementary Education in India*, New Delhi: Oxford University Press.

Tooley, James and Pauline Dixon (2007) 'Private Schooling for Low-Income Families: A Census and Comparative Survey in East Delhi, India', *International Journal of Educational Development*, 27, pp. 205–17.

United Nations Development Programme (UNDP) (2009) *Human Development Report 2009 Overcoming Barriers: Human Mobility and Development*, New York: Palgrave Macmillan.

UN Millennium Project (2005) *Towards Universal Primary Education: Investments, Incentives and Institutions*, London: Earthscan.

Wratten, E. (1995) 'Conceptualizing Urban Poverty', *Environment and Urbanization*, 7 (1), pp. 11–36.

PART III
Issues of Weaker Sections in the Inclusive Growth Strategy

6
Electric Light and Minorities: The Provision of Semi-public Goods to Weaker Sections in India

Norio Kondo

Introduction

This chapter is an attempt to examine the relation between the provision of semi-public goods and the status of religious minorities in India. Among these religious minorities,[1] the focus is on the Muslim communities since the socio-economic status of Muslims, which is thought to have gradually deteriorated since independence, is a very important issue in India today.

India's independence was achieved through partition with Pakistan. As is well known, the partition happened along religious lines and resulted in a terrible massacre of innocent people, both Hindu and Muslim. Independent India, therefore, designated herself a secular nation-state, separating religion and politics. The Indian National Congress government, especially under Nehru, was very careful to prevent any deterioration in the communal situation, which was, by and large, avoided until the 1970s in spite of sporadic communal riots. However, relations between Hindus and Muslims became strained again after the 1980s with a series of events, such as the Shah Bano case (1985) and the enactment of the *Muslim Women (Protection of Rights on Divorce) Act* in 1986 by the Rajiv Gandhi government, the re-emergence of the Ayodhya issue, the rise of the Hindu nationalist party, the Bharatiya Janata Party, and the resulting destruction of Babri Masjid in Ayodhya, which led to widespread communal riots in 1992. Behind the communalization of Indian politics, there was a lessening of secular values and the decline of the Indian National Congress. The rise of communalism and the frequent communal riots in the cities, in which around 80 per cent of the casualties were Muslims, have highlighted the worsening social conditions of Muslims.

On the other hand, with the recent rapid economic growth after the introduction of economic liberalization in 1991, it has been easy to see the difference between those who have been able to ride the surge in economic growth and those who have not. The former include a rich class, including the Hindu middle class in the cities. The latter are socio-economically weaker sections of society, such as the Scheduled Castes (SCs), the Scheduled Tribes (STs),[2] and the Muslim communities. This contrast has also underlined the relatively disadvantaged status of the Muslim communities. This is especially so because there has been no strong affirmative action programme for the improvement of conditions for Muslims in comparison to other weaker sections, namely, the SCs and the STs (Ahmad, 1993: 64; Zainuddin, 2003; Hasan, 2004). For example, reservations for electoral representatives at various levels such as Parliament and the State Assemblies, as well as reservations for public service and higher education, have been provided to SCs and STs since independence. Although some Muslim 'castes' are included in the list of 'Other Backward Classes (OBCs)'[3] and are in a position to receive the benefits of reservations for recruitment to government offices or higher educational institutions, the number of Muslims who actually receive these benefits is considered to be very small. First, this is because the OBCs category includes a large number of castes and Muslim communities constitute a small proportion of the whole. A second reason is because the social and educational status of Muslims is, by and large, lower than other castes or communities, even within the OBCs category, which means that Muslims are disadvantaged in terms of receiving the benefits of reservation in comparison to the more advanced castes or communities, since there is no sub-division within the OBCs category.

Thus, at present, Muslim communities are seen to be politically depressed and socio-economically backward. If the situation of Muslim communities is to be rapidly improved, sufficient provision of socio-economic facilities might be necessary. Quite often such facilities can be provided only by the government or by public utilities under the government. In many cases, these facilities have the character of being public or semi-public goods. This chapter thus tries to examine the relation between the provision of an important semi-public good and the Muslim communities, mainly in urban areas. Among semi-public goods, we focus on the provision of electric light.

In the developing world, electric light is a symbol of modernity and development. It is a big step forward for a household to shift from a kerosene lamp to an electric light. With electric light, children can study and housewives can do their housework at night. Electric light means modernization for a society. So, it is very important to study it in order to see whether there is any systematic correlation between the provision or non-provision of electric light and being a Muslim. If there is any correlation, the reasons, which will partly reveal a social structure of disparity, have to be considered. It might be mentioned that in an ordinary household the installation of electric light is synonymous with getting electricity. This is because the first thing a household does after getting electricity is to install an electric light. Whether an electric light is installed or not is a good indicator of actual electrification. So, in this chapter, 'electric light' is used almost as a synonym for 'electricity' or 'electrification in the household', and vice versa.

This chapter is constructed as follows. In the following section, the situation surrounding Muslim communities is explained. The declining social status of Muslim communities and government policies are outlined first and the importance of the provision of a basic social infrastructure is explained. In the third section, the theoretical background of the relation between ethnic divisions and the provision of public goods is briefly surveyed and data are presented to examine certain hypotheses. In the fourth section, the results of regression and their analysis are presented. In the concluding section, some implications will be drawn.

Muslims and social infrastructure

Muslims' socio-economic backwardness and government policies

According to the decennial population census, Muslim population ratios in 1971, 1981, 1991, and 2001 were 11.2 per cent, 11.4 per cent, 12.1 per cent and 13.4 per cent, respectively. Muslims were 69.2 per cent of the non-Hindu population in 2001. Although Muslims are the most numerous of the religious minorities, Muslim communities are, no doubt, the most backward when compared to other minorities and Hindus. According to the National Sample Survey of 1999–2000 (the 55th round), the percentages of the population below the poverty line for Hindus, Muslims, Christians, and Sikhs are 27.80 per cent, 27.22 per cent, 19.82 per cent and 2.95 per cent, respectively, in rural areas. In the urban area, they are 21.66 per cent, 36.92 per cent, 11.84 per cent and 10.86 per cent, respectively (Ministry of Minority Affairs, 2007: 25). Muslims are economically far more backward than Christians and Sikhs. They are also in a more backward position than the caste Hindus, if SCs and STs are excluded from the Hindu category. Muslims are, especially, the poorest communities in urban areas. Besides, Muslims are the only communities that are poorer in urban areas than in rural areas.

Various socio-economic indicators for Muslims have come close to those of SCs and STs, which occupied 16.2 and 8.1 per cent of the population, respectively, in 2001. For example, the average literacy rate of Muslim is 59.1 per cent compared to the SCs' 54.7 per cent and the STs' 47.1 per cent, while Hindus, as a whole, show 65.1 per cent literacy in 2001. The literacy gap between Muslims and SCs, which, together with the STs, are traditionally considered to be the most backward section of Indian society, is narrowing. According to the National Sample Survey of 2004–5 (the 61st round), the literacy of Hindu-General, Hindu-OBCs, Hindu-SCs/STs, and Muslims are 80.5 per cent, 63.4 per cent, 52.7 per cent and 59.9 per cent respectively. But it is important that in the younger age group, the literacy of SCs/STs is slightly higher than Muslim. In the age cohort of six to 13, the literacy of SCs/STs and Muslim are 74.7 per cent and 74.6 per cent. Similarly, in 14–15 year-old age group, they are 80.0 per cent and 79.5 per cent, while in the 16–17 age range, they are 78.6 per cent and 75.5 per cent (Government of India, 2006a: 54).

The relatively declining social status of the Muslim communities was explicitly and politically noticed for the first time in the central government during the era of the Janata Party government, under which the National Minorities Commission was created in 1978. After the collapse of the Janata government, the new Congress government under Prime Minister Indira Gandhi set up a high-level committee, headed by Dr V. A. Sayid Mohammad, to study the problems of minorities and other weaker sections in 1980. Dr Gopal Singh later became the head of this committee. Its report was submitted to the government in 1983, but the report was not made public for a long time. The reasons why it was not published are not clear, but it is presumed that there was a fear that the revelation of the 'backwardness' of Muslims might cause negative political repercussions for the Congress government that had seen Muslims as an important base of support. Besides, in the early 1980s, Indira Gandhi had tried to woo the Hindu majority for electoral reasons. The revelation of Muslim 'backwardness' and the resultant demand for a government response to improve the condition of Muslims might have been considered counter to Indira Gandhi's strategy. The Rajiv Gandhi government, by and large, followed the same strategy, but at the same time tried to retain the electoral support of Muslims, which later seems to have been an impossible task.

In the early 1990s, when the Congress Party returned to power, some reforms were made under Prime Minister P. V. Narasimha Rao in order to ameliorate the feelings of minority communities. The National Minorities Commission was reorganized in 1993 and became the

'National Commission for Minorities', with statutory status. Although the Commission has only limited authority to make recommendations and has no jurisdiction over similar state-level commissions, its recommendations and reports have the effect of facilitating government action to some extent. In the 1995/6 report, for example, the Commission revealed that the percentage of Muslims in the police forces of the 21 states/union territories governments and the six paramilitary forces of the central government were quite low when considering the ratio between India's different populations. On the basis of this finding, the Commission asked the Ministry of Home Affairs of the Government of India and state governments to relax the criteria for the recruitment of Muslims just as they do for SCs and STs (National Commission for Minorities, 1997: 143–6, 173–4). Furthermore, in 1999, the Commission requested the Registrar General of India to collect the population data on the basis of religion in the 2001 population census in order to clarify the condition of religious minorities (National Commission for Minorities, 2001: 137–8). Accordingly, the 2001 population census data showed, for the first time, the distribution of religious minority populations up to the sub-district level, their literacy and work status up to the district level, etc. These figures, again, revealed the low socio-economic status of Muslims.

Other investigations have also revealed the backwardness of the Muslims' situation and their lower presence in public organizations. On the basis of a survey of more than 33,000 people conducted in the 'Human Development Survey of India' in 1993/4, the National Council of Applied Economic Research, for instance, showed that Muslim's socio-economic position was better *vis-à-vis* SCs and STs, but generally worse than ordinary Hindus (Shariff, 1999). In 1996, the Planning Commission showed the percentages of Muslims employed on the railways, state governments and among higher officials in various departments to be quite low. This tenuous presence on the part of Muslims also was verified in a study by Niraja Gopal Jayal (Jayal, 2006: 164).

The government's concern for Muslims' socio-economic status, by and large, seems to have been evolving along with the needs of electoral politics, especially that of the Congress Party. A typical example seems to have been the Prime Minister's High Level Committee For Preparation of Report on Social, Economic and Educational Status of the Muslim Community of India, which was appointed in 2005 under the United Progressive Alliance (UPA) government led by Prime Minister Dr Manmohan Singh of the Congress. The Committee, chaired by Justice Rajindar Sachar, submitted their report in 2006 ('Sachar Committee' hereafter). It is the most comprehensive report so far on various aspects of the situation of Muslim communities, showing Muslims' disadvantaged position in terms of their economic status, employment, education, health and their presence in governments and public organizations, etc. The UPA government's concerns for the minorities were also shown in the creation of the Ministry of Minority Affairs in 2005.

Along with the growing recognition of Muslims' backwardness, several policies have emerged for the improvement of circumstances of Muslim communities. In 1994, for example, the National Minorities Development and Finance Corporation was constituted under the Companies Act, 1956, at the national level, to render financial assistances specifically to minorities. The Corporation is under the Ministry of Minority Affairs now. In a few states, similar financial corporations for minorities were incorporated by state governments before the establishment of the National Minorities Development and Finance Corporation. The attitude of the UPA government towards minorities seems to be much more positive. In 2005, the UPA government announced the *Prime Minister's New 15-Point Programme for Welfare of Minorities* (Government of India, 2006b), which consisted of several programmes for the socio-economic development of minorities, especially Muslims,[4] but it is not clear if these programmes are effective enough to produce rapid improvements in conditions for minorities.

Finally, of several policy measures for the betterment of minorities, the most controversial is reservations for Muslims. Although several Muslim communities can avail themselves of reservations as OBCs, the number of Muslims who actually receive this benefit is considered to be small, as explained before. This is the basic reason why the argument for giving a separate reservation to Muslim communities as a whole has intensified. The controversy has now been precipitated by the introduction of the report of the National Commission on Religious and Linguistic Minorities headed by Justice Ranganath Misra ('Misra Commission' hereafter) to the Parliament in December 2009, which had already been submitted to the central government in 2007. The course of the argument on reservations for minorities is not clear at this moment, but it is certain that the coverage of reservations for minorities might be very limited, even if it is successfully introduced, compared to those for SCs and STs, in view of the already complicated reservations system.

Electric light, as a basic social infrastructure and Muslim communities

As shown in the above section, in spite of declining socio-economic conditions for Muslim communities, the policies of both central and state governments seem to have been far from satisfactory in terms of any improvement in the situation, at least, so far. Those policy measures which directly deliver benefits/services of education, employment, reservations for public office, etc., to minorities do not seem to have worked efficiently and effectively, so it is important to emphasize other indirect but possibly effective policy measures, such as the provision of better social facilities, which promote socio-economic development. Among such facilities, 'electricity', which is represented by 'electric light' in this chapter, has significant and unique features. As mentioned, electricity is an important element that has multiple effects on the modernization of society.

In a survey of the electrification of tribal villages in Bihar, for example, quite a few people felt that the arrival of electricity was a good thing and that their social status had risen when they got electricity in the form of an electric light or power for an agricultural pump-set. Wherever electricity was used for agricultural purposes, additional income was generated. Although many problems were found, such as red tape in the Electricity Board and high-handedness in giving connections to people, corruption, maladministration in billing, etc., the advent of electricity contributed to the improvement or awakening of the rural society (Sachchidananda and Verma, 1983: 78, 171, 175).

The improvement in economic conditions through electrification was also observed in rural areas in Madhya Pradesh and, to a lesser degree, in Uttar Pradesh, according to a study based on 5,000 households (Ranganathan and Ramanayya, 1998).

In developing countries, the provision of basic facilities is the responsibility of the government or semi-governmental organizations to quite a large extent. Although electricity cannot be said to be a pure public good with complete non-competitiveness and non-excludability, it might be regarded as a semi-public good when the government guarantees the universal availability of electricity to all residents on the grounds that it is a basic social infrastructure. Although it is true that at present the power distribution network has not been extended to the every corner of the country, and the supply of power is far from sufficient, especially in rural areas, the government of India clearly intends to cover all households with a power distribution network in the near future. In 2005, it announced the National Electricity Policy, which is aimed at achieving access to electricity for all households in the next five years and at completely meeting the nation's demand for power by 2012 (Government of India, 2005: para 2.0). If electricity should be universally available, there should be no disparity in the availability of electricity between communities. However, the real situation appears to be different.

There are few studies on the relation between the provision of electricity and communities in India. The survey of the National Council of Applied Economic Research, mentioned above, revealed the poor accessibility of Muslims to electricity. Those whose households have electricity connections were 30.0 per cent among Muslims compared to 43.2 per cent among Hindus (including SCs and STs) (Shariff, 1999: 63).[5] A study conducted by the Jahangirabad Media Institute and others, on the other hand, did not show a substantial difference in the provision of electricity between Muslims and non-Muslims either in urban or rural areas. Rather the condition of Muslims seems to be slightly better than others (Jahangirabad Media Institute *et al.*, 2006: 80, 94), but it would be risky to conclude that Muslim communities are not disadvantaged in terms of electricity provision. This is because the basis of the sampling appears to be biased. Therefore, its comparison between Muslims and others seems to be questionable. Actually, Muslims constituted 87 per cent of the 4,854 samples.

On the other hand, the studies in the Sachar Committee report appear to be more credible because the data from the National Samples Survey (NSS) or population census are more reliable. The Sachar Committee report shows, on the basis of NSS 55th and 61st round data, that, in both the years 1999/2000 and 2004/5, for those villages where Muslims and the SCs/STs live in larger numbers, the villages were likely to be least electrified. Besides, on the basis of 2001 census data, the Sachar Committee report also shows that the share of villages with no electricity increases substantially as the size of the village falls and the share of the Muslim population rises (Government of India, 2006a: 146–7). Thus, the studies in the Sachar Committee report demonstrate that Muslim communities are disadvantaged when it comes to the provision of electricity in rural areas; but the studies in the Sachar Committee report are not sufficient for several reasons. The results only show a simple association between two variables. Some important control variables are not taken into consideration. For example, the level of economic development of the household or the locality is definitely an important variable when explaining the level of electrification, but this is not included in the analysis. Besides, its focus is on rural areas.

In this chapter, I would like to concentrate my research mainly on urban areas for two reasons. The first is because urban areas are much more electrified; therefore, it is easier for urban residents, irrespective of their community, to get physical access to electrical wires and connections than in rural areas. This means that getting access to electricity is less dependent on the physical or geographical location of the resident in an urban area compared to a rural area, so we need not make much of physical factors in the analysis when we concentrate on data from an urban area. On the other hand, when we analyze the same issue in a rural area, it might be necessary to have appropriate control variables, representing, for example, the distance from the nearest electrical wire or distribution transformer. This information would be very difficult to get.

Another reason is that, as will be explained in the next section on the theoretical background, it might be important to take into consideration the heterogeneity or social relations of communities in a local society in order to examine the relation between Muslim communities and the provision of public or semi-public goods. The social relations between communities, for example, whether friendly or hostile, is much more observable and discernible in urban areas than in rural areas, which means that the effect of social heterogeneity or of the social relations of communities on the provision of semi-public goods might be more discernible in urban areas. For example, the problems of communal riots or the segregation of communities is more serious in urban areas. The cumulative effect of communal conflicts or tensions is the concentration of a particular community in a particular locality (Kirmani, 2008), which is sometimes called 'ghettoization'. The ghettoization of Muslims is particularly acute in cities that have experienced severe communal riots, like Ahmadabad (Jahangirabad Media Institute *et al.*, 2006: 107–12; Shani, 2007: 128). Such segregation, or ghettoization in its extreme form, might have an effect on the provision of basic services and facilities. So, studying the problem of disparities between Muslims and other communities is more important for urban areas. In addition, there is the fact that more Muslims live in urban areas than in rural areas, as is shown in Table 6.1.

Table 6.1 Percentage of urban population (%)

	1961	1971	1981	1991	2001
All	17.9	19.9	23.7	25.7	27.8
Muslim	27.1	28.8	34.0*	35.5*	35.7

Note: * The figures are partly estimated because the censuses were not conducted in Assam in 1981 and in Jammu and Kashmir in 1991 because of political unrest.
Source: Calculated from censuses: 1961, 1971, 1981, 1991 and 2001.

Theoretical background and data

Theory of ethnicity and the allocation of public goods[6]

Before entering into an empirical analysis, we need to survey the theoretical background. There seem to be basically two streams that explain the relation between the provision of public goods and ethnic communities. One relates ethnic heterogeneity to the provision of public goods. According to this type of thinking, ethnic heterogeneity leads to less provision in terms of public goods. There are a few hypotheses connected to this.

First, the provision of public goods will be less in an ethnically heterogeneous society or locality because the preferences of one community concerning public goods differs from those of another, and this impedes collective action on the part of heterogeneous communities as a whole to extract a higher level of public goods from the government. On the basis of this theory, Alesina *et al.* found that ethnic heterogeneity was inversely related to the share of spending in productive public goods, such as education, roads, etc., in US cities (Alesina *et al.*, 1999).

Second, divisions or cleavages in social networks might explain the poor provision of public goods in an ethnically heterogeneous society. An ethnically homogeneous society might have advantages when acting collectively in order to get public goods because common social networks, in terms of culture, language, historical experience, etc., facilitate social communication and cooperative action when such a society demands public goods from the government. In addition, social sanctions on free-riders are stronger in a homogeneous society. In an ethnically heterogeneous society, on the other hand, social networks are segmented or divided, which makes social communication between different ethnic groups less effective and weakens social sanctions to other ethnic groups.

Miguel and Gugerty found, in a study of a local society in rural western Kenya, that ethnic diversity was associated with lower voluntary school funding, worse school facilities and fewer community social sanctions (Miguel and Gugerty, 2005). In India, Banerjee *et al.* found that social fragmentation based on the Hindu caste system and the presence of religious minorities was likely to result in a lower level of provision of public goods, such as education, public transportation, tap water supply and power supply. They considered this lower provision to be due to conflictual social relations, together with other elements in the historical background, like the skewed land tenure system that has its origins in colonial times (Banerjee *et al.*, 2005).

This second theory might be sub-divided into what Habyarimana *et al.* have called the 'technology mechanism' and the 'strategy selection mechanism'. Both theories are the same to the extent that the lack of both cooperative behaviour and social sanctions on free-riders in a heterogeneous society explains the poor provision of public goods. However, the two theories differ when it comes to the factors explaining this lack of provision. In the former case, the lack of both common cultural resources and mutual 'findability' of co-ethnics in the social networks in the heterogeneous society is the reason given for the lack of both cooperative behaviour and social sanctions. In the latter case, the very fact that individuals will select different strategies of interaction depending on the ethnicity of the people with whom they are interacting is what explains the lack of both cooperative behaviour and social sanction in heterogeneous society. An individual may expect people from different ethnic groups to adopt a strategy which might be worse than that chosen by people of the same ethnic group. In this case, the selection of strategies of social interaction by individuals, which depends on the ethnicity of others, tends to reduce both cooperative behaviour and social sanctions between different ethnic communities (Habyarimana *et al.*, 2007).

They showed, on the basis of experimental games conducted in a slum in Uganda, that the strategy selection mechanism was the most effective in explaining the association between a higher ethnic diversity and lower public goods provision, but they admitted that the difference between the technology and strategy selection mechanisms seemed to be subtle, particularly concerning the role of sanctioning (*ibid.*: 711). So, in this chapter I will not distinguish between the two mechanisms, but rather include the two in the category of social network theory. Social networks based on ethnicity are still an important social entity for collective political action in India. Chandra, for example, shows this in her study of the growth of the Bahujan Samaj Party in Uttar Pradesh, which is based on the support of SCs (Chandra, 2004).

The above theories, both of which are included in the category of 'heterogeneity theory', explain the lower provision of public goods through ethnic heterogeneity, but there will be factors other than ethnic heterogeneity which might explain a lower level of provision of public goods. If an ethnic community is socially and politically disadvantaged for historical or social reasons, the community's ability to get public goods from the government might be weaker. The action of articulating the political demands of members and of projecting them to a supplier is called 'voice' by Hirschman (1970: 30–9). If the ability of a community to raise its voice to a supplier of public goods, namely, the government or a public organization, is weak, it will be difficult for the community to get more public goods. For example, to obtain electricity connections in a locality, an effective voice will be necessary. Without a strong voice from residents by themselves or through their representatives, it is difficult to get electrical wires or distribution transformers promptly.

There can be several reasons for a weak voice. The voice of a community might be weak because of a special historical reason. The partition in 1947 between India and Pakistan, for example, made Muslims in India socially vulnerable. The voice of a community might be weak since the community does not have the socio-economic resources to mobilize its members. For instance, the community might not be wealthy enough to give financial support to their candidates in an election campaign. The community might not be strong enough to precipitate collective action to raise its 'voice' against government due to a lack of internal mechanism to put social sanctions on dissidents. It might be because of a weak social network and a lack of mutual trust among members, due to internal cleavages or a split in the leadership, namely, a lack of social capital (Coleman, 1990: 300–21; Putnam et al., 1993).

This weak voice theory focuses on a particular community, not on the relation between communities. It might overlap with social network theory to the extent that social communication and sanctions have important roles, but, in the weak voice theory, the focus is on social communication and sanctions within the community, not between communities. In India, the SCs and STs are typical of such communities, which is why special affirmative policies are applied to improve their socio-economic situation. Muslim communities also seem to be in a very weak position today (Alam, 2008), but they differ from SCs and STs in that they have been unable to obtain the benefits of the strong affirmative policies and actions that are provided for SCs and STs. Betancourt and Gleason found that, on the basis of district data for the 1970s and 1980s in India, the levels of provision of health service in the form of doctors and nurses and of educational service in the form of teachers were, by and large, lower for SCs and Muslims even after taking into account the effect of the different situations in the states (Betancourt and Gleason, 2000).

The relative importance of the heterogeneity theory and the weak voice theory might depend on the social structure of a particular society. In the case of India, Banerjee and Somanathan have insisted, on the basis of 1971 and 1991 data, that the social heterogeneity that had been emphasized in recent empirical literature on public goods was relevant but not overwhelmingly important. It is interesting that political heterogeneity in terms of fragmentation in their share of the political parties' vote in an election did not affect the provision of most of the public goods examined. Rather, their study seems to have shown the importance of the weak voice theory. They found that, among the three weaker sections – namely the SCs, the STs and the Muslims – the Muslims and the STs were more disadvantaged, while the SCs improved their access to public goods between 1971 and 1991 (Banerjee and Somanathan, 2007).

Finally, it must be emphasized that the role of the government is very important in every theoretical framework because the government is the main provider of public goods. If the government discriminates against a particular community, the community will get less, even if the local society is homogeneous and has a well-integrated, strong voice with effective social sanctions. In India's case, although it is a fact that some sections of Muslims feel discriminated against or alienated, most ordinary Muslims seem to have confidence in their governments (Mayer, 1983; Haqqi, 1989). Also, it can be said that there is no clear evidence for a discriminatory attitude at the higher levels of government. But such an attitude might be observed sometimes at the level of lower officials or staffs in government or public organizations.[7]

In the next section, I would like to explain the data and variables used to examine both theories. The dependent variable is 'electric light', which is the percentage of households using electricity as their main source of lighting. I will construct an indicator of communities' heterogeneity, namely an index of 'diversity', on the basis of the ratio in terms of population between SCs, STs and Muslims. The latter three variables are also to be used as independent variables in order to check the weak voice theory.

Data and variables

First of all, I have to make the coverage of my study clear. Although the studies already mentioned, such as the Human Development Survey of India in 1993/4 or Sachar Committee report, are revealing and suggestive, they are not enough to describe the exact situation surrounding Muslims. In order to depict the situation, this study has to take into account a few points. First, as pointed out already, it will be better if we concentrate on the urban data. Second, we have to focus on the state because the state is the fundamental unit of government that provides public goods. More importantly, there is a possibility that the social and political situation of Muslims is widely different between different states. We will conduct a regression analysis on the basis of both pooled samples consisting of several states and samples from each state, but the latter will be more important for an understanding of the real situation.

Four states were selected. First, Bihar, Uttar Pradesh and West Bengal were chosen on the basis of their Muslim population. The absolute numbers, as well as the percentage of the Muslim population in these states, is large and, therefore, worth studying, and the fact that these three states are geographically contiguous might have some merit in a statistical analysis because this contiguity might, to some extent, provide a common social background. If the three states were geographically separated, we could not expect such commonality and might have to prepare additional control variables to absorb the differences. Also, I added Gujarat as a state to contrast it with the other three states. Although the percentage of the Muslim population of Gujarat is below the national average, the state is unique with respect to its minorities' problems. Muslim communities are in a sensitive position in Gujarat, where there have been several communal riots. The biggest riot in 2002 spread to rural areas. Gujarat is economically the most developed of the four states, while Bihar is the most underdeveloped.

The percentages of the Muslim population of the four states are shown in Table 6.2, together with those for the SCs and STs. The table shows Muslim percentages as sub-district-based averages and town averages. The 'sub-district' and 'town' are the units of observation in the regression analysis. The former includes Taluk (in the case of Gujarat), the Community Development (CD) block or tehsil (in the case of Uttar Pradesh). 'Town' is synonymous with an urban area[8] and is the main target in our statistical analysis in this chapter. The geographical area of a sub-district unit consists of both a town area and a rural area. Namely, the data for a sub-district unit includes the data for towns within the sub-district. The number of these units in each state is shown in Table 6.2. Since the picture at town level can be understood more properly when compared to the overall picture, I will conduct a sub-district analysis at the beginning of the regression analysis.

The equation (1) below is the basic model based on the theoretical survey mentioned above. The provision of public goods, namely, 'electric light', is to be explained by control variables, ethnic groups belonging to weaker sections and ethnic heterogeneity. The weaker sections include 'Muslim',[9] 'SCs' and 'STs'. There will be no opposition to the fact that these three groups are the most vulnerable or weakest sections in Indian society. It might be necessary to include 'SCs' and 'STs' in the equation in order to clarify the position of 'Muslim'. This is because, in

Table 6.2 Average percentage of the population of Hindu and weaker sections in four states, 2001 (%)

Gujarat

	No. of samples	Hindu	Muslim	SCs	STs
Taluk	226	90.67	8.14 (7.16)	7.21 (3.80)	17.91 (29.12)
Town	242	82.40	15.19 (14.60)	6.89 (4.59)	5.94 (9.29)

Bihar

	No. of samples	Hindu	Muslim	SCs	STs
CD block	533	84.89	14.91 (12.90)	16.37 (6.07)	0.97 (3.13)
Town	130	80.80	18.65 (12.48)	11.50 (4.62)	0.45 (0.81)

Uttar Pradesh

	No. of samples	Hindu	Muslim	SCs	STs
Tehsil	300	82.31	16.88 (11.89)	22.17 (6.88)	0.06 (0.03)
Town	704	65.61	33.26 (23.26)	14.28 (8.16)	0.03 (0.43)

West Bengal

	No. of samples	Hindu	Muslim	SCs	STs
CD block	341	70.26	26.25 (21.99)	25.83 (13.80)	7.92 (10.30)
Town	375	80.12	18.64 (23.63)	19.61 (12.64)	2.03 (3.57)

Notes: [1] CD block = Community Development block. The data for 'town' are covered in the data for taluk/CD block/tehsil.
[2] Figures in parentheses are the standard deviations.
Source: Calculated from Census, 2001.

the competition to get public goods, the SCs and STs might be strong rivals for Muslims in the affirmative policy environment that is meant for the SCs and STs. The percentage of the population of each community on the basis of the 2001 population census is used to represent their respective weights.

It should be noticed here that, in the towns, the variable STs might not be an appropriate independent variable to explain 'Electric light'. First, as is shown in Table 6.2, the percentage of the population of STs is, by and large, very small in the towns, although the percentage in Gujarat is a little higher than in the other states. It might be difficult, therefore, to conclude that the minuscule population of the STs affects the installation of electricity in the towns. Second, the increase in the STs population in the towns seems to be due to their migration from rural areas. In the 1961 census, the STs populations in urban areas in

Gujarat, Bihar, Uttar Pradesh and West Bengal were 2.59 per cent, 2.81 per cent, 0.0 per cent, and 0.56 per cent, respectively, which are much lower than those shown in Table 6.2, except for Bihar.[10] When people from the STs migrate to the towns for work, they might settle in areas where they can easily access the facilities they need, such as electricity. If this is so, the STs population might be a dependent variable to be explained by 'Electric light' in the towns. Namely, 'Electric light' affects the STs population, not vice versa. So, I will include 'STs' in the regression analysis for sub-districts, but not in the analysis of the towns.

The index of ethnic heterogeneity is constituted as 'Diversity' and constructed from the ratios of the three weaker sections, namely, 'Muslim', 'SCs', 'STs' and other. It is the Herfindahl Index as used in other studies, which is shown in Table 6.3.

$$\text{Electric light} = XA + b_m \text{Muslim} + b_{SC}\text{SCs} + b_{ST}\text{STs} + b_d \text{Diversity} + \text{constant} \quad (1)$$

where:

X: control variables, A: coefficient vector for X.
b_i: coefficient for 'i' {i = Muslim, SCs, STs, Diversity}, and,
if the dataset is that for towns, 'b_{ST}STs' is to be removed.

It goes without saying that it is important to select appropriate control variables. In view of the availability of data, I included population size and good housing as control variables. Population size is important because electricity is more likely to be installed in the bigger towns. The natural logarithm of the population size of the sub-district or town in the 2001 census is calculated as an indicator of size. The association of the two variables is shown in Figure 6.1, shown later. Also, good or economically developed houses or localities will stand a better chance of getting electrical wiring or distribution transformers installed in their area. According to a survey, higher-income households had better access to electricity (Ranganathan and Ramanayya, 1998: 3182). As shown in Table 6.3, an indicator of the modernity of a house is created as a composition of the variables of 'roof', 'wall' and 'floor'. The 'roof', for example, shows the percentage of households whose roof is made of brick, stone, or concrete. The variables 'wall' and 'floor' are also formed in the same way. 'Good house' is the first factor in the factor analysis based on the three variables. The original data concerning the materials of 'roof', 'wall' and 'floor' are collected in the house-listing census of

Table 6.3 Variables

Dependent variables	Explanation	Source
Electric light	Percentage of households whose main source of lighting is electricity (%)	Housing Census, 2001
Independent variables		
Population size	Size of population: natural logarithm of population size = ln (population)	Census, 2001
Good house	Composite variable showing proportion of households whose house is made of modern or steady materials. This consists of the first factor among the following three variables in the factor analysis (principal-components factor method). 1. 'roof': percentage of households whose roof is made of brick, stone, or concrete 2. 'wall': percentage of households whose wall is made of burnt brick, stone, or concrete 3. 'floor': percentage of households whose floor is made of brick, stone, or cement	Housing Census, 2001
Muslim	Percentage of the Muslim population (%)	Census, 2001
SCs	Percentage of the scheduled castes population (%)	Census, 2001
STs	Percentage of the scheduled tribes population (%)	Census, 2001
Diversity	Variable showing the *diversity*/heterogeneity of weaker sections and others Diversity = $1 - (\text{Muslim}/100)^2 - (\text{SCs}/100)^2 - (\text{STs}/100)^2 - [1 - (\text{Muslim} + \text{SCs} + \text{STs})/100]^2$	Census, 2001
Instrumental variable		
Drinking water	Percentage of households that get drinking water from a tap within the premises or near the premises ('near premises' is considered to be a tap within 100 metres for urban areas and within 500 metres for rural areas)	Housing Census, 2001

2000 which was conducted as part of the 2001 census operation. The dependent variable, 'Electric light', which is the percentage of households whose main source of lighting is electricity, is also adopted from the house-listing census.

It has to be pointed out that the control variables might be endogenous. Of the two control variables, electricity may explain 'size of population'. This is because the availability of electricity may lead to a growth in population, especially in small towns. People may migrate to a locality where modern facilities are available. Electricity is an essential modern facility for both households and enterprises. I will treat 'size of population' as a possible endogenous variable. In order to correct the effects of endogeneity, an Instrumental Variable (IV) estimation is conducted. The instrumental variable adopted is 'drinking water', which is the percentage of households getting drinking water from a tap within the premises or near the premises. This information is also from the house-listing census. A tap is a modern method for many people to get clean drinking water. It has a clear correlation with the control variables. Another control variable, 'Good house', might also be an endogenous variable, but the regression with 'Good house' as an instrumented variable does not produce a clear result. The reason may be that the installation of electricity in the locality does not necessarily cause residents to construct a 'Good house'. On the contrary, those who have a 'Good house' are likely to demand electrification. So, I will treat the 'size of population', rather than 'Good house', an instrumented variable, with 'drinking water' as instrumental variable.

The variables used in the regression are shown in Table 6.3, together with definitions of the variables and data sources.

If the heterogeneity theory holds true, the coefficient for 'Diversity' ($= b_d$) in the equation (1) is negative and statistically significant. The more heterogeneous the locality is, the fewer the public goods that are provided, namely, the ratio of households with electric lights, is. This will reveal that, because of the different preferences among communities or because of cleavages in social networks, the heterogeneous composition of the local society makes it difficult for the collective actions of the local population to be organized in order to make strong demands for public goods.

On the other hand, if the weak voice theory is correct concerning Muslim communities, the coefficient for 'Muslim' ($= b_m$) in the equation (1) is negative and statistically significant. The more Muslims live in the locality, the lower the number of households with electric lights. This will show that Muslim communities are in a weak position when making demands for public goods because of their socio-political weakness.[11]

Before going into an explanation of the result, I would like to clarify the relation between 'Electric light', urbanization and 'size of population'.

Figure 6.1 consists of graphs showing the relations between 'Electric light', on the one hand, and 'Urban population' (per cent) as well as 'Size of town', on the others, in the four states in 2001.[12] The graphs on the left-hand side show a scatter plot of electric light *vis-à-vis* urban

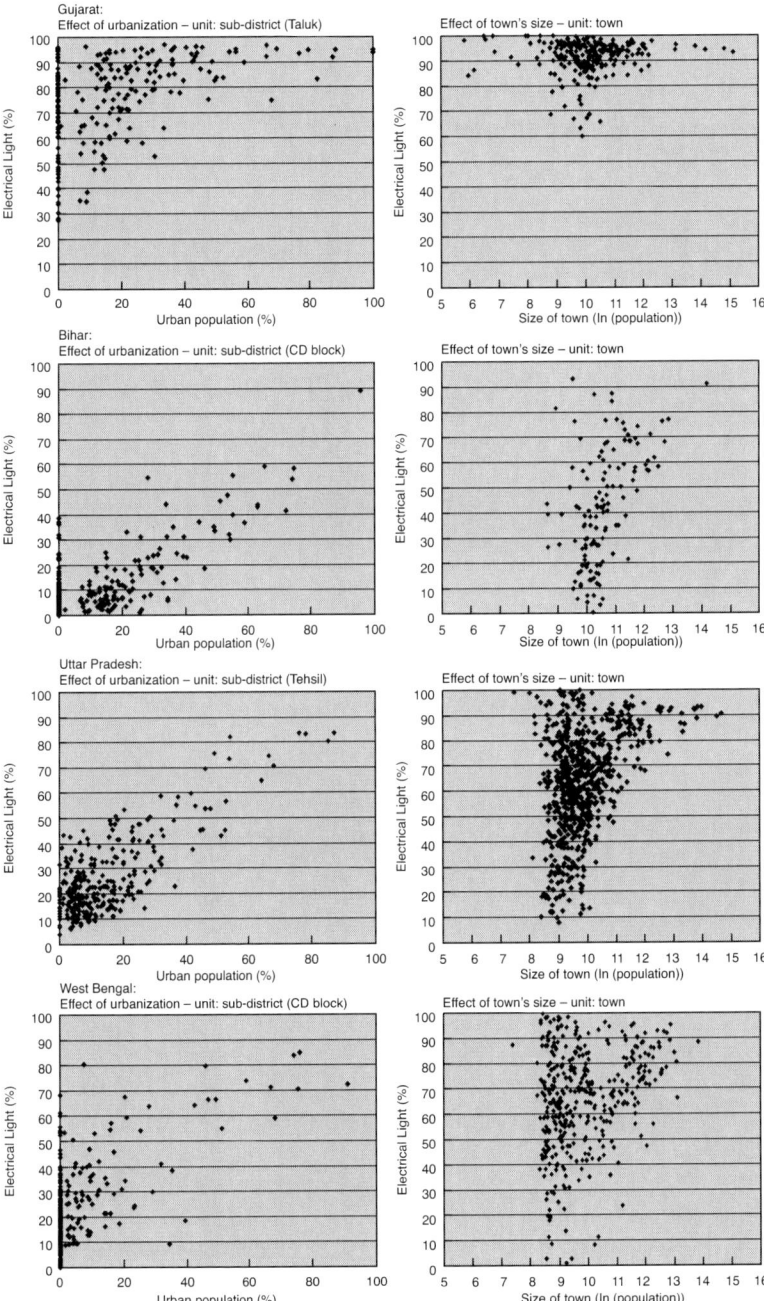

Figure 6.1 Houses with electric light *vis-à-vis* urban population/size of town, 2001
Sources: Housing Census 2001 and Census 2001.

population on the basis of sub-district data, which cover, as explained, the town data. It is very clear that there is a strong association between the two variables. Electrification and urbanization go hand in hand. It is also obvious from the graphs that there are clear differences between states. The more developed a state is, the more electrified a locality is, even if the level of urbanization is the same. A rural area in Gujarat is more electrified than an urban area in Bihar. Concerning the effect of population size, this is not so obvious, when compared to that of urbanization, but it is still sufficiently clear in view of the graphs on the right-hand side. The bigger the town is, the more electrified it is. The differences between the states are also obvious. Especially in the case of Gujarat, the distribution of the plots is concentrated in the upper portion of the graph, showing that towns in Gujarat are highly electrified. This means that the explanatory power of the independent variables will be much lower in Gujarat.

In the next section, the results of the regression analysis are examined.

Results and analysis

Analysis based on the pooled samples of four states

Tables 6.4 and 6.5 are the results of regression on the basis of the pooled samples of the four states in terms of the town and sub-district data, respectively. The 'STs' are not included as an independent variable in regressions of the town dataset, for the reason explained above. Dummy variables for Bihar, Uttar Pradesh and West Bengal are included to absorb the differences between the states, while the dummy for Gujarat is not, because the constant is included in the regression. Based on both sub-district and town data, the weak voice theory is statistically significant in the case of Muslims. The disadvantaged position for Muslims, when it comes to getting electric light, is robust both at the sub-district and town levels. It is clearer in the towns in view of the comparison of t-values between Tables 6.4 and 6.5.

The case for the SCs is clear at the sub-district level with both the OLS and IV showing SCs' disadvantaged position at the sub-district level, but at the town level, the result is not clear. The signs of the coefficients for SCs are opposite one another if we compare the results on the basis of OLS with those on the basis of IV.

Concerning the STs, the sub-district level analysis exhibits a robust result showing that STs are disadvantaged in the sub-districts, which constitute 90.6 per cent of the rural and 9.4 per cent of the urban population in our dataset. Roughly, this means that they are disadvantaged in rural

Table 6.4 Electric light – weaker sections and diversity: sub-district level analysis in Bihar, Gujarat, Uttar Pradesh and West Bengal

Dependent variable: electric light	OLS (with robust standard errors)				Instrumental variable estimation (with robust standard errors) Instruments: Muslim, SCs, STs, diversity, good house, Bihar, Uttar Pradesh, West Bengal, drinking water			
Independent variables	Coefficient	Robust standard error	t	P > |t|	Coefficient	Robust standard error	t	P > |t|
Population size	2.783	0.672	4.14	0.000	43.67	15.66	2.79	0.005
Good house	9.359	0.391	23.91	0.000	4.482	1.829	2.45	0.014
Muslim	-0.106	0.0236	-4.50	0.000	-0.441	0.138	-3.20	0.001
SCs	-0.159	0.0375	-4.23	0.000	-0.209	0.0839	-2.50	0.013
STs	-0.119	0.0318	-3.75	0.000	-0.185	0.0653	-2.84	0.005
Diversity	22.30	3.210	6.95	0.000	4.134	9.878	0.42	0.676
Bihar	-70.40	1.146	-61.46	0.000	-58.96	5.133	-11.49	0.000
Uttar Pradesh	-55.22	1.423	-38.81	0.000	-93.53	14.92	-6.27	0.000
West Bengal	-54.85	1.585	-34.59	0.000	-44.53	5.354	-8.32	0.000
Constant	38.91	8.213	4.74	0.000	-442.03	183.86	-2.40	0.016
N	1400				1400			
F (9, 1390)	907.31				130.20			
Prob > F	0.000				0.000			
R-squared	0.8665				–			
Root MSE	10.041				21.486			
Maximum VIF among independent variables	3.75 (for 'West Bengal')				–			

Note: State dummy variable 'Gujarat' is dropped to include the constant.

Table 6.5 Electric light – weaker sections and diversity: town-level analysis in Bihar, Gujarat, Uttar Pradesh and West Bengal

Dependent variable: electric light	OLS (with robust standard errors)				Instrumental variable estimation (with robust standard errors) Instrumented: population size Instruments: Muslim, SCs, diversity, good house, Bihar, Uttar Pradesh, West Bengal, drinking water			
Independent variables	Coefficient	Robust standard error	t	P > |t|	Coefficient	Robust standard error	t	P > |t|
Population size	1.985	0.298	6.65	0.000	24.95	4.530	5.51	0.000
Good house	11.88	0.414	28.71	0.000	4.709	1.468	3.21	0.001
Bihar	-48.74	1.527	-31.93	0.000	-59.00	3.398	-17.36	0.000
Uttar Pradesh	-23.78	1.019	-23.33	0.000	-19.32	2.686	-7.19	0.000
West Bengal	-22.68	1.132	-20.04	0.000	-20.24	3.046	-6.65	0.000
Muslim	-0.179	0.0248	-7.22	0.000	-0.193	0.0376	-5.13	0.000
SCs	-0.198	0.0549	-3.60	0.000	0.292	0.137	2.13	0.033
Diversity	9.042	3.645	2.48	0.013	-18.60	9.041	-2.06	0.040
Constant	72.00	3.280	21.95	0.000	-153.5	44.28	-3.47	0.001
N	1451				1451			
F (8, 1442)	410.79				78.690			
Prob > F	0.000				0.000			
R-squared	0.6803				–			
Root MSE	12.892				27.07			
Maximum VIF among independent variables	2.71 (for 'Uttar Pradesh')				–			

Note: State dummy variable 'Gujarat' is dropped to include constant.

areas in relation to the provision of electric light. It is understandable that the STs are disadvantaged in rural areas because their villages are often located in remote areas.

Comparing the *t*-values for Muslims, SCs and STs in the sub-district level analysis, it can be said that Muslims are slightly more disadvantaged than the SCs and STs.

The role of 'Diversity' is not clear. In the sub-district, the coefficient of diversity is positive and statistically significant on the basis of OLS but not statistically significant on the basis of IV. In the towns, it is positive and statistically significant in OLS, but it is negative and statistically significant in IV. The heterogeneity theory does not appear to hold true in the pooled samples.

The relations of the SCs, as well as diversity, to electric light in the towns should be carefully checked again in each state.

Finally, both the population size and a 'Good house' are, by and large, positively and significantly correlated to the provision of electric light, as expected.

Next, we must proceed to an analysis of each state separately so that we do not fall into the trap of 'fallacy of composition'.

Analysis of each state

Tables 6.6, 6.7, 6.8 and 6.9 are the results of the regression for each state.

First, concerning Gujarat, the result is not as clear as had been expected. The SCs are negative and statistically significant in OLS, but not significant in IV. There are no clear tendencies regarding Muslims. Although Muslim communities, especially in urban areas, are socially and politically in a difficult position in Gujarat after several communal riots, this difficulty is not reflected in the provision of electricity. Diversity is positive and statistically significant in OLS, but not significant in IV at 5 per cent level. Concerning the control variables, although population size is not relevant, 'Good house' contributes to electrification. As shown in Figure 6.1, the towns in Gujarat are highly electrified overall, so, in general, it will be difficult for these independent variables to discern the level of electrification in the towns.

Second, in Bihar, we cannot discern any significant variables concerning the weak voice and heterogeneity theories in both OLS and IV. 'Muslim', SCs and diversity do not make a difference in the provision of electric light. A sample survey of the socio-economic and educational status of Muslims in Bihar showed that, in urban areas, 47.2 per cent of Muslim households have an electricity connection compared to

Table 6.6 Electric light – weaker sections and diversity: town-level analysis in Gujarat

Dependent variable: electric light	OLS (with robust standard errors)				Instrumental variable estimation (with robust standard errors) Instrumented: population size Instruments: Muslim, SCs, diversity, good house, drinking water			
Independent variables	Coefficient	Robust standard error	t	P > |t|	Coefficient	Robust standard error	t	P > |t|
Population size	−0.318	0.275	−1.16	0.249	−6.334	6.850	−0.92	0.356
Good house	4.486	0.485	9.25	0.000	6.300	2.250	2.80	0.006
Muslim	−0.0416	0.0306	−1.36	0.176	0.0465	0.101	0.46	0.646
SCs	−0.249	0.115	−2.17	0.031	−0.0741	0.203	−0.37	0.715
Diversity	5.936	3.004	1.98	0.049	9.777	5.536	1.77	0.079
Constant	94.85	2.691	35.24	0.000	151.9	65.70	2.31	0.022
N	242				242			
F (5, 236)	20.74				12.00			
Prob > F	0.000				0.000			
R-squared	0.4058				–			
Root MSE	5.326				9.088			
Maximum VIF among independent variables	1.85 (for 'diversity')				–			

Table 6.7 Electric light – weaker sections and diversity: town-level analysis in Bihar

Dependent variable: electric light	OLS (with robust standard errors)				Instrumental variable estimation (with robust standard errors) Instrumented: population size Instruments: Muslim, SCs, diversity, good house, drinking water			
Independent variables	Coefficient	Robust standard error	t	P > |t|	Coefficient	Robust standard error	t	P > |t|
Population size	6.999	1.690	4.14	0.000	42.71	25.25	1.69	0.093
Good house	14.42	1.542	9.35	0.000	1.725	8.331	0.21	0.836
Muslim	0.149	0.160	0.93	0.355	0.594	0.464	1.28	0.203
SCs	0.130	0.371	0.35	0.726	2.497	1.814	1.38	0.171
Diversity	−31.61	22.37	−1.41	0.160	−210.6	138.8	−1.52	0.132
Constant	−21.74	18.56	−1.17	0.244	−355.8	233.8	−1.52	0.131
N	130				130			
F (5, 124)	48.46				6.010			
Prob > F	0.000				0.000			
R-squared	0.6191				–			
Root MSE	14.23				30.68			
Maximum VIF among independent variables	2.96 (for 'diversity')				–			

Table 6.8 Electric light – weaker sections and diversity: town-level analysis in Uttar Pradesh

Dependent variable: electric light	OLS (with robust standard errors)				Instrumental variable estimation (with robust standard errors)			
					Instrumented: population size Instruments: Muslim, SCs, diversity, good house, drinking water			
Independent variables	Coefficient	Robust standard error	t	P > |t|	Coefficient	Robust standard error	t	P > |t|
Population size	3.370	0.434	7.77	0.000	32.061	7.148	4.49	0.000
Good house	13.95	0.519	26.88	0.000	4.215	2.426	1.74	0.083
Muslim	−0.0786	0.0315	−2.50	0.013	−0.216	0.0694	−3.11	0.002
SCs	−0.0402	0.0839	−0.48	0.632	0.615	0.219	2.81	0.005
Diversity	−5.700	6.010	−0.95	0.343	−52.29	16.92	−3.09	0.002
Constant	36.15	5.258	6.87	0.000	−230.6	65.51	−3.52	0.000
N	704				704			
F (5, 698)	272.71				45.85			
Prob > F	0.000				0.000			
R-squared	0.6096				–			
Root MSE	12.68				28.46			
Maximum VIF among independent variables	1.83 (for 'SCs')				–			

Table 6.9 Electric light – weaker sections and diversity: town-level analysis in West Bengal

Dependent variable: electric light	OLS (with robust standard errors)				Instrumental variable estimation (with robust standard errors)			
					Instrumented: population size Instruments: Muslim, SCs, diversity, good house, drinking water			
Independent variables	Coefficient	Robust standard error	t	P > |t|	Coefficient	Robust standard error	t	P > |t|
Population size	0.227	0.535	0.42	0.672	9.013	2.732	3.30	0.001
Good house	11.70	0.838	13.95	0.000	9.782	1.253	7.81	0.000
Muslim	−0.376	0.0449	−8.37	0.000	−0.273	0.0571	−4.78	0.000
SCs	−0.238	0.0866	−2.75	0.006	−0.0297	0.115	−0.26	0.796
Diversity	10.73	6.530	1.64	0.101	10.93	8.105	1.35	0.178
Constant	70.33	6.848	10.27	0.000	−22.27	29.22	−0.76	0.447
N	375				375			
$F_{(5, 369)}$	130.86				80.40			
Prob > F	0.000				0.000			
R-squared	0.6283				–			
Root MSE	12.38				16.06			
Maximum VIF among independent variables	1.94 (for 'SCs')				–			

Note: The sample for 'Kolkata (Municipal Corporation)' is excluded because the population of 4.57 million is too large for it to be compared with the other samples.

72.0 per cent of the general population. Although, ostensibly, this seems to mean that Muslims are disadvantaged when it comes to the provision of electricity, the situation was said to be due to the economic distance between Muslims and the general population (Asian Development Research Institute 2006: 53).[13] Taking their incomes into account, there might be no substantial disadvantage due to their being Muslim. There seems to be some socio-political background behind this. Bihar was governed by Janata Dal or Rashtriya Janata Dal, led by Laloo Prasad Yadav and his wife, from 1990 to 2005.[14] During this period, the interests of Muslims were cared for, because Muslims, as well as the Yadav caste, provided an important base of support for the parties. Concerning diversity, although the signs are negative in line with heterogeneity theory, it is not statistically significant in both OLS and IV. The two control variables, population size and good house, are significantly correlated in OLS but not in IV.

Third, the Uttar Pradesh data clearly show Muslims' disadvantaged position with respect to the provision of electric light in towns. The coefficients for Muslims are negative and statistically significant in both OLS and IV. One important reason might be the much more dispersed distribution of Muslims among the towns. As shown in Table 6.2, the standard deviation of the distribution of Muslims among the towns is much larger than those for Gujarat and Bihar. That is to say, for example, one town has a much higher percentage of Muslims in the population while another town has a very low percentage. Such a big difference makes the effect of being a Muslim statistically more likely to appear. Suppose the distribution is completely homogeneous among the towns, we cannot observe the effect. On the basis of the dispersed distribution of the Muslim populations in the towns, it has become clear that Muslim communities are disadvantaged in terms of getting electric light. The basic reason for this might be the lower socio-political status of these Muslim communities in the towns. The gradually deteriorating socio-economic condition of Muslims after independence, as well as the communalization of society after the 1980s, due to Ayodhya issues, etc. (Hasan, 1998: chapter 5), might be important reasons for the deteriorating socio-political environment for Muslims in the towns.

On the other hand, the SCs' coefficient is not significant in OLS, but significant and positive in IV. Although the position of the SCs is not clear in the regressions, their condition does not seem to be deteriorating in the towns, at least. This might be related to the fact that the political status of the SCs has been improving, the symbol of which is the rise of the Bahujan Samaj Party from the 1990s onward (Pai, 2002). Concerning diversity, it is not significant in OLS, but significant and negative in IV. The heterogeneity theory seems to hold true on the basis of IV, but the result is not robust. Among the control variables, it is clear that 'Good house' contributes to the provision of electric light.

Fourth, the West Bengal data also shows a clear case of the Muslims' weak voice on the basis of OLS and IV. Their weakness is clearer here than in Uttar Pradesh. One important reason might be the same as in the case of Uttar Pradesh, namely, the highly dispersed distribution of the Muslim population among the towns, which can be seen in Table 6.2. As has been explained in the case of Uttar Pradesh, the fact that the Muslim population is dispersed makes it easy for their relatively greater inability to get electric lights to show up in the regression analysis. This inability seems to be due to the weak socio-political status of Muslims, the historical origins of which can be traced back to the colonial era (Siddiqui, 1989). Although the Left Front government, which has been in power in West Bengal since 1977, has to be praised for having prevented communal riots, it seems not to have been so active in improving the socio-economic status of this minority (Dasgupta, 2009). The SCs seem to be disadvantaged in OLS, but this is not clear in IV. Concerning diversity, it does not have any significant relation to the provision of electric light. Finally, it is very clear that towns with many good houses are likely to have more electric lights.

Finally, it must be mentioned that there seems to be no major contradiction between our analysis of the pooled samples and that of each state's sample. The Muslims' position of disadvantage is confirmed in the datasets for Uttar Pradesh and West Bengal, as well as in the pooled samples. Although the coefficients for Muslims are not statistically significant in the cases of Gujarat and Bihar, there are specific reasons that are particular to these states. Concerning the SCs, although the associations of the SCs with electric light are negative and significant at the sub-district level in both OLS and IV, they are neither stable nor robust at the town level in the pooled samples as well as at the level of each state. It can be said that the SCs are disadvantaged in rural areas, but the situation is not clear in urban areas.

In any case, it can be said that although there are limitations in terms of explanation, due to the social and political structure of each state, the weak voice theory in relation to Muslim communities can be supported in the present Indian situation.

Diversity is, by and large, neither stable nor robust. The coefficients of diversity are negative and significant in line with heterogeneity theory in a few regressions, but they are positive or statistically not significant in other cases. So, the heterogeneity theory cannot be supported firmly on the basis of the present dataset.

Concluding remarks

In this chapter, the weak voice theory and the heterogeneity theory, with regard to the provision of electric light, are examined with special reference to Muslim communities. As mentioned above, the weak voice theory is, by and large, supported, in spite of some limitations in terms of explanation that depend on the socio-political structure of each state.[15]

The weak position of Muslims has been an explicit part of the political agenda since the end of the 1970s. The Congress government, under Mrs Indira Gandhi, sent to Chief Ministers of the states the so-called *Prime Minister's 15-Point Programme on Minorities* on the subject of the welfare of minorities. The programme consisted of three main sections, namely, 'Communal Riots', 'Recruitment to State and Central Services' and 'Other Measures' (Gandhi, 1983). After 23 years, the new 15-point programme was published in 2006. The *Prime Minister's New 15-Point Programme for Welfare of Minorities* consists of four main sections, namely, (A) Enhancing Opportunities for Education, (B) Equitable Share in Economic Activities and Employment, (C) Improving the Living Conditions of Minorities and (D) Prevention and Control of Communal Riots (Government of India, 2006b). Comparing the two 15-point programmes, it is obvious that the priority for policy is to shift from social security to socio-economic development. The evidence of Muslims' weak position in terms of basic social facilities, which this chapter has revealed, presents a clear case for such a shift.

The question is: what kinds of special affirmative action measures are more appropriate for reducing the gap between Muslims and other communities? Reservations for Muslims, which are recommended by the Misra Commission, will assuage the feelings of Muslims, but there will only be a limited number of beneficiaries from the communities. On the other hand, socio-economic assistance, especially better provision of basic public facilities, as well as education, may become much more important in an era of economic development that is centred on the private sector. As far as urban areas are concerned, improving the urban infrastructure in areas where Muslims are concentrated is an urgent task. This is, first, because, as this chapter has revealed, they are disadvantaged in towns compared to other sections of the population. Second, the development of an urban infrastructure is expected to lead to socio-economic development in these areas, which will facilitate socio-economic interaction among the various communities. Besides, if the urban areas where Muslims are in a majority are to be redeveloped, this should be done in such a way that the redevelopment facilitates socio-economic communication and interaction among the different communities, so that the 'ghettoization' of Muslims does not occur. The strengthening of socio-economic ties between Muslims and other communities will be a necessary condition for the stabilization of local society.

Notes

1. According to the 'National Commission of Minorities Act, 1992', Muslims, Christians, Buddhists, Sikhs and Parsis are recognized as minorities at the national level. In the states, Jains are recognized legally as a minority in Maharashtra, Karnataka, Madhya Pradesh, Rajasthan, Uttar Pradesh, Chhattisgarh, Jharkhand, Uttarakhand and Delhi.
2. 'Scheduled Castes' are the castes recognized by the Constitution of India as special groups of people, who can receive the benefits of special affirmative policies because of their history of being discriminated against as untouchables. 'Scheduled Tribes' are also constitutionally recognized tribes for special affirmative policies because of discrimination in their history and their social backwardness. It goes without saying that both SCs and STs consist of a variety of castes or tribes, which makes it very difficult to rally SCs or STs as a whole to make collective and strong demands.
3. 'Other Backward Classes' are a collective category for those people who do not have such historically discriminated background, either of untouchability or of being regarded as backward tribes, like the SCs and the STs, but they are still socially and educationally backward. The Indian government implemented the reservation of posts in the central government for OBCs in 1993.
4. The new 15-point programme mainly consists of several educational and employment promotion schemes. A characteristic feature of the programme is a budgetary arrangement that reserves 15 per cent for minorities. This is a programme that follows on from Mrs Indira Gandhi's 15-Point Programme for the Welfare of Minorities in 1983. The Rajiv Gandhi government also communicated the importance of this programme in his letter to Chief Ministers in 1985.
5. In the same way, accessibility to the public distribution system for food grain is 21.8 per cent in the case of Muslims and 34.1 per cent for Hindus (Shariff, 1999: 259).
6. Hereafter, I will include the concept of 'semi-public goods' in the public goods category in order to simplify the argument, but this will not damage the logic of the argument.
7. There is a criticism that government schemes for minorities are rarely implemented with sincerity and often funds meant for minorities are diverted (Kashif-Ul-Huda, 2009: 19).

8. In the Census of India 2001, the definition of an urban area was adopted as follows: (a) All statutory places with a municipality, corporation, cantonment board or notified town area committee, etc., (b) A place satisfying the following three criteria simultaneously:(i) a minimum population of 5,000; (ii) at least 75 per cent of the male working population engaged in non-agricultural pursuits; and (iii) a density of population of at least 400 per sq km (1,000 per sq mile) (www.censusindia.gov.in/Metadata/Metada.htm, accessed 5 January 2010).
9. As mentioned before, the census of 2001 is epoch-making because the detailed data on religion up to the sub-district or town level has been made available to the public. It is thanks to this that the analysis of this chapter has become possible.
10. The change in the definition of 'STs' has to be taken into account when comparing the 1961 and 2001 census data. Still, the increase in the proportion of the ST population in the towns between the two censuses might, to some extent, be due to their migration.
11. Generally, it is very important for local people, irrespective of whether they are Hindus or Muslims, to make strong collective 'demands' in order to get public goods promptly. Without such demands by local people, it might be difficult to get an electric connection promptly. I heard such opinions quite often from leaders in a few villages during my field visit in Dharbangha, Bihar, in September 2009. According to these leaders, their villages got electrical wires or distribution transformers after prolonged demands were made of the Bihar State Electricity Board or the Dharbangha district administration.
12. In 2001, the urbanization of Gujarat, Bihar, Uttar Pradesh and West Bengal, in terms of the population, was 37.36, 10.46, 20.78 and 27.97 per cent, respectively.
13. The sample sizes of the survey are 6,573 households in rural areas and 1,586 in urban areas.
14. There was a brief break in their rule in 2000.
15. I have conducted the same regression analysis with 'drinking water' as a dependent variable. The results are, by and large, the same as for 'Electric light'.

References

Census of India, 2001

Housing Census, 2001

Government of India (Office of the Registrar General) (2003a) *Census of India 2001 – Tables on Houses, Household Amenities & Assets: Uttaranchal, Uttar Pradesh, Jharkhand, Bihar (CD)*, New Delhi (Data Product No. 00-031-2001-Cen-CD).

_____ (2003b) *Census of India 2001 – Tables on Houses, Household Amenities & Assets: Gujarat, Maharashtra, Goa, Dadra & Nagar Haveli, Daman & Diu (CD)*, New Delhi (Data Product No. 00-035-2001-Cen-CD).

_____ (2003c) *Census of India 2001 – Tables on Houses, Household Amenities & Assets: Sikkim, West Bengal, Orissa, Andaman & Nicobar Islands (CD)*, New Delhi (Data Product No. 00-033-2001-Cen-CD).

Census, 2001

Government of India (Office of the Registrar General) (2004a) *Census of India 2001 – Primary Census Abstract: Daman & Diu, Dadra & Nagar Haveli, Gujarat (CD)*, New Delhi (Data Product No. 00-65-2001-Cen-CD).

_____ (2004b) *Census of India 2001 – Primary Census Abstract: Uttar Pradesh (CD)*, New Delhi (Data Product No. 00-56-2001-Cen-CD).

_____ (2004c) *Census of India 2001 – Primary Census Abstract: West Bengal, Orissa (CD)*, New Delhi (Data Product No. 00-60-2001-Cen-CD).

_____ (2005) *Census of India 2001 – Primary Census Abstract: Uttaranchal, Bihar, Jharkhand (CD)*, New Delhi (Data Product No. 00-57-2001-Cen-CD).

_____ (2006) *Census of India 2001 – Table name: C-1 Population by Religious Community (C0101) (CD)*, New Delhi.

Articles and books

Ahmad, Ausaf (1993) *Indian Muslims: Issues in Social and Economic Development*, New Delhi: Khama.

Ahmad, Imtiaz (ed.) (1983) *Modernization and Social Change among Muslims in India*, New Delhi: Manohar.

Alam, Javeed (2008) 'The Contemporary Muslim Situation in India: A Long-Term View', *Economic & Political Weekly*, 43 (2), 12 January, pp. 45–53.

Alesina, Alberto, Reza Baqir and William Easterly (1999) 'Public Goods and Ethnic Divisions', *Quarterly Journal of Economics*, 114 (4), November, pp. 1243–84.

Ansari, Iqbal A. (ed.) (1989) *The Muslim Situation in India*, New Delhi: Sterling.

Asian Development Research Institute (2006) *Socio-Economic and Educational Status of Muslims in Bihar* (A study sponsored by Bihar State Minorities Commission), Patna: Asian Development Research Institute.

Banerjee, Abhijit and Rohini Somanathan (2007) 'The Political Economy of Public Goods: Some Evidence from India', *Journal of Development Economics*, 82, pp. 287–314.

Banerjee, Abhijit, Lakshmi Iyer and Rohini Somanathan (2005) 'History, Social Divisions and Public Goods in Rural India', *Journal of the European Economic Association*, 3 (2–3), pp. 639–47.

Betancourt, Roger and Suzanne Gleason (2000) 'The Allocation of Publicly-Provided Goods to Rural Households in India: On Some Consequences of Caste, Religion and Democracy', *World Development*, 28 (12), pp. 2169–82.

Chandra, Kanchan (2004) *Why Ethnic Parties Succeed: Patronage and Ethnic Headcounts in India*, New York, NY: Cambridge University Press.

Coleman, James S. (1990) *Foundations of Social Theory*, Cambridge, MA: Harvard University Press.

Dasgupta, Abhijit (2009) 'On the Margins: Muslims in West Bengal', *Economic & Political Weekly*, 44 (16), 18 April, pp. 91–6.

Gandhi, Indira (1983) *Prime Minister's Fifteen-Point Programme on Minorities*. in *Readings on Minorities: Perspectives and Documents*, Vol. II, ed. Iqbal A. Ansari, 1996, New Delhi: Institute of Objective Studies (Prime Minister's letter dated 11 May 1983 to the Home Minister and copies to all Members of the Council of Ministers regarding the problems of minorities).

Government of India (Ministry of Power) (2005) *National Electricity Policy*, New Delhi (*The Gazette of India*, Extraordinary, Part I – Section 1, www.powermin.

nic.in/indian_electricity_scenario/national_electricity_policy.htm, accessed 10 January 2010).

Government of India (Prime Minister's High Level Committee) (Chairperson: Rajindar Sachar) (2006a) *Social, Economic and Educational Status of the Muslim Community of India*, New Delhi: Cabinet Secretariat ('Sachar Committee' in this chapter).

Government of India (2006b) *Prime Minister's New 15 Point Programme for Welfare of Minorities*, New Delhi (www.ncm.nic.in/points_programme.html, accessed 20 December 2009).

Habyarimana, James, Macartan Humphreys, Daniel N. Posner and Jeremy M. Weinstein (2007) 'Why Does Ethnic Diversity Undermine Public Goods Provision?', *American Political Science Review*, 101 (4), November, pp. 709–25.

Haqqi, S. A. H. (1989) 'Muslims in India: A Behavioural Introduction', in Iqbal A. Ansari (ed.), *The Muslim Situation in India*, New Delhi: Sterling.

Hasan, Mushirul (2004) 'Muslims in Secular India: Problems and Prospects in Education', in Mushirul Hasan (ed.), *Will Secular India Survive?*, New Delhi: imprintOne.

Hasan, Zoya (1998) *Quest for Power: Oppositional Movements and Post Congress Politics in Uttar Pradesh*, Delhi: Oxford University Press.

Hirschman, Albert O. (1970) *Exit, Voice, and Loyalty: Responses to Decline in Firms, Organizations, and States*, Cambridge, MA: Harvard University Press.

Jahangirabad Media Institute and ActionAid-India, and Indian Social Institute (2006) *National Study on Socio-Economic Condition of Muslims in India*, New Delhi: Indian Social Institute.

Jayal, Niraja Gopal (2006) *Representing India: Ethnic Diversity and the Governance of Public Institutions*, Basingstoke: Palgrave Macmillan.

Kashif-Ul-Huda (2009) 'How Not to Do Minority Welfare', *Economic & Political Weekly*, 44 (36), 5 September, pp. 19–21.

Kirmani, Nida (2008) 'History, Memory and Localised Constructions of Insecurity', *Economic & Political Weekly*, 43 (10), 8 March, pp. 57–64.

Mayer, Peter B. (1983) 'Tombs and Dark Houses: Ideology, Intellectuals and Proletarians in the Study of Contemporary Indian Islam', in Imtiaz Ahmad (ed.), *Modernization and Social Change among Muslims in India*, New Delhi: Manohar.

Miguel, Edward and Mary Kay Gugerty (2005) 'Ethnic Diversity, Social Sanctions, and Public Goods in Kenya', *Journal of Public Economics*, 89 (11–12), pp. 2325–68.

Ministry of Minority Affairs (Government of India) (Chairman: Ranganath Misra) (2007) *Report of the National Commission for Religious and Linguistic Minorities*, New Delhi: Alaknanda Advertising ('Misra Commission' in this chapter).

National Commission for Minorities (1997) *Third Annual Report – Financial Year 1995–1996*, New Delhi: Government of India Press.

_____ (2001) *Annual Report for 1999–2000*, New Delhi: Government of India Press.

Pai, Sudha (2002) *Dalit Assertion and the Unfinished Democratic Revolution: The Bahujan Samaj Party in Uttar Pradesh*, New Delhi: Sage.

Putnam, Robert D., Robert Leonardi and Raffaella Y. Nanetti (1993) *Making Democracy Work: Civic Traditions in Modern Italy*, Princeton, NJ: Princeton University Press.

Ranganathan, V. and T. V. Ramanayya (1998) 'Long-Term Impact of Rural Electrification: A Study in UP and MP', *Economic and Political Weekly*, 33 (50), 12 December, pp. 3181–4.

Sachchidananda and K.K. Verma (1983) *Electricity and Social Change*, Patna: Janaki Prakashan.

Shani, Ornit (2007) *Communalism, Caste and Hindu Nationalism: The Violence in Gujarat*, New York, NY: Cambridge University Press.

Shariff, Abusaleh (1999) *India Human Development Report*, New Delhi: National Council of Applied Economic Research.

Siddiqui, M. K. A. (1989) 'Muslim Education in Calcutta', in Iqbal A. Ansari (ed.), *The Muslim Situation in India*, New Delhi: Sterling.

Zainuddin, Sayyed (2003) 'Islam, Social Stratification and Empowerment of Muslim OBCs', *Economic and Political Weekly*, 38 (46), 15 November, pp. 4898–901.

7
Challenges for Inclusive Sustained Employment: An Attempt to Organize Female Embroidery Homeworkers in Delhi

Mayumi Murayama

Introduction

In India, which has begun to experience high economic growth, it has become critical for the government and for society at large to make this growth more inclusive by ensuring decent employment and better economic and social security. The Indian National Congress, at the head of the United Progressive Alliance (UPA) government that came to power in 2004 with the promise of benefiting *aam aadmi* (common people), achieved a second and even larger victory in the general election of 2009. The post-election assessments report that the victory owed much to the government's employment creation measures, namely the National Rural Employment Guarantee Act (NREGA) of 2005,[1] which legally ensures 100 days of manual work a year to any willing household at the statutory minimum wage. Since NREGA covers only rural areas, there has been a call for measures to tackle the problems of urban employment, including expanding NREGA to the urban areas.

The problems of urban employment primarily concern unorganized workers in the non-agricultural sector, who numbered 167 million people in 2004/5 (NCEUS, 2007: 14). According to the National Commission for Enterprises in the Unorganized Sector (NCEUS), which was constituted in 2004 under the first UPA government, unorganized workers consist of those working in unorganized enterprises or households, excluding regular workers with social security benefits, and workers in the formal sector without any employment/social security benefits provided by the employer. In this definition, the unorganized sector refers to all unincorporated private enterprises owned by individuals or households engaged in the sale and production of goods and services operating on a proprietary or partnership basis and employing less than ten workers in total. In a nutshell, they are workers without adequate legislative or other support with regard to their employment and/or conditions of work (*ibid.*: 3). Besides the large number at any specific point in time, what is striking is that this category's workers have been increasing over the years in which the country has begun to experience higher economic growth.

This chapter is a case study of embroidery homeworkers in a resettlement colony in Delhi. Delhi, for a long time a parochial town, despite being the seat of political power for 300 years, is now undergoing vibrant changes economically and socially. As the site of the Commonwealth Games in October 2010, the city was transformed into a 'world-class city', overwhelmed by an unprecedented construction boom. Infrastructure development, with modern amenities, such as metro, shopping malls, hotels and apartments were vigorously promoted. Right beside this progress, however, one could not help noticing that the city or the country has large-scale poverty, and that a substantial contribution to this progress was made by the sheer labour power of the men and women least likely to enjoy the comforts of these symbols of 'progress'.

While workers on the construction sites and in the streets are visible to onlookers, there are a massive number of other, invisible workers who are engaged in various types of production and services at home. The nature of their work is varied and covers a wide range of industries ranging from textiles, engineering, chemicals, food processing and so forth, to different types of personal services. They are home-based workers. Home-based workers consist of two types of worker: (1) independent employers or own-account workers (purely self-employed) and (2) dependent sub-contract workers (*ibid.*: 5). The second category of workers is termed 'homeworkers' under the ILO definition we cite below. Whereas the first category of home-based workers include economically better-off workers who provide various professional and technical services, homeworkers are considered to lie at the bottom of the working class because of their lower wages, which are usually in the form of piece rates, than those doing equivalent work outside. They also lack any legal protection. The focus of this chapter is on this second type of home-based worker.

In India, there are more than 8 million homeworkers. The NCEUS, established as part of government efforts to fulfil their manifesto to improve the welfare and wellbeing of workers in the informal sector, acknowledges the need for a special focus on homeworkers on two grounds. They state, 'Firstly, a significant share of women workers belong to this segment, and, secondly, therefore, they warrant separate treatment from a policy point of view' (*ibid.*). The NCEUS, however, was not the first to identify the problems of female homeworkers. The issue has been addressed ever since the 1970s, initially by the non-governmental initiatives such as the Self-Employed Women's Association (SEWA) (Bhatt, 2006; Rose, 1992; Kitamura, 2004). *Towards Equality*, the official document prepared by the Committee on the Status of Women in India prior to the first United Nations International Women's Year in 1975, discovered contrasting trends. First, household industries, such as hand weaving, oil pressing, rice pounding, leather, tobacco processing and so on, which were the major sources of women's employment, had declined over time as a result of competition from factory production and, second, some establishments resorted to farming out work to be done by women at home as a strategy to avoid falling under the purview of labour laws (Government of India, 1975: 170).[2] To some extent, the Committee detailed homeworkers' conditions in the *bidi* (indigenous hand-rolled cigarette), match and *Chikan* (a traditional embroidery style mainly from Lucknow, Uttar Pradesh) industries. In 1988, *Shramshakti*, the report of the National Commission on Self-employed Women and Women in the Informal Sector, was published. The report underscored the necessity to raise wages and to improve the implementation of labour laws for homeworkers. Further, it recommended the enactment of a new law specific to homeworkers in order to give them greater visibility and tailored to the peculiar conditions of homework in which the direct employer–employee relationship in the conventional legal sense is missing and workers are spread over a large area in dispersed locations (Government of India, 1988: 115–17).

The above-mentioned official reports and their recommendations have been substantiated by several micro studies which have highlighted the exploitative nature of home work on the basis of case or sector studies and, collectively, their findings indicate the increasingly large numbers of women and sectors entering the system of home work (Mies, 1982; articles in Singh and Kelles-Viitanen, 1987; Prasad and Prasad, 1990 – to mention a few of the earlier studies). More recent research corroborates the earlier research and finds that, even after several studies have been conducted and recommendations made, the conditions of homeworkers have seen little improvement (Mazumdar, 2007; All India Democratic Women's Association, 2009; Ghosh, 2009). The consequences of the dismal conditions of homeworkers have not been confined only to the homeworkers' individual wellbeing, they have also been affecting the children of the homeworkers' households, as many of the children are also involved in home work as unpaid labour. This has resulted in capability deprivation in terms of their education and health, particularly for the girls (Biggeri *et al.*, 2009).[3]

Furthermore, on the basis of an empirical analysis of NSSO data, Rani and Unni (2009) found that between 1994/5 and 2000/1, there was a sharp growth in male home-based workers, including homeworkers, whereas there was a slight decrease in female home-based workers.[4] The increase in male home-based workers took place in industries facing import penetration, but not in export-oriented industries. In the latter sector, the women's share remained high. They presume the reason for the differences can be found in the cost-cutting measures adopted by the two sectors. They have also presented the insightful finding that macro-policy changes have affected male home-based workers but not female home-based workers, whose choice to become home-based workers is better explained by a micro model which examines the effects of individual social attributes such as age, education, caste, religion, residence, whether rural or urban, marital status, number of young children and so forth.

The last two studies suggest a necessity to extend our scope of analysis to other household members than female homeworkers in order to examine the multifarious implications of home work and to draw up comprehensive approaches to solve their problems.

These studies have delineated the important characteristics and problems of homeworkers and some of them have described painstaking efforts to improve their situation. Nevertheless, if we consider the contribution made by the homeworkers to the economy and to their households, there is still a dearth of information about the homeworkers, even compared to other types of female workers, such as factory workers or domestic workers. As for the protection of their labour rights, enactment of a separate law is said to be under consideration. Moreover, while there are common features which characterize the basic nature of homework as will be described in more detail in the following section, the economic, social and cultural contexts in which individual homeworkers live vary, as do the interventions undertaken by any outsiders, as well as their challenges and outcomes. This chapter analyzes a programme for embroidery homeworkers in Delhi carried out by SEWA Delhi on the basis of a survey conducted by the author from October to November in 2009. In a nutshell, the SEWA Delhi's approach is a direct intervention at the bottom of the global value chain. Through their experiences, we can see how an NGO can make a dent in the race to the bottom and improve the work and livelihoods of a particular group of homeworkers. Finally, we can reflect on what challenges remain in their approach in the way of incorporating invisible homeworkers into more inclusive and sustained employment.

The chapter consists of six sections. This introductory section is followed by a brief discussion, in the second section, on conceptual issues and the problems that result from these issues for the homeworkers. The third section presents an overview of homeworkers in India – the scale, characteristics and historical factors which gave rise to the current contours of the Indian homeworkers' situation. The export-oriented ready-made garment industry is given special focus as it provides the national and global contexts in which the embroidery homeworkers of our case study are situated. The fourth and fifth sections describe the experiences of SEWA Delhi's embroidery programme and identify its effects and problems. The findings are summarized and a wider applicability of the model is reviewed in the concluding section.

Theorizing homeworkers

The ILO Convention C177, adopted in 1996, defined a homeworker as one who carries out work (1) in his or her home or in other premises of his or her choice, other than the workplace of the employer; (2) for remuneration; (3) which results in a product or service as specified by the employer, irrespective of who provides the equipment, materials or other inputs used, unless this person has the degree of autonomy and economic independence necessary to be considered an independent worker under national laws, regulations or court decisions. In the Convention, the term 'employer' is assigned to refer to 'a person, natural or legal, who, either directly or through an intermediary, whether or not intermediaries are provided for in national legislation, gives out home work in pursuance of his or her business activity'. In other words, the employer–employee relationship is not bound by a legal or direct contract. Instead, it is deemed to exist on a realistic relationship between those who issue the primary orders and those who follow those orders. The Convention requires ratifying states to adopt, implement and periodically review a national policy on home work aimed at improving the situation of homeworkers. The fundamental principle is to ensure treatment for homeworkers which is equal to that for those engaged in the same or a similar type of work in an enterprise, in terms of the right to establish or join an organization of their own, protection against discrimination, safety and health, remuneration, statutory social security protection, access to training, a minimum age for admission to employment or work, and maternity protection. As of today, only six countries, namely,

Finland, Ireland, Albania, the Netherlands, Argentina and Bulgaria have ratified the Convention. It should be noted that, although India has not ratified the Convention, like the majority of the countries in the world, the country, represented by SEWA, was the prime mover in getting the Convention adopted (Prügl and Boris, 1996).

Homeworkers are sometimes called 'industrial homeworkers', 'disguised wage workers' or 'dependent subcontract workers'. A typical example is a seamstress who gets pre-cut materials from a manufacturer or an intermediary, sews the garments together at home, and is paid by the piece upon returning the finished products (Prügl and Tinker, 1997: 1472). Although the existence of homeworkers has been a common phenomenon for centuries and in many countries, it was only in 1996 that the ILO Home Work Convention was adopted. While movements to improve the conditions of homeworkers in individual countries began much earlier, collective initiatives across countries and regions began in the early 1990s. According to Elisabeth Prügl and Eileen Boris, behind the surge of interest in home-based work lay structural changes in the organization of international capitalism which were detrimentally affecting women's economic position. One notable change was the progressive decentralization of production processes around the world (Prügl and Boris, 1996: 5). It should be noted, however, that while the issue of women working in global factories as a consequence of these processes entered the academic limelight and became a focus of labour activism as early as the late 1970s, the issue of homeworkers, which had expanded in scope and depth along with the increase in subcontracting work, had to wait another decade to be noticed. This means that two significant perspectives should be kept in mind when we discuss the issue of homeworkers: first, that the issues are relatively less explored in terms of research and action to redress the problems and, second, and more importantly, the problems of homeworkers are not a carry-over from a state of affairs that we can characterize as being one of pre-industrialization, pre-liberalization or pre-globalization, but, instead, are part of the very process and consequences of ongoing global and national changes.

There are two key factors that have caused the neglect of the issue of homeworkers and have rendered it difficult to address their problems. The first one is related to stereotypical and gendered perceptions about work and a worker which do not fit the nature of home work and homeworkers, who are predominantly women and do the work at home side by side with other reproductive work, such as household chores and care work.[5] This has resulted in non-recognition of their economic contributions and their rights as workers. As is well known, feminist scholars have questioned the gendered notions of work and space and have argued that the notion of work should not be limited to waged work and that places and spaces of work stretch from factories and offices to the community, the streets and the home. Nevertheless, the conventional notion persists, not only among policy-planners and society as a whole but also among the female homeworkers themselves. Their home-based work is often perceived as subsidiary to household work, and women identify themselves as housewives or daughters rather than as workers.

The second problem concerns the legal conceptualization of the employment status of homeworkers vis-à-vis employees and self-employment. Elisabeth Prügl states that in most countries homeworkers do not have a separate legal status and therefore have to fit into the category of employee in order to qualify for protection under labour laws (Prügl, 1996: 206). According to Prügl and Tinker (1997: 1475), the legal tradition generally relies on two criteria to gauge the employment status of an employee: subordination and economic dependence. Subordination is related, first, to whether a provider of work exerts control on a worker in terms of their working hours, their place of work, any discipline involved, etc. and, second, whether the worker is under the direction of a work-provider as to how the work should be performed. On the other hand, economic dependence measures whether a worker is solely dependent on the work-provider or whether there are opportunities for taking risks and for making a profit or loss. The status of home-based workers or homeworkers is often ambiguous in the light of these criteria. They are usually under the direction of a work-provider but are not under his/her direct supervision and, although economic dependence generally holds true for a large number of homeworkers, there is still some scope for a worker to exercise their own discretion. The ambiguities of a homeworker's status, as lying between being employees and self-employment have negative consequences for them when it comes to availing themselves of existing legal provisions. Moreover, due to these factors, the number of homeworkers has been grossly underestimated in official statistics (Chen *et al.*, 1999: 605).

Overview of homeworkers in India

Scale and characteristics

Like the majority of countries in the world, homeworkers have not been properly captured by the official statistics of India. Sample surveys by the National Sample Survey Organization (NSSO), the most referred-to source of information, divide workers according to three types of status: self-employed, regular-salaried/wage employee and casual labour. The self-employed category is further classified into three sub-categories: own-account worker, employer and helper. Homeworkers are included in the category of self-employed, but, other than the NSS Employment and Unemployment Survey 1999–2000 (55th round), which asked some specific questions regarding a person's place of work and the nature of their contract, no direct estimation of the number and proportion of homeworkers has yet been made (NCEUS, 2007: 5).

In 1999/2000, about 12 per cent of self-employed workers were homeworkers. They numbered 8.2 million persons, with women constituting 58.5 per cent, or 4.8 million persons (*ibid*.: 57). With regard to rural–urban distribution, rural areas account for 61 per cent (5 million); the rest lived in urban areas. The concentration of female homeworkers in rural areas was slightly higher at 63 per cent (*ibid*.: 241, Appendix A1.4). Of the 365 million workers (employed) that year, homeworkers accounted for only 2 per cent of the total. Nevertheless, the representation of homeworkers among urban female workers is as high as about 10 per cent, which is not a negligible amount.[6]

If we look at the prevalence of homeworkers among self-employed workers in the unorganized manufacturing sector (in entities with less than ten workers in total, according to the NCEUS (2007: 3) definition), among the nearly 22 million workers, 32 per cent were homeworkers. The share of homeworkers was 20 per cent in the case of male workers, while nearly 50 per cent of female self-employed workers in unorganized manufacturing were homeworkers. The dominance of homeworkers was highest among urban female workers at 52 per cent (*ibid*.: 58). The industries where home-based employment dominates or accounts for a proportion equal to industrial shed-based employment are handlooms, *bidi*, artistic metal ware, *agarbathi* (incense stick), and so on (*ibid*.: 70).

Table 7.1 shows the degree of control of production for non-agricultural home-based workers – that is, whether they produce under given specifications. Here we can observe that independent home-based workers constitute only half of all non-agricultural home-based workers. In both rural and urban areas, around one third of the home-based workers are under the subordination of work-providers and the degree of subordination is higher among female workers. They are predominantly paid on piece rates rather than on the basis of a contract. Gender disparity also exists in the mode of payment, since 80 per cent and 76 per cent of rural and urban female workers, respectively, are paid on piece rates, while the ratios among rural and urban male workers are 64 per cent and 63 per cent.[7] Among unorganized manufacturing homeworkers, about 70 per cent

Table 7.1 Extent of control of production for non-agricultural sector home-based workers (%)

	Wholly	Mainly	(Wholly+ mainly)	Partly	No	Others	Total
Rural male	19.9	4.8	24.7	4.4	63.6	7.3	100.0
Rural female	41.8	4.6	46.4	2.8	47.5	3.3	100.0
Rural total	29.9	4.7	34.6	3.7	56.3	5.4	100.0
Urban male	19.6	5.7	25.3	4.7	63.1	6.9	100.0
Urban female	36.4	6.6	43.0	4.3	47.7	5.0	100.0
Urban total	26.6	6.1	32.7	4.5	56.7	6.1	100.0

Note: Including the status of both principal and subsidiary. The term 'home-based workers' refers to those whose workplace is their own dwelling.
Source: Compiled from Table 14, NSSO (1999b).

(68 per cent for men and 71 per cent for women), were involved in vertical subcontracting, rather than horizontal subcontracting. The difference in the two arrangements is related to the provision of production materials. While horizontal subcontracting contracts out work without providing production materials and thus leaves some independence to the workers, which is similar to the situation for independent self-employed workers, vertical subcontracting creates a more dependent production relationship and is closer to the situation for a wage worker, except with regard to the lack of supervision. This again indicates the strong dependency of home-workers on work-providers and the resultant vulnerability and insecurity of their work (*ibid.*: 59).

Historical evolution

The degree of prevalence and the characteristics of home-based work differ from country to country as they are a reflection of the process and state of each individual country's development as well as of policy stances *vis-à-vis* economic development, labour and social issues. In the case of India, the existence of vast traditional household industries, the impact of colonization, modernization and commercialization, slow and uneven industrialization in the post-independence period, the impact of globalization, and the liberalization of the economy since the 1980s are the major economic factors which have drawn the contours of home work in India today.[8] Moreover, gender roles and ideologies accorded to women individually and socially, which defined their mobility, their responsibility for reproductive work, the required level and nature of their education and skills, and the notion of 'suitable jobs' for women have had determining effects on their work options.

Although home-based work as the traditional work of artisans and service castes has existed for centuries, many household industries went into decline under colonial rule. Among the more affected were labour-intensive industries in which the workforce was predominantly female, such as hand-spinning, weaving, paper, jute articles, etc. (Government of India, 1975: 153; Banerjee, 1989). Goods produced by home-based work lost their market in the face of a combination of commercialization and competition from goods produced by the modern factory sector inside and outside the country. The mechanization of what were earlier manual production processes, for instance, from rice-pounding to rice mills, and a shortage of low-cost materials for production further reduced the demand for female labour. The inception of modern factory production, such as in jute and textiles, further undermined traditional home-based production. Although some women constituted a section of the modern factory workforce, they remained unskilled or semi-skilled workers (Government of India, 1975: 151). Furthermore, a larger number of women stayed outside the modern factory sector because of the social and cultural restrictions that were imposed upon them, as well as the poor living conditions for factory workers, which also hindered women's family migration, let alone single migration, as in the case of the jute industry in Calcutta (Banerjee, 1989; Sen, 1999).

According to Prasad and Prasad (1990), the origin of the present-day putting-out system or subcontracting to homeworkers goes back to the Mughal period. By the mid-18th century, some traditional industries and home-based work became organized to cater to an expanding overseas market. Initially, the merchants, acting as middlemen for foreign companies, gave advances to the artisans and bought back the products in a system called *dadni*. Under the *dadni* system, producers still had considerable control over their production in terms of arranging their own materials and deciding on the production process. However, their dependence on middlemen gradually grew. The latter, on behalf of European merchants, placed orders, and later they also supplied designs and materials, and decided on the production process (ibid:. 3–4). With the spread of the putting-out system, which was quite advantageous for work-providers, home work continued to exist or rather expanded in closer links with different modes of production, such as the modern factory sector and small-scale enterprises through putting-out and subcontracting as part or all of the production process. As in the case of the *bidi* industry, some industries changed from factory-based production to the putting-out system to evade the extra costs of labour welfare that were imposed by the Factory Act enacted in 1952 (ibid:. 27). A similar process of shifting from the formal sector to home work was effected under the Indian Bidi and Cigar Workers (Conditions of Employment) Act of 1966 (Prügl, 1996: 204). The abundant supply of female labour and their limited mobility has worked in favour of work-providers to reduce piece rates. As Jeanne Hahn puts it, 'women did not cease to be productive workers, but the simultaneous erosion of many of their traditional occupations and the emergence of a male-dominated waged work force obscured their visibility' (Hahn, 1996: 222).

Another important change has taken place since the 1980s. It is now a well-known fact that the liberalization and globalization of the economy has accelerated the informalization of employment by way of the closure and down-sizing of public sector employment and the increasing use of cheap and flexible labour, such as casual, contract workers and female workers, especially in export-oriented, labour-intensive industries. The process has also led to a greater use of industrial homeworkers as they are the cheapest form of labour and are unprotected by labour laws. Rani and Unni (2009) found that India's recent economic reforms have caused an increase in male home-based workers as a result of cost-cutting measures by firms, while the participation of females in home-based work remained high and was little affected by these macro-policy changes. Nevertheless, the indirect effects of the increase in male home-based work may well have been substantial on women and other family members at the household level. It is documented in several studies that the loss of employment or downward mobility from more secure employment to one that is less secure and with low returns among male breadwinners has forced many women to take on home-based work to supplement their household's income (Bhatt, 2006: 8; Kiso, 2008: 55).

Embroidery homeworkers in the export-oriented ready-made garment industry

The export-oriented ready-made garment industry is a typical example of how economic globalization and liberalization have played a pivotal role in the diffusion of home work, especially among women in developing countries. While numerous detailed studies have been conducted on female factory workers in various countries, few of these studies have shed light on homeworkers, the 'weaker link' in the global value chain (Carr *et al.*, 2000: 129; McCormick and Schmitz, 2002).

There is no accurate information on how many homeworkers are involved in the ready-made garment industry. The NCEUS states that a large part of the production is outsourced to home-based workers (NCEUS, 2007: 70). In India, the export-oriented garment industry emerged in the 1960s. Unlike many other major exporters – Bangladesh, for instance, which largely relied on imported mill-made raw materials – India's export garments gained initial popularity in the USA and Europe in the early 1970s through handloom garments and other indigenous fabrics. Since the mid-1980s, a rise in the popularity of knitwear garments and the gradual replacement of handlooms by mill-made garments has occurred. In 2007/8, India's garment exports reached about $9.7 billion, accounting for about 6 per cent of India's total export earnings.[9]

Although capacity expansion and investments in technical modernization began in the late 1980s and 1990s, India's garment sector today consists of a large number of small firms and a decentralized and networked production structure, partly because of state policy, which kept the ready-made garments industry reserved for the small-scale sector with an investment ceiling being imposed upon it until 2001. Today, India has several garment hubs across the country. Each hub is independent in terms of sourcing raw materials and labour, and has developed unique product specialities (Murayama, 2008: 65–6). It is assumed that this specific development process and the structure of the export garments industry, along with the rich artisan tradition and skills, which are in demand to produce the exquisite hand-worked, embellished clothing and accessories that attract fashion-conscious consumers, have given rise to the enormous pool of garment homeworkers in India. According to Rao and Husain (1987), they are involved in different types of work, such as cutwork, embroidery, crochet, tracing and button stitching (59). The geographical dispersal of homeworkers seems paradoxically to be broad in contrast to the tiny space of the homeworkers' actual 'workplace' and their limited mobility. The homeworkers in our survey have been taking orders from export houses located not only inside Delhi proper but also from those in Faridabad (Haryana) and Noida (Uttar Pradesh), although they themselves, have little knowledge of where their products are delivered and sold.

Interventions by SEWA Delhi in organizing embroidery homeworkers

Organization and activities related to the embroidery programme

SEWA Delhi was established in 1999 as an independent organization promoted by SEWA Bharat – the All-India Federation of Self-employed Women's Association – which has ten member organizations spread across eight states.[10] SEWA Delhi started setting up Self-help Groups (SHGs) and has since been working with women workers, such as street vendors, embroidery workers, construction workers and domestic workers. In 2007, the membership totalled 13,570 and, in 2008/9, it reached around 28,000. While promoting SHGs, they came to know of the conditions of the embroidery workers in Sundernagri, where their embroidery workers' programme was later implemented. According to them:

> Although skilled in embroidery work, the women here still used to receive work on a piece-rate basis from the moneylenders or contractors, who did not pay them the fair rates for their labour. Being poor and illiterate, they were literally voiceless.
>
> In this context, SEWA Delhi intervened to remove the chain of middlemen and directly link the members to new companies.[11]

The Embroidery Centre was set up in October 2005. The objectives of the Centre are: (1) empowering women artisans by bringing them into the mainstream, (2) eliminating the middlemen and protecting the workers from exploitation, (3) linking the women to mainstream markets, (4) enhancing the income level of the women workers and (5) making the enterprise self-sustainable and forming a cooperative that could be owned, managed and controlled by the women.[12] The initial idea of the programme was conceived at a meeting of the National Home Workers Group, which was promoted by the Ethical Trading Initiative (ETI), based in London. ETI is a coalition of companies, trade unions and NGOs established in 1998 with the purpose of improving the lives of workers in global supply chains by promoting responsible corporate practice. Big retailers, such as GAP, Monsoon and Next, as well as SEWA, are members of ETI. SEWA was involved in preparing the guidelines for applying and implementing the ETI base code with homeworkers.

SEWA Delhi approached GAP to implement this initiative. Subsequently, an export house, which worked for GAP, gave SEWA their first small order, and the house promised that they would give them more orders if SEWA Delhi could provide high-quality products. Initially, the work started with only eight or nine women homeworkers, but now around 500 women are involved in the work of two main centres established in Sundernagri and Rajiv Nagar. To promote the interests of the homeworkers, three sub-centres have been established, one in Nand Nagri, adjacent to Sundernagri, and two near Rajiv Nagar.

Sample making, quality checks, the distribution of materials,[13] record keeping and training are all carried out at the centres. Record keeping covers information related to production, daily reports and payments. Individual members are given a passbook, which registers the pieces taken and delivered as well as their wages.[14] Members are also given individual tag numbers and they stick the tag number to the back of the stitched garments. Until October 2009, each centre consisted of seven members of staff, including a *Sathi* (a grassroots leader from the same locality who mobilizes more embroidery workers to join the programme), supervisors/trainers/record keepers/material distributors and a centre coordinator. In addition to these centre-based staff, a production supervisor and a programme coordinator look after the technical side of production and the overall functions of the programme, respectively. Except for the production supervisor and the programme coordinator, the staff all belong to the local community. The staff of the centres were, until recently, all women, except for one, a driver who moves between the centres and the export houses.[15] The aim was to persuade female homeworkers to come out to the centres and to assure male family members that the centre was a safe place for women. In the centres, weekly meetings are held to inform the members about weekly or bi-weekly production targets. The agenda of the weekly meetings ranges from discussions about SEWA's objectives and programmes to talk about problems related to production. Sometimes experts, such as a lawyer, are called into the meeting to disseminate information and provide counselling about social and economic issues, such as divorce, property shares and the obtaining of ration cards. There are members called *Aageban* who represent all the members and are appointed by SEWA Delhi. They are usually selected on the basis of criteria such as some degree of literacy, the ability to speak up on issues, their activities as a member and their knowledge of the business. There are four *Aageban* in Sundernagri Centre. Representation from different residential blocks and religious communities are taken into consideration at the time of selection. *Aageban* are consulted on important issues about the programme.

Besides the embroidery programme, SEWA Delhi runs a Gender Resource Centre (GRC) in the same locality. GRC is part of the *Bhagidari* (partnership) programme of the social welfare department of the Delhi government. Their work is mainly to provide various kinds of training and access for local residents to various government welfare schemes. The SHGs were registered as a cooperative, the Mahila SEWA Urban Credit and Thrift Society Limited, in 2007. Members have been encouraged to open an account, although SEWA Delhi does not pressurize anyone, especially those whose income is low and not so regular. For those who have an account, a fortnightly payment of wages (on a piece-rate basis) is made through the cooperative's bank accounts and in cash for those who do not have an account. Currently, 90 members from the two centres have accounts.

Production process of the embroidery programme

The products that the embroidery workers of SEWA Delhi produce are all exported to the US and the EU market through the export houses. From 2005 to the present, SEWA Delhi has interacted with more than ten export houses. However, their engagement fluctuates, dependent as it is on the orders. There is no sustained relationship with a particular export house.

SEWA Delhi's principle on wages is to ensure statutory minimum wages. The minimum daily wages in Delhi at the time of the survey were set at Rs 151 (approximately US$3.3), Rs 158 (US$3.5) and Rs 168 (US$3.7) for unskilled, semi-skilled and skilled workers, respectively. Nevertheless, maintaining this standard is one of the organization's most difficult tasks, because there are abundant sources of labour besides SEWA Delhi, and there is competition from the *thekedars* (middlemen). There are two types of rates offered by the export houses, one open (i.e., fixed rates by the export houses) and the other closed. In the case of closed rates, SEWA Delhi conducts a time and motion study with five members at the centre and on the basis of the derived average rates; they negotiate with the export houses. The export houses have their own rates, which are offered by other *thekedars* and which are likely to be minimum market rates. Approximately 30 to 40 per cent of all the orders are on open rates. SEWA Delhi takes orders on open rates during the lean season.[16] An example mentioned by the programme coordinator is that if SEWA Delhi's rate, calculated from the time and motion study, is Rs 10 and the rate offered by an export house is Rs 4, SEWA takes the order if the negotiation ends up at, for instance, Rs 7. According to the programme coordinator, the possibility of negotiating the price partly depends on the type of work. Heavy styles with a lot of embroidery work may be negotiable, but light styles are not.

When a new order comes, members first make a sample at the centre. After approval from the staff, they take the materials back home. Some gifts, such as utensils and lunch boxes, but not cash, are provided to members as an incentive to meet production targets.[17] Quality control is done by the staff and, in some cases, by the quality controllers of the export houses, who visit the centre occasionally.

The challenge of dual objectives

The approach of SEWA Delhi towards the embroidery homeworkers can be summarized thus: to ensure enhanced piece rates and to nurture collective strength among hitherto isolated workers. Moreover, an important premise of their programme is the acknowledgement of the reasons why women prefer home-based work, so SEWA Delhi tries to maintain the flexibility and advantages of home-based work in their work model. Simultaneously, SEWA Delhi is trying to develop a business culture among the members so that the programme will become a financially sustainable business entity on its own. These dual objectives are easier said than done. The programme coordinator stated in our first meeting that the balance between the social and economic objectives is the most difficult goal to achieve. For instance, while some export houses insist on the daily delivery of finished products, members who prefer to remain home-based workers cannot be forced to take orders or to come out of their homes. In the global supply chain, the time allowed for outsourced embroidery work is set at a minimum since it constitutes the bottom of the chain. This severely circumscribes SEWA Delhi's ability to manage the production process. One consequence of these constraints has been a fluctuation in the labour supply and a resulting decrease in orders from export houses.[18]

When our research was about to start, SEWA Delhi was planning to expand its membership of embroidery workers, because they found that a shortage of production capacity was the major obstacle to the further development of the programme. In their understanding, the reasons of the labour shortage were as follows. First, some members take orders from *thekedars* alongside orders through SEWA Delhi. Second, some members are sometimes not available as they visit their villages. As a long-term solution, SEWA Delhi has been trying to increase production capacity by providing training at both the centres and the GRC. However, as a short-term solution, they conducted a mapping survey to identify potential members and assess their skills in and around the centres. They also sought advice from an expert who is knowledgeable about social entrepreneurship and sustainable business models in the social sector. Out of the meeting, some practical suggestions were made with regard to relationships with existing members as well as with the export houses, in addition to the induction of new members and the exploration of a domestic market for their products. The suggestions even included a proposal to establish a production centre where women could sit and do their work outside their homes. On this, the coordinator of SEWA Delhi showed some reluctance, saying that he would not like to create a factory model and he would rather like to ensure the liberty and flexibility of home-based workers.[19] In the meeting, another officer expressed her opinion that members might perceive

SEWA Delhi as a sophisticated middleman, and that members have not understood SEWA's goals and objectives.

What came out of the meeting and subsequent hearings was the necessity for a more detailed survey of existing members regarding their household situation and their perception about the programme and SEWA Delhi as a whole. On the basis of further discussions with SEWA Delhi, our survey was conducted with three main objectives; first, to garner information about the social and economic conditions of each member, second, to identify whether they are engaged in work other than work through SEWA Delhi and if so, why, and, third, to assess how they perceive their engagement with SEWA Delhi. For these purposes, we defined three sample groups: active SEWA Delhi members, non-active SEWA Delhi members, who in our definition have not taken work from the centre for the last six months and, finally, embroidery homeworkers who are not working with SEWA Delhi but have made other arrangements. The survey was carried out with members of the Sundernagri Centre, and we tried to cover all the active members. This turned out to be 146 members. From the old member list kept at the centre, we were able to trace 78 non-active members.[20] As a control group, we collected information from 70 non-SEWA embroidery workers in Sundernagri. According to the mapping survey done by SEWA Delhi earlier, there are more than 500 households that have women with embroidery skills in Sundernagri. Due to time and financial constraints, the selection of the sample of non-SEWA embroidery workers was not based on a systematic sampling method, but, instead, was rather arbitrary. We used a snowballing technique, although geographical dispersion within the colony was taken into account. The aim was chiefly to make a rough comparison with SEWA members and to get a better idea of their work with contractors and their reasons for not engaging with SEWA Delhi's embroidery programme.

Survey findings

Socio and economic profile of embroidery workers and their households

Sundernagri is a resettlement colony in the North-East District of Delhi. According to a recent survey conducted by the GRC, there were more than 12,000 households and about 62,000 people living in 15 blocks in the colony in 2008. The colony was first developed in about 1976, with a plot of 25 square yards for each household. With the expansion of the colony, there sprang up three unauthorized blocks in what were then empty spaces. The original residents of the colony were those who faced the forced demolition of their residences in Old Delhi during the Emergency (1975–7) and some migrants from Uttar Pradesh, which borders the colony. Presently, the latter group accounts for the large majority of residents in Sundernagri, as 78 per cent of our sample households are of Uttar Pradesh origin, while 13 per cent originated from Delhi. The majority of the houses are *pucca* (permanent) buildings although *jhuggis* (makeshift dwellings) also exist on the periphery. Around 90 per cent of our sample workers reside in *pucca* houses. Almost three-quarters live in their own houses or in houses owned by close relatives, while the rest live in rented houses with an average monthly rent of Rs 1,500 (approximately US$33). Nevertheless, residential space per capita is extremely small as the average household size is as many as 6.2 persons, in contrast to the Delhi average of 5.1 persons or 5.7 persons for the North-East District, according to the population census of 2001.

Table 7.2 shows the demographic characteristics of our sample households compared to the situation in Delhi as well as in the North-East District, although information for the latter is out of date due to the absence of more recent data. There are several notable features. The first is the high sex ratio (number of females per 1,000 males) among our embroidery workers' households. The North-East District recorded the highest sex ratio of 849 among the nine districts of Delhi in 2001. In our sample, women outnumber men in all three types of households. Second, the embroidery homeworkers are predominantly Muslim. The aforementioned GRC survey finds the share of Muslim households in Sundernagri is 42.3 per cent. Therefore, the concentration of Muslims is higher in the colony than in Delhi, as well as in the North-East District, on average, and is again higher among embroidery homeworkers. One reason for the high sex ratio may be the high share of Muslim households in our sample. The religion-wise sex ratio of our sample tallies with the higher sex ratio among Muslim households (1,158) than Hindu households (1,096). It should be noted, however, that in our sample, the child sex ratio is lower than the Delhi and the North-East District, on average, in the case of non-SEWA Delhi workers' households, despite the fact that more than 90 per cent of them are Muslims. Third, the female literacy rate of our sample is higher than average when compared to Delhi and the North-East District, the latter recording the lowest female literacy rate in Delhi in 2001. This, however, may be due to outdated data for Delhi and the North-East District. What is more evident is the relatively low literacy rate among males in the embroidery homeworkers' households. Lastly, female household

Table 7.2 Household characteristics

	SEWA active (n = 146)	SEWA non-active (n = 78)	Non-SEWA (n = 70)	Total (n = 294)	Delhi 2001[1]	North-East District 2001[1]
Average household size (persons)	6.1	6.5	6.0	6.2	5.0	6.0
Sex ratio (no. of females per 1,000 males)	1153	1070	1269	1155	821	849
Sex ratio for 0–6 years	1155	1222	846	1099	868	875
Literacy rate (above 7 years) (%)	79.1	75.1	75.9	77.2	81.7	77.53
Male literacy rate (above 7 years) (%)	82.4	79.7	79.4	81.0	87.3	84.78
Female literacy rate (above 7 years) (%)	76.2	70.6	73.4	74.0	74.7	69.94
Share of Muslim households (%)	52.1	60.3	92.9	63.9	11.7	27.2
Share of SC/ST households (%)	26.2	23.1	2.9	19.8	16.9	16.7
Share of migrant households (%)[2]	11.0	3.9	14.5	9.9		
Share of migrant households (%)[3]	37.7	32.5	30.4	34.6		
Average monthly household income (Rs)	6219	7161	5767	6284		
Average per capita monthly income (Rs)	1026	1106	957	1020		
Average no. of income earning members	2.5	2.8	2.8	2.7		
Male	1.2	1.5	1.3	1.3		
Female	1.3	1.3	1.5	1.4		
Share of households with savings (%)	85.4	78.2	63.8	78.4		
Share of households with debts (%)	21.4	25.0	18.6	21.7		
Share of households sending remittances (%)	19.2	11.5	18.6	17.0		

Notes: [1] Data for Delhi and North-East District refer to the share of the population, not to that of households.
[2] Less than 10 years stay in Delhi.
[3] Less than 10 years stay in current residence.

members are engaged in income-generating work on more or less equal terms to males with regard to their work participation.

We can discern some differentiation among the three categories of embroidery homeworkers from the same table. One is the higher share of Hindus as well as scheduled caste households among SEWA Delhi members than among non-SEWA Delhi workers. Second, the literacy rates for both males and females are highest among active SEWA Delhi members, whereas the female literacy rate is lowest among non-active SEWA Delhi members. Third, the share of migrant households, defined in terms of the duration of their stay in Delhi being for less than ten years, is highest among non-SEWA Delhi households. Between active and non-active SEWA Delhi member households, active member households have a higher share of migrant households. If we turn to the share of migrants in the present locality, the share is highest among active SEWA Delhi households. Therefore, as far as social indicators are concerned, we can roughly conclude that the active members of SEWA Delhi belong to socially weaker and more vulnerable sections of the locality, although their literacy rate is quite high. This last feature may be related to their degree of awareness and understanding about SEWA Delhi's programme. We will discuss this in more detail, subsequently. Lastly, the average monthly household as well as per capita income shows that it is highest in the case of non-active SEWA Delhi households and lowest among non-SEWA Delhi households. However, the differences in the mean income between SEWA Delhi households, including both active and non-active and non-SEWA Delhi households, as well as between active and non-active SEWA Delhi households, are not statistically significant. This suggests that we need to explore factors other than the size of a household's income to explain the different levels of involvement with the programme.

Now let us examine the profiles of female embroidery homeworkers in these three sample households (see Table 7.3). Embroidery homeworkers are quite young, as their average age is in the 20s. The average age is significantly lower in the case of non-SEWA Delhi workers than for both active and non-active SEWA Delhi workers. It should be noted that there are many cases of daughters or daughters-in-law being members of SEWA Delhi, when the actual work is done with the participation of older women in the households. Nevertheless, according to the progamme coordinator, older women tend to prefer other home-based work, such as *charkha* (spinning thread for handlooms), *bindi* (forehead decoration), or bangle making. The proportion of never-married workers is significantly higher among non-SEWA Delhi workers.

Table 7.3 Social profile of embroidery workers

	SEWA active	SEWA non-active	SEWA all	Non-SEWA	Total
Average age (years)	27.3	29.3	28.0	24.2	27.1
	(n = 150)	(n = 79)	(n = 229)	(n = 72)	(n = 301)
Marital status (%)					
Never married	32.7	26.6	30.6	51.4	35.5
Married	64.7	64.6	64.6	45.8	60.1
Divorced/separated	1.3	3.8	2.2	1.4	2.0
Widow	1.3	5.1	2.6	1.4	2.3
Total	100.0	100.0	100.0	100.0	100.0
	(n = 150)	(n = 79)	(n = 229)	(n = 72)	(n = 301)
Education (%)					
Illiterate	24.8	26.6	25.4	23.6	25.0
Literate but no formal education	3.4	1.3	2.6	4.2	3.0
Primary	12.8	20.3	15.4	13.9	15.0
Middle	28.9	29.1	28.9	29.2	29.0
Secondary	22.8	16.5	20.6	22.2	21.0
Higher secondary	5.4	5.1	5.3	2.8	4.7
Bachelor's degree	2.0	1.3	1.8	4.2	2.3
Total	100.0	100.0	100.0	100.0	100.0
	(n = 149)	(n = 79)	(n = 228)	(n = 72)	(n = 300)
Average years of experience in embroidery work for income generation	4.4	5.7	4.8	7.1	5.4
	(n = 150)	(n = 74)	(n = 224)	(n = 69)	(n = 292)

On the other hand, the levels of education are quite similar for all three types of workers. Despite the lower average age, non-SEWA workers have significantly more experience in embroidery work as a method of earning money than SEWA Delhi workers. Among SEWA Delhi workers, the active members have fewer years of experience.[21] Therefore, SEWA Delhi's embroidery programme is thought to cater to the needs of those who are new to the work.

Why have they taken up embroidery home work as their means of income generation? Our sample shows that, but for one case, none of them had prior working experience other than home-based work, such as *bindi* and bangle making. The major reasons commonly mentioned by the three categories of workers are that home-based work can give them flexibility to manage household chores and child-rearing while also allowing them to increase their household income. Family restrictions on taking outside work were referred to by about 40 per cent of the workers, with a slightly higher share of non-SEWA workers mentioning this as a reason. This, however, does not mean that the workers themselves are totally reluctant to take outside work. A government job is perceived as a favourable alternative by about 60 per cent of workers, followed by a private job (about 50 per cent), whereas factory work (11 per cent) and domestic work (1 per cent) are much less desirable choices for them, although the latter options are still relevant for some.

Differences between SEWA Delhi's work and work with middlemen

Table 7.4 shows average monthly earnings by embroidery workers and their contributions to the household income. As a caveat, it should be noted that the figures are based on declarations by the respondents themselves. In the case of non-active SEWA Delhi workers, figures are related to their earnings when they were engaged in embroidery work in the recent past, thus they are not totally comparable.

The average monthly earnings from embroidery work are highest for non-SEWA workers, although the differences between SEWA Delhi workers and non-SEWA workers are not statistically significant. Nevertheless, the average daily earnings per worker are significantly lower in the case of the non-SEWA Delhi workers. It is assumed that, in non-SEWA households, lower per capita earnings are more often inflated in the figure of average monthly earnings by embroidery workers mentioned earlier, as minor workers' earnings are included under those of major workers.[22] Similarly, the level of satisfaction with their wages is lower among non-SEWA workers.[23]

Table 7.4 Earnings by embroidery workers

	SEWA active	SEWA non-active[2]	SEWA all	Non-SEWA	Total
Average monthly income of embroidery workers (Rs)[1]	930	952	936	1047	964
Contribution to household income by embroidery homework in total (%)	(n = 145) 22.8	(n = 50) 17.0	(n = 195) 22.1	(n = 67) 24.4	(n = 262) 21.2
Share of households with more than 50% of total contributions from embroidery homework (%)	(n = 138) 9.4	(n = 51) 5.9	(n = 189) 8.5	(n = 69) 11.6	(n = 258) 8.9
Average minimum daily earnings (Rs)[1]	(n = 138) 37	(n = 51) 38	(n = 189) 37	(n = 69) 30	(n = 258) 36
Average maximum daily earnings (Rs)[1]	(n = 149) 71	(n = 74) 69	(n = 223) 71	(n = 60) 55	(n = 283) 67
Average daily earnings (Rs)[1]	(n = 149) 54	(n = 74) 53	(n = 223) 54	(n = 60) 42	(n = 283) 51
Average daily working hours[1]	(n = 149) 7.1	(n = 74) 6.9	(n = 223) 7.0	(n = 60) 7.0	(n = 283) 7.0
Average hourly earnings (Rs)[1]	(n = 149) 7.6	(n = 74) 7.8	(n = 223) 7.7	(n = 60) 6.1	(n = 283) 7.3
Average monthly working days[1]	(n = 149) 24	(n = 74) 26	(n = 223) 25	(n = 60) 24	(n = 283) 25
Share of workers with subsidiary home-based work (%)	(n = 148) 33.3	(n = 73) 34.2	(n = 221) 33.6	(n = 56) 31.9	(n = 277) 33.2

Notes: [1] Figures are per worker.
[2] Earnings of non-active SEWA Delhi members include both those involved in embroidery work at present and earnings members recalled of the time that they were engaged in embroidery work.

There is no doubt that the women's earnings have become important increments to their household's finances. Positive gains are felt more with respect to personal use, the contribution to a family business, the education of children and the quality of food, but less with respect to the repayment of debts and the raising of money for remittances or dowries, probably because there is less of a need in these cases. Economic gains have also led to some psychological and attitudinal changes on the part of the homeworkers, as a large majority of them perceive positive changes in terms of their mobility, their status in the community and their self-perception. However, changes in family relationships are relatively limited, as around 80 per cent of them find no changes in this regard.

Fewer changes in family or gender relationships can be partly attributed to the fact that their contribution to the household income remains as low as 20 per cent despite the fact that they spend seven hours a day at this work, in addition to other reproductive work at home. As we can see from Table 7.4, calculated hourly wages are dismally low. Although wages offered by SEWA Delhi are higher than the wages non-SEWA Delhi workers are getting, they are still below the statutory minimum wages.[24] Moreover, a majority of workers, whether SEWA Delhi workers or non-SEWA Delhi workers, feel that piece rates have declined over the last year. In fact, one third of the workers are engaged in additional home-based work such as tailoring, *bindi* and bangle making, which are piece-rate jobs offered by the *thekedars*. With respect to embroidery work, while all non-SEWA Delhi workers are taking work from *thekedars*, 12 per cent of the active members and 3 per cent of the non-active members also, at present, engage themselves in embroidery work that is provided by the *thekedars*. They say that the main reason for taking work from the *thekedars* is that SEWA Delhi cannot provide regular work.

Of those who have worked with both SEWA Delhi and the *thekedars*, we asked about the differences they saw between the two. Around 90 per cent of those responding said that there were differences. Of them, 66 per cent of the active SEWA Delhi and 52 per cent of the non-active members viewed the work with SEWA Delhi favourably. As we have seen before, a positive assessment about SEWA Delhi's programme is made chiefly regarding the wages they offer. However, in other respects, such as the timing of payments, which are made on demand in the case of the *thekedars* in contrast to the fortnightly payments made by SEWA Delhi, and the regularity of work orders, the *thekedars* fare better.[25] Other advantages of *thekedar* work are that work is delivered to the home and that the *thekedars* are less strict when it comes to quality. If we turn to the situation of non-SEWA Delhi workers, however, not all of them are satisfied with working for the *thekedars*. Of those mentioned, 36 per cent have contentions with the *thekedars*. The most prominent problem is late payment and lack of transparency in payment. This is followed by low piece rates and irregularity with respect to work orders. Therefore, generalizations are difficult with respect to the work with *thekedars*. However, these responses indicate that SEWA Delhi and *thekedars* have both advantages and disadvantages in the eyes of the workers and neither is absolutely superior to the other.

Workers' perceptions of SEWA Delhi

Let us look into the worker's relation with SEWA Delhi more closely. Our survey found that some members of SEWA Delhi stopped taking orders from the organization temporarily in the past due to three major reasons: irregularity in the supply of work, late payments and longer time spent to get work. These incidents were more frequent in the case of non-active members, happening with nearly 50 per cent of them, whereas the figure for active members was only 17 per cent. Besides, personal as well as family imperatives, illness and staff behaviour were cited as reasons. Notwithstanding all these problems, 94 per cent of the active members and 63 per cent of the non-active members expressed their willingness to stay in touch with SEWA Delhi, even when immediate economic gains are not available – that is, work orders from the organization are suspended for a period. Since SEWA Delhi workers, particularly active members, predominantly depend on work orders from the organization, this may suggest that they derive some importance from their engagement with SEWA Delhi that lies beyond just the economic benefits, although we cannot deny workers' expectation of better wages from SEWA Delhi in the longer term.

As we have seen before, the clearest difference between work through SEWA Delhi and through *thekedars* is that, in the former, the workers are exposed to an environment other than that of their homes. Have these experiences made any differences in the workers' consciousness? Of the active members and of the non-active members, 70 per cent and 60 per cent, respectively, are articulate about what they have learned from their engagement with SEWA Delhi. Of them, 90 per cent in both groups referred to positive gains. The most frequently cited comment (about 55 per cent of both groups) was the idea that women should be self-reliant. The value of self-reliance seems to have been strongly coined among SEWA Delhi members. Significant attitudinal differences

Table 7.5 Differences in perception

	SEWA active	SEWA non-active	SEWA all	Non-SEWA	Total
	(n = 146)	(n = 78)	(n = 224)	(n = 70)	(n = 294)
Ready to do embroidery work outside home (%)	33.6	30.8	32.6	12.9	27.9
Girls should be educated as much as boys (%)	100.0	100.0	100.0	95.7	99.0
Expectations for daughters to take work outside (%)	78.1	78.2	78.1	62.9	74.5

between SEWA Delhi members and non-SEWA Delhi workers are also discerned with respect to their willingness to do embroidery work outside, as well as to let daughters take a job outside, as demonstrated in Table 7.5.

For non-SEWA Delhi workers, we asked whether they knew about SEWA Delhi's embroidery programme. In fact, 57 per cent knew about it and 44 per cent of them had visited the centre. However, they have refrained from joining the programme due to reasons such as the distance to the centre, the non-availability of work and the time spent in getting work.

Conclusion

This chapter has described the problems and needs of homeworkers on the basis of the experiences of embroidery homeworkers involved in SEWA Delhi's programme compared to those working with *thekedars* (middlemen). One of the most important findings of our survey is that a large majority of the embroidery homeworkers, whether involved in the programme or not, are under severe time constraints, but that even with this limitation they are always eager to take more orders. Around 90 per cent of the workers in our survey expressed their willingness to take on more work.

For a certain section of embroidery homeworkers in Sundernagri, SEWA Delhi's embroidery programme has provided opportunities; for some, to do work with better piece rates and, for others, to learn skills for income generation or to acquire new ideas about women's self-reliance. As we have discussed in the preceding section, the programme did begin to generate unmistakable psychological and attitudinal changes among active members. This has been effected through their association with other members and staff, and their participation in various activities taking place at the centres and not at home. Nevertheless, it is certain that the prerequisite for any continuation in the process of their empowerment lies in the sustainability and expansion of the programme from the economic vantage point. As we discussed before, the lack of a regular supply of work has been the biggest disadvantage of the programme in the eyes of SEWA Delhi members. Moreover, for those workers who desire to do as much work as possible while managing household work and taking care of family members, time spent to get work – for example, visiting the centre, sometimes more than once a day and waiting for the supply of new orders to reach the centre and be distributed among members – is, they say, a 'waste of time'.

These problems are fully acknowledged by SEWA Delhi. Those in charge of the programme said more than once to me that if only export houses could promise a long-term supply of work to SEWA Delhi, they could plan work schedules lest members should remain idle or go to *thekedars* for lack of work. However, in reality, there has been no steady relationship with the export houses. Since the programme started, SEWA Delhi has worked with more than ten export houses. However, as of November 2009, they were receiving orders from only three export houses. The reasons for this non-engagement are varied. Some are unavoidable, such as the closure of a company or its moving to a distant location, while other reasons are related to the nature of the terms and conditions the export houses demand. For instance, it is impossible for SEWA Delhi to meet the requirements of a company when they want products to be delivered the same day they place the order. Overall, according to the programme coordinator, export houses are reluctant to give orders to SEWA Delhi because there are so many *thekedars* who can supply them at cheaper rates. I asked how the ETI might be effective in this regard. Her answer was that unless retailers exert pressures over the export houses every time they place an order, there is little that one can do to enforce the initiative.

While continuing to make efforts to approach more export houses, SEWA Delhi's ongoing strategy is to increase production capacity by mobilizing more embroidery homeworkers to join their programme so that they can secure larger orders. A plan to establish two new centres, one in New Ashok Nagar and another in Aligaon, which are in geographical proximity to the industrial clusters of Noida and Faridabad, respectively, is now being implemented. It is also planned that the technical dimensions of the programme (i.e., securing orders and distributing them among the centres) will be centrally and more effectively managed from the Centre of Excellence to be set up in New Ashok Nagar. It remains to be seen, however, as to what extent this supply-led economic strategy increases the volume of work for individual members without compromising the social objectives of the organization.

When we turn our attention to the situation of other homeworkers in general, what lessons can we draw from the model of SEWA Delhi's embroidery programme? The model requires substantial costs and devoted intervention by non-profit-making third parties who can connect dispersed homeworkers and enterprises. Moreover, an entity, whether in the form of a programme, a cooperative or a company, needs to be of a certain size in terms of production capacity and to be sided with extra influence, such as a buyers' code of conduct over enterprises which place the orders, in order to be able to compete with the *thekedars*, who have cost advantages. Even then, it is hard to make such an entity financially sustainable, let alone one owned and managed by the homeworkers themselves. With regard to these goals, SEWA Delhi is still only halfway.

Therefore, it is difficult to expect immediate replications of the model in other sectors and areas on a large scale. Nevertheless, it is not impossible to draw some useful lessons from the experiences of the model. One is the importance of establishing centres that give training in various skills and social awareness, especially in close vicinity to potential homeworkers. This training can have various effects on female homeworkers of different traits and orientations. We have seen that among the active SEWA Delhi members generational changes are underway, not so much in practice yet but at least in their perceptions regarding women of the younger generation working outside the home. If the collective strength of varied skills and orientations can be effectively integrated with some efforts to connect those workers to the market, we can but expect that invisible home-based work will become more visible and that homeworkers will demand their due share with a larger voice in the mainstream economic sphere.

Notes

1. It was renamed the Mahatma Gandhi National Rural Employment Guarantee Act in October 2009.

2. The number of women engaged in household industry decreased from 4.6 million in 1961 to 1.3 million in 1971, according to census figures (Government of India, 1975: 170). Household industry is defined as an industry conducted by the head of the household himself/herself and/or by members of the household at home or within the village in rural areas, and only within the precincts of the house in cases where the household lives in an urban area.
3. Their survey of homeworker households engaged in the making of *bidi*, *agarbathi* and garments in states such as Uttar Pradesh, Karnataka, Tamil Nadu and Madhya Pradesh finds that 32 per cent of children aged five to 14 were working and over 80 per cent of them were involved in home work (Biggeri *et al.*, 2009: 50).
4. Rani and Unni (2009) used 'home-based workers' as their analytical category. This included own-account workers working on household premises, homeworkers and wage workers working for wages or salaries in enterprises located in the employer's home.
5. According to Prügl (1996), in half of the countries for which she found statistics, at least 90 per cent of the homeworkers were women. Among them, India was the only exception in that women account for less than 60 per cent of the home-based labour force (214, note 11). Chen *et al.* (1999) summarize the trend from the literature (606).
6. Computed from Table 46 (NSSO, 1999a) and Table 14 (NSSO, 1999b). The figure refers only to non-agricultural sector homeworkers.
7. Table 16 (NSSO, 1999b).
8. See Prasad and Prasad (1990) and Hahn (1996) for succinct accounts of the evolution of women's home work in India.
9. Department of Commerce data.
10. www.sewabharat.org/membersandprojects_organization.htm (accessed 16 December 2009). The states where the activities of SEWA Bharat have spread include Gujarat, Delhi, Madhya Pradesh, Uttar Pradesh, Bihar, Rajasthan, Kerala, Uttarakhand and West Bengal.
11. SEWA Bharat, *Annual Activity Report 2007*.
12. Cited from the brochure of SEWA Delhi, 'Weaving the World: Women Home-Based Workers of Delhi'.
13. All the raw materials are provided by export houses and SEWA Delhi's staff fetch them and deliver the finished products. This is one of the difficulties SEWA Delhi faces since it is both costly and time-consuming.
14. The passbook system started in October 2007. Until then, payment records for the members had been written on loose sheets.
15. In November 2009, male staff were hired for delivery of raw materials and finished products. Since the export houses are scattered in and around Delhi and due to traffic congestion in the city, it was increasingly difficult for young and mostly single female staff to do this work.
16. From May to September they receive winter-season orders and from October to March, summer-season orders.
17. The members prefer to receive their rewards in kind rather than in cash since they can then show their achievements more clearly to family members, friends and neighbours, according to the programme coordinator.
18. According to an embroidery-in-chief of an export house, the problem with SEWA Delhi is that their production capacity is too small and therefore the

company has to subcontract through other *thekedars* simultaneously. At the time of interview, there were four such *thekedars* working for the company in Delhi besides SEWA Delhi (interview by the author, 30 June 2009).
19. Interview by the author, 7 July 2009.
20. Members registered with Sundernagri Centre include residents in Nand Nagri, which adjoins Sundernagri.
21. The mean difference between the active and non-active SEWA Delhi workers is significant at a 90 per cent level of confidence.
22. At the time of the survey, the average number of female embroidery homeworkers per household was 1.1 persons (active SEWA Delhi), 0.8 persons (non-active SEWA Delhi) and 1.2 persons (non-SEWA Delhi).
23. About 80 per cent of SEWA Delhi workers were satisfied with their wages, while the figure was 40 per cent among non-SEWA workers.
24. Legally, the Minimum Wages Act, 1948, also applies to piece-rate homeworkers.
25. Information from non-SEWA workers shows that about 70 per cent of them receive wages whenever they ask for them.

References

All India Democratic Women's Association, Delhi State Committee (2009) *Report on the Condition of Work of Home Based Women Workers in Delhi*, Delhi: All India Democratic Women's Association, Delhi State Committee.
Banerjee, Nirmala (1989) 'Working Women in Colonial Bengal: Modernization and Marginalization', in Kumkum Sangari and Sudesh Vaid (eds), *Recasting Women: Essays in Indian Colonial History*, New Delhi: Kali for Women.
Bhatt, Ela R. (2006) *We are Poor but So Many: The Story of Self-Employed Women in India*, New Delhi: Oxford University Press.
Biggeri, Mario, Santosh Mehrotra and Ratna M Sudarshan (2009) 'Child Labour in Industrial Outworker Households in India', *Economic and Political Weekly*, 44 (12), pp. 47–56.
Carr, Marilyn, Martha Alter Chen and Jane Tate (2000) 'Globalization and Home-Based Workers', *Feminist Economics*, 6 (3), pp. 123–42.
Chen, Martha, Jennefer Sebstad and Lesley O'Connell (1999) 'Counting the Invisible Workforce: The Case of Homebased Workers', *World Development*, 27, (3), pp. 603–10.
Ghosh, Jayati (2009) *Never Done and Poorly Paid: Women's Work in Globalising India*, New Delhi: Women Unlimited.
Government of India (GOI) (1975) *Towards Equality: Report for the Committee on the Status of Women in India*, New Delhi: Department of Social Welfare, Ministry of Education and Social Welfare.
Government of India (1988) *Shramshakti: Report of the National Commission on Self Employed Women and Women in the Informal Sector*. New Delhi: National Commission on Self Employed Women and Women in the Informal Sector.
Hahn, Jeanne (1996) '"Feminization Through Flexible Labour": The Political Economy of Home-Based Work in India', in Elisabeth Prügl and Eileen Boris (eds), *Homeworkers in Global Perspective: Invisible No More*, New York and London: Routledge, pp. 219–38.

Kiso, Junko (2008) 'Job Loss and Job Opportunities of Factory Workers in Ahmedabad: Flexible Labour Rithink', in Hiroshi Sato and Mayumi Murayama (eds), *Globalization, Employment and Mobility: The South Asian Experience*, Basingstoke: Palgrave Macmillan, pp. 31–61.

Kitamura, Yuri (2004) *Indo no hatten to jenda: josei NGO niyoru kaihatu no paradaimu tenkan* (Development and Gender in India: Development Paradigm Shift by Women's NGO), Tokyo: Shinyosha (in Japanese).

Mazumdar, Indrani (2007) *Women Workers and Globalization: Emerging Contradictions in India*, Kolkata: Stree.

McCormick, Dorothy and Hubert Schmitz (2002) *Manual for Value Chain Research on Homeworkers in the Garment Industry*, Sussex: Institute of Development Studies.

Mies, Maria (1982) *The Lace Makers of Narsapur: Indian Housewives Produce for the World Market*, London: Zed.

Murayama, Mayumi (2008) 'Female Garment Workers in India and Bangladesh in the Post-MFA Era', in Hiroshi Sato and Mayumi Murayama (eds), *Globalization, Employment and Mobility: The South Asian Experience*, Basingstoke: Palgrave Macmillan.

NCEUS (National Commission for Enterprises in the Unorganized Sector) (2007) *Report on Conditions of Work and Promotion of Livelihoods in the Unorganized Sector*, New Delhi: NCEUS.

NSSO (1999a) *Employment and Unemployment Situation in India 1999–2000*, National Sample Survey Organization, Government of India.

NSSO (1999b) *Non-Agricultural Workers in Informal Sector Based on Employment – Unemployment Survey 1999–2000*, National Sample Survey Organization, Government of India.

Prasad, Anuradha and K. V. Eswara Prasad (1990) *Home-based Workers in India*, Noida: National Labour Institute.

Prügl, Elisabeth (1996) 'Biases in Labour Law: A Critique from the Standpoint of Home-Based Workers', in Elisabeth Prügl and Eileen Boris (eds), *Homeworkers in Global Perspective: Invisible No More*, New York and London: Routledge, pp. 203–71.

Prügl, Elisabeth and Eileen Boris (1996) 'Introduction' in *Homeworkers in Global Perspective: Invisible No More*. eds. Elisabeth Prügl and Eileen Boris. New York and London: Routledge: 3–17.

Prügl, Elisabeth and Irene Tinker (1997) 'Microentrepreneurs and Homeworkers: Convergent Categories', *World Development*, 25 (9), pp. 1471–82.

Rani, Uma and Jeemol Unni (2009) 'Do Economic Reforms Influence Home-Based Work? Evidence from India', *Feminist Economics*, 15 (8), pp. 191–225.

Rao, Rukmini and Sahba Husain (1987) 'Invisible Hands: Women in Home-based Production in the Garment Export Industry in Delhi', in Andrea Menefee Singh and Anita Kelles-Viitanen (eds), *Invisible Hands: Women in Home-Based Production*, New Delhi: Sage, pp. 51–67.

Rose, Kalima (1992) *Where Women are Leaders: The SEWA Movement in India*, New Delhi: Vistaar.

Sen, Samita (1999) *Women and Labour in Late Colonial India: The Bengal Jute Industry*, Cambridge: Cambridge University Press.

Singh, Andrea Menefee and Anita Kelles-Viitanen (eds) (1987) *Invisible Hands: Women in Home-Based Production*, New Delhi: Sage.

PART IV

Perspectives for Overcoming Underdevelopment: A Case-Study of Bihar

8
Historical Origins of Underdevelopment and a Captured Democracy: An Analytical Narrative of Bihar

Kazuki Minato

Introduction

Bihar, a Hindi-belt state with a population of 104 million, has always remained a complete puzzle to observers of Indian affairs. This is because, compared to the other regional states of India, it seems to have followed a quite different path of economic and political development over the past few decades.

The long-lasting stagnation of Bihar's economy, for instance, presents a sharp contrast to the unprecedented speed with which the Indian economy as a whole has grown in recent years. Consequently, progress in poverty reduction has been far more sluggish; thus the absolute level of poverty continues to be much higher in Bihar than in the rest of India. To make matters worse, a wide variety of socio-economic data clearly show that Bihar is lagging behind even other relatively underdeveloped states such as Uttar Pradesh, Madhya Pradesh, Orissa and Assam.

On the other hand, its 'political stability' does stand out in India's democracy, where voters are more likely to be scathing about the performance of incumbent governments and, as a result, frequent government changes are the rule rather than the exception. In Bihar, though, Lalu Prasad Yadav and then his wife Rabri Devi (as a figurehead after Lalu's resignation as the Chief Minister of Bihar due to corruption charges against him) swept successive State Assembly elections and dominated state politics between 1990 and 2005. This is all the more exceptional in Indian democratic politics since the Lalu–Rabri regime was so lawless, anarchic and corrupt that not only major opposition parties but the mainstream media have critically dubbed it the 'jungle *raj*' (i.e., 'jungle rule'). Even before the 15-year-long rule of the Lalu–Rabri duo, despite widespread kidnappings, politically motivated murders and atrocious caste/class violence and communal riots, the Indian National Congress had managed to retain power in the northern state ever since Independence, except for several years.

Above all, however, the most peculiar feature of Bihar is that the prolonged stagnation of its economy has coexisted with such 'political stability' in a competitive democracy over a long period of time. Indeed, we cannot find this unusual tendency in any other state of India. This observation in turn leads us to ask the following fundamental questions about Bihar's political economy. First, in spite of a relatively long tenure, why did successive state governments fail so miserably to adopt and implement sensible policies that could promote economic growth and poverty reduction? Second, why were incumbent state governments rarely voted out of power by the electorate, even though their performance was completely disappointing on almost all fronts? Last but not least, what was the critical driving force behind the paradoxical coexistence of economic stagnation and persistent inertia in democratic politics during the past decades?

In this chapter, I analyze the mechanism through which idiosyncratic patterns of economic and political development have gone hand in hand over the last few decades. In doing so, I examine in a logical manner the politico-economic underpinnings of perpetual poverty and inequality in Bihar. The analytical narrative presented in this chapter makes it clear that, through a shaping of both the incentives that drive politicians and voters with different caste/class backgrounds and the constraints under which they operate, the complementary relationship between particular historical legacies – colonial land tenure institutions and a rigid socio-economic hierarchy based on an age-old caste system – has a profound influence on long-term economic and political consequences in the state.

At present, there is a ray of hope among the people of Bihar, as well as among many observers of Indian affairs, that the state will be put on the road to development now that the notorious 'jungle *raj*' has finally been replaced by Nitish Kumar of the Janata Dal (United) as a result of the State Assembly elections in November 2005. On the contrary, however, I claim that such an optimistic view lacks historical perspective and thus pays too little attention to continuity before and after the emergence of the new state government. In other words, despite enormously high expectations for the Nitish Kumar government, the analysis of this chapter reveals that it will be a daunting task to get rid of the deep-rooted causes of persistent poverty and inequality in Bihar. To illustrate this point, I take as examples recent controversies over two important policy issues: land reform and welfare schemes for the poor and marginalized. These episodes demonstrate that, even if Bihar succeeds in escaping from its prolonged economic stagnation at the macro level, the fruits of economic growth will not reach the great majority of the landless and marginal peasants in the rural areas, and the gap between the haves and the have-nots will widen further.

More generally, the analytical narrative presented in this chapter contributes to and complements quantitative research, such as Banerjee (2004), Banerjee and Iyer (2005, 2010), Banerjee and Somanathan (2007) and Iyer (2010), among others. This empirical literature convincingly demonstrates the long-term effect of historical institutions on current socio-economic outcomes, but it is by and large silent about any specific mechanism behind some of the causal relationships involved. For example, Banerjee and Iyer (2005, 2010) present empirical results that establish the adverse impact of a landlord-based system of revenue collection during the colonial period on agricultural investments and productivity, and the provision of public goods (e.g., schools, hospitals, paved roads, electricity, etc.) after Independence. It seems fair to argue, however, that Banerjee and Iyer (2005, 2010) never successfully illuminate a specific mechanism through which the colonial legacy has had a significant influence on long-term economic consequences. The analytical narrative of this chapter, therefore, intends to bridge this wide gap.

The remainder of this chapter is organized as follows. The second section analyzes the underlying reason why the long-lasting stagnation of Bihar's economy has coexisted with its 'political stability' in the setting of a competitive democracy and stresses the crucial role of certain historical legacies as a distinctive feature of Bihar's political economy. In the third section, it is argued that, although a large number of people have had high hopes for the future of Bihar since the emergence of the Nitish Kumar government, it will be quite difficult to break the vicious circle in which the state has been trapped over the past decades. To show that the burden of historical legacies remains extremely heavy in the state, the following two sections detail recent episodes concerning the bitter controversy over the Nitish Kumar government's policy initiatives. The fourth section examines the enactment of new legislation to protect sharecropper rights, and the fifth section analyzes the welfare measures that have exclusively targeted the weaker sections of society, especially the so-called *Mahadalits*, who have been identified by the state government as 'the most deprived amongst the scheduled castes ... in terms of educational, economic, socio-cultural and political status' (Government

The political economy of underdevelopment in Bihar

The state of Bihar is by far the poorest of the major regional states of India. Its Net State Domestic Product (NSDP) per capita is just about one fifth that of Haryana, one of the most economically advanced states, and even less than 40 per cent of the All-India Net National Product per capita.[1] In addition, although different studies have reported somewhat different estimates on the extent of poverty reduction, they do agree, regardless of the method used, that the absolute level of poverty continues to be much higher in Bihar than in the rest of India. According to estimates by the 55th round of the National Sample Survey, nearly 40 per cent of the population in the third most populous state of India lived below the poverty line in 1999–2000, a significantly higher percentage than the national average of 28.6 per cent.

Bihar has also been left far behind in terms of human development such as education, health and gender equality. For example, the overall literacy rate in the state was 47.0 per cent in 2001, while it was 65.4 per cent in India, and the literacy rates of the weaker sections of society are even grimmer. In Bihar, 66 per cent of women and 72 per cent of scheduled castes were illiterate (Government of Bihar, 2009: 146–8).

Bihar's economy is still predominantly agrarian. The 2001 census shows that about 90 per cent of people live in villages and that more than 80 per cent of the population is engaged in agriculture and allied activities. On the other hand, the primary sector generates only a quarter of the state's NSDP, and lately this figure has been in constant decline (Figure 8.1). This is largely because agriculture has remained relatively stagnant, while rapid growth has been concentrated primarily in urban sectors such as construction, communications, trade, etc. All these figures imply that there exists a huge economic disparity between a handful of urban areas and the vast majority of rural areas. In fact, the incidence of rural poverty was 41.1 per cent in 1999–2000, substantially higher than the urban level at 24.7 per cent (Deaton and Drèze, 2002). Also, it follows directly from these figures that the urban–rural gap has been widening rapidly.

Therefore, it is quite obvious that, for India's most impoverished state, increasing agricultural productivity has always been the key to reducing prevalent poverty and inequality. Nevertheless, successive state governments in Bihar have never carried out measures involving

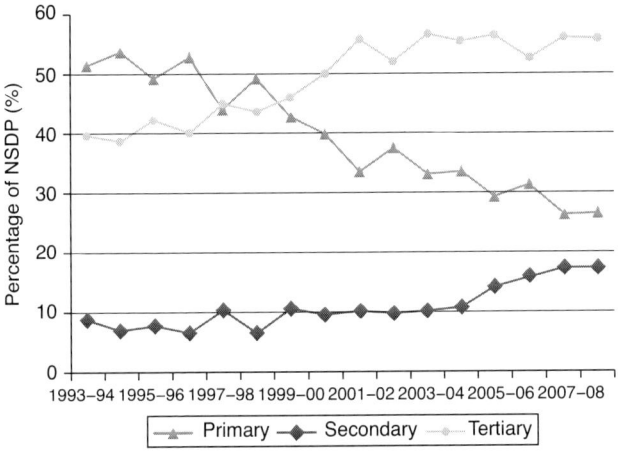

Figure 8.1 Sectoral composition of Bihar's economy
Source: Central Statistical Organization.

agrarian reform in any serious way, whereas the Left Front government in neighbouring West Bengal, which has been in power since 1977, initiated a land reform programme called 'Operation Barga' nearly three decades ago.

In West Bengal, Operation Barga succeeded in recording the names of 1.6 million sharecroppers and in giving them security of tenure and the heritable right of cultivation. In addition, about a million acres of vested land were distributed among 2.5 million beneficiaries who were landless or marginal peasants (Bandyopadhyay, 2003, 2009). Some empirical studies in economics, such as Besley and Burgess (2000), Banerjee, Gertler and Ghatak (2002), and Bardhan and Mookherjee (2009), confirm the positive effects of the land reform on agricultural productivity in West Bengal. As shown in Figure 8.2, even though it cannot be attributed solely to Operation Barga, the widening divergence in agricultural productivity (measured by rice yield) between the adjoining states since the 1980s reflects, at least to some extent, the profound impact of the Left Front government's effort to transform agrarian relations in West Bengal.

Now the question is how we can explain the continuation of government inaction in this Hindi-belt state. It seems to be all the more unusual that this kind of inaction has persisted in the setting of a competitive democracy. To answer this fundamental question, I argue three points in the following subsections.

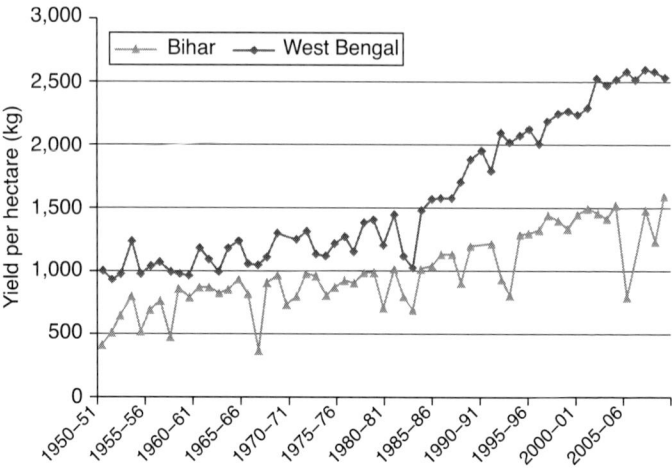

Figure 8.2 Rice yields in Bihar and West Bengal
Source: Indiastat (www.indiastat.com/).

Distortions of pro-poor policy

First, a number of 'good' economic policies, which are usually recommended as part of a development strategy by international institutions and foreign aid agencies, are not necessarily politically viable, even in the setting of a competitive democracy. If they can be expected to harm the interests of people with political power, policies that are indispensable for enhancing economic growth and reducing severe poverty and inequality are easily distorted by political pressure on the state government. Also, even when a state government has decided to adopt these 'good' policies, poor governance and a low quality of public administration prevent proper implementation.

This is certainly true of land reform. In Bihar, due to large inequalities in land ownership, most of the land cultivated by small and marginal farmers has been leased. One survey, for example, illustrates that in Bihar around 80 per cent of the land cultivated by scheduled caste and scheduled tribe households was leased (World Bank, 2005: 15). Accordingly, the state government has enacted a series of tenancy reforms since Independence, but the status of tenants in Bihar has remained vulnerable in terms of rents and security of tenure. In fact, the implementation of these tenancy protection measures has been so ineffective that landlords have flouted the laws in dealing with *bataidars* (or sharecroppers), who are of a low caste or scheduled caste background (Frankel, 1989; Kohli, 1992; World Bank, 2005).

Another typical example is the Public Distribution System (PDS), through which food grains, sugar and kerosene are distributed to consumers at relatively lower prices. Even though it is part of a most basic social safety net for the impoverished, it has never worked well in Bihar. The reality is that, although quite a few non-qualifying households have been able to obtain benefits from the PDS, many qualified poor households have not received the food subsidies (World Bank, 2005: 78–80). Moreover, as documented in Mooij (2001), a large number of people with power at the local level, including PDS dealers, civil servants and politicians, have kept cards entitling households below the poverty line to food grains and they have siphoned off below-the-poverty-line (BPL) grains for sale on the black market. Obviously, this corruption in the PDS has had devastating effects on a large number of households below the poverty line. Unfortunately, one still comes across similar stories very frequently.[2]

In Bihar, more generally, deficiencies in public service delivery have been largely responsible for terrible social sector outcomes, such as a lack of education, poor health conditions and inadequate access to sanitation and drinking water (World Bank, 2005: 63–78). Apart from the PDS, other poverty alleviation programmes and welfare schemes have also been plagued with bureaucratic apathy and pervasive corruption.[3] This has had a disproportionate impact on the poor, who are more critically dependent on the provision of public goods.

Economic and political dominance of landed castes

Second, landowning upper and upper backward castes have succeeded in keeping their position centre stage in the political struggle for control of the state in Bihar.[4] As is clearly illustrated in Table 8.1, the minority of the elite castes in the traditional caste hierarchy is over-represented among the Members of the Legislative Assembly (MLAs).

The political dominance of landed castes comes from the fact that each major political party has had its own core support base among upper and upper backward castes. For example, the Yadavs, along with the Muslims, were strongly in favour of the Rashtriya Janata Dal (RJD) in past elections (Table 8.2). This Muslim–Yadav alliance (i.e., the so-called 'MY factor') enabled the Lalu–Rabri duo's reign to continue for 15 years, thanks to the numerical significance of these two communities in Bihar (Table 8.1). As will be discussed shortly, however, support for the RJD among Muslim voters has been declining and has shifted to the Congress in recent elections. Presumably, this is one of the most important reasons for the poor performance of the RJD and its allies and thus for the end of the Lalu–Rabri regime. Moreover, although it seems

Table 8.1 Caste and political representation in Bihar

Castes and communities	(a) Caste composition		(b) Caste and community of the MLAs					
	Old Bihar	New Bihar	1980 INC	1985 INC	1990 JD	1995 JD/RJD	2000 RJD	2005 Nov. JD(U)+BJP
Upper castes	13.7	17.7	36.5	38.5	34.5	21.8	23.1	30.0
Brahman	5.0	6.4	12.3	10.8	8.3	3.1	3.1	4.9
Rajput	4.4	5.7	11.4	14.5	12.7	9.5	11.4	14.0
Bhumihar	3.0	4.1	9.8	10.5	11.1	5.8	7.1	9.5
Kayastha	1.2	1.5	1.8	1.5	1.2	2.2	1.2	1.6
Upper backward castes	20.2	24.8	29.0	25.3	34.2	43.6	35.2	34.5
Yadav	11.7	14.6	13.8	14.5	19.1	25.8	20.7	22.6
Koeri	4.4	5.7	2.8	2.8	4.0	6.8	5.9	4.9
Kurmi	3.5	3.8	6.2	5.2	4.9	5.8	4.6	4.5
Baniya	0.6	0.7	6.2	2.8	6.2	5.2	4.0	2.5
Lower backward castes	18.2	21.3	1.5	1.8	0.6	3.1	5.2	5.3
Muslims	13.8	16.8	8.9	10.2	6.2	7.1	9.3	9.5
Scheduled castes	15.9	18.3	14.5	14.8	14.8	15.1	14.8	16.9
Scheduled tribes	9.9	0.6	8.6	8.9	9.0	8.2	8.9	–

Notes: All figures are in per cent. In November 2000, the state of Jharkhand was carved out of the southern part of Bihar. In (a), 'Old Bihar' refers to Bihar before the bifurcation, while 'New Bihar' refers to Bihar after the bifurcation. In (b), either a ruling party or a ruling coalition is indicated below each year of the State Assembly elections. INC and JD stand for the Indian National Congress and the Janata Dal, respectively. The 2000 State Assembly elections were held before the bifurcation of Bihar and Jharkhand.
Sources: Census of India, 1931; and Robin (2009).

that the Yadavs still remain loyal to the RJD and its allies, turnout in the 2009 Lok Sabha elections was much lower among the Yadavs than among other communities such as the Kurmis, Koeris and Muslims (Kumar and Ranjan, 2009: 143–4).

On the other hand, the Janata Dal (United) (JD(U)) has had its core support base among two upper backward castes, the Kurmis and the Koeris, and the upper castes have tended to vote for the Bharatiya Janata Party (BJP). In both the 2005 November State Assembly elections and the 2009 Lok Sabha elections, nearly two-thirds of the upper caste and the Kurmi–Koeri voters voted for the JD(U)–BJP alliance (see Table 8.2).

Table 8.2 Voting patterns of upper castes, upper backward castes and Muslims

	Upper castes	Kurmi-Koeris	Yadavs	Muslims	
	JD(U)+BJP	JD(U)+BJP	RJD+	RJD+	JD(U)+BJP
1996 Lok Sabha	77	69	81	61	6
1998 Lok Sabha	75	56	74	68	4
1999 Lok Sabha	71	71	76	77	19
2000 Assembly	49	50	80	52	8
2004 Lok Sabha	63	64	68	79	9
2005 February Assembly	50	40	78	47	–
2005 November Assembly	65	61	75	58	9
2009 Lok Sabha	65	62	65	30	9

Notes: All figures are in pre cent. Figures reported below JD(U)+BJP are the shares of the vote for the Janata Dal (United)–Bharatiya Janata Party alliance, while figures reported below RJD+ are the shares of the vote for the Rashtriya Janata Dal (the Janata Dal before 1998) with its allies. The RJD contested various elections in alliance with different political parties. For more details on the electoral alliances of the RJD, see Kumar and Ranjan (2009). Occasionally, different sources present somewhat different estimates of voting patterns even in the same elections, but the qualitative implications of the different estimates are essentially the same for our purposes.
Sources: CSDS Team (1999); Kumar (1999, 2000, 2005, 2007); and Kumar and Ranjan (2009).

Another reason for the predominance in state politics of the landowning forward and upper backward castes is that their major political forces have attempted to mobilize the weaker sectors of society, such as the lower backward castes and the scheduled castes, by focusing on their identity of 'backwardness,' and these sectors have not been able to represent themselves through their own political organizations.[5] In particular, the RJD has been somewhat successful in consolidating these communities by assuring empowerment or 'social justice', but its competitive edge has been eroded in recent elections (Table 8.3). Now the JD(U)–BJP and the RJD and its allies have been engaged in fierce electoral competition to consolidate these swing voters. This capture of democracy by the minority of the elite castes has been one of the most significant reasons for policy distortions in Bihar over the past decades.

The crucial role of historical legacies

Third, historical legacies have played a major role in the seemingly inconsistent and contradictory coexistence of low growth performance, a high incidence of poverty and substantial socio-economic inequality on the one hand, and persistent inertia in a competitive democracy on the other.

252 Origins of Underdevelopment and Democracy

Table 8.3 Voting patterns of lower backward castes and scheduled castes

	Lower backward castes		Scheduled castes	
	RJD+	JD(U)+BJP	RJD+	JD(U)+BJP
1996 Lok Sabha	37	36	31	28
1998 Lok Sabha	26	41	32	22
1999 Lok Sabha	30	45	39	44
2000 Assembly	35	25	31	29
2004 Lok Sabha	38	36	42	28
2005 February Assembly	24	26	23	20
2005 November Assembly	22	48	20	15
2009 Lok Sabha	12	58	31	29

Notes: All figures are in pre cent. Figures reported below JD(U)+BJP are the shares of the vote for the Janata Dal (United)–Bharatiya Janata Party alliance, while figures reported below RJD+ are the shares of the vote for the Rashtriya Janata Dal (the Janata Dal before 1998) with its allies. The RJD contested various elections in alliance with different political parties. For more details on the electoral alliances of the RJD, see Kumar and Ranjan (2009). Occasionally, different sources present somewhat different estimates of voting patterns even in the same elections, but the qualitative implications of the different estimates are essentially the same for our purposes.
Sources: CSDS Team (1999); Kumar (1999, 2000, 2005, 2007); and Kumar and Ranjan (2009).

In Bihar, the distribution of landholdings is extremely skewed towards the upper castes and, to a lesser extent, towards the upper backward castes. Therefore, although it is an oversimplification to think of the upper castes as big landowners, the backward castes as middle peasants and the scheduled castes as poor labourers, there still exists a considerable correlation between the caste hierarchy and landownership (see Table 8.4).[6] This inequality originates from the *zamindari* system, a landlord-based system of land revenue collection that was set up by the British in India (Frankel, 1989: 55–66; Roy, 2006: 46–60).

In addition, the elite castes who hold land have had a definite advantage in the caste-ridden politics of Bihar, which is known throughout India for its rigid caste structure because 'caste identities are embedded and influence much of Bihar's social, economic, and political life' (Kohli, 1992: 207). Each group among the landed castes (especially the Yadavs) is relatively numerous. In contrast, the lower backward castes and the SCs are much more fragmented, and the size of each sub-group is quite small, although the weaker sections, taken together, compose a larger group (see Table 8.1). This skewed distribution of caste groups makes all the difference in the intense electoral competition in Bihar, where the number of contestants has always been large and the winner's margin of victory (i.e., the difference between the share of the vote of

Table 8.4 Landownership by caste in Bihar

	Castes and communities				
	Upper castes	Upper backward castes	Lower backward castes	Muslims	Scheduled castes
Number of households	3,405	4,664	7,605	11,079	4,155
Average land-holdings (hectares)	1.82	0.94	0.29	0.17	0.12
% of landless households	19.50	25.24	67.00	70.95	80.43

Note: This survey was conducted in five districts of Bihar: East Champaran, Kishanganj, Bhagalpur, Madhubani, and Rohtas.
Source: Institute of Developing Economies–Asian Development Research Institute joint field survey, 2008–9.

the winner and that of the runner-up) has been constantly shrinking (Figure 8.3).

In sum, land tenure institutions from the colonial period have provided a substantial economic advantage to the landed castes and their numerical significance has given them a great electoral advantage in the fiercely competitive, caste-ridden politics of Bihar. This has, in turn, provided them with the indispensable political leverage that has ensured their control over land and thus their economic ascendancy in a predominantly agrarian society.

It is well worth stressing that it is the complementary relationship between these two historical factors that has created the dire consequences in Bihar. If the distribution of land were more equal, there would be fewer obstacles to the adoption and implementation of policies for pro-poor growth, especially agrarian reform. Also, if the landholding forward and upper backward castes were either relatively less numerous or more fractured, they could not retain the crucial political leverage that they need to ensure their economic dominance in a semi-feudal agrarian society.

The burden of historical legacies

In November 2005, as a result of the Bihar Assembly elections, the Lalu–Rabri regime was finally brought to an end. A coalition government

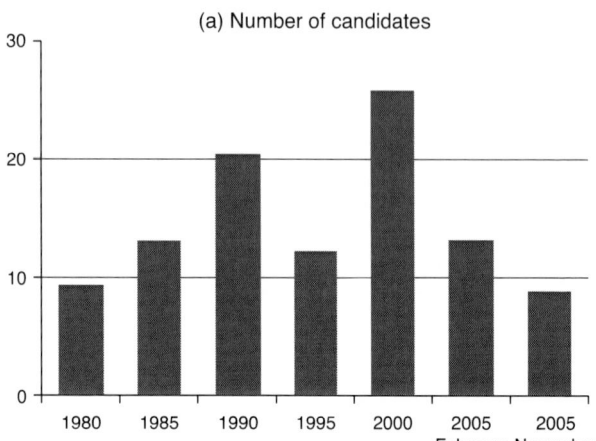

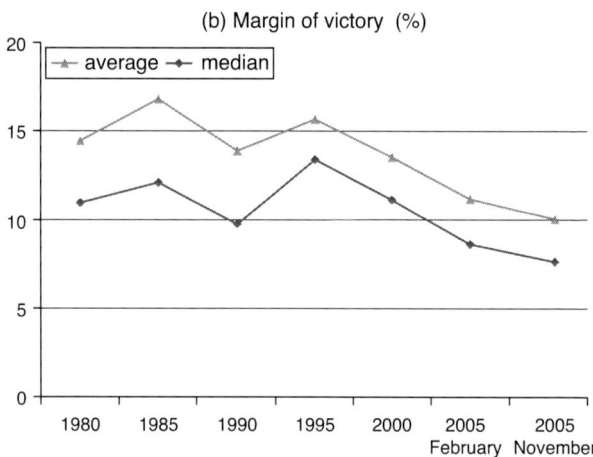

Figure 8.3 Measures of electoral competition in the Bihar Assembly elections
Source: Election Commission of India (www.eci.nic.in/eci_main/index.asp).

led by the Janata Dal (United) with the Bharatiya Janata Party replaced a 15-year-long rule, and Nitish Kumar of the JD(U) assumed office as the Chief Minister of Bihar (Table 8.5).

In this election, the JD(U)–BJP alliance campaigned vigorously on the platform of caste-blind development and good governance and, in doing so, attempted to discredit the Lalu–Rabri reign as one that was

Table 8.5 Important dates and events in Bihar politics, 2005–9

2005	February	As a result of the Bihar Assembly elections, no political party or coalition of parties was in a position to form a state government. The Rashtriya Janata Dal, which had retained control of the state for 15 years under the leadership of Lalu Prasad Yadav, lost 40 seats, compared to the previous election.
	7 March	Bihar was brought under President's rule.
	November	State Assembly elections were held again. The Janata Dal (United)–Bharatiya Janata Party alliance secured a majority by winning 143 out of 243 seats (JD(U) 88, BJP 55). The RJD managed to win only 54 seats, 21 seats fewer than in the February elections.
	24 November	Nitish Kumar of the JD(U) assumed office as the Chief Minister of Bihar. The JD(U) were in coalition with the BJP.
	15 December	The Chief Minister announced that a Land Reforms Commission and an Administrative Reforms Commission would be set up.
2006	3 April	The Bihar Panchayati Raj (Amendment) Bill, 2006 was passed by the State Assembly. This legislation provided for a 20 per cent reservation for extremely backward classes and for a 50 per cent reservation for women in panchayati raj institutions.
	19 June	The Bihar Land Reforms Commission was formed under the chairmanship of Debabrata Bandyopadhyay, a retired Indian Administrative Service officer of the West Bengal cadre.
2007	June	The State Land Reforms Commission submitted its interim report over *bhoodan* land to the state government.
	30 August	The State Mahadalit Commission was formed under the chairmanship of Vishwanath Rishi.
	November	The State Mahadalit Commission submitted its first interim report and recommendations.
2008	April	The State Mahadalit Commission submitted its second interim report and recommendations.
		The State Land Reforms Commission submitted its final report to the state government. This suggested the enactment of new legislation to protect sharecroppers, a land ceiling and the computerization of land records. After its submission, however, the state government neither laid the report before the State Assembly nor made it public.
	October	The National Commission for Scheduled Castes, which was headed by former Bihar Governor Buta Singh, termed the State Mahadalit Commission 'unconstitutional' for excluding some Dalit sub-groups.
2009	May	The JD(U)–BJP alliance swept the Lok Sabha elections in Bihar. It won 32 out of 40 seats (JD(U) 20, BJP 12), while the RJD–LJP combine secured only four seats (RJD 4, LJP 0).

(*continued*)

Table 8.5 Continued

Date	Event
28 July	The state government decided to include the Pasi and Dhobi in the list of Mahadalit castes on the basis of a recommendation by the State Mahadalit Commission. Except for the Ravidas (Chamar) and Dusad (Paswan) castes, the other 20 scheduled castes were identified as Mahadalits.
29 July	The Chief Minister announced welfare schemes under the Bihar Mahadalit Vikas Mission.
September	In the Bihar Assembly by-elections, the JD(U)-BJP combine managed to retain only six out of 18 seats (JD(U) 4, BJP 2). The RJD–LJP alliance won eight seats (RJD 5, LJP 3), while the Indian National Congress secured two seats and the Bhahujan Samaj Party and an independent one each.
1 October	At Amausi village in Khagaria district, 16 people were shot dead, allegedly by Musahars over a land dispute. Of the 16 villagers killed, 14 were Kurmis and two Koeris. While Musahars are Mahadalits, both Kurmis and Koeris are upper backward castes.
5 October	BJP leader and Deputy Chief Minister Sushil Kumar Modi told reporters that there was no recommendation by the State Land Reforms Commission to give land rights to tillers and that the opposition had made a concerted effort to create confusion among landed farmers.
20 October	Chief Minister Nitish Kumar declared that the state government had no plans to implement the recommendations of the State Land Reforms Commission.
21 October	RJD chief Lalu Prasad Yadav demanded that the Chief Minister come clean on the issue of land reforms and end vacillation on legislation regarding sharecropper rights.
4 November	A section of BJP MLAs and MPs revolted against their party leader and Deputy Chief Minister Sushil Kumar Modi for his statement reportedly expressing his intention to include sharecroppers under the Kisan Credit Card Scheme.
17 November	The state government decided to accord the status of Mahadalit to the Ravidas, which meant that the Dusads were the only scheduled caste off the Mahadalit list. The state cabinet requested the State Mahadalit Commission to immediately submit a report on the socio-economic status of the Dusad community.
24 November	A state-wide bandh called by the CPI-ML (Liberation) was carried out to press for the implementation of land reforms along the lines of the recommendations of the Land Reforms Commission and an end to corruption in the Public Distribution System. The RJD, together with parties on the left, supported the bandh.
17 December	The Dalit Ekta (Unity) Rally, called by the LJP, was held in the state capital Patna to censure the state government's policies on the Mahadalit issue.
31 December	The state government announced that each Mahadalit family would be given Rs 20,000 to purchase homestead land under a housing scheme.

characterized by empty political rhetoric, gross misgovernment and economic stagnation:

> Lalu [Prasad] Yadav led the Janata Dal to victory in 1990 by riding the mandir wave, assuring protection to the Muslims who were terrified after the 1989 Bhagalpur massacre and by promising empowerment to the backward castes. Over the years, though, 'social justice' has come to resemble little more than empty rhetoric and misgovernance has led to social and economic indicators of development steadily declining in the state ... The upsurge in Naxalism in parts of the state reflects the emptiness of the RJD's slogan of empowerment and needs to be dealt with by the new government. The JD(U)–BJP alliance won by very intelligently positing the contest not as one between personalities or between caste alliances, but as a choice between development and governance on the one hand and social empowerment and chaos on the other.[7]

Since coming to power, the Nitish Kumar government has announced a slew of policy initiatives, and this has triggered optimism about the future of Bihar among the people of the state as well as among observers of Indian affairs. According to a large-scale sample survey conducted by the Centre for the Study of Developing Societies (CSDS) in 2009, an overwhelming majority of people (88 per cent) evaluated the performance of the JD(U)–BJP government as satisfactory, and nearly 70 per cent of the respondents rated Nitish Kumar as the best Chief Minister that Bihar has had in the last 20 years (Kumar and Ranjan, 2009: 144). Moreover, this survey showed that the JD(U) leader was one of the most popular Chief Ministers in India at that time.[8]

In the 15th Lok Sabha elections held in April–May 2009, the popularity of the Nitish Kumar government was definitively reconfirmed by the landslide victory of the JD(U)–BJP combine in Bihar. It won 32 out of 40 seats (JD(U) 20, BJP 12), whereas the Rashtriya Janata Dal–Lok Janshakti Party alliance managed to secure only four seats (RJD 4, LJP 0). The editorial of India's leading newspaper, the *Hindu*, commented on the election results as follows:

> In the rush of pre-election predictions and analyses, if there was unanimity of opinion on any one State, it was on Bihar. That the outcome would favour the Janata-Dal (United)–Bharatiya Janata Party alliance was never in doubt, thanks mainly to the State's visible transformation under the stewardship of Chief Minister Nitish Kumar.

In a space of about three years, Bihar has shed its basket case, badlands image to emerge as a State on the threshold of hope and progress, a change reflected in Mr Kumar's phenomenal approval ratings ... The simple fact is that Mr Kumar has put Bihar back on the India map. The State has ceased to be the butt of jokes, and its people have been freed of the hopelessness and despair that had become their lot. It must be emphasized that there is more to Verdict-2009 than simple [caste] arithmetic.[9]

Nevertheless, despite high expectations for the Nitish Kumar government and the future of Bihar, it will still be quite a daunting task to transform the deep-seated structure of Bihar's economy in a drastic fashion and, as a consequence, eradicate continuing poverty and inequality. This is for at least two reasons.

First, the prospects for sweeping agrarian reforms remain quite bleak because, in spite of the recent change in the state government, the landholding forward and upper backward castes have stayed centre stage in the political struggle for control of the state. In fact, as documented thoroughly in Robin (2009), the share of each caste group has altered only very slightly, thus the landholding forward and upper backward castes still account for 64.5 per cent of the Members of the Legislative Assembly, even after the November 2005 Assembly elections (see Table 8.1). This study also points to the dramatic reallocation of political power in favour of the upper castes from the evidence that nearly 40 per cent of the cabinet members of the Nitish Kumar government have come from these elite castes, whereas they represented less than 15 per cent in the Rabri Devi government in 2000 (Robin, 2009: 93–4).

Second, contrary to the key campaign plank of the JD(U)–BJP combine, the welfare measures for deprived sections of society, which have been launched by the Nitish Kumar government, have actually been far more caste-based than caste-blind. With these welfare schemes, the state government has placed a premium on consolidating the underprivileged along caste lines to form a stable winning coalition rather than on improving their socio-economic status. Furthermore, the benefits of these schemes will not be able to reach the target groups because of the poor governance and low quality of public administration that have always been a serious hindrance to the effective delivery of public services in Bihar since the Congress was in power before the Lalu–Rabri duo's regime.

To demonstrate the validity of these claims that emphasize continuity rather than discontinuity before and after the demise of the notorious 'jungle *raj*', I take for examples, in the following sections, two recent controversies over important policy issues: the protection of *bataidari* (or sharecropper) rights, and the state government's welfare schemes for the weaker sections of society, particularly the *Mahadalits*. These episodes show that even if Bihar succeeds in escaping from its prolonged economic stagnation at the macro level, the socio-economic structure that has caused persistent poverty and inequality will remain intact in the rural areas and thus the fruits of economic growth will not reach the great majority of landless and marginal peasants.

Much ado about nothing: the protection of *bataidari* rights

Only three weeks after assuming office, Chief Minister Nitish Kumar announced that the state government was going to set up a Land Reforms Commission. In June 2006, the Commission was formally constituted and Debabrata Bandyopadhyay, a retired Indian Administrative Service officer of the West Bengal cadre, was appointed as chairman. The selection of the former bureaucrat as head of the Commission seemed to send a clear message that the new state government intended to execute agrarian reforms in a serious manner, since he has been credited with carrying out Operation Barga, the land reform measures implemented under the Left Front government in neighbouring West Bengal.

In June 2007, the Land Reforms Commission submitted to the Chief Minister its interim report over *bhoodan* land (or land donated by big landlords to the landless after Independence). Subsequently, the final report was submitted in April 2008. This recommended specific measures on agrarian reform. These included the enactment of new legislation to protect sharecroppers, the stringent application of a cap on landholdings at 15 acres for both agricultural and non-agricultural land, and the computerization of land records. In these reports, however, the Bandyopadhyay Commission did not propose any transfer of ownership to sharecroppers. Therefore, by any standard, the recommendations can be considered to be more moderate than radical.

At the same time, rumours about land reforms were constantly spreading across rural Bihar. Soon after the commission submitted its interim report, it was reported that landed farmers were scared of losing control and ownership rights to their land and that, driven by such fears, the landed gentry in a couple of districts had started throwing sharecroppers off their land to prevent any chance of this happening.[10] Sensing the widespread fear of potential land reforms among the landowning forward and upper backward castes, the state government became so cautious that they neither tabled the final report of the Bandyopadhyay Commission in the state legislature nor made it public after its submission in April 2008. Nonetheless, the rumour mills never stopped running. In fact, the Nitish Kumar government ended up facing a harsh backlash after the final report was made available to the Members of Legislative Assembly on the last day of the monsoon session and the media started to report the specific recommendations of the Land Reforms Commission in July 2009.[11] To make things even more complicated, opposition parties, including the left, harshly accused the state government of having been reluctant to lay the report before the Assembly, and they demanded the urgent implementation of the report's recommendations.[12]

In September 2009, just a few months after their sweeping victory in the Lok Sabha elections in Bihar, the Nitish Kumar government suffered a major setback. In the Bihar Assembly by-elections, the JD(U)–BJP combine won only six out of 18 seats. In particular, the JD(U) could manage to retain no more than four out of the 11 seats it had held earlier, while the BJP retained its two seats. On the other hand, the RJD–LJP alliance succeeded in winning eight seats (RJD 5, LJP 3). Since the by-elections for the 18 seats were spread all over the state and were thus seen as a mini-referendum on the incumbent state government, the poor performance of the ruling alliance was seen to represent people's disappointment with the Nitish Kumar government.[13]

A number of political observers have argued that the shock defeat of the JD(U)–BJP alliance could be attributed to widespread discontent among the landed interests (or the upper and upper backward castes), who were important constituencies for the ruling alliance, the reason for this discontent being the recommendations for land reform, especially the protection of sharecropper rights. Indeed, some members of the ruling coalition agreed in substance with this perspective and, in fact, it is almost impossible to find an alternative explanation for why the results of the State Assembly by-elections were so totally different from the clean sweep of the JD(U)–BJP combine in the Lok Sabha elections only a few months before.[14]

In the end, on 20 October, Chief Minister Nitish Kumar declared that the Bihar government had no plans to implement the recommendations of the Land Reforms Commission. The Chief Minister stressed that the state government ruled out legislation on sharecropper rights and that no one in the state would lose ownership rights over land. 'In Bihar, the land mass is fragmented and we need massive consolidation before discussing rights or land reforms. We need to examine the entire issue in the light of existing sharecropper laws,' he added. Furthermore, the

Chief Minister accused the RJD supremo, Lalu Prasad Yadav, of spreading the rumour among upper caste villagers that Nitish would take away their land.[15]

Even after this clear statement by the Chief Minister, however, the dust did not settle very quickly. In the beginning of November, a section of BJP members revolted against their party leader and Deputy Chief Minister, Sushil Kumar Modi. The rebels condemned a statement he had made which reportedly expressed his intention to include sharecroppers under the Kisan Credit Card Scheme, and they sought his immediate removal from his post. 'Mr Modi's statement advocating Kisan Credit Cards for sharecroppers is irresponsible and will harm the party's interests,' one of his ministerial colleagues said.[16] The Deputy Chief Minister was forced to clarify the situation and state that the distribution of Kisan Credit Cards to sharecroppers had nothing to do with the transfer of land ownership rights to them. 'There is no confusion on the issue of land reforms in [the] BJP and we have opposed left parties many times for using the issue of land reforms to serve their political ends,' the BJP leader affirmed.[17]

But the opposition parties made the most of this opportunity to attack the state government and appeal to the rural poor. On 24 November 2009, on the completion of four years of the Nitish Kumar government, a state-wide *bandh* (or strike) was called by the Communist Party of India (Marxist–Leninist) Liberation (CPI-ML (Liberation)) and carried out under a series of demands that included the implementation of land reforms in line with the recommendations of the Bandyopadhyay Commission as well as a call to put a check on corruption in the Public Distribution System. The RJD, together with parties on the left, supported the bandh, although its chief was rumoured to have told upper castes that they would be deprived of their lands by the state government. Also, it was reported that the left parties had decided to make land reforms a major poll issue in the State Assembly elections due in October–November 2010.[18]

Divide et impera: welfare schemes for the underprivileged

In Bihar, as has already been pointed out, political competition for control of the state has become fiercer and more subtle. For this reason, the state government has been under much more pressure to deliver a fair share of 'development' to poor and marginalized sections of society because, as indicated by their voting patterns in recent polls, the underprivileged – scheduled castes (SCs), lower backward castes and

Muslims – have formed a large mass of swing voters (see Tables 8.2 and 8.3). Hence, in order to build a larger constituency and win elections, it is no longer sufficient for political parties just to manipulate these voters' identity of 'backwardness' through the use of empty political rhetoric, as Lalu Prasad Yadav did constantly.

Accordingly, the Nitish Kumar government has launched a wide array of welfare schemes for the underprivileged since it came to power in November 2005. However, in contrast to the key campaign plank of the JD(U)–BJP alliance, these policies have obviously been caste-based rather than caste-blind. In fact, although a number of welfare measures are indeed targeted at the weaker sections of society, the state government has divided these sections into SCs, lower backward castes and Muslims and aimed a different set of schemes at each specific community (Government of Bihar, 2009: 184–92, 2010: 194–207). Therefore, the state government's welfare schemes for the underprivileged seem to have been shrewdly engineered to consolidate those swing voters along caste lines and, as a consequence, to construct a stable winning coalition.

The use of this 'divide-and-rule strategy' by the Nitish Kumar government has been clearest in its interventions for the SCs, whom neither the JD(U)–BJP combine nor the RJD have been very successful in mobilizing in recent elections (Table 8.3). In August 2007, the state government formed the State Mahadalit Commission under the chairmanship of Vishwanath Rishi. The primary objective of the commission was to identify the most deprived of the SCs and promote their development in terms of their educational, economic, socio-cultural and political status. This sub-group of the SCs was named *Mahadalits* and, initially, 18 out of the 22 SCs in Bihar were identified as Mahadalits.

The State Mahadalit Commission submitted two interim reports to the state government in November 2007 and April 2008, recommending specific measures to improve the socio-economic status of the Mahadalits. In July 2009, the Chief Minister announced a large variety of welfare schemes under the Bihar Mahadalit Vikas (or Development) Mission and said that these programmes would be initiated, beginning in August. The schemes included the Land for Housing Scheme, the Mahadalit Awas Yojna (the provision of houses for Mahadalit families), the Mahadalit Water-supply Scheme, the Mahadalit Toilet Construction Scheme, the Mobile Public Distribution System, the Mukhyamantri Jeevan Drishti Programme (the provision of a radio for Mahadalit families and of TV sets to community centres), the Mukhyamantri Mahadalit Poshak Yojna (the provision of school uniforms and other materials worth Rs 700 per child in class 1 to 5 in government schools), etc.[19]

Table 8.6 Caste composition of scheduled castes in Bihar

Name of caste	Population	% of SCs	Recommendation of the Mahadalit Commission
Bantar	101,223	0.78	1st recommendation
Bauri	2,096	0.02	1st recommendation
Bhogta	12,659	0.10	1st recommendation
Bhuiya	568,403	4.37	1st recommendation
Chaupal	100,111	0.77	1st recommendation
Dabgar	3,590	0.03	1st recommendation
Dom,Dhangad	155,383	1.19	1st recommendation
Ghasi	674	0.01	1st recommendation
Halalkaor	3,960	0.03	1st recommendation
Hari, Mahtar, Bhangi	181,784	1.40	1st recommendation
Kanjar	1,620	0.01	1st recommendation
Kurariar	6,567	0.05	1st recommendation
Lalbegi	809	0.01	1st recommendation
Musahar	2,112,136	16.22	1st recommendation
Nat	38,615	0.30	1st recommendation
Pan, Sawasi	3,653	0.03	1st recommendation
Rajwar	213,795	1.64	1st recommendation
Turi	33,638	0.26	1st recommendation
Dhobi	647,491	4.97	2nd recommendation
Pasi	711,389	5.46	2nd recommendation
Ravidas (Chamar)	4,090,070	31.42	3rd recommendation
Dusad (Paswan)	4,029,411	30.95	Not identified as Mahadalit
Total	13,019,041	100.00	

Sources: Government of Bihar (2009, 2010) and the website of the Bihar Mahadalit Vikas Mission (www.mahadalitmission.org/).

Indeed, all these welfare measures for the Mahadalit castes look quite excellent on paper, but the identification of 'the most deprived among the SCs' has actually been rather arbitrary and politically motivated. In July 2009, in addition to the 18 SCs who were initially identified as Mahadalit castes, the state government decided, on the basis of a recommendation from the State Mahadalit Commission, to include both the Pasis and the Dhobis in the list of Mahadalits. In November 2009, four weeks after the Chief Minister said no to land reforms as a result of the JD(U)–BJP's shocking defeat in the Assembly by-elections, the state government also accorded the status of Mahadalit to the Ravidas (Chamars), the largest Dalit sub-caste in Bihar. This decision meant that the Dusads (Paswans), the second largest Dalit sub-caste, were the only SC who were not included in the Mahadalit list (see Table 8.6). But why has only the Dusad caste, of all the SCs, remained out of the Mahadalit fold? One obvious reason is that the ruling coalition intended to isolate the Lok Janshakti Party in the Dalit politics of the state since the LJP chief, Ram Vilas Paswan, is a Dusad and thus the Dusad community has been likely to vote *en bloc* for his party.

Needless to say, the 'Mahadalit agenda' of the Nitish Kumar government has been a very contentious issue and quite a few people have levelled various charges against it. In October 2008, for instance, the National Commission for Scheduled Castes, which was headed by former Bihar Governor Buta Singh, termed the State Mahadalit Commission 'unconstitutional' for excluding some Dalit sub-groups from the Mahadalit list. The main opposition parties, especially the LJP, have echoed this accusation. Also, they have condemned the JD(U)–BJP government's Mahadalit agenda as being 'divisive'. Responding to the state government's decision to leave only the Dusads off the Mahadalit list, Ram Vilas Paswan denounced the move, saying, 'He [the Chief Minister] is now bent on extending his vote base by creating bifurcations within the Dalit fraternity.'[20]

Apart from welfare schemes for the Mahadalit castes, the Nitish Kumar government has aggressively wooed other weaker sections of the community. One of its prime targets has been the lower backward castes (or the extremely backward classes). In April 2006, for example, the State Assembly passed the Bihar Panchayati Raj (Amendment) Bill, 2006, which provided for a 20 per cent reservation for extremely backward classes and for a 50 per cent reservation for women in panchayati raj institutions. Moreover, 15 per cent of the cabinet members of the JD(U)–BJP government came from the lower backward castes, whereas they represented no more than 2 per cent in the RJD government in 2000 (Robin, 2009: 93).

The Nitish Kumar government has also offered a sop to the Muslims (in particular, *pasmanda* or backward Muslims), who used to contribute to the continuation of the Lalu–Rabri regime but have lately abandoned the RJD. Nevertheless, this strategy has by and large been unsuccessful so far, judging from the fact that in the 2009 Lok Sabha elections, the ruling alliance received only 9 per cent of the Muslim vote, while the RJD–LJP alliance and the Congress won 31 per cent and 29 per cent, respectively.[21] Presumably, the reason for the ruling coalition's continued unpopularity lay in feelings of wariness about the BJP among Muslim voters.[22]

In spite of all these welfare programmes being targeted at swing voters in Bihar's electoral politics, it is somewhat questionable how much these schemes will contribute to improvements in their socio-economic status because the poor quality of governance and public administration can prevent effective implementation of the programmes. In Bihar, as was argued in the second section, deficiencies in public service delivery have been largely responsible for terrible social sector outcomes, such as a lack of education, poor health conditions and inadequate access to sanitation and drinking water.

Moreover, it seems to be very difficult for the state government to transform its lower-level bureaucracy into an efficient machine of public administration over a short period of time. This is largely because the local powers-that-be have benefited from the malfunctioning system of social service delivery and thus have no incentive to fix it on their own. Another important point is that in Bihar the incompetence and ineffectiveness of the state's bureaucratic arm is a negative legacy of past state governments. The poor quality of governance and public administration, which has always been a serious hindrance to the effective delivery of public service, originates from the time when the Congress was in power, before the Lalu–Rabri duo's 'jungle *raj*' (Frankel, 1989; Kohli, 1992). These observations imply that grants for social programmes will remain easy prey for capture by local strongmen and that, as a consequence, the benefits of the schemes are unable to reach the weaker sections of society.

Conclusion

In this chapter, I have demonstrated how and why, over the past few decades, Bihar has followed a quite distinctive path of economic and political development when compared with that of other regional states in India. We have been led to the politico-economic underpinnings of persistent poverty and inequality in the Hindi-belt state.

The analytical narrative in this chapter has clearly illustrated that through a framing of the incentives driving both politicians and electorates with different caste/class backgrounds, together with the constraints under which they operate, the combination of two historical factors – colonial land tenure institutions and a rigid socio-economic hierarchy based on a caste system – has played a significant role in determining long-term economic and political consequences in Bihar. It has also been suggested that, although quite a few people have had high hopes for the Nitish Kumar government after the demise of the 15-year-long Lalu-Rabri regime, it will be quite difficult to break the vicious circle in which the state has been trapped over such a long period of time. Two accounts of the fierce controversy over the JD(U)–BJP government's recent policy initiatives have shown vividly that, due largely to the capture of democratic politics by the landholding upper and upper backward castes, the semi-feudal agrarian structure, which is a fundamental politico-economic factor underpinning both long-lasting economic backwardness and socio-economic inequality, remains intact in present-day Bihar. Thus, it is quite misleading to put too much emphasis on discontinuity before and after the emergence of the Nitish Kumar government.

As the state government has boasted, Bihar's economy has recently recorded unprecedentedly high growth rates. During the five years from April 2004 to March 2009, the average annual growth rate for the Net State Domestic Product (at constant prices) stands at 10.8 per cent, which makes Bihar one of India's fastest-growing states, along with the industrially developed state of Gujarat.[23] However, as the *Economic Survey* admits, this rapid growth has been concentrated primarily in urban sectors such as construction, communications, trade, hotels and restaurants, while the agricultural sector has remained relatively stagnant and suffered from very high volatility (Government of Bihar, 2009, 2010).

Furthermore, regardless of these economic statistics, it follows from the analysis of the current chapter that even if the state manages to escape from prolonged economic stagnation, the fruits of economic growth will be concentrated in the urban areas, where only 10 per cent of Bihar's total population lives, and the great majority of landless and marginal peasants in the rural areas will be left further behind. Bihar's economy as a whole will indeed take off in the near future, but it will surely be accompanied by a widening gap between the haves and the have-nots.

Acknowledgements

I would like to thank Shigemochi Hirashima, Takeshi Kawanaka, Ajay Kumar, Kazuya Nakamizo, Hiroshi Sato and two anonymous referees for helpful comments and suggestions. I am also grateful to Shigemochi Hirashima for providing me with data on caste-wise landownership in Bihar. Needless to say, however, I am solely responsible for any remaining errors and for the conclusions and interpretations presented.

Notes

1. In 2007–08, Bihar's NSDP per capita at factor cost (at constant prices with 1999–2000 as a base year) was Rs 8,703, while Haryana's NSDP per capita and the All-India Net National Product per capita were Rs 39,796 and Rs 24,295, respectively (Reserve Bank of India, 2009: 37–9).
2. 'Bihar Hunger Deaths: Lower Level Bureaucracy Apathetic', *Hindu*, 23 August 2009; 'Villagers Bust a Major PDS Racket in Bihar', *Hindu*, 22 November 2009; 'Mahadalit Families in Bihar Living in Starvation', *Bihar Times*

(online), 19 January 2010; 'Failed PDS Starves Gaya's Maha Dalits', *Hindu*, 24 May 2010; etc.
3. This is particularly true of the Mahatma Gandhi National Rural Employment Guarantee Scheme. See, for instance, 'Major Irregularities in NREGA Implementation in Bihar', *Hindu*, 8 October 2009; 'Bihar Villagers Burn MGNREGS Job Cards', *Hindu*, 9 February 2010; 'Women MNREGA Workers Denied Their Due in Katihar, Given Tougher Tasks', *Hindu*, 23 March 2010; 'Bihar at the Bottom in Providing Work under NREGA', *Bihar Times* (online), 22 April 2010; 'Drèze: Bihar a Dismal Laggard in MGREGS', *Hindu*, 23 April 2010; etc.
4. The term 'upper castes' refers to the Brahmans, Rajputs, Bhumihars and Kayasthas. These elite castes are also called 'forward castes' or 'twice-born castes'. 'Upper backward castes' include four other backward classes (OBCs): the Yadavs, Kurmis, Koeris and Baniyas. Nevertheless, this chapter focuses on the first three castes as upper backward castes because, compared to them, the Baniyas are not numerous in Bihar (Table 8.1). For a brief profile of these castes, see Kohli (1992: 207–12).
5. The lower backward castes are also called the lower OBCs or the extremely backward classes (EBCs), and these terms are used interchangeably.
6. Kohli (1992: 210) has explained that population growth and the division of landholdings through inheritance have been responsible for a trend whereby the backward castes are not middle peasants but rather small landowners and landless labourers, and the forward castes are not big landowners but rather medium-sized and small landowners.
7. 'End of Lalu Raj', *Economic and Political Weekly*, 26 November 2005.
8. According to the CSDS survey, Naveen Patnaik in Orissa was the most popular Chief Minister, followed by Nitish Kumar in Bihar. Both of them were preferred by more than 60 per cent of respondents in each state. For more details on the survey, refer to 'How India Voted: Verdict 2009', *Hindu*, 26 May 2009.
9. 'A Vote for Nitish', *Hindu*, 22 May 2009.
10. 'Land Reforms: Bihar Farmers Afraid of Bengal Repeat', *Indian Express*, 3 July 2007.
11. 'New Law Mooted to Protect Share-Croppers in Bihar', *Hindu*, 1 August 2009; and 'Panel Suggests Sweeping Land Reforms in Bihar', *Times of India*, 12 August 2009.
12. See, for example, the article by Dipankar Bhattacharya, the general secretary of CPI-ML (Liberation), 'Implement Bandyopadhyay Commission Recommendations for Land Reforms in Bihar', *Bihar Times* (online), 7 August 2009.
13. 'Poor Show by JD(U) in Bihar By-Elections', and 'Setback for NDA in Bihar By-Elections', *Hindu*, 18 September 2009.
14. 'Crack in Nitish Formula, Wooing Extremely Backward Backfires', *Indian Express*, 19 September 2009; 'Government Will Take a Fresh View on Land Reforms: Nitish', *Hindustan Times*, 22 September 2009; 'Post-Poll BJP Grumbling Becomes Vocal in Bihar', *Hindu*, 23 September 2009; etc.
15. 'Nitish Says No to Land Reforms', *Times of India*, 20 October 2009; and 'Dealing "Bataidari", Mahadalit Cards', *Indian Express*, 8 December 2009. For the reaction of Debabrata Bandyopadhyay to the state government's decision, see Bandyopadhyay (2009).

16. 'Cracks in Bihar BJP Unit, Revolt against Dy CM Modi', *Hindu*, 4 November 2009; and 'Sharecroppers Issue Haunts Bihar BJP', *Bihar Times* (online), 5 November 2009.
17. 'Modi Clarifies Stand on Kisan Credit Card', *Bihar Times* (online), 5 November 2009.
18. 'ML to Make Land Reforms a Major Poll Issue', *Times of India*, 21 October 2009; and 'Bardhan's Call to Bihar Farmers', *Hindu*, 6 June 2010.
19. For more information on the Bihar Mahadalit Vikas Mission, see the website of the programme (www.mahadalitmission.org/docs/data/BMVM_YOJNA_en.pdf).
20. 'Non-Inclusion of Paswans in Maha Dalit Angers Paswan', *Hindu*, 19 November 2009. It is worth noticing that whereas Ram Vilas Paswan has always behaved as an important leader representing the entire Dalit community in Bihar, all the SCs have not necessarily voted *en bloc* for the LJP. In the 2009 Lok Sabha elections, for example, the LJP failed to attract Dalit sub-castes other than the Dusads. Moreover, only 50 per cent per cent of the Dusads voted for the RJD–LJP alliance (Kumar and Ranjan, 2009: 143). Therefore, it seems fair to argue from these voting patterns that 'the Dalit fraternity', which the LJP chief has claimed to represent, is in fact an imaginary concept.
21. 'How India Voted: Verdict 2009', *Hindu*, 26 May 2009.
22. The JD(U) has never welcomed Gujarat Chief Minister Narendra Modi, one of BJP's star campaigners, to Bihar because it has been afraid that his Hindutva leanings may spoil the JD(U)–BJP alliance's prospects in elections. During the campaign for the 2009 Lok Sabha elections: 'Why should Narendra Modi come to Bihar? The state BJP is competent to handle its campaigning job. Moreover, we have our own Modi [Deputy Chief Minister Sushil Kumar Modi of the BJP] whose political credentials are no less,' said Chief Minister Nitish Kumar. See 'Bihar BJP Shuns Hindutva, Plays Development Tune', *Economic Times*, 11 April 2009; 'You Can't Enjoy Sweets and Say You Don't Like Sugar', *Hindu*, 13 June 2010; and 'Coalitions and Contradictions', *Hindu*, 17 June 2010.
23. As a matter of fact, a number of seasoned researchers have doubted this figure. See, for example, 'Has India's Poorest State Turned the Corner?', *BBC News* (online), 17 January 2010.

References

Bandyopadhyay, Debabrata (2003) 'Land Reforms and Agriculture: The West Bengal Experience', *Economic and Political Weekly*, 38 (9), pp. 879–84.

Bandyopadhyay, Debabrata (2009) 'Lost Opportunity in Bihar', *Economic and Political Weekly*, 44 (47), pp. 12–14.

Banerjee, Abhijit (2004) 'Who Is Getting the Public Goods in India? Some Evidence and Some Speculation', in Kaushik Basu (ed.), *India's Emerging Economy: Performance and Prospects in the 1990s and Beyond*, New Delhi: Oxford University Press.

Banerjee, Abhijit, Paul J. Gertler and Maitreesh Ghatak (2002) 'Empowerment and Efficiency: Tenancy Reform in West Bengal', *Journal of Political Economy*, 110 (2), pp. 239–80.

Banerjee, Abhijit and Lakshmi Iyer (2005) 'History, Institutions and Economic Performance: The Legacy of Colonial Land Tenure Systems in India', *American Economic Review*, 95 (4), pp. 1190–213.

Banerjee, Abhijit and Lakshmi Iyer (2010) 'Colonial Land Tenure, Electoral Competition, and Public Goods in India', in Jared Diamond and James A. Robinson (eds), *Natural Experiments of History*, Cambridge, MA: Belknap Press of Harvard University Press.
Banerjee, Abhijit and Rohini Somanathan (2007) 'The Political Economy of Public Goods: Some Evidence from India', *Journal of Development Economics*, 82 (2), pp. 287–314.
Bardhan, Pranab and Dilip Mookherjee (2009) 'Productivity Effects of Land Reform: A Study of Disaggregated Farm Data in West Bengal, India', mimeo.
Besley, Timothy and Robin Burgess (2000) 'Land Reform, Poverty Reduction and Growth: Evidence from India', *Quarterly Journal of Economics*, 115 (2), pp. 389–430.
CSDS Team (1999) 'Sharp Polarisation in Bihar', *Frontline*, 16 (25), pp. 36–8.
Deaton, Angus and Jean Drèze (2002) 'Poverty and Inequality in India: A Re-Examination', *Economic and Political Weekly*, 37 (36), pp. 3729–48.
Frankel, Francine R. (1989) 'Caste, Land and Dominance in Bihar: Breakdown of the Brahmanical Social Order', in Francine R. Frankel and M. S. A. Rao (eds), *Dominance and State Power in Modern India: Decline of Social Order*, Vol. 1, Delhi: Oxford University Press.
Government of Bihar (2009) *Economic Survey 2008–09*, at www.finance.bih.nic.in/Documents/ESR-2008-09-EN.pdf
Government of Bihar (2010) *Economic Survey 2009–10*, at www.finance.bih.nic.in/Bud2010/Economic-Survey-2010-English.pdf
Iyer, Lakshmi (2010) 'Direct versus Indirect Colonial Rule in India: Long-term Consequences', *Review of Economics and Statistics*, 92 (4), pp. 693–713.
Kohli, Atul (1992) *Democracy and Discontent: India's Growing Crisis of Governability*, Cambridge: Cambridge University Press.
Kumar, Sanjay (1999) 'New Phase in Backward Caste Politics in Bihar', *Economic and Political Weekly*, 34 (34 and 35), pp. 2472–80.
Kumar, Sanjay (2000) 'The Return of the RJD', *Frontline*, 17 (6), pp. 27–30.
Kumar, Sanjay (2005) 'Bihar Assembly Elections: RJD Needs an Alliance for Victory', *Economic and Political Weekly*, 40 (3), pp. 190–3.
Kumar, Sanjay (2007) 'The New Alliance Made the Difference in Bihar', in Ramashray Roy and Paul Wallace (eds), *India's 2004 Elections: Grass-roots and National Perspectives*, New Delhi: Sage.
Kumar, Sanjay and Rakesh Ranjan (2009) 'Bihar: Development Matters', *Economic and Political Weekly*, 44 (39), pp. 141–4.
Mooij, Jos (2001) 'Food and Power in Bihar and Jharkhand: PDS and Its Functioning', *Economic and Political Weekly*, 36 (34), pp. 3289–99.
Reserve Bank of India (2009) *Handbook of Statistics on the Indian Economy*, at www.rbidocs.rbi.org.in/rdocs/Publications/PDFs/FHB100909_Full.pdf
Robin, Cyril (2009) 'Bihar: The New Stronghold of OBC Politics', in Christophe Jaffrelot and Sanjay Kumar (eds), *Rise of the Plebeians? The Changing Face of Indian Legislative Assemblies*, New Delhi: Routledge.
Roy, Tirthankar (2006) *The Economic History of India 1857–1947*, New Delhi: Oxford University Press.
World Bank (2005) *Bihar: Towards a Development Strategy*, at www.go.worldbank.org/0DK3NTTT70

9
Interstate Disparity in India and Development Strategies for Backward States

Prabhat P. Ghosh

Introduction

During the last six decades since independence, the long-term growth rate of the Indian economy has been at least moderate at around 5 per cent. Even more comforting is the fact that, during the last two decades, the economy has escaped from the 'Hindu' rate of growth of barely 3–4 per cent to reach a decent growth rate of above 7 per cent. The last two decades have also seen an appreciable reduction in demographic growth rate, leading to a speedier growth of per capita income. But this positive description of the aggregate Indian economy is somewhat misleading, as the equity outcomes of this growth process have been very skewed. What possibly has contributed most to such (in)equitable outcomes is the sectoral composition of the overall growth; during the entire post-independence period, the agricultural sector in India has grown at less than half of the growth rate of the non-agricultural sector. This sectoral disparity would not have mattered if the growth was accompanied by a substantial shift of population from the low-productivity agricultural sector to the rapidly growing industrial sector. But that was not the case; between 1951 and 2001, the share of rural population has decreased by just 16 percentage points. Consequently, the source of livelihood of close to two-thirds of the country's population even now continues to be the low-productivity agricultural sector. As an obvious consequence, this sectoral disparity between agricultural and non-agricultural sector has been translated into rural–urban disparity and, second, depending on the relative size of the agricultural or rural sector in different states, the growth process has also widened regional disparity. The regions with relatively larger agricultural sectors have fallen behind, others with some industrial base have marched ahead, frustating one of the 'stated' objectives of the Indian planning – that is, reduction in regional disparity. This negative trend is in complete contrast to India's development experience in any other field, where the progress might have been of varying magnitude – but nowhere has the trend been in the 'opposite' direction.

The present study is an attempt to analyze this issue of regional disparity in India from a number of relevant perspectives. In the second section, the study reviews the existing studies on the issue to characterize the long-term trends in regional disparity, covering both the periods of planning and liberalization. With a view to looking at the causes behind the trend, the third section of the study presents a critique of the India's overall development strategy and the critical role of the asymmetric federalism in India towards widening of the regional disparities, a phenomenon inherited from the colonial period. In the next, fourth section, the focus of the study is the state of Bihar, which lies at the bottom of the development ladder among all Indian states. Taking the 25-year period since the early 1980s, the growth process in Bihar is analyzed in terms of both its economic and social disadvantages. In view of the discussion in the third section, holding national development strategies and asymmetric federalism as the prime factors behind regional disparities, one would expect reversal of the trend of widening regional disparities only through a change in those policies. Unfortunately, such a change is least likely in the present political configurations. That leaves the disadvantaged states with the only option of rethinking their 'own' development strategies to improve their conditions, within the scope of the 'limited autonomy' that they enjoy. The main components of such an alternative development strategy, with special reference to Bihar, are suggested in the fifth section. The chapter finally ends with a concluding section, collecting the main findings of the study.

Trends in regional disparity

Besides economic stagnation, the Indian economy was also characterized by wide regional disparity at the time of Independence. The regions that had undergone significant economic transformation during colonial rule were all around the three seats of colonial power – Calcutta, Bombay and Madras. Outside these, there were only a few regions where because of reasons other than trade (for example, location of military establishments) or some highly specific conditions leading to the development of a local capitalist class (for example, the textile industry in Ahmadabad), some significant economic transformation had taken place. On the one hand, the colonial administrative machinery had caused limited economic development of India by separating the link between economic and political power. This meant that, at the turn of the twentieth century, Indian capital could emerge only in and around the 'capitalist enclaves', the rest of the country still dominated by pre-capitalist social relations. On the other hand, the Indian commercial classes were protected from the wrath and struggles of the exploited and the oppressed through the 'rule of law', enforced uniformly by an elaborate police force and judicial structure. The same administrative-judicial institutions, later combined with a discriminatory electoral franchise, provided a convenient means of depriving the peasantry of their crops, resources, customary security and personal protection. That the existing regional disparities like social inequalities and sectoral disparities at the time of Independence were the consequences of such economic policies and were almost wholly unrelated to the resource endowments of different regions is apparent from the fact that the central Indian plateau, where the mineral resources of the country are concentrated, was one of the poorest regions of the country. So was the Gangetic Plain, which is endowed with extremely fertile agricultural land along with rich biodiversity, except certain parts of Bengal, the seat of colonial establishment till 1912.

It was, therefore, not surprising that within the realm of economic policy, right from the 1st Five-Year Plan, the goal of 'balanced regional growth' was considered politically as important as the goal of aggregate growth (Kumari, 2006). Up to the 4th Five-Year Plan, towards this goal, three basic strategies were undertaken – (1) according priority to agriculture, irrigation and community development, which all related to the rural sector where development deficits were most stark, (2) providing equitable infrastructural facilities (power, roads, communications, educational and health institutions) in all regions and (3) locating new enterprises, whether public or private, based on the need to address regional disparity. It must be noted that these strategies did yield results, leading to a reduction of regional disparity in the early period of planning, although the long-term trend in regional disparity in India has been one of widening. Taking the period from the 1950s to the 1980s and using a weighted coefficient of variation (CV), Mathur (1994) concluded that regional disparity in India had lessened during the 1950s and up to the mid-1960s, but had thereafter widened steadily. Because of the reorganization of the states in 1956, other studies on long-run trends in regional disparity refer to periods, starting from 1960–1 or a year later. In one such study (Chaudhuri, 2000), regional disparity is measured as the CV of per capita state domestic product (PCSDP) indices, taking the all-India per capita gross domestic product (PCGDP) as 100. Starting with 1961–2, the CVs of PCSDP indices are computed at five-year intervals, which again show that it steadily increased from 18.2 in 1961–2 to 35.4 in 1997–8. In another exhaustive study (Dasgupta *et al.*, 2000), covering the period 1970–1 to 1995–6 and using the CV of PCSDP as the measure of interstate disparity, it was concluded that 'Indian states have diverged in terms of per capita real state domestic product (PCSDP) over the 25 years under consideration'. Apart from establishing the widening of regional disparity, the study also showed that it is the low-income states that have exhibited lower growth rates in SDP, another important aspect of the dynamics of regional disparity in India. Since the liberalization has meant a major paradigm shift in the source of economic growth, some authors have compared the growth performance of different state economies during the 1980s and 1990s, that is, in the immediate pre- and post-reform decades. Based on the CVs of growth rates of SDP, it is observed that regional disparities were more in the 1990s than in the 1980s; these disparities are still more in terms of the growth rates of PCSDP, since low-income states are also at the lower end of the demographic transition (Ahluwalia, 2002; Bhattacharya and Sakthivel, 2004). That the process of liberalization has accentuated the trend in widening of regional disparity in India is also corroborated by two studies (Nagaraj *et al.*, 1998; Ahluwalia, 2002), both showing that the Gini coefficient of PCSDP was 0.152 in the beginning of the 1980s, and rose to 0.171 in the beginning of the 1990s, and increased faster thereafter to reach 0.239 in 2003–4. The following conclusions thus emerge about the trend of regional inequalities in India since independence:

1. Independent India inherited an economy which had wide regional disparities because of colonial interests; its few relatively developed regions consisted of industrial and trading enclaves mainly around the port cities. Removal of regional disparity has been constantly underlined in all plan documents. But, except during the early years of planning, interstate disparity in India has steadily widened. One should emphasize here that this is the only aspect of India's development experience where actual 'progress' has been in the 'opposite' direction. Further, although the phenomenon of widening regional disparity has been a feature since the mid-1960s, the process of economic liberalization has certainly accentuated it.
2. The trend in regional disparity in India also shows that the regions that were poor (rich) earlier are the ones that continue to be poor (rich) now. Such a secular homogeneity among the poorer and richer

regions of India probably signifies a close relation between the overall national growth strategy both in the pre- and post-liberalization periods and its regional outcomes.

3. The division of the major states in India into the three broad groups of high-, middle- and low-income states since the 1970s interestingly generates three almost contiguous zones. At the top, one finds four states (Punjab, Haryana, Gujarat and Maharashtra) which, but for the location of Rajasthan, would mean a contiguous zone of relative prosperity, all in the western half of the country. The middle-income states (Tamil Nadu, Kerala, Karnataka, Andhra Pradesh and West Bengal) again form a contiguous zone in the southern part of the peninsula, except for West Bengal. That leaves four Hindi heartland states (Rajasthan, Madhya Pradesh, Uttar Pradesh and Bihar) to form a contiguous zone of poor states, with one of its remaining members (Orissa) just bordering the Hindi heartland and another (Assam) located at a distance. This geographical pattern of prosperity has no association with the natural endowment of the different states.

Development strategy, asymmetric federalism and regional disparities

The Indian economy has grown at a long-term rate of 4.39 per cent, covering the entire post-independence period of 1950–2000 (Sivasubramoniom, 2004). This might be a moderate pace, but the estimated growth rates of earlier and later sub-periods clearly indicate the generation of a growth momentum since the 1980s, when it had grown at 5.71 per cent, compared to only 4.06 per cent in the 'strong' planning era (1951–65) and still lower at 3.12 per cent during the 'weak' planning era (1965–80). However, although the growth rate increased substantially during the following two decades, when the direct role of the state in promoting growth was indeed declining, it would be erroneous to conclude that the state had been an obstacle to growth during earlier periods.

Within the framework of Indian planning and the federal structure of its constitution, the developmental role of the state had clear impacts not only on the expansion of the overall economy, but also on the composition of growth in both agricultural and non-agricultural sectors. The latter had grown at twice the rate for the former (Sivasubramoniom, 2004; Krishna, 2004). For the entire post-Independence period (1950–2000), the non-agricultural sector had grown at 5.8 per cent, compared to only 2.6 per cent for agriculture. For both these sectors, the core of the development strategy had included substantial state interventions through public investment in a number of highly capital-intensive basic industries, apart from the investments in irrigation, roads and power. In addition, state intervention also included administered prices for a number of basic inputs, often through subsidies. All these were obviously 'promotive' interventions. It was only in the large industrial sector where the state exercised 'regulatory' intervention in the realm of geographical or sectoral destination of investments.

For the non-agricultural sector, the most important component of state intervention was the public investment in infrastructure and basic industries. Starting with a share of around a quarter during the early 1950s, the contribution of the public sector in total gross capital formation in India had risen to nearly half by the middle of the 1980s; thereafter, of course, it started decreasing because of the economic reforms (Chaudhuri, 1998). The huge investments that infrastructure and basic industries usually demand were beyond the capacity of the private sector in the initial years after Independence and the strategy of the public investment in these sectors was to 'crowd in' private investment in remaining sectors of the non-agricultural economy. Together with this investment support, the state had also followed a policy of administered prices, which amounted to subsidizing many of the industrial inputs like steel and energy. Thus, along with the ropes of regulation, restricting the free play of private capital in terms of entering sectors or regions of its choice, the state had indeed provided the industrial sector, which was none-too-strong at the time of Independence, with considerable patronage through huge public investment.

The core element of state's development strategy for the agricultural sector was the 'Green Revolution'. Unlike the strategy of industrialization which had remained unaltered throughout the planning period, the state had to change its policy of agricultural development during the mid-1960s when a serious food shortage in the urban areas (a wage-goods bottleneck) started unsettling the growing industrial sector. At this point, the agricultural development strategy changed to 'concentrate' only in those areas where, thanks to earlier investment in agriculture, facilities for assured irrigation were substantial. Such areas covered barely one fifth of the cultivated area in the country, mostly in the north-western region. As a result of water-seed-fertilizer technology, all subsidised, the Green Revolution enabled the Indian economy to attain self-sufficiency in food grains. This self-sufficiency was, however, a limited phenomenon. It did not imply adequate food for all; instead, it only meant adequate food for those who had the purchasing power for the same, leaving a large majority of hungry households without purchasing power.

Thereafter, the agricultural production levels in India have been sufficient to meet the entire urban food demands and also help to create a large food stock, the two together ensuring that the industrial economy does not suffer from any food supply constraint (as it did during the 1960s) even in the face of serious crop failures.

Both these core elements of India's development strategy are 'sector-specific' and hence expected to be 'region-neutral', more so the strategy of industrialization. But, much to the disadvantage of Hindi heartland states, this neutrality was only apparent, not real. Both the strategies of industrialization and agricultural growth had displayed asymmetric geographical distribution of resources in favour of states that were already better off because of historical reasons.

To consider the strategy of industrialization first, one may note that, at least initially, it had implied favourable investment patterns in at least two Hindi heartland states of Bihar and Madhya Pradesh, because of their rich mineral resources. But this initial advantage was more than offset by the policy of 'freight equalization', which ensured availability of basic industrial inputs like coal and steel at same prices throughout India. This promoted the growth of industries in those regions where the industrial economy was already relatively large (to take advantage of the external economies) and deprived remaining regions of India, including even those areas of Hindi heartland which had natural 'comparative advantage' for industrialization. The enormous loss that the mineral rich states, including Bihar, suffered because of this policy of freight equalization has at times been highlighted by the political leaders of these deprived regions, but, surprisingly, an economic analysis of the consequences of the policy of freight equalization in terms of regional disparities has not been attempted.

In the case of the Green Revolution, it might be noted that the 'economic motive' behind the strategy was not agricultural growth as such, but only ensuring adequate supply of food grains to the urban market to meet the food demands of industrial workers. Failure to ensure this causes wages to rise, threatening the profit levels of the industrialist. For this limited objective, it was not at all necessary to promote agricultural growth throughout India; coverage of barely one fifth of the cultivated area in the country under the Green Revolution was sufficient to attain the goal. Apparently, it could be argued that, once a region (initially uncovered by the new technology) could manage to erect an adequate irrigation infrastructure, the benefits of the substantially subsidized new technology were as much within its access as for the areas already covered. But, unfortunately, once the limited objectives of meeting the food demand of the industrial sector were served, public investment in agriculture started declining, even in absolute size, from the late 1970s onwards (Rao, 2006); consequently, the spread of the Green Revolution, after its initial success in selected areas, was very slow elsewhere in the country. This is how, parallel to regional disparities in industrial development caused by freight equalization, there arose regional disparities in agricultural development caused by the Green Revolution. Surprisingly, again, the existing literature on the Green Revolution is wholly oblivious of this consequence of the all-important agricultural growth strategy.

It is very rational to treat the above notes on the overall national development pattern, particularly its agricultural part, as the reference point for an analysis of the regional development patterns. A striking feature of India's development experience since independence is the continued duality of its economy. This problem of duality (the coexistence of a large labour-surplus subsistent agricultural sector along with a much smaller but modern industrial sector) was first analyzed by Lewis (1958) and his model also visualized that, with an emphasis on agricultural growth, a substantial transfer of labour from agriculture to industry would fuel a sustained expansion of the modern sector to absorb productively the surplus labour in agriculture. This is obviously an agenda for a 'structural transformation' of the economy and all that Lewis had done was to indicate a pathway for that transformation. One could possibly identify an alternative pathway for the same development agenda (not easy at all, as the literature on dual economies clearly indicates), but any development of a largely subsistence economy is unlikely (nay, impossible) without 'breaking' this duality. Quite surprisingly, the development pattern of the Indian economy in general has not been analyzed much along this framework of duality. A notable exception to this trend is a study by Patnaik and Chandrashekhar (1998) which underlines how, after the initial success of the Green Revolution, the Indian economy is made to miss Lewis pathway of transformation of subsistence agricultural sector, because of the following three paradoxical trends:

1. The real net domestic product per head of rural population has remained nearly constant and the current per capita food production in India is barely 10–15 per cent higher than it was in the early 1950s. If one takes out the Green Revolution areas (less than one fifth of country's total cultivated area), then it is very likely that per capita food production is indeed declining. This is exactly the opposite of what Lewis's model envisaged as a necessary condition for breaking the sectoral duality.

2. Irrespective of the growth rates of aggregate output in different regions, the shift of labour from agriculture to non-agriculture is extremely slow. In about 50 years since Independence, urbanization has gone up by barely 16 percentage points; not only is the absolute size of rural population today larger, but rural workers per acre of gross (not just net) cultivated area is also higher, taxing the carrying capacity of land. The expected sectoral shift of workers/population would have been, in any case, slow in backward regions; but even in the fast-growing regions of the country, the shift was only marginally higher.
3. Because of sluggish domestic demand, a phase of deceleration in industrial growth gripped the Indian economy after the Green Revolution, which indeed had freed the industrial sector of the critical problem of inadequate supply of food for its workers. The industrial sector later revived after liberalization when the export market tried to supplement domestic demand; but, as was noted earlier, the pace of widening of regional disparities also increased during this later period.

These three observations, taken together, indeed present a most comprehensive description of the development 'pattern' of the Indian economy, seen from the perspective of either structural change or its distributive outcomes. The first observation clearly indicates how, after it had ensured a steady supply of food for the urban workers, the rural economy was made to remain insulated from its urban counterpart. In the face of much higher growth rates of the urban economy, this insulation only meant further dualization of the Indian economy, which was already a dual one to start with. This, in a sense, is a structural 'retrogression'. This insulation would not have mattered much if the insulated subsistence economy was becoming steadily smaller. But, as the second observation indicates, this was certainly not the case. With its low productivity, the rural economy had to support a large and growing population, thereby allowing an acute problem of distribution – both within rural economy and between rural and urban areas – the regional disparities being the reflection of the same phenomena. Finally, the third observation underlines that the growth of agricultural/rural economy is not merely an issue of inequality and poverty; it is also a critical condition for aggregate economic growth per se through its immediate implication for sustained domestic demand.

Along with this agricultural growth pattern, the economy has also witnessed geographical distribution of industrial investment favouring the states that already had a sizeable industrial sector for historical reasons. The resulting regional economic disparities can be best expressed when per capita SDP (state domestic product) of different states are expressed as percentages of per capita GDP (gross domestic product) at national level (Das Gupta, 2007) for different years. Two conclusions easily emerge from the comparison of these income figures. First, the relative income rankings of the different states have remained largely unchanged, especially for the richer states. Second, except during the 1960s, the overall inequality among states has been steadily increasing, denoted by the substantial increase in the ratio of per capita SDP of the richest and the poorest states, from 1.9 in the beginning of 1960s to 3.6 at the end of 1990s. It is not difficult to realize that this widening of the regional disparities was an 'inherent' component of the development strategy of the state at the central level. First, the states at the regional levels had no participation in the investment decisions of the state at the central level, either for the policy of industrialization or for the policy of agricultural development pursued during the entire post-Independence period. Second, because of varying natural endowment in different regions and their growth pattern in earlier (colonial) period, the 'sector selectivity' of the development strategy of the state at the central level was certain to be translated into 'region selectivity', causing regional disparities to widen over the decades.

One is certain to wonder at this point how, in spite a federal constitution, the state at the central level in India is endowed with so much political and economic power. This asymmetric nature of India's federal structure has received some attention in recent years in the context of fiscal dimension of the structure (Rao and Singh, 2004). The fiscal directives allow the central government to mobilize far more resources than it spends directly and this automatically puts it in an advantageous position *vis-à-vis* policy formulation. In addition, the Constitution also divides the economic affairs of the overall state in such a manner that, in crucial sectors like industrial development, the central government is allowed to act as the primary authority. Further, the scope of discretion is indeed very large in both fiscal and economic matters and thus asymmetry emerges both out of 'provisions' and 'practices' in federal issues. Many of the wide regional disparities in India could be attributed to such unforeseen practices of federalism. In analyzing the relative powers of the central and state governments, one should make a distinction between unequal arrangements or asymmetry that are transparent and rule-based and those that are opaque and discretionary. The first may be:

> built into the constitutional arrangement itself [and] ... this type of asymmetry is transparent and rule based and plays an important role

in building the nation. In contrast, the second type of asymmetry can simply be the result of administrative and political power play in a federation [which] ... can have serious repercussions for the future of Federalism. (*Ibid.*)

The inequitable impact of the strategies of industrialization and Green Revolution, both of which seem to rest on discretionary privileges of the state at the centre, were not limited to only some loss of resources for the deprived regions; they also meant loss of certain development opportunities for them. As regards industrialization, it must be remembered that it was an easier challenge during the early decades after Independence, when the support of public investment was substantial and the competitive forces were relatively fewer. For the other major development agenda, such as transformation of the agrarian economies, the loss is probably even larger for the poorer states. As the experience would show, structural transformation of traditional agrarian economies has generally been possible when an 'external' impetus for growth was present, like the demand for food in urban areas leading to agricultural growth in Green Revolution areas. With that objective already met, the said external impetus disappeared for remaining areas of the country. Thus, just as the Green Revolution helped transform the agrarian economy of certain regions, by so doing, it also caused 'detachment' of the rest of the agrarian economies from the industrial sector, the only source of an external impetus. It is in this sense that the national strategies of development have strong negative structural implications for the disadvantaged regions.

Analysis of long-term trends in interstate disparity shows that it has been widening continuously since the 1960s; but, during the 1990s, the process has been faster. This is apparently paradoxical – for, if the earlier regional disparities were indeed caused by the development strategies of the state, its much smaller role during the 1990s should have at least arrested that trend of widening regional disparities. The reason it did not happen is because poorer states, when left to the forces of the market, were bypassed even more than when development was state-sponsored. By the beginning of 1990s, the poorer states in India were not only so *vis-à-vis* their income levels; they also had inadequate infrastructure, poorer social development and their governments were much incapacitated because of weak financial bases, all leading to structural deteriorations of their economies.

Growth of the Bihar economy

Notwithstanding the constitutional provisions of the federalism in India allocating the different social and economic sectors between the central and state governments, the 'core' of the development strategies in India, as shown above, has always been decided at the central level, mainly through the sectoral allocation of resources, the regional allocations being only a by-product of that exercise. This is so because, within the existing structure of fiscal federalism, the central (state) government mobilizes more (less) resources than it needs for its direct needs, leaving the central government with a surplus, a substantial part of which is spent/distributed using its own 'discretion'. In this framework, the regional-level state governments have only 'limited autonomy'. If the state-level governments had indeed any autonomy, at least some of the poorer states would have exercised it to their advantage to break away from the historical trend.

Aggregate and sectoral growth rates

It is very rational to treat the above observation on overall national development pattern as the point of departure for an analysis of the regional developments in Bihar. Taking the last two and a half decades into account, it might be observed that the composition of the group of high-, medium- and low-income states in India has remained unaltered from the beginning of 1980s, with Bihar being at the bottom (Table 9.1). Staying within their respective groups, some of the Indian states did improve their relative position; however, Bihar has remained at the bottom of this ranking throughout the period under consideration. If one compares the growth rate of the national and Bihar economies separately for the 1980s (1980–1 to 1989–90) and the period since the 1990s (1993–4 to 2003–4), it first emerges that the latter has been growing at a slower rate during both periods. The most distressing part of this trend is that, during the post-reform era since the 1990s, the economic growth rate of Bihar has been barely 3.42 per cent, just above the population growth rate, resulting in a growth rate of barely 0.92 per cent of per capita income. In the previous decade, it had broadly followed the national trend – a moderate growth rate of the non-agricultural sector, accompanied by an agricultural growth rate of 2.21 per cent, the two together resulting in an overall growth performance which was inferior to the national average, but not strikingly so. While the difference between the growth rates of Bihar and the national economy was a only 0.92 percentage points during the pre-reform period of the 1980s,

Table 9.1 Per capita GSDP of major Indian states

States	Annual average for 1980–1 to 1982–3		Annual average for 1990–1 to 1992–3		Annual average for 2003–4 to 2005–6	
	Amount (Rs)	Percentage of India	Amount (Rs)	Percentage of India	Amount (Rs)	Percentage of India
Punjab	3,174 (1)	178.7	4,286 (1)	179.1	33,022 (3)	142.3
Haryana	2,705 (2)	152.3	3,843 (3)	160.6	35,128 (1)	151.4
Maharashtra	2,695 (3)	151.7	3,931 (2)	164.3	33,277 (2)	143.4
Gujarat	2,280 (4)	128.4	3,118 (4)	130.3	30,182 (4)	130.1
West Bengal	1,871 (5)	105.3	2,448 (9)	102.3	22,850 (9)	98.5
Tamil Nadu	1,743 (6)	98.1	2,579 (5)	107.8	27,027 (6)	116.7
Karnataka	1,739 (7)	97.9	2,462 (7)	102.9	24,002 (7)	103.5
Kerala	1,683 (8)	94.8	2,158 (6)	90.2	28,059 (5)	120.9
Andhra Pradesh	1,673 (9)	94.2	2,312 (8)	96.6	23,994 (8)	103.4
Madhya Pradesh	1,529 (10)	86.1	1,882 (11)	78.6	14,829 (13)	63.9
Assam	1,485 (11)	83.6	1,719 (12)	71.8	17,037 (11)	73.4
Uttar Pradesh	1,449 (12)	81.6	1,833 (13)	76.6	12,151 (14)	52.4
Rajasthan	1,416 (13)	79.7	2,129 (10)	89.0	17,122 (10)	73.8
Orissa	1,371 (14)	77.2	1,639 (14)	68.5	15,952 (12)	68.8
Bihar	1,080 (15)	60.8	1,291 (15)	53.9	7,418 (15)	32.0
India	1,776	100.0	2,393	100.0	23,199	100.0

Note: Figures for (1980–1 to 1982–3) and (1990–1 to 1992–3) are based on 1980–1 prices. The figures for (2003–4 to 2005–6) are based on current prices.

Source: EPW Research Foundation (2009).

it had become 2.92 percentage points during the post-reform period. Indeed, the growth rate of the Bihar economy during the post-reform era was the lowest of any of the states of India in any of the decades. Clearly, the sharp deterioration was caused by the performance of the non-agricultural sector and this is very likely the consequence of the strategy of liberalization. A substantial number of the industries in erstwhile Bihar were located in the mineral-rich Jharkhand region, which now forms a separate state. Thus, in the present state of Bihar, the industrial sector is very small and the non-agricultural sector comprises mostly tertiary activities. The growth rate of this non-agricultural economy of Bihar was halved during the post-reform period; for the national economy, the rate actually increased, albeit marginally.

From the perspective of structural change, the duality of the Indian economy between its agricultural and non-agricultural sector stands out as critical, both in the context of growth and structural change. During the entire post-Independence period, this duality has indeed been reinforced for two reasons: first, during this period, the agricultural economy grew at a much slower rate and, second, the transfer of population from the agricultural to non-agricultural sector during this long period was only marginal. Such slower growth of output of the agricultural sector, unaccompanied by any migration of workers from the rural areas, obviously weakens the 'natural' distributive mechanism in the economy and thereby deepens its structural weakness. We have computed a simple 'index of duality' for the national and Bihar economy for three years – 1980–1, 1990–1 and 2000–1 – to identify the trend in this structural weakness (Table 9.2). It clearly emerges from these computations that Bihar economy, in spite of being the poorest, is more dual than the national economy. Second, although the economic duality has been continuously intensified in the entire Indian economy, the process was a little faster in Bihar. During the 1980s, the process was faster in Bihar because of a larger difference between its agricultural and non-agricultural growth rates than in India as whole; during the post-reform period, however, it was basically because of a shift of part of the agricultural workforce to the non-agricultural sector for India as a whole, with no such shift being observed in Bihar. Whatever might be the trend, it is quite well known that, without breaking its duality, a steady growth for an overwhelmingly agricultural economy is not possible. The economic distance between the agricultural and non-agricultural sectors gets easily translated into 'social' distance between the rural and urban people and, as shown later in this chapter, this social distance is large in India and still larger in Bihar.

Table 9.2 Index of duality of economy of Bihar and India

State/Year	Agriculture		Non-agriculture		Index of duality
	Percentage share in		Percentage share in		
	Output	Workforce	Output	Workforce	
Bihar					
1980–1	48.0	79.1	52.0	20.9	4.09
1990–1	40.6	78.0	59.4	22.0	4.86
2000–1	37.5	77.0	62.5	23.0	5.58
India					
1980–1	35.7	66.5	64.3	33.5	3.58
1990–1	32.1	67.0	67.9	33.0	4.30
2000–1	24.3	61.4	75.7	38.6	4.95

Note: Index = (share in total output of non-agricultural/share in total workforce of non-agricultural)/(share in total output of agricultural/share in total workforce of agricultural).
Sources: EPW Research Foundation (2009), Government of India (2003) and census reports of 1981, 1991 and 2001.

Human development

In conformity with its ranking with respect to per capita income (Table 9.1), Bihar also ranks at the bottom with respect to its Human Development Index (HDI) in 1981, 1991 and 2001 (Table 9.3), as computed by the Planning Commission (Government of India, 2002). It is, however, quite pleasing to note that, although economic growth in Bihar has lagged far behind the national average, its HDI and that of India for both rural and urban population have increased at nearly the same pace during the two decades. Throughout this period, the HDI for Bihar has been about 20 per cent lower than the national HDI. The Planning Commission used eight indicators for human development: infant mortality rate, life expectancy at birth, percentage of children attending school, literacy rate, percentage of households with *pucca* houses, percentage of households with access to safe drinking water, percentage of households below the poverty line and per capita expenditure. Of these eight indicators, the situation in Bihar is comparatively better with respect to 'availability of safe drinking water' and 'life expectancy'. In 2001, 86.6 per cent of Bihar's population had the provision for safe drinking water, compared to 78.0 per cent for India; as regards life expectancy, it was nearly the same in Bihar and India (62.8 and 62.9 years). Bihar's position, however, was much worse with regard to 'per capita expenditure' and 'poverty ratios'. A second important feature of HDI for Bihar emerges when one considers the rural and urban indices

Table 9.3 Human Development Index of major Indian states, 1981, 1991 and 2001

States	1981		1991		2001
	Rural	Urban	Rural	Urban	Combined
Punjab	0.386 (2)	0.494 (2)	0.447 (2)	0.566 (2)	0.537 (2)
Haryana	0.332 (3)	0.465 (5)	0.409 (4)	0.562 (3)	0.509 (5)
Maharashtra	0.306 (5)	0.489 (3)	0.403 (5)	0.548 (6)	0.523 (4)
Gujarat	0.315 (4)	0.458 (6)	0.380 (6)	0.532 (7)	0.479 (6)
West Bengal	0.264 (8)	0.427 (9)	0.370 (7)	0.511 (9)	0.472 (8)
Tamil Nadu	0.289 (7)	0.445 (7)	0.421 (3)	0.560 (4)	0.531 (3)
Karnataka	0.295 (6)	0.489 (4)	0.367 (8)	0.523 (8)	0.478 (7)
Kerala	0.491 (1)	0.544 (1)	0.576 (1)	0.628 (1)	0.638 (1)
Andhra Pradesh	0.262 (9)	0.425 (9)	0.344 (9)	0.473 (12)	0.416 (10)
Madhya Pradesh	0.209 (15)	0.395 (11)	0.282 (14)	0.491 (11)	0.394 (12)
Assam	0.261 (10)	0.380 (14)	0.326 (11)	0.555 (5)	0.386 (14)
Uttar Pradesh	0.227 (12)	0.398 (10)	0.284 (15)	0.444 (5)	0.388 (13)
Rajasthan	0.216 (14)	0.386 (12)	0.298 (12)	0.492 (10)	0.242 (9)
Orissa	0.252 (11)	0.368 (15)	0.328 (10)	0.469 (13)	0.404 (11)
Bihar	0.220 (13)	0.378 (14)	0.286 (13)	0.460 (14)	0.367 (15)
India	0.263	0.442	0.340	0.511	0.472

Note: The figures in parentheses denote the ranking of the states.
Source: Planning Commission (2002).

separately. Interestingly, the HDI for rural Bihar enjoys a rank of 13 among the 15 major states of India, ahead of both Uttar Pradesh and Madhya Pradesh, for both 1981 and 1991 (separate estimates for rural and urban areas are not available for 2001).

Poverty ratios

Taking the poverty ratios in rural areas first, it is noticed that the latest estimate (2004–5), shows this to be 42.2 per cent in Bihar, compared to 28.7 per cent for India as a whole (Table 9.4). The level of rural poverty in Bihar is the third highest in the country, only the states of Jharkhand and Orissa reporting still higher ratios. This is, of course, no comfort to Bihar because, being a part of the Gangetic Plain, its soil fertility and water resources are much higher than those of Jharkhand and Orissa, a substantial part of whose areas fall in the relatively infertile plateau region of the country. In absolute terms, the above poverty ratios imply about 35 million people living below the poverty line in rural Bihar, out of a total of about 230 million poverty-striken people in rural India. However, it is comforting to note that the poverty ratio decreased here from 64.7 per cent in 1983 to 42.2 per cent in 2004–5, a substantial drop

Table 9.4 Poverty ratios in Bihar and India

Sector	Years	Poverty ratios Bihar	India
Rural	1983	64.7	46.5
	1987–8	54.2	39.0
	1993–4	56.6	37.2
	2004–5	42.2	28.7
Urban	1983	61.6	43.6
	1987–8	63.8	38.7
	1993–4	40.7	32.6
	2004–5	38.1	25.9

Source: Reports of NSSO Surveys of relevant rounds.

of 22.5 percentage points. The decrease in rural poverty ratio in India during the same period was 17.8 percentage points – from 46.5 per cent in 1983 to 28.7 per cent in 2004–5. This reduction in rural poverty was a steady process in India as a whole, but somewhat paradoxically, the rural poverty ratio in Bihar increased between 1987–8 (54.2 per cent) and 1993–4 (56.6 per cent). In the absence of such an atypical phenomenon, the rural poverty ratio would have probably registered a steeper fall in Bihar between 1983 and 2004–5. Indeed, between 1993–4 (56.6 per cent) and 2004–5 (42.2 per cent), the fall in rural poverty ratio was as much as 14.4 percentage points, the highest in the country. If one prepares an estimate of 'annual reduction of poverty' from the available estimates, it will be observed that this speed of reduction has been lower in Bihar than in India as a whole during the 1980s; however, between 1993–4 and 2004–5, this pace has been much higher in Bihar. Thus, the overall rural poverty situation in Bihar can be described by two major observations: first, it is still the worst in the country, apart from Jharkhand and Orissa; and, second, a redeeming one, that the poverty ratio is dropping at a faster rate in Bihar in recent years.

As regards the urban areas in Bihar, the poverty ratio there in 2004–5 was 38.1 per cent, compared to 25.9 per cent for India. The difference between Bihar and India with respect to urban poverty ratio, one may note, is smaller than observed for the rural poverty ratio. This is primarily because urban economies are relatively more homogeneous and hence interregional differences are comparatively less. Apart from the expected fact that the urban poverty ratio is higher in Bihar, one may also note that the pace of reduction in Bihar's urban poverty during the 1990s is much slower than in India as a whole. Between 1993–4 and 2004–5, the urban poverty ratio in Bihar has decreased by only 2.6 percentage points (from 40.7 to 38.1 per cent); for the national economy, this reduction is 6.7 percentage points (from 32.6 to 25.9 per cent). This is again expected, as liberalization has entailed a larger difference between Bihar and India in terms of the growth rates of their non-agricultural sectors.

Literacy and education

With respect to most of the development indicators, Bihar ranks at the lowest among all the states of India. But one indicator that hinders most its development prospects is probably its very low literacy level. As per the 2001 census, Bihar had a literacy rate of 47.0 per cent, only a little higher than the national literacy rate in 1981 (Table 9.5). In other words, the state is nearly two decades behind the nation *vis-à-vis* the literacy status. Between 1991 and 2001, the literacy rate increased in Bihar by 9.3 percentage points (37.7 to 47.0 per cent); at this pace, total literacy in Bihar is more than half a century away.

The only redeeming feature of this otherwise dismal literacy scenario in Bihar is a reduction in gender disparity in literacy rates, both during the 1980s and 1990s. In 1981, the female literacy rate of 16.5 per cent was 65 per cent lower than the male literacy rate of 46.6 per cent; in 1991, this ratio has come down to 57 per cent and, in 2001, to a still lower level of 45 per cent. In addition, although the spread of literacy in Bihar has always lagged behind the national rate, the 1990s saw a faster spread of literacy than during the 1980s.

The most immediate reason for slower spread of literacy in Bihar is probably its poor educational infrastructure. At the present low level of

Table 9.5 Literacy rates in Bihar and India

	Male			Female			Overall		
	1981	1991	2001	1981	1991	2001	1981	1991	2001
Literacy rates									
Bihar	46.6	52.5	60.3	16.5	22.9	33.6	31.6	37.7	47.0
India	56.4	64.1	75.9	29.8	39.3	54.2	43.6	52.2	65.4
Decadal increase									
Bihar	—	5.9	7.8	—	6.4	10.7	—	6.1	9.3
India	—	7.7	11.8	—	9.5	14.9	—	8.6	13.2

Source: Census of India, 1981, 1999 and 2001.

income, a rapid increase in literacy rates is unlikely in the absence of adequate public expenditure on education. The rapid increase in literacy rates in some of the Indian states has generally been a consequence of supply impetus, like in Rajasthan in recent decades. But, unfortunately, such supply impetus has actually been weakening in Bihar since the 1980s. For example, for the most important stage of elementary education, the number of primary and middle schools per 10,000 population in Bihar has recorded a negative growth rate both during the 1980s and 1990s, the fall being sharper in the earlier decade (Panchmukhi, 2004). Interestingly, such a negative trend is visible even at the national level, but, fortunately, the pace of decline is a little slower. The manpower base of this educational infrastructure, as indicated by the number of teachers per institution, also experienced a negative growth in Bihar during the 1990s, though not during the preceding decade. These trends clearly show that the withdrawal of the state from the all-important sector of elementary education had started even before the introduction of economic reforms during the 1990s. This is primarily because of the incapacitation of the state resulting from the weakening of public finances that had started from the early 1980s in Bihar.

Fortunately, in recent years, the central government has been financing an ambitious elementary education programme (Sarva Shiksha Abhiyan) which might improve the literacy scenario, especially in rural areas, across the country – including Bihar. One will have to wait till the next census in 2011 to know the impact of the programme.

Health status

For an overwhelmingly large section of the Indian population, health needs are indeed more immediate than their educational needs. The absence of literacy and formal education may restrict a person's choice with respect to livelihood and other life-supporting activities, but in the absence of good health, it will not be possible to utilize even the limited choices that a person may have. Second, without strengthening human life as a biological phenomenon, efforts to enrich its other dimensions, social or cultural, are probably meaningless.

Earlier, an absence of a strong relationship between growth performance and trends in human development was noted. In the context of health status, one can again notice that there could be factors, other than economic growth, substantially influencing human development. As regards infant mortality rate (IMR) for rural areas, the present figure of 59 per thousand for Bihar is only slightly worse than the national average of 61. The figures for the early 1980s and 1990s further indicate

Table 9.6 Infant mortality rate and expectation of life in Bihar and India

		1981–3	1991–3	2001–6	Improvement during 1980s	1990s
Infant mortality rate (per 1,000 live births)						
Bihar	Rural	114	74	59	40	15
	Urban	61	47	44	14	2
India	Rural	116	86	61	30	25
	Urban	65	52	37	13	15
Expectation of life (years)						
Bihar	Male	55.2	60.8	65.7	5.6	4.9
	Female	52.9	60.1	64.8	7.2	3.7
India	Male	55.6	60.6	63.9	5.0	3.3
	Female	56.4	61.7	66.9	5.3	5.2

Source: Government of India (2007).

that this relatively better status of Bihar *vis-à-vis* IMR has existed in the past also (see Table 9.6). However, in case of IMR for urban areas, it is 37 for India as whole, compared to a much higher figure of 44 for Bihar. Interestingly, the urban IMR in Bihar was actually a little lower than the national average in the 1980s and early 1990s; that advantage, however, no longer exists. From the overall trend in IMR in Bihar and India during the 1980s and 1990s, it also emerges that the improvements have been much slower in the 1990s, a phenomenon particularly lamented by the UNDP Report (UNDP, 2006).

That Bihar enjoys a health status relatively better than that which its income levels would indicate is also apparent when one notes that, according to the most recent estimate, the expectation of life in Bihar is 61.4 years for males and 59.5 years for females; for India as a whole, the corresponding estimates are 61.6 years (males) and 63.3 years (females). However, one should note here that the gender disparities in health status, as indicated by the estimates of expectancy of life, is much wider in Bihar where average female life is much shorter; according to the usual demographic pattern, it is males who generally have a shorter life, as observed in India as a whole. From a comparison of the estimates of life expectancy in 1981–3, 1991–3 and 2001–3, it clearly emerges that Bihar and India experienced a similar upward trend during the 1980s. Indeed, during this decade, the pace of improvement was faster in Bihar. The 1990s, however, witnessed a clear deceleration in improvement in health standards, more so in Bihar. Quite alarmingly, the expectation of life for females has actually decreased during this decade in Bihar.

Towards an alternative development strategy

To begin with, one may first note that the prospects of an alternative development strategy in India, to address particularly the problems of regional inequality, are brighter now than ever before. There are at least two clear indicators of such enhanced prospects taking hold in the nation as a whole. The first of these indicators is a realization on the part of the national planners that the accelerated growth of the economy during the period of liberalization has been highly selective in terms of its sectoral, regional and social coverage, and the welfare consequences of this growth process have been far less than expected. As a response to this lapse, the national planning exercise now underlines 'inclusive growth' as one of its key goals, along with the earlier goal of 'accelerated growth'. This major change is widely reflected in India's 11th Five-Year Plan document.

The second important phenomenon, which is likely to make this inclusive growth possible through an alternative development strategy, is the threatened food security of the country, as experienced during recent years. Thanks to the Green Revolution, India reached a comfortable situation where it was able to meet the effective demand for food to avert any shortage of food in the urban market or the emergence of a famine-like situation. Unfortunately, that comfort level is now low and a wage-goods bottleneck has reappeared in the economy (similar to the one in the early 1960s), as evidenced through the soaring food prices in recent times. The situation clearly demands a response where the agricultural sector receives a much higher priority, covering the entire country, particularly fertile regions like Bihar.

In the specific case of Bihar, there is also a third factor enhancing the prospects of an alternative development strategy: an exceptionally strong urge for development, a consequence of the radical changes in the social base of governance in the state. Until the 1980s, the political power at the state level was largely at the hands of traditional elites, comprising the land-rich households and the upper castes. But the 1990s saw the emergence of the middle layers of the population in the political arena to pursue the twin political goals of 'social justice' and 'economic development'. For a number of socio-political reasons, it was the agenda of social justice that gained precedence over economic development during the 1990s; but the continued neglect of the latter agenda could not be tolerated by the people and the present government was elected almost solely on the basis of its promised development initiatives.

The above triad of forces – a policy of inclusive growth announced by the central government, threatened food security in the Indian economy and the emergence of a political leadership in Bihar for which development is the single most important agenda – obviously calls for a new thrust for development in the state which, in turn, demands an alternative development strategy. Three crucial points need to be kept in mind in outlining this alternative strategy. The starting point is to recognize that, given the breadth of poverty, action needs to focus on creating and expanding income opportunities for the rural poor, the majority of them primarily engaged in agriculture. Urban poverty in Bihar, as often underlined, is a spillover of rural poverty. A second point is to recognize that improved human capabilities and their wider spread are crucial for raising the productivity and hence income of the poor. Improvements in education, health and nutrition are not simply definitions of welfare status, but also crucial human capital needed for sustaining this status through growth. Finally, access by the poor to productive capital assets is fundamental to engagement in productive activities. Given the dominance of agriculture in the provision of livelihoods for the poor, access to land is pivotal. This calls for reforms in the tenural system and, simultaneously, creation of non-land assets for the poor. In view of the foregoing considerations, one can delineate the following four major action areas as part of an alternative growth strategy in Bihar:

1. *Primary attention to agricultural growth.* Remembering that nearly nine-tenths of the Bihar's population live in rural areas, earning their livelihood mainly from agriculture, one cannot visualize an accelerated and inclusive growth process where agriculture is not accorded the centre stage. Since the agricultural production process is labour intensive, the growth of the sector is automatically inclusive. Indeed, a faster reduction of rural poverty in recent years in Bihar, as noted before, is precisely because of a higher growth rate of its agricultural sector. Additionally, one may also note here that the problem of threatened food security in India can also be met only through a higher resource allocation for the agricultural sector. By virtue of being a part of the Gangetic Plain, water resources in Bihar are abundant and the required level of agricultural investment to enhance agricultural growth is much less here, compared to most other regions of India.

   Pursuit of productivity growth in agriculture requires four critical interventions. The first is to create conducive conditions to promote long-term investments in the sector to improve its productivity; in the context of Bihar, this implies investment in irrigation infrastructure so that the entire cultivated area enjoys the benefits of assured irrigation. Second is to build and strengthen the credit markets for financing investment as well as agricultural operations. The bulk of the rural economy depends to a large extent on informal credit arrangements. The strengthening of credit system is not just a matter of mobilizing financial resources; more important is an understanding of the system, which will ensure minimum default of payments. The third area is that of facilitating the adoption of technological innovations for raising both land and labour productivity. Finally, to unleash the full potential of the rural economy, the tenural system should at least be reformed, if not a redistribution of land, to free the rural economy from its persistent feudal social relations.

2. *Strengthening of human development.* Investment for a healthy and educated workforce holds an important key not only to the overall growth of the economy, but also to enhance the capacity of the poor to earn a decent income. In spite of the emergence of private players in this sector, the government still has a pivotal role to play in strengthening the supply of these services. The rationale for the continued pivotal role of governments in health and education services is based on at least two considerations. First is the limited income of the large sections of the needy population who cannot afford to buy these services from the private players. Thus, private health and education services remain restricted to only a small segment of the population with adequate income. The second reason is the existence of significant externalities from health and education expenditures. The social returns from such expenditures include higher awareness about causes and remedies for different diseases, a rise in social and political interaction through literacy and numeracy, and skills that have higher social than private returns.

The main adjustments to current policy practices include the restructuring of budgets in favour of education (elementary and secondary) and health; improving the flow of health information; and raising the quality of education by providing more inputs in the form of textbooks and other learning devices. The recent trend towards decentralization of management of these services augurs well, not only for enhanced accountability and hence cost-effectiveness, but also for encouraging local initiatives.

3. *Improving infrastructure for market integration.* Long periods of neglect of the road network, due to curtailment of development budgets to

achieve fiscal balance, has led to its serious deterioration in Bihar. The resulting poor mobility, in turn, has hampered efficiency in production, supply responsiveness and market integration. State interventions can play the most effective role in promoting growth and alleviating poverty through improvement in road infrastructure – first through building major roads connecting the smaller towns (rurban centres) with the major consuming centres, and then developing feeder or arterial roads to reach the interiors of the rural areas which are also production points. The second important area of infrastructure is communications. The value of information flow for raising productivity and improving education and health status is well known. Finally, the improvement of infrastructure includes the availability of power through rural electrification and other forms of energy.

4. *Improving the efficiency of poverty alleviation programmes.* Poverty alleviation programmes have been a major component of government expenditure, both at central and state levels, since the 1970s. Indeed, over the years, there have not only been newer programmes under this head, but their resource base has also increased continuously. Of particular importance among these programmes are the Public Distribution System (PDS), National Rural Employment Guarantee Programme (NREGP), Indira Awas Yojana (IAY) housing scheme, Integrated Child Development Scheme (ICDS), among others, for each of which the budgetary provisions are very substantial. Many of these programmes are also seen to be at least moderately effective in some other states of India, but their working has been rather poor in Bihar. Since the government is already spending a substantial part of its scarce resources on these programmes, it needs to pay special attention to improve the implementation of these schemes. The two major interventions required for improving the efficiency of poverty alleviation programmes are: encouraging people's participation in them through panchayati raj institutions and, second, designing an effective information and monitoring system, encompassing the working of the schemes right up to village level.

Conclusion

The phenomenon of substantial regional inequality has been a part of the overall Indian economy for a long time; it has been widening in the recent decades. It is indeed a reflection of the national strategy of growth where the regions that were better off to start with have continued to grow faster, leaving the disadvantaged regions even more disadvantaged. It is, therefore, not surprising that the relative ranking of the different states in India have remained nearly unaltered since the 1970s. Bihar just happens to be bottom of this ranking.

On the issue of why Bihar's economy has been continuously experiencing low growth, especially since the 1990s, it is relevant to remember the expected roles of the state and the market in the development initiatives. Before liberalization, Bihar's economy suffered, first because of the policy of freight equalization and then because of being left out of the scope of the Green Revolution. The second area of discrimination was, of course, related to the abandoning of the agenda for structural change in the agrarian sector, a case of wilful default of the local agrarian polity and a convenient default of the national industrial polity. In any case, all these discriminations occurred because of the state, either directly or indirectly. During the 1990s, when the market was expected to replace the state as the main initiator of growth impulses, Bihar's disadvantage was actually deepened. Thus, Bihar, with its small industrial sector, was unable to exploit the opportunities of market-led growth.

Fortunately, the prospects of an alternative development strategy to address the problems of regional inequality in India, in particular, is brighter today than ever before for at least three reasons. First, the national planning exercise now underlines inclusive growth as one of its key goals, along with the earlier goal of accelerated growth. The second important indicator, a boon in disguise, is the threatened food security of the nation, which should force the planners to pay more attention to agricultural growth, benefiting states like Bihar. Finally, the present government of Bihar was elected on the basis of its promised development initiatives, providing a strong political base for its development agenda.

The above triad of forces obviously calls for a new thrust for development in Bihar which, in turn, demands an alternative strategy. The study underlines four pillars of this development strategy in terms of: a high priority for agricultural growth, increasing human capabilities, improving infrastructure for market integration and, finally, improving the efficiency of all poverty alleviation programmes. Except for the last of these pillars, all others require the resources of state government. Thus, even in an era of liberalization, the states of the poorer regions have a substantial developmental responsibility. Once the development process takes off and gains momentum through appropriate state interventions, the strong market forces are almost certain to emerge, providing the fillip for a sustained growth process of presently disadvantaged regions like Bihar.

References

Ahluwalia, M. S. (2002) 'State Level Performances under Economic Reforms in India', in Anne Krueger (ed.), *Economic Policy Reforms and the Indian Economy*, Chicago, IL: University of Chicago Press.

Bhattacharya, B. B. and S. Sakthivel (2004) 'Regional Growth and Disparity in India: Comparison of Pre and Post-Reform Decades', *Economic & Political Weekly*, 39 (10), pp. 1071–7.

Chaudhuri, S. (1998) 'Debate on Industrialisation', in T. J. Byres (ed.), *The Indian Economy: Major Debates since Independence*, Oxford, New Delhi: Oxford University Press.

Chaudhuri, S. (2000) 'Economic Growth in States: Four Decades", *Money and Finance*, October–December.

Das Gupta, C. (2007) 'State and Capital in Independent India: From Dirigisme to Neoliberalism', PhD thesis, University of London.

Dasgupta, D. P., R. Maiti, R. Mukherjee and S. Chakravarti (2000) 'Growth and Inter-State Disparities in India', *Economic & Political Weekly*, 35 (7).

EPW Research Foundation (2009) *Domestic Product of States in India: 1960–61 to 2006–07*, Mumbai: EPW.

Government of India (2002) *National Human Development Report, 2001*, New Delhi: Planning Commission.

Government of India (2003) *Economic Survey, 2002–03*, New Delhi.

Government of India (2007) *Health Information of India of 2006*, New Delhi.

Krishna, K. L. (2004) *Patterns and Determinants of Economic Growth in Indian States*, Working Paper No. 144, New Delhi: ICRIER.

Kumari, A. (2006) *Balanced Regional Development in India: Issues and Policies*, New Delhi: New Century.

Lewis, W. A. (1958) 'Economic Development with Unlimited Supply of Labour', Manchester School of Economic and Social Studies, 12 (2).

Mathur, A. (1994) *Regional Economic Development and Policy in India*, New Delhi: Har-Anand.

Nagaraj, R., A. Varoudakis and M. A. Veganzones (1998) 'Long Run Growth Trends and Convergence across Indian States', OECD, Technical Paper, No. 131.

Panchmukhi, P. R. (2004) *Bulletin of Educational Data Bank: Vol. 1 (Elementary Education)*, Mumbai: Himalaya.

Patnaik, P. and C. P. Chandrashekhar (1998) *India: Dirigisme, Structural Adjustment and the Radical Alternative*, in D. Baker, G. A. Epstein and R. Pollin (eds), *Globalisation and Progressive Economic Policy*, Cambridge: Cambridge University Press.

Planning Commission (2002) *National Human Development Report, 2001*, Oxford, New Delhi: Planning Commission.

Rao, C. H. Hanumantha (2006) *Agriculture, Food Security, Poverty and Environment*, New Delhi: Oxford University Press.

Rao, M. G. and N. Singh (2004) *Political Economy of Federalism in India*, New Delhi: Oxford University Press.

Sivasubramonian, S. (2004) *The Sources of Economic Growth in India: 1950–51 to 1999–2000*, New Delhi: Oxford University Press.

UNDP (2006) *Human Development Report, 2006*, New York, NY: UNDP.

Index

Key: **bold** = extended discussion; f = figure; n = note; t = table.

affirmative action programme 10
agricultural labour 21, 29(n7),
　74–84, 90
agriculture xvii–xviii, 2, 11, 16, 17,
　23t, 27, 29(n5), 30, 31, 46, 59,
　266, 268, 274, 284t, 290
　fertile land 272
　crop failures 276
　growth rate (Bihar) 281
　investment and productivity
　　245
　labour-surplus subsistent 277
　off-farm employment 29(n7)
　slow growth, low
　　productivity 270
　see also land distribution
All-India Debt and Investment Survey
　(AIDIS, NSSO) 67, 86, 91, 93,
　97, 107
alternative development strategy
　(Bihar) **290–3**, 294
　agricultural growth **291–2**, 294
　human development **292**, 294
　infrastructure (market integration)
　　292–3, 294
　poverty alleviation **293**, 294
Andhra Pradesh (AP) 6f, 38f, 43t,
　44f, 50t, 53t, 55f, 58(n12,
　n14), 68–71f, 106(n6), 114;
　115–26f; 116, 117, 274, 282t,
　285t
Anganwadi 159, 159t
Arunachal Pradesh 69, 70f, 71f,
　106(n6); 115–26f; 121
Aschauer, D. A. 58(n8), 59
Assam (AS) 6f, 38f, 43t, 44f, 50t,
　58(n12, n14), 55f, 68–71f,
　106(n6), 115–26f, 243, 274,
　282t, 285t
assets
　changes (1980s, 1990s) **65–73**

composition (rural India, 2002–3)
　72f
under-reporting bias 67
asymmetric federalism 271
　and regional disparities **274–80**
Ayodhya 175, 202

Bahujan Samaj Party 185, 202–3,
　256t
Bandyopadhyay Commission 255–6t,
　259–61, 267(n11–12)
bank branches 18, 99, 102t, 103t
　licensing policy (1977–) 89–90,
　　93–4, 99
　loss-making 90
　number 98, 100, 101, 105
　number (access to financial
　　services) 93
　openings 106(n3)
　population group-wise distribution
　　(1969–2005) 94f
Beck, T. 93, 98–9, 100, 106
below poverty line 51
BPL children 141t, 142, 167(n10)
BPL households 249, 284
BPL population 99, 102t, 137,
　166(n1)
　(1973–2005) 97, 98f
　Bihar 246, 285
　Muslims 177
　types of measurement 106(n5)
Bhandari, A. K. 99–100, 104, 106
Bharatiya Janata Party (BJP) 175,
　250–8, 260–5, 267(n14),
　268(n16, n22)
Bihar xvii, xviii, 6f, 12, 13, 15,
　21–31, 38f, 43, 43t, 44f, 50t,
　58(n12, n14), 68, 68–71f,
　106(n6); 115–26f; 124, 125,
　158, 169 (n30–1), 190, 192,
　206(n12), 207

297

Bihar – *continued*
  aggregate and sectoral growth rates 281–4
  bifurcation (loss of Jharkhand, 2000) 29(n4), 43, 45, 49, 167(n6), 250n, 283
  'butt of jokes' 258
  constraints for provision of infrastructure 50–6, 58–9 (n16–22)
  democracy versus low growth, poverty, inequality 251
  divide et impera (welfare schemes) 261–5, 268(n19–22)
  economic duality index 283, 284t
  economic growth (2004–9) 266, 268(n23)
  economic stagnation 243, 244, 245, 266, 294
  economy 'predominantly agrarian' 246
  education 287–8
  electric light and minorities 197, 199t, 202, 203
  electric light and minorities (results and analysis) 194–7, 206(n13–14)
  electricity consumption 43t, 51
  electrification 194
  'fertile region' 290
  financial dependence upon central government 52
  fiscal deficits/fiscal deterioration 52, 292–3
  fiscal transfers versus own revenue (2006–7) 53t
  further research 57
  'growth of economy' 281–90
  health status 288–90
  historical legacies 253–9, 267(n7–9)
  house with electric light vis-à-vis urban population/size of town (2001) 193f
  human development 246, 284–5
  inequality 6–7, 266
  infrastructure 16, 56
  investment constraints 55, 59(n20–1)
  'jungle *raj*' 27

land prices (1998–2008) 83
land reform 63
landownership by caste 253t
literacy 6, 287–8
migrants to Delhi 139, 140–1
natural resources: lost to Jharkhand (2000–) 22, 29(n4)
NSDP 246, 268(n1)
obstacles to reform 258–9
overcoming under-development (case study) 1–2, 22–7, 29–30, 241–95
per capita GSDP (1980–2006) 282t
Plan expenditure and provision of infrastructure 54–6, 58–9(n19–22)
political economy 244, 246–53, 266–7(n1–6)
political events (2005–9) 255–6t
'political stability' 243, 244, 245
population 51, 243
population (Muslim) 188, 189t
poverty ratios 285–7
public finances 'weakening' 288
public goods (electricity) 188
relative income gap with other states (1999–2006) 50t
revenue capacity per capita (2006–7) 53t
rice yields (1950–2006) 248f
rural areas 14
sectoral composition 247f
social sector 'undeveloped' 51, 58(n17)
socio-economic structure 259
state government (current) 294
'state left behind' 51–2, 58(n16–18)
state revenue 52–4
swing voters 251–2t, 262, 264–5
trapped as poorest Indian state 281, 282t
tribal villages 181
under-development and captured democracy 243–69
BIMARU 51, 160, 162t
birth (health care) 19, 118–19, 120f, 126, 135t

birth certificates 158t, 158, 161t, 163, 164, 165, 169(n29–31)
BRICs (Brazil, Russia, India and China)
Burgess, R. 74, 86, 99, 100, 102, 106, 247, 269

caste 6–7, 13, 17, 20, 24, 26, 29(n5, n7), 35, 74, 75t, 77t, 79–81t, 136, 138, 142, 146, 153–7, 162t, 163–5, 167(n15), 184, 207, 213, 219, 244, 248, **249–51**, 257, **258**, 262, 265, 266, 267(n4–5)
  Bihar **252–3**
  land-ownership 252, 253t
  school drop-outs 147
  see also Mahadalit castes
censuses 2, 182
  (1931) 250n
  (1961) 183n, 189–90, 206(n10), 238(n2)
  (1971) 177, 183n, 238(n2)
  (1981) 177, 183n
  (1991) 129, 177, 183n
  (2001) 6, 43, 44n, 139, 140, 177, 183n, 189n, 190, 191t, 193n, 206(n8, n10), **206–7**, 287, 287n
Central and Centrally Sponsored Schemes (CSS) 52, 59(n19)
central government 22, 27, 28, 54, 56, 59(n19, n22), 112, 178, 180–1, 205(n3), 281, 288, 291, 293
  active intervention required 57
  employees 127
  ministries 52
  'regulatory' intervention 275
  relative powers (versus state governments) 279–80
  role (economic) 274–5
Central Government Health Schemes (CGHS) 127
Central Plan and Centrally Sponsored Scheme 14
Chhattisgarh (2000–) 58(n13), 68–71f, 114, 121, 124; 115–26f; 121, 124, 125, 205(n1)
children 9, 15, **19–20**, 41, 130f, 176, 227
  Delhi slums (educational disparity) **136–71**

health 112
infants 129
life-cycle 159, 171
out-of-school: drop-outs **147–50**, 151, 158–63, 165, 168(n21–5)
out-of-school: never attending **150–1**, 158–63, 165
out-of-school: probability 163
over-age pupils 149f, **149–50**, 158, 160, 162t, 163, 168(n21–5)
pre-school age 20, 113, 159, 159t, 161t, 163, 165
pupil–teacher ratios 144t
coefficient of variation (CV) 39–40, 40f, 272–3
  method of calculation 58(n5)
colonial legacies 245, 252–3, 265, 271, 273
regional disparity 271–2
communal rioting 21, 175, 183, 188, 203, 204, 244
consumption xvii, 7, 12, 16, 57(n4), 65, 85(n5)
  Lorenz curve 66f, 66–7
  personal data 57(n4)
convergence theory 37, 59
  beta-convergence (β) 37, 38, 49, 58(n6)
  sigma-convergence (σ) 39–40, 58(n6)
corruption 28, 243, 249, 256t, 261, 267(n3)
credit xvii, 9, 17t, 62–3, 91, 292
  rural poor 90

decentralization 14, 19
Delhi 106(n6), 115–26f, 137, 166(n1), 205(n1)
  embroidery homeworkers (attempt to organize) **210–40**
  school education (structure) 166(n4)
  slum population 139
Demirgüç-Kunt, A. 88, 93, 98–9, 100, 106
democracy xvi, 8, 12, 27, 207, 248
demography 270, 273, 278, 289
development strategies **10–12**
  asymmetric federalism and regional disparities **274–80**
  backward states **270–95**

development strategies – *continued*
  'core' (decided at central level) 281
  interstate disparities widening 279
  national 271, 280
  'sector selectivity' versus 'region selectivity' 279
  'sector-specific', 'region-neutral' 276
Disparity
  income 7, 16, 35, 56, 98, 106
  inter-state and intra/state 36–40; *see also* intrastate disparities
economic duality (Bihar and India) 283, 284t
  literature 277
economic growth 1, 3–4, 13
  correlation coefficient (industry versus agriculture) 11
  empiricism 60
  failure to promote (Bihar) 244
  impact of financial development 88
  infrastructure and 40–4, 58(n7–13)
  infrastructure and interstate disparity 35–61
  interstate disparity 4–5
  jobless 21
  literature (interstate disparities) 36
  low 27
  market-led 14
  national strategy 293–4
  non-agricultural 62–87
  post-independence era 274–5
  pro-poor 253
  relationship with financial development 98
  relationship with financial inclusion 99
  sustainable 41
economic liberalization 37, 56, 60, 273, 274, 278, 283, 287, 290, 294
education xvii, 9, 12, 18–20, 22, 23t, 41, 90, 180–1, 184, 186, 204, 205(n4), 233, 235t, 246, 249, 265, **287–8**, 291–3
  disparity (Delhi slum children) **136–71**

elementary 19
household decision-making 140
literature 136, 142
percentage attending school 284
primary (elementary) 24, 25t, 136, 167–8(n17), 170, 288
primary (universalization) 137, 151, 166, 170, 171
private 171
privatization 137, 144
public versus private provision 19
secondary 288
electricity 23n, 25–6, 41, 58(n15), 166(n5), 245
state-wise infrastructure provision **42–4**, 58(n10–13)
transmission and distribution (T&D) loss 42, 58(n11)
electricity consumption 45–8, 51, 99
  per capita 42, 58(n10)
  validity as proxy for infrastructure endowments (defended) 46
Employee State Insurance Scheme (ESIS) 127
employment xvii, 2, 9, 15, 20, **21–2**, 23t, 24, 31, 62, 64, 65, 73, 83–6, 141, 151, 179–81, 190, 205(n4)
  challenges **210–40**
  inclusive sustained **210–40**
  non-agricultural 206(n8)
  public sector 220
  state and central services 204
  urban 210
Ethical Trading Initiative (ETI, London, 1998–) 222, 236
extremely backward classes (EBCs) 255t, 264, 267(n5)

federalism 127, 281, 295
  asymmetric 279–80
Fifteen-Point Programme for Welfare of Minorities (Gandhi, 1983) 204, 205(n4), 207
finance, institutional versus non-institutional 17, 29(n2)
financial inclusion
  definition 17, 88, 104
  explicit policy objective (RBI, 2005) 91

history (India) 89–93, 104–5, 106(n1–3)
 literature 88, 89
 measurement 101
 phase 1 (1980s) 89–90
 phase 2 (1990s to March 2005) 89, 90–1
 phase 3 (April 2005–) 89, **91**
 poverty conditions **93–8**, 106(n4–5)
 relationship with economic growth and infrastructure development 99
fiscal federalism 61, 281
fiscal transfers 53t, 58(n18)
 'vertical' versus 'horizontal' distribution 52
Five-Year Plans
 first 54
 first to fourth 272
 see also Plan expenditure
Five-Year Plan (eleventh, 2007–12) 8, 13, 18, 30, 36, 54, 57, 60
 Approach Paper 8–9
 per capita outlay versus levels of state income 53t, 53–4, 55f
 'Report to People' (PM's foreword) 9
food security 290, 291, 294
'freight equalization' 27, 276, 277, 294

Gadgil formula 58(n19)
Gandhi, Indira 178, 205(n4)
GAP (retailer) 222
garments 215, 238(n3)
 assumptions 221
 export-oriented, ready-made **220–1**, 238(n9)
 knitwear 221
gender 6–7, 9, 12, 20, **21–2**, 29(n7), 136, 138, 141t, 142, 146, 156, 157, 164, 165, 167(n15), 215–16, 233, 246
 homeworkers (degree of subordination) 217, 218t
 homeworkers (mode of payment) 217, 238(n7)
 school drop-outs 147
Gender Resource Centre (GRC), SEWA Delhi 223, 225, 226, 227
General Credit Card 91

ghettoization 183, 205
Gini coefficient 5f, 5, 7, 16, 38–9, 39f, 57(n3–4), 66–72
governance 111, 248, 254, 257, 258, 264–5, 290
government schools 24, 146, 158, 165, 167(n14)
 average monthly expenditure 152t
 costs **152–6**, 168(n26)
 Delhi 144t, 145t
 deteriorating quality 144–5
 expenditure 146, 167–8(n17)
 monthly expenditure (explanation via OLS technique) 154–5, 155t
 out-of-pocket expenditure 156
 quality 146–7, 168(n18)
Green Revolution 11, **275–8**, 280, 290, 294
 regional disparities 277
gross domestic product (GDP)
 contribution of informal sector 21
 growth rate xvi
 per capita (PC GDP) 99, 100, 273
Gujarat (GJ) 6f, 21, 38f, 43, 43t, 44f, 50t, 53t, 55f, 55, 58(n12, n14), 68–71f, 106(n6), 115–26f, 189, 190, 192, 206(n12), 266, 268(n22), 274, 282t, 285t
 electric light and minorities **197**, 198t, 202, 203
 electric light and minorities (results and analysis) **194–7**
 electrification 194
 house with electric light *vis-à-vis* urban population/size of town (2001) 193f
 Muslim population 188, 189t
 public goods (electricity) 188

Haryana (HY) 6f, 38f, 43, 43t, 44f, 50t, 53t, 55f, 58(n12, n14), 68–71f, 106(n6), 115–26f, 127, 274, 282t, 285t
 electricity consumption 51
 NSDP 246, 268(n1)
 wealthiest state 51
Hausman test 47t, 101, 103t
haves versus have-nots **8**, 9

health   xviii, 12, **18–20**, 23n, 136, 159, 159t, 166, 166(n2), 180, 213, 234, 246, 249, 265, 291–3
  Bihar versus India   **288–90**
  maternal   112
  outpatient care (household health expenses)   **122–5**, 124–6f
  'Health for All' programme (2002)   111, 128
  health insurance   128
    formal scheme required   127
    private   19, 127
  health service/health care   9
    provision   186
    provision (public versus private)   19
    three-tier system   111
    utilization   112, 127
  health shocks   75, 78, 82, 112, 115
    need for finance mechanisms for the poor   112
  heterogeneity theory   21, 185, 186–7, 192, 197, 202
  Hindi (language)   157–8, 158t, 161t, 163, 243, 247, 265
  'Hindu rate of growth' (Raj Krishna)   3, 35, 270
  historical legacies
    Bihar   **251–3**, 267(n6)
    burden (Bihar)   **253–9**, 267(n7–9)
  homeworkers   22, **210–40**
    children   212
    data deficiencies   213, 216–17, 220
    definition (ILO, 1996)   211, 214
    discrimination   214
    embroidery (export-oriented garment industry)   **220–1**, 238(n9)
    evolution   **218–20**, 238(n8)
    exploitation   212
    female   20, **21–2**
    legislation 'under consideration'   213
    literature   238(n5)
    neglect of issue (two factors)   **215–16**
    non-agricultural sector   217, 218t, 238(n6)
    overview   **216–21**, 238(n6–9)
    rural–urban distribution   217
    scale and characteristics   **216–18**, 238(n6–7)
    status ambiguity   216, 218
    theory   **214–16**
    unorganized manufacturing   217–18
  hospitalization   112, 113, **119–22**, 124–5, 125f, 126, 129, 130f
    out-of-pocket (OOP) expenditure   119, 122, 123f
    reimbursement (by government)   120, 122, 123f
    reimbursement (private)   120, 123f
  hospitals   19, 25, 26t, 30(n7), 111, 127, 128, 245
    government-run   123–4
    private   121
  housing   24, 141, 146, 167(n8), 195–6t, 197, 198–201t, 203, 256t, 262
    percentage of households with pucca houses   284
    pucca (permanent)   227
  human development   295
    Bihar   292, 294
    Bihar and India   **284–90**

immunization   159, 159t, 161t, 163–5
incentives   160, 162t, 164, 169(n32), 265
inclusive growth   16, 290, 291, 294
  approaches/constraints   3
  bibliography   30–2
  challenges   **12–14**
  definition   1
  existing literature   1, 2, 8
  government understanding   **8–10**
  political processes   2
  pre-reform versus (1991–) post-reform   12–13
  versus PRSP   2
  'threefold approach'   **1–2**
Inclusive Growth Strategy (IGS, 2006–)   xvi–xvii
  background   **3–8**, 28–9(n1)
  income-asset relationship   **33–108**
  issues of weaker sections   **20–2**, **173–240**
  key components   9
  objectives   xviii, 7

income inequality/disparity 7, 16, 35, 56, 98, 106
  initial level of state income 37
  interstate 15, **36–40**, 49
  intrastate disparities 6, 57
Indian National Congress 8, 175, 210, 244
  Bihar 249, 250t, 256t
  'Congress Party' 178, 179, 258, 265
  electoral politics 179
industrial sector 43, 278, 280, 283, 294
  growth 270
  modern 277
  public investment 275
inequality/disparity 3, 10, 26, 27, 248, 278
  asset 65–73
  Bihar 244, 251
  consumption *see* consumption
  economic 2
  income *see* income under Disparity
  literature 57(n1), 59–61
  obstacles to eradication 258
  persistent 265–6
  regional 270–1
  rural–urban 35, 270
  social 12
  socio-economic 1, 8, 251
  structural bottlenecks 28
infant mortality rate (IMR) 284, 288–9, 289t
inflation rate 18, 45t, 45–6, 47t, 49, 101–5
infrastructure xvii, 8, 9, 14, 24, 27, 32, 138, 272
  health inequality **114–16**, 117–18f, 128(n2)
  market integration **292–3**, 294
  Plan expenditure **54–6**, 58–9(n19–22)
  public investment 275
  social and physical 2
  state-wise provision (electricity) **42–4**, 58(n10–13)
  urban 204–5
inpatient care 124, 125f, 127
institutional births 117, 120f
Integrated Child Development Services (ICDS) 159, 293

International Labour Organization: Convention (C177, 1996)
  definition of homeworker 211, 214
  India 'prime mover' 215
  ratification 214–15
interstate disparities 6
  descriptive analysis **36–40**, 57–8(n2–6)
  economic growth, infrastructure, and **35–61**
  initial income levels 37–8
  solution 57
  widening **37–40**, 56, 279, 280, 293
  see also inequality
irrigation 12, 23n, 29–30(n7), 41, 43, 272, 275–7, 292

Jammu and Kashmir (JK) 6f, 38f, 43t, 44f, 58(n12, n14), 106(n6), 115–26f
Janata Dal (United) or JD(U) 244, 250–8, 260, 262–5, 267(n13), 268(n22)
Japan 4, 86
  land reform 63, 85(n1), 86
  post-war occupation 85(n1)
Jharkhand 29(n4), 43, 43t, 44f, 49, 50t, 52, 53t, 55f, 68–71f, 115–26f, 158, 169(n30), 205(n1), 250n, 269, 283, 285, 286

Karnataka (KT) 6f, 38f, 43t, 44f, 50t, 53t, 55f, 55, 58(n12, n14), 68–71f, 83, 106(n6), 114; 115–26f; 116, 117, 205(n1), 238(n3), 274, 282t, 285t
Kerala (KE) 6f, 38f, 43t, 44f, 50t, 52, 53t, 55f, 58(n12, n14), 68–71f, 106(n6); 115–26f; 116, 117, 274, 282t, 285t
  inequality **6–7**
  land reform 85(n1)
  literacy 6
  social welfare 14
Kisan Credit Card (KCC) scheme 17, 91, 256t, 261, 268(n16–17)

304 Index

Kumar, Nitish. 27, 244–5, 254–62, 264–6, 267(n14), 268(n22)
  land reform and *bataidari* rights 259–61
  popularity 257–8, 267(n8–9)

labour 16, 66, 225
  informalization 28
  manual 84, 210
  public sector 2
  seasonal 24
  shift to non-agriculture 'extremely slow' 278
  unlimited supply 277, 295
land xviii, 28, 29(n5), 141, 157, 167(n8), 168(n20), 272, 290
  area owned 74–82
  buyers versus non-buyers 76, 77t, 78, 82–5
  buyers and sellers 74
  'guidance value' 83
  market price 62–3, 63–4
  market transactions 17
  non-agricultural demand 73, 84
  rent-to-price ratio 83
  sellers versus non-sellers 78, 79t, 82
land distribution changes and non-agricultural growth xvii–xviii, 2, 7, 15, 16–17, 62–87
  changes (1980s, 1990s) 65–73
  data deficiencies 67
  literature 83
  mean comparisons 76–8, 79t, 84
  methodology and data 73–6, 85(n3–7)
  policy implications 84, 85
  probit regression 78, 80–2
  relationship with non-agricultural growth 73
  results 76–82
  variables 74, 75t
land prices 65, 73, 78, 82–3, 86
  distance to town (effect) 83
land reform 17, 63, 65, 67, 74, 86, 247, 248, 253, 255–6t, 258, 263, 267(n10–15), 268, 269, 291, 292
  Bihar 245, 259–61, 267–8(n10–18)
  laws (1948–92) 75t, 75–82, 84, 85, 85(n7)

land redistribution
land tenure 184, 291, 292
  colonial 244, 265, 268
landholdings 15, 26, 251
  cap/ceilings 67, 255t, 259
  division by inheritance 267(n6)
  under-reporting bias 67
landlessness 17, 27, 29(n7), 62, 63, 65, 73, 83, 84, 85, 245, 253t
landless and marginal households
landownership 17, 73, 266
  by caste (Bihar) 253t
  versus caste hierarchy 252
  increase in inequalities 63
  route out of poverty 62
land transaction
latrines **114**, 115f, 116, 135t, 166(n5)
Levine, R. 88, 98, 107
life expectancy 18, 284
  Bihar versus India (1981–2006) 289t, **289–90**
literacy 18, 48, 179, 222, 223, 227–9, 230t, 292
  Bihar 246
  Bihar versus India **287–8**
  gender disparity 287, 287t
  Muslims 178
  slum areas of Delhi and Mumbai 139
Lok Janshakti Party (LJP) 255–6t, 257, 260, 264, 268(n20)
Lok Sabha elections
  (1996–2009) 251t
  (2004) 210
  (2009) 210, 250, 251t, 257, 260, 264, 268(n20–2)
Lorenz curve 38–9, 39f, 65–7, 57(n3), 72

Madhya Pradesh (MP) 6f, 16, 38f, 43t, 44f, 50t, 51, 53t, 55f, 58(n12, n14), 67, 68, 68–71f, 106(n6); 115–26f; 125, 181, 205(n1), 208, 238(n3), 243, 274, 276, 282t, 285t, 285
  bifurcation (loss of Chhattisgarh, 2000) 45, 49, 58(n13)

Mahadalit castes 245, 255–6t, 259, 262–4, 266(n2), 267(n15), 268(n19–20)
Maharashtra (MH) 6f, 38f, 43t, 44f, 50t, 53t, 55f, 58(n12, n14), 68–71f, 106(n6), 115–26f, 205(n1), 274, 282t, 285t
 manufacturing 2, 11, 42, 46, 60, 64
 homeworkers 217
 market integration 292–3
Martinez Peria, M.S.
medical expenditure (household) 75t, 75, 77t, 78, 79–81t, 82, 85(n5)
micro-insurance 128
migrants 227, 228t, 229
 links with place of origin 141, 167(n9)
 school drop-outs 147
 visits to place of origin 157, 158t
migration xvii
 'adversely affects school attendance' 165
 to areas with electricity 191–2
 domestic (within India) 29(n7)
 duration (effect on school attendance) 160
 educational disparity (Delhi slum children) 136–71
 internal 59
 international 29(n7)
 long–duration 140
 reasons 141
 rural–urban 20, 138 141, 166, 167(n7), 169, 189–90, 206(n10), 283
 urban to urban 167(n7)
Minimum Wages Act (1948) 239(n24)
Misra Commission 180, 204
mukhiya (heads of *Gram Panchayat*) 22, 23t, 25, 26t, 29(n7)
Mukhyamantri Jeevan Drishti Programme 262
Mukhyamantri Mahadalit Poshak Yojna 262
Muslim Women (Protection of Rights on Divorce) Act (1986) 175
Muslims xvii, **20–1**, 29(n7), 141t, 142, 143, 146, 154, 155t, 155, 157, 160, 162t, 163–4, 170, 188–92, 195–6t, 198–201t, 205(n1), 206(n11), 228t, 250–1t, 253t, 262, 264
 electric light (as basic social infrastructure) 180–3, 205(n5)
 embroidery homeworkers 227
 lack of affirmative action 176
 percentages living in urban areas (1961–2001) 183t
 social infrastructure **177–83**, 205(n4–5)
 socio-economic status 197, 202, 203, 208
 socio-economic backwardness and government policies **177–80**, 205(n4)
 status (social and educational) 176
 weak voice theory 'statistically significant' 194

National Commission for Enterprises in Unorganized Sector (NCEUS) 21, 31, 210, 211–12, 240
National Commission for Minorities (1993–) 178–9
National Electricity Policy (2005–) 181
National Health Policy (1985) 111
National Rural Employment Guarantee Act (NREGA, 2005) 210, 237(n1)
National Rural Employment Guarantee Programme (NREGP) 9, 293
National Rural Health Mission (NRHM, 2005–) 111–12, 116
National Sample Survey (NSS) 2, 142
 55th round (1999–2000) 177, 182, 217, 238(n6), 240, 246
 58th round (2002) 166(n3)
 59th round (2003) 64
 60th round (2004) **112–13**
 61st round (2004–5) 147–8, 150, 178, 182
National Sample Survey Organization (NSSO) 64–7, 69, 70–1n, 83–4, 86–7, 91, 92n, 107, 216–17, 218n, 285n
Naxalites 8, 59(n20), 257

Nehru, Jawaharal.   xvi, 11, 175
  'Tryst with Destiny' speech (1947)
    12
net state domestic product (NSDP)   5f,
    5, 16, 36, 37n, 85(n2), 101–4,
    246, 268(n1)
  Bihar (2004–9)   266, 268(n23)
  deflators   45, 46
  non-agricultural   69
  non-agricultural (growth rate)
    71f, 74–85
  per capita   68–9
net state domestic product: real per
    capita   6n, 38–9, 39–40f, 50t,
    50, 57(n3), 58(n5)
  growth rate   37
  initial level   44–5, 47t, 49
  six-year average   44
  ten-year average   44–6, 47t, 48
NGOs   15, 28, 145, 145n, 167(n14),
    213, 222
non-agricultural growth
  changes in land distribution and
    62–87
  high rates (versus market for
    land)   65
non-agricultural sector   210, 274–5,
    281, 283, 284t, 287
nutrition   137, 159, 169(n32), 233,
    291

Orissa (OR)   6f, 16, 38f, 43, 43t, 44f,
    50t, 52, 53t, 55f, 58(n12, n14),
    68–71f, 106(n6), 114, 115–26f,
    243, 267(n8), 274, 282t, 285t,
    285, 286
other backward classes (OBCs)   15,
    20–1, 29(n7), 74, 75t, 77t,
    79–81t, 141t, 142, 147, 150,
    154–5, 155t, 160, 167(n15),
    176, 178, 205(n4), 267(n4), 269
  definition   205(n3)
  Hindu versus Muslim   21
out-of-pocket expenditure   124f
  education   156
  inpatient care   119, 123f
outpatient care   124f, 126f, 127, 135t
  household health expenses and
    finance   **122–5**, 124–6f

Pande, R.   99, 100, 102, 106
parents
  motivation (children's education)
    20, 154, 155t, 155, 161t, 163,
    164, 166
  negative perceptions about
    education   150, 151t
  visits to place of origin   161t, 163
perinatal health   112, **116–19**, 120–2f,
    127, 128(n3)
Plan expenditure
  and provision of infrastructure
    54–6, 58–9(n19–22)
  see also Five-Year Plans
Planning Commission   4, 28(n1),
    52, 54, 58–9(n19), 60, 166(n1),
    167(n10), 170, 179, 284, 285n
polio   159, 159t, 161t, 165
poverty   xviii, 13, 21, 25, 60, 66, 86,
    136, 137, 211, 278
  estimation methodology   166(n1)
  inter-temporal aspects   67
  migrants   167(n7)
  migrants versus non-migrants   138
  paths out of   62
  persistent   265
  relationship with health   xvii
  rural   62, 246
  urban   9, 246
  urban (conceptualization)   138, 171
poverty alleviation   8, 11, 14, 16, 27,
    136, 291
  empirical analysis (state-wise data)
    88–108
poverty-alleviation programmes   249,
    293, 294
poverty headcount ratio   68n, 97,
    101, 105, 137
poverty reduction   xvi, xvii–xviii, 4,
    28–9(n1), 42, 60, 83, 85, 86,
    243, 244, 246, 248, 269
  Bihar   22
  financial inclusion measures
    17–18
  interstate disparity   4–5, 31
  obstacles   258
  'one of major goals of financial
    inclusion'   93
  semi-elasticity   100

Poverty Reduction Strategy Paper (PRSP, IMF/World Bank)   xvii, xviii, 2
  versus 'inclusive growth'   2
prenatal health care   19, 116–19, 119f, 128(n3), 135t
  versus birth and postnatal expenditure   118–19, 121–2f, 126, 128(n3)
primary health care   123
Primary Health Centres (PHCs)
  'gross under-utilization' (2005)   111
Prime Minister's New Fifteen-Point Programme for Welfare of Minorities (2006)   180, 204, 205(n4), 208
priority sector lending   89, 90
private reimbursement   124f
private sector   11, 14, 15, 18, 28, 29(n3), 55, 56, 204, 275
private tuition fees   152, 152t, 153, 154, 155t, 156
privatization   13
  education   137
Public Distribution System (PDS)   12, 249, 256t, 261, 266–7(n2), 269, 293
public–private partnerships (PPP)   13–14, 15, 18, 30, 138
Punjab (PJ)   6f, 38f, 43, 43t, 44f, 50t, 51, 52, 53t, 55f, 55, 58(n12, n14), 68–71f, 106(n6), 114; 115–26f; 120–1, 127, 274, 282t, 285t

Rajasthan (RJ)   6f, 16, 38f, 43t, 44f, 50t, 58(n12, n14), 51, 53t, 55f, 67, 68–71f, 106(n6), 115–26f, 205(n1), 274, 282t, 285t, 288
Rao, Narasimha P.V.   178
Rashtriya Janata Dal (RJD)   202, 206(n14), 249–51, 252t, 255–6t, 257, 260–2, 264, 268(n20), 269
regional disparity   xvi, xvii, 24
  see also interstate disparities
Regional Rural Banks (RRBs)   89–90
reservation system   21, 176
  see also affirmative action programme

Reserve Bank of India (RBI)   85(n2), 89, 92n, 94–8n, 99–100, 106(n3), **107**
  Annual Policy Statement 2005–6   91
  RBI Bulletin   101, 102t
resettlement colony   226
revenue
  state   52–54
  village   24, 29(n5),
roads   23t, 24–5, 25t, 29(n7), 41, 58(n9), 90, 166(n5), 184, 245, 275, 292–3
  density   45–9
  influencing factors   46
  length   99
  road quality   46, 48
  traffic congestion   238(n15)
  types   29(n6)
rural areas/rural India   7–8, 9, 15, **16–17**, 18–19, **22–7**, 29(n2), 41, 51–2, 57, 57(n4), 58(n9), 59(n20), 61, 69f, 89–99, 105, 113, 130f, 136–7, 157, 169, 171, 177, 191t, 194–7, 206(n13), 207, 213, 238(n2), 245, 266, 272, 291, 293
  communal riots   188
  composition of assets (2002–3)   72f
  definition   106(n4)
  development programmes   24–5, 26t
  electrification   181, 182–3, 208
  HDI   285t
  health inequality   112
  homeworkers   217
  infant mortality rates   288–9, 289t
  lack of health insurance   127–8
  literacy   288
  NREGA (2005–)   210
  poverty ratios   102–4
  poverty ratios (Bihar versus India, 1983–2005)   **285–6**, 286t
  quacks   123
  real domestic product per head   277

Sachar Committee report (2006)   179–80, 182, 187, 208
sanitation   12, 19, 24, 112, **114**, 115f, 116, 126, 135t, 144t, 166(n2, n5), 249, 265

scheduled castes (SCs) 6, 7, 9, 10, 15, 20–1, 17, 25, 26t, 29(n7), 74–82, 136, 141t, 142–3, 147, 150, 154–5, 155t, 160, 167(n15), 176–80, 182, 185–90, 191t, 194–203, 228t, 229, 245, 248, 250t, 251–2, 253t, 256t, 261–3, 268(n20)
  composition (Bihar) 263t
  definition 205(n2)
  illiteracy (Bihar) 246
  rural versus urban 203
  voting patterns (Bihar, 1996–2009) 252t
  see also Mahadalit castes
Scheduled Commercial Banks (PRBs)
scheduled tribes (STs) 7, 10, 15, 20–1, 74–82, 136, 141t, 142–3, 147, 150, 154–5, 155t, 160, 167(n15), 176–80, 182, 186–90, 194–7, 228t, 248, 250t
  change in definition 206(n10)
  definition 205(n2)
school attendance 20, 24, 165, 168–9(n27–32)
  current 159–64
  Delhi slums 142–3, 167(n11–12)
  effect of child's place of birth 160
  effects of migration 157
  estimation 159–60, 169(n32)
  framework of analysis 156–9, 168–9(n27–31)
  initial 159–65
  literature review 156–9, 168–9(n27–31)
  logit analysis 159
  migration-related issues 158t
  policy implications 138–9
  rural–urban disparity 137
  type of school 145t
  versus 'school enrolment' 167(n11)
school costs 152–6, 168(n26)
  direct versus indirect 152
Self-Employed Women's Association (SEWA) 212, 214, 215, 240
  see also SEWA Delhi

self-employment 17, 21, 62, 90, 91, 211, 216, 217, 218
  income 75, 85
  women 212
Self–Help Groups (SHGs) 17, 29(n7), 221–2, 223
SHG–Bank linkage programme **90–1**, 105
SEWA Delhi (1999–) 213–14, 238(n13)
  approach towards homeworkers (summary) 224–5
  embroidery homeworkers **221–6**, 238–9(n10–20)
  late payments 234
  lessons 237
  members: active versus non-active 226, 228t, 229–37, 239(n21–2, n25)
  members: versus non-members 228t, 229–33, 235t, 235, 239(n22–3)
  membership 221–2
  production capacity 'too small' 225, 238–9(n18)
  reasons for not joining 235
  'sophisticated middleman' 226
  two new centres planned 236–7
  wages 233, 234, 235
  work (advantages versus disadvantages) **231–4**, 239(n22–5)
  work (irregularity of supply) 234, 235, 236
  workers' perceptions **234–5**
Shah Bano case 175
Singh, Manmohan xvi–xvii, 36, 179
  budget speech (1991) xviii
slums 28
  definition (1956) 166(n2)
  notified versus non-notified 166–7(n5)
social inequality xvi–xvii, xviii, 17
social security 22, 204, 210, 214, 223
'socialistic state of society' xvi
sugar 249

Sundernagri (North-East Delhi)   222, 235
  basic facts   **226–7**
supply chain (global)   222, 225

Tamil Nadu (TN)   6f, 38f, 43t, 44f, 50t, 53t, 55f, 58(n12, n14), 68–71f, 106(n6), 114; 115–26f; 116, 117, 238(n3), 274, 282t, 285t
thekedars (middlemen)   224, 225, 236–7, 239(n18)
  advantages of work provided   233–4
  late payment   234

unconditional (absolute) convergence   37, 38
underclass   169
Union Government   1, 14, 16, 18, 19
  understanding of 'inclusive growth'   **8–10**
  see also central government
United Progressive Alliance (UPA)   9, 36, 179–80
unorganized sector   21–2, 29(n3), 91, 210, 240
  characterization   210–11
urban area/s   9, 18, **19–20**, 51–2, 57, 57(n4), 63, 73, 92–9, 105, 111, 113, 130f, 177, 187–8, 191t, 194, 204–5, 206(n13), 213, 238(n2), 266
  Bihar   246
  cities   176
  definitions   106(n4), 206(n8)
  demand for food   280
  electrification   182–3
  food supplies   275–7
  HDI   285t
  homeworkers   217
  infant mortality rates   289t, 289
  poverty ratios (Bihar versus India, 1983–2005)   286t, **286–7**
  renewal   xvii
  school learning facilities   144t
  slums   20

Uttar Pradesh (UP)   6f, 13, 16, 21, 31, 38f, 43t, 44f, 49–52, 53t, 55f, 55, 58(n12–14), 68–71f; 115–26f; 124, 158, 169(n30–1), 181, 185, 190, 192, 206(n12), 205(n1), 208, 227, 238(n3), 243, 274, 282t, 285t, 285
  bifurcation (loss of Uttarakhand, 2000)   45, 49, 58(n13), 167(n6)
  electric light and minorities   200t, **202–3**
  electric light and minorities (results and analysis)   **194–7**
  house with electric light *vis-à-vis* urban population/size of town (2001)   193f
  migrants to Delhi   139, 140–1
  Muslim population   188, 189t
  public goods (electricity)   188
Uttarakhand (2007–)   58(n13), 68–71f, 158, 169(n30), 205(n1)
  migrants to Delhi   140–1
Uttaranchal (2000–2007)   115–26f

villages   13, **22–7**, 29(n5–6), 41, 87, 106(n3), 113, 129–30, 134, 158, 169, 181–2, 206(n11), 225, 238(n2), 246, 261, 266(n2), 293

wages   11, 23t, 85, 85(n6), 212, 223, 238(n4), 239(n25), 276
  agricultural   83–4
  low   232t, 233
  'remuneration'   214
  statutory minimum   210, 224, 233, 239(n24)
water   90, 285, 291
  drainage   166(n5)
  drinking water   12, 166(n5), 195–6t, 198–201t, 206(n15), 249, 265, 284
  drought   17
  flooding   29(n7), 59(n20)
water sources   114–15, 116f, 135t
  within-state variation   115
weak voice theory   21, 186–7, 192, 197

West Bengal (WB)   6f, 21, 38f, 43t, 44f, 50t, 53t, 55f, 58(n12, n14), 68–71f, 106(n6); 115–26f; 116, 117, 125, 190, 192, 206(n12), 248, 255t, 268, 269, 274, 282t, 285t
   electric light and minorities   201t, **203**
   electric light and minorities (results and analysis)   **194–7**
   house with electric light *vis-à-vis* urban population/size of town (2001)   193f
   land reform   17, 85(n1), 247, 259
   Muslim population   188, 189t
   public goods (electricity)   188
   rice yields (1950–2006)   248f
women   xvii, 9, 15, 22, 28, 90, 176, 211, 255t, 267(n3)
   embroidery homeworkers   **210–40**
   life expectancy   289t, **289–90**
   number involved in household industry (1961–71)   238(n2)
   poverty   17
   self-reliance   234–5, 236